6/10

D0884482

ENCYCLOPEDIA OF PASTA

California Studies in Food and Culture
Darra Goldstein, Editor

ORETTA ZANINI DE VITA

ENCYCLOPEDIA OF

pasta

TRANSLATED BY MAUREEN B. FANT
WITH A FOREWORD BY CAROL FIELD

University of California Press   *Berkeley Los Angeles London*

The publisher gratefully acknowledges the generous
support of the General Endowment Fund
of the University of California Press Foundation

University of California Press, one of the most distinguished
university presses in the United States, enriches lives around
the world by advancing scholarship in the humanities, social
sciences, and natural sciences. Its activities are supported by
the UC Press Foundation and by philanthropic contributions
from individuals and institutions. For more information, visit
www. ucpress.edu.

University of California Press
Berkeley and Los Angeles, California

University of California Press, Ltd.
London, England

© 2009 by The Regents of the University of California

Library of Congress Cataloging-in-Publication Data

Zanini De Vita, Oretta, 1936–
  [Pasta, atlante dei prodotti tipici. English]
  Encyclopedia of pasta / Oretta Zanini De Vita ; translated by
Maureen B. Fant ; with a foreword by Carol Field.
     p. cm. — (California studies in food and culture ; v. 26)
  Includes bibliographical references and index.
  ISBN 978-0-520-25522-7 (cloth : alk. paper)
   1. Pasta products—Italy—Encyclopedias.   2. Pasta
products—Italy—History.   3. Cookery (Pasta).   I. Title.
  TX394.5.Z35 2009
  664'.755—dc22

                                              2009010522

Manufactured in the United States of America

17 16 15 14 13 12 11 10 09
10 9 8 7 6 5 4 3 2

The paper used in this publication meets the minimum require-
ments of ANSI/NISO Z39.48-1992 (R 1997) (Permanence of Paper).

64.
AN
009

To my husband, Carlo De Vita

The regions of Italy and their capitals

CONTENTS

FOREWORD

[CAROL FIELD]

How long have Italians been eating pasta? Some report the depiction of pasta-making tools in Etruscan tombs. Others argue that the Roman poet Horace was the first to write about pasta with his mention of *laganum,* a possible ancestor of today's *lasagna.* Scholars long ago exploded the myth that Marco Polo brought pasta to Italy from China, observing that Sicilians were eating homemade pasta long before he was born. They were most likely referring to *busiata,* an early form of *spaghetti* made by rolling dough around a reed or blade of grass that was then swiftly pulled out, leaving a long pasta pierced with a hole down the middle. Later Italians used knitting needles for the same purpose, and members of old Albanian communities in the south still employ metal umbrella spokes.

Fast forward to 2009. It doesn't take an expert to confirm that pasta is Italy's most famous and popular food, the country's preeminent contribution to its culinary culture. But it has taken an extraordinary scholar to break new ground with this encyclopedia on the hundreds of shapes in which pasta is formed.

To track down the components of her astonishing volume, Oretta Zanini De Vita, an impeccable researcher and detective of pasta from its earliest appearances in Italy, has compiled the first thorough compendium of the country's most basic food. Indefatigable and undeterred by the complexity of her task, she traced multiple forms of pasta in their geographical, regional, and historical contexts and noted lexical and gastronomic differences from village to village and region to region.

Her most compelling strategy was the decision to begin by interviewing many of the country's oldest citizens, intent on capturing their memories of an era before the changes wrought by the prosperity of the last fifty years. She listened for local nuances and names and probed for recollections of earlier times when people were poorer, ingredients were fewer, and sauces and stuffings often relied on the imaginative use of whatever grew wild in the fields or was left in the larder.

Pasta can be short or long, handmade or factory made, stuffed or not, floating in broth or tossed with sauce. It can be made of durum wheat or soft-wheat flour with eggs and/or water. Some shapes speak of the poverty of rural areas. *Abbotta pezziende*, "feed the beggar," probably belongs to the pasta category named as much for wish fulfillment as for form. Some shapes are named for everyday objects, such as *cenci*, "dusting rags," and *chianche*, the large, flat paving stones popular in Puglia.

Some are flavored with whatever the rural landscape provides. *Cadunsei*, from the alpine Val Camonica in Lombardy, are half-moon *ravioli* filled with a mixture of chopped chicken giblets cooked with onion, carrot, and celery and flavored with peach pits from local trees. Smoky-flavored *orecchiette al grano arso* are made with flour produced from grains collected from the fields after they were harvested and burnt.

Envision the golden *tajarin* of Piedmont, which calls for mixing twenty egg yolks with a kilogram of flour. Hold up a thin sheet of *tagliatelle* dough and look through it. Sheets of hand-rolled *pasta fresca* can speak of privilege and promise in the fineness of its dough and the riches of its sauces, such as those made with sweetbreads, truffles, mixtures of meat, and chicken livers.

Pasta may be the country's preeminent food, but that doesn't make it a unifying dish. Indeed, for something that begins with such simple ingredients—flour, water, salt, and sometimes eggs—it is both astonishing and gastronomically thrilling to realize that those few basic elements are formed into a dazzling variety of shapes, some with fillings and some not, and then tossed with a wide range of sauces. Unifying? If anything, the hundreds of divergent pasta shapes accentuate Italy's regional differences and draw attention to the distinctions that define precise local identities.

We all know some of the names—*fettuccine* and *ravioli, tortelli* and *tagliatelle*—but variant doughs and shapes within such well-known categories can swap names as well as ingredients. *Fettuccine* sumptuously sauced with giblets in Rome changes character in nearby towns where the dough is made with whole-wheat flour and bran and the pasta is renamed *lane pelose* (hairy wools), for the coarse texture of the bran in the whole grain. Around Orvieto, *fettuccine* with goose *ragù* was served at the time of the threshing lunch. For Christmas Eve, the same pasta, dressed with honey and walnuts, became *maccheroni*. Multiply all these shapes and name changes by thousands of times, and add the specific festivals for which dishes are served and the religious rituals that include them, and you can see how fractured and complex the world of pasta is.

Still, after occupying Naples in 1860, General Giuseppe Garibaldi said "it will be *maccheroni*, I swear to you, that will unify Italy." In fact, it is *spaghetti* that more closely meets that description, but the sauces that dress them still keep their geo-graphical beginnings.

You should not be hungry when you open this book. The smell of slivered leeks sautéed in butter, white truffle shavings over egg-rich *tagliarini,* slow-stewed meats with ribbons of pasta will rise up off the page. You will learn techniques for making and shaping more than thirteen hundred forms of pasta, though this is not a recipe book. You will travel up and down the peninsula, learning about villages and hamlets, cities and towns, all over the country, but this is not a guide-book. And although this is much more than a reference book, you will learn the history and culture of each form and its variations, confirmed by Oretta Zanini De Vita through her many informants, archival documents, inventories, tax reg-istries, and books from the Renaissance forward. As you read, you will encounter flavors and tastes that stir the appetite and evoke memories, and at the same time synthesize immense amounts of information in a way that deepens and enriches your knowledge about Italy's culinary patrimony.

This is a treatise of extraordinary learning and compelling information wrapped inside a great appreciation of the history and meaning of pasta. It is clear that Oretta Zanini De Vita agrees with the writer Giuseppe Prezzolini, who said that *"spaghetti* have the same right or more to belong to Italian civilization that Dante has."

PREFACE TO THE ENGLISH-LANGUAGE EDITION

[ORETTA ZANINI DE VITA]

Wheat flour and water. For more than a thousand years, Italian hands have crafted this simple dough into hundreds of different shapes with a creative genius that no other noodle-eating people in the world has rivaled. To me, this heritage is an Italian gift to gastronomic culture on a par with what the Florentine Renaissance gave to art. I am thus proud and delighted that the results of my research are now available to English-language readers.

This book is about the traditional shapes of Italian pasta—the long, the short, the layered, the rolled, the stretched, and the stuffed. A mixture of wheat flour and water recognizable as pasta has existed in many parts of the world since antiquity, but the quantity and the variety of the forms found on the Italian peninsula and islands, served in so many ways, are unique.

My research aimed to sort out and clarify this vast repertoire of shapes and their often ambiguous and confusing names. During a period of about ten years, this work took me throughout Italy to consult documents in public and private archives and in municipal and private libraries and, even more important, to interview hundreds of elderly people whose recollections confirmed what I had read in the written sources.

Because the industrialization of pasta making has, to an extent, altered the traditional nomenclature and shapes, it was essential to consult these oral sources of the old ways. And so I endeavored to record—region by region, valley by valley—whatever remained of this immense and uniquely Italian heritage. The first Italian edition of my results was published in 2004 by the Italian Institute of Rural Sociology.[1]

During the preparation of the English-language edition, non-Italians (as well as more than a few Italians) asked Maureen and me the same two questions over and over. The first, Is it true that Marco Polo introduced noodles into Italy? And the second, Are you going to talk about what sauces go with what shapes?

The answer to the first question is a resounding no. Dried pasta, the kinds made with durum wheat, is found in Italy from about A.D. 800. It was, in fact, the Muslim occupiers of Sicily who spread the manufacturing and drying technique.[2] By the twelfth century, pasta produced in Sicily and Sardinia was being exported to mainland Italian territory and northern Europe, where it was marketed by the powerful maritime republics of Genoa and Pisa. Documents exist to prove this, should there be anyone left—and it appears that there is—who still believes that Marco Polo introduced noodles into Italy in 1296 on his return to Venice from China. In reality, by that time, people throughout Italy had been eating pasta for at least a century.[3] Marco Polo does relate an encounter with the Chinese noodle and uses the word *pasta* to describe it, clearly being already familiar with both term and concept.[4] The notion that *spaghetti* began in the Far East seems to have originated as recently as 1938, in Minneapolis, as a marketing gimmick in an article by one L. B. Maxwell in the trade publication *Macaroni Journal*.[5]

As to the question on sauces, foreigners who are intimidated by the strength and tenacity of Italian food habits, beliefs, and prohibitions will be surprised to learn that the pairing of shapes and sauces is mostly due to tradition. Of course there are a few guidelines—for example, chunky sauces do better on short tubes than on long strings. But by and large, the sauces and condiments are dictated by what people have always done. The shapes in this book are traditional foods, often poor or, if enriched with such expensive ingredients as fish or meat, reserved for rare and important occasions. Sauces were invented from what was on hand. Pairings became first traditional, then canonical, so that today the matching of, say, clam sauce with *rigatoni* instead of *spaghetti*—a combination with which there is nothing inherently wrong—still has the power to shock. But this book is not about modern usages, whether codification of the traditional ways or the experiments of creative chefs. Nor does it give recipes or advice to modern cooks. It is a record of what ordinary people did and do and have always done with the available resources. Necessity became tradition, and tradition would appear to have entered the national DNA to the point that Italians instinctively match shape and sauce and get it right.

Tradition, of course, has always been guided by three factors: local products, their seasons, and, most of all, the liturgical calendar. In areas where vegetables were plentiful, the different pasta shapes, everywhere served mostly in soups, came to be paired with various kinds of vegetables. Legumes, on the other hand, are grown everywhere, and are paired with pasta everywhere as well.

The widespread use of the tomato in home kitchens, which began in the early nineteenth century, has brought about a certain uniformity, and since its arrival, tomato sauce has been the most emblematic condiment for *pastasciutta*, although seasonal vegetables and local cheeses are still used in many parts of the country. In

Puglia, for example, *orecchiette* are sometimes dressed with tomato sauce, yes, but when the splendid local turnip greens *(cime di rapa)* are in season, no one would use anything else. Religious traditions too have influenced how pasta is served, and are treated at length in the individual entries (see, for example, *tagliolini* for the rituals of Ascension Day in the Vulture area). Meat in sauces was reserved almost exclusively for feast days, and usually involved cuts that were difficult to cook any other way, especially giblets and offal in general. When tradition called for an important cut of meat (always, and still, cooked very slowly over a practically invisible flame), the meat was (and is) served separately as a main course. And the same goes for sauces made with fowl, such as duck or goose.

I will take this opportunity to thank some of the people who have helped me in my work, and first among them are the numerous older people, especially women, some of whom are no longer living, who shared their memories. Next, I owe a grateful mention to my late husband, Carlo De Vita, to whom this book is dedicated. Among so much else, including his moral support during the years of research, he provided material help in reading antique documents and explored the patents section of the Archivio Centrale dello Stato (the Italian national archive) with me. The incomparable Tommaso Lucchetti consulted documents in Umbria and the Marche on my behalf, and Laura Celentano accompanied me on research trips to Basilicata. Last but not least, the pasta makers, notably Benedetto Cavalieri and the entire Martelli family, provided precious information and insights that helped me to put into focus the links between the ancient art of home pasta making and the modern pasta industry.

For the English edition, I thank first of all Maureen B. Fant, who has translated my work with intelligence and rare skill, making even its most abstruse parts comprehensible to non-Italian readers. This is my first publication in the United States, and it has been a privilege and pleasure to work with Darra Goldstein, Sheila Levine, and Dore Brown, of the University of California Press. Our diligent, and diplomatic, copyeditor, Sharon Silva, has been inspiring. Luciana Marini, artist, and Stefano Filippi, photographer, worked closely with me to provide just the right images, and they too have my thanks.

To all, *grazie infinite*.

Notes

1. I am grateful to the institute, and to its president, Corrado Barberis, for graciously authorizing this English edition.
2. See *spaghetti* entry, page 257.

3. G. Prezzolini, *Maccheroni & C.* (Milano: Rusconi, 1998), 67 ff.

4. Paolo Rivalta, ed., *Il libro di Marco Polo detto il Milione* (Torino: Einaudi, 1960), 179. In a subsequent chapter, Marco recounts that the Tartars in their peregrinations had to "dry" their milk like pasta! That certainly implies that the traveler was also familiar with dried pasta, which indeed Venetians had been eating for quite some time.

5. S. Serventi and F. Sabban, *La pasta. Storia e cultura di un cibo universale* (Roma-Bari: Laterza, 2000), 14.

TRANSLATOR'S PREFACE

[MAUREEN B. FANT]

One very good reason to learn the Italian language is to enjoy the works of Oretta Zanini De Vita in the original. In fact, it's a very good reason to study Italian geography, literature, and history. Writing with humor and charm, Oretta thinks nothing of reporting the opinion of a four-hundred-year-old author as though she had just put down the telephone, and sends the reader to the remotest villages of the most distant alpine valleys as though they were marked in bold on any map. In other words, she puts even educated Italian readers through their paces—with a smile.

To make the going easier for English-language readers, Oretta and I have added a glossary (including notes on translation choices), a bibliography, and many new notes and explanations in the text. To cover everything, however, would have made this an encyclopedia of Italian culture, not a biography of 310 traditional pasta shapes and their innumerable variations. Readers who want to follow up on the many allusions can do so easily in any number of reference books and atlases, while those who just want to know what a pasta shape is like, where it is or was made, and some of the names by which it is called will find all they need in these pages—along with plenty of folklore, anecdotes, literary excerpts, and the author's opinions.

A few aspects of the translation warrant explanation.

PASTA NAMES. The star of this book is the pasta shape. Each entry heading is the principal name by which a given pasta shape or group of similar, or similarly named, shapes is known. Other names for the same or similar shape are given in the text. Sometimes the names are normal Italian words used fancifully, such as *spaghetti*. A speaker of Italian knows this means "little strings," even if a ball of twine is not the first thing that springs to mind. But most Italian speakers would not know that, say, *blecs* means "patches" without reading the text. Where there is a clear and literal Italian meaning for a pasta name, its English translation is usually given at the beginning of the Remarks section of each pasta entry. Where the pasta name is a dialect word or otherwise requires lengthy explanation, this is covered in Remarks as well. Sometimes nobody knows what a pasta name means or what its etymology is. In other words, English- and Italian-language readers are often in the same boat.

Some pasta names are both specific enough to have their own entries and comprehensive enough to be used generically. Where translation would not be too forced, I have tried to use English equivalents (noodle or flat noodle instead of *tagliatella*) in the text, but in most cases anyone reading this book will understand that *ravioli* are something stuffed and *spaghetti* something stringy.

It is impossible to translate all the entry headings even into standard Italian, much less into English. Therefore, in order to give some quick idea of what an entry is like, Oretta and I formulated six broad categories of pasta shapes and assigned one of them to each entry heading:

- *pasta corta* Short forms, both factory made and homemade, such as *penne* or *rigatoni*, but also, say, handmade *trofie*.
- *pasta lunga* Long forms, such as *spaghetti* and *tagliatelle*, of course, as well as handmade shapes, such as *pici*.
- *pasta ripiena* Stuffed pasta, that is, *ravioli* and the like, as well as, rarely, certain pastas layered with sauce and baked, such as *vincisgrassi*.
- *pastina* Tiny shapes that are cooked in broth.
- *gnocchi/gnocchetti* Usually small, dumplinglike forms, but also some rustic long forms.
- *strascinati* Variations on the traditionally handmade, and today also factory-made, pasta disk dragged—*strascinato*—across a wooden board by hand or with the aid of a traditional utensil. *Orecchiette* are the most famous example.

Names that can apply to many shapes, such as *maccheroni* and *lasagne,* are so labeled, and shapes that cannot be shoehorned into any of the six classifications are designated "unusual shape." The category assignments should often not be taken too literally: one man's *gnocchetto* may be another man's *strascinato*. This is not an exact science. An index of pasta names, including the alternative names for the entry headings as well as other pastas mentioned, is given at the end of the book.

GEOGRAPHIC DIVISIONS. Readers who wish to follow the pasta shapes around their home territories would be well advised to keep a detailed atlas of Italy to hand, such as those published by the Touring Club Italiano. After only a few pages of this book, it will be clear that the important geographic divisions are valleys, hills or mountains, segments of the seacoast, lakeshores, or some other area formed by physical features, often obscure, rather than by political boundaries. Place names without precise political boundaries, especially river valleys, often lack clear-cut names in Italian. And Italian editorial (and probably cartographic) usage values nuance over the consistency so relentlessly pursued by the English-speaking world. In choosing to translate, or not, the names of the valleys so important to this book, I have tried to adopt the form a reader is most likely to find in the index of a good atlas of Italy. Sometimes only the name of the river will be listed, sometimes the valley (as one, two, or three words, sometimes under V, sometimes under the name of the river). Speaking solely of river names, only the Tiber, Tevere in Italian, has an English translation.

A word about Italy's political divisions is also needed. The present-day Republic of Italy has twenty *regioni,* or "regions," most of whose boundaries date to the 1970s, some later. The gastronomic divisions of Italy do not, however, always correspond to the modern map, and regional attributions should never be taken too literally. Also, some Italian regions have been formed from more than one geographic entity, such as Emilia-Romagna or Friuli–Venezia Giulia, and others that were formerly joined have been split into two regions, such as Abruzzo and Molise. The regions of Sicily and Sardinia each comprise numerous islands, not just the large ones.

Adding to the complexity are the ancient regional names, traditionally dragged in to serve as English equivalents of Italian. Examples are Latium, an ancient region that only partially corresponds to the modern Lazio, and ancient Calabria, which has nothing whatsoever to do with its modern namesake, an area roughly equivalent to the ancient Bruttium.

Where only half the name of a double region appears, it is not an omission. In fact, only that half is meant—"Emilia" alone means only the Emilia half of the region (where Bologna and Modena are located); "Romagna" used alone means only the piece on the Adriatic side, where Rimini and Ravenna are the best-known cities. "Friuli" means the northwest part of the region of Friuli–Venezia Giulia, and "Venezia Giulia" refers only to the southeastern part (which contains the regional capital and most famous city, Trieste).

Beneath the regional level come the provinces, each bearing the name of its capital city. Municipalities are subdivided into any number of villages, towns, *frazioni* (fractions), and *borghi* (hamlets). Unless it is obvious that the urban area is meant, all names of cities should be taken to include their surrounding area, possibly as far as the provincial boundaries.

The names of regions are given in English where English equivalents exist, otherwise in Italian, but not Latin. Only the names of the largest cities, whose English names are household words, are translated. For the adjective form of all place names, I have preferred to use English.

SAINTS' AND FEAST DAYS. Saints' names are given in English except when they are part of an Italian proper name, such as a place name or a church name, or when a saint's English equivalent is either nonexistent or highly obscure.

MEASUREMENTS. Inch equivalents are given with the original centimeters, but are rounded off because the precise sounding "5 cm" really just means "a couple of inches" in the home kitchen.

ORGANIZATION OF THE BOOK. Each entry, corresponding to a pasta shape, is divided as follows.

INGREDIENTS: This is a list of the usual traditional ingredients. If it sometimes seems vague or ambiguous, it is because people used what they could lay hands on.

HOW MADE: This is descriptive of traditional methods. It is not (necessarily) intended as a recipe.

ALSO KNOWN AS: Almost all the pastas are known by many, many names. No list can be exhaustive.

HOW SERVED: The principal traditional ways are included. Modern chefs are devising all kinds of new ways to serve traditional pastas, but that is for another book.

WHERE FOUND: Again, these are the main places. Comprehensiveness is not possible. Lovers of parallel lists—all provinces, all cities—will have to loosen up here. The list of sightings of a given pasta may well consist of a region, the outskirts of a city in a different region, and a valley somewhere. In cases in which a pasta is found throughout Italy without clear associations with a given place, it is noted as "widespread."

REMARKS: These are notes on the shape's history, documentation, literary allusions, etymology, folklore, and anecdotes.

Oretta and I consider ourselves very fortunate indeed that our book is being published by University of California Press and thank Darra Goldstein, Sheila Levine, and Dore Brown for their wise and good-humored counsel throughout the months of translation and editing. As we prepared the draft, we often wondered who they could possibly find to copyedit a book like this, with its history, its geography, its literature, and its rolling and twisting of dough into the most outlandish shapes. Oretta doubted that a single copyeditor could combine the culinary expertise and cultural breadth needed for the task, while I feared that no one could possibly have the strength, patience, and restraint I knew the job required. But there was no need to worry. We are obliged to the press for assigning just such a jewel, Sharon Silva, of whom we are in awe and to whom we are profoundly grateful.

Oretta Zanini De Vita has been my friend here in Rome for more than twenty years, and much of what I know about Italian food and its history has come from listening to Oretta talk and from translating her work. She is the classic walking encyclopedia of Italian social history and so much more, and gives her pearls for the asking. It would be hard to find another person so well suited to this topic, and it has been a privilege for me to help bring her work to an international readership.

And speaking of walking encyclopedias, my friend Leofranc Holford Strevens, in Oxford, has replied within minutes to all my most desperate e-mail queries on everything from Albanian diacritical marks to Greek citations. Thanks, too, as always, to the irreplaceable Howard Isaacs, my partner for the 1998 *Dictionary of Italian Cuisine*. I could never have translated this book without that earlier work, and I blessed him every time I found exactly the term I sought over these last months. And of course I have been greatly helped by my husband, Francesco Filippi, whose passion for pasta takes second place to no man's.

VOYAGE IN THE PASTA UNIVERSE

The Reasons for This Research

[ORETTA ZANINI DE VITA]

Pasta may be the unchallenged symbol of Italian food, yet no in-depth research has ever been done on its many shapes. Recent cookery texts are stuck mainly on the nobler stuffed pastas, with little attention to their form, and recipes nowadays almost always call for factory-made pasta. One small exception is Luigi Sada and his 1982 *Spaghetti e compagni*,[1] where he talks about the shapes of homemade pasta in Puglia, his home region. A century earlier, the work of the Sicilian ethnologist Giuseppe Pitré[2] repeats the names given in Perez's 1870 *Vocabolario siciliano-italiano*.[3] These, however, refer in particular to the so-called pastas *d'ingegno*, or what the Sicilians called *d'arbitrio*, that is, to the first pastas manufactured with the ancestors of modern industrial machinery. There were others, especially in the 1800s, who tried to impose some order on the world of pasta shapes, but they eventually threw in the towel. With no written sources—many of the operators were illiterate—and the difficulty of testing sources directly, they abandoned the project.

The scholars who have studied food over time have largely relied on early printed texts. I chose a different way. First, I sought oral sources for what remains alive in memory of the pasta-making tradition, and then corresponding evidence in printed texts. It has been a long and exhausting journey. I traveled to small towns and talked with samplings of very old people, trying to jog their memories about the pasta-making traditions and rituals of the past. Even though much has changed, a great deal remains. Also, many people today are trying to reclaim this past and fix it in the collective memory. Important in this regard is the work of associations and other organizations laboring on the spot, many established ad hoc, such as the Accademia del Pizzocchero di Teglio, dedicated to preserving the *pizzocchero* of the Valtellina. I was aided by housewives' family recipe collections, too, but only where I was able to verify their statements on the ground.

My interviews with these older people also made me more aware of how rapidly the agrarian landscape had been transformed and how the grain varieties once essential to the making of pasta and other foods had disappeared with the entry onto the market of superior varieties from other countries. Their stories vividly confirmed what had emerged from the succession of Italian inquests into the country's economic situation between the 1800s and the 1950s: until just after World War II, the country had eaten "green," that is, only vegetable soup, with pasta as a rule reserved for the tables of the middle and upper classes in towns and cities and only occasionally for the feast-day tables of the poor.

Greater prosperity and better living conditions in some areas can be inferred from the ingredients used in the local pasta. For example, in Tuscany, *frascarelli* contained eggs; in Piedmont, the old farm wealth was visible in the typical egg-rich *tajarin,* sometimes even made only with yolks. In Bologna, where *pasta all'uovo* was well rooted, factory production in the early 1900s was already linking the name of the city to particular pasta shapes.[4]

The widespread prosperity of today has brought a reversal of the old order: the pasta that we eat almost daily is usually factory made, and modern and advanced techniques for preservation have made possible the broad distribution of vacuum-packed fresh pastas, whose consumption is growing rapidly. In the course of my research, I identified more than thirteen hundred pasta names, counting both factory made and homemade, which represent almost as many different shapes or sizes, though some variations are, of course, small.

A Terminological Tower of Babel

A current Italian-language dictionary defines the word *maccherone* as *"pasta alimentare*[5] of diverse formats depending on regions of provenance." But the definition takes little account of the myriad shapes that constellate the Italian pasta universe.

A true *pastario*—a catalog of pastas—that is, one that includes homemade pastas and that covers all of Italy, has never been attempted. Exceptions are certain publications[6] and the catalogs of various industrial producers, which refer specifically only to the cold and numerous shapes extruded through dies, but which also include numerous reminiscences of homemade formats of yesteryear. The classic printed texts, from the 1400s on, include clusters of pasta terminology here and there. For certain pastas, we know the name but not the shape. Some books shed light on the presence of pastas in a well-delimited territory. Skimming the index of the precious sixteenth-century book by Giovan Battista Rossetti,[7] *scalco* of Lucrezia d'Este, duchess of Urbino, we find *macaroni all'urbinata,* which the author sometimes cooks in milk, distinguished from the *macaroni ferraresi* (of Ferrara), which are made of bread. He mentions *gnocchetti di Genova,* which he distinguishes from French ones, and he notes *vermicelli* made with hard-boiled egg yolks; *maccaroni d'anguilla* (of eel), called *sblisegotti; canellini bergamaschi; maccaroni* of bread; and others of stale bread crumbs. Whatever the format of these pastas, the *scalco* knew exactly where they came from. *Tortelli* appear both large and small, down to *tortelletti piccolissimi.* There are *tortelli di zucca,* fried ones filled with eel, those with marzipan, and—a very precious piece of information—the *tortelli* of Lombardy, attesting the early diffusion of stuffed pasta in that region.

Even recent studies exclude the myriad of small sculptures made with water, flour, and a pinch of salt by the expert hands of the housewives of other times. The popular imagination has gradually christened them with endearing names, such as *farfalline* (little butterflies), *nastrini* (little ribbons), *margherite* (daisies), or, with an eye to the barnyard, *creste di gallo* (coxcombs), *galletti* (small roosters), *corna di bue* (ox horns), and *denti di cavallo* (horse's teeth). Then come *occhi* (eyes) *di lupo* (wolf), *di pernice* (partridge), *di passero* (sparrow), and on down, smaller and smaller, until we get to *occhi di pulce* (flea) and *punte d'ago* (needle points). The weather contributed, too, with *tempestine* (little storms) and *grandinine* (little hailstones), and the lame in the village became pastas called *gobbini* and *stortini.* From the forest came *folletti* (elves) and *diavoletti* (imps), and on humid summer evenings, *lucciole* (fireflies) and *lumachelle* (snails). Saints and demons populate the Italian pasta universe, too, linked to sagas, legends, beliefs, and superstitions.

Some epic names commemorate Italy's wars in Africa. Libya inspired *tripolini* (from Tripoli), which entered the market in 1911, and *bengasini* (from Benghazi). Abyssinia gave its name to *abissini,* and *assabesi* honor the purchase of the port of Assab by the Genoese Rubattino Shipping Company in 1869. These names do not always denote the pasta format itself. Sometimes they refer to the shape of African headdresses, or to the rings (*anelli*) the women of Benghazi wore in their ears, though more often the terms are assigned without precise reference. There is a vast category of pastas named for the House of Savoy as well, on the Italian throne from the Unification until the end of World War II, and thus we still have today *mafaldine* (named for Princess Mafalda), *regine* (queens), and *reginelle* (its diminutive), all of them factory-made *tagliatelle* with a ruffled edge, like the popular image of a queen's crown.

The advent of industry introduced names that reflected the then-emerging science of machinery, and thus we have *ruote* (wheels), and the smaller *rotelle, rotelline, eliche* (propellers), and even *dischi volanti* (flying saucers)—all words of a recent past.

Ravioli and Tortelli

The terms *raviolo* and *tortello,* along with such related terminology as *anolino, agnolino, cappelletto, tortellaccio,* and the like, have caused great confusion over time.

Today, the differences are especially, but not only, geographical: the *cappelletto* is from Romagna, the *anolino* from Parma, the *agnolino* from Mantova, the *tortellino* from Bologna, the *agnolotto* from Piedmont, and so on. Rather than enter into the merits of linguistic problems that do not concern my work, I will instead simply set forth, in chronological order, the texts consulted.

In the earliest sources, the *raviolo* is a pasta wrapping filled with meat or other foods, folded into a triangle. Giambonino da Cremona,[8] writing in the late thirteenth century, collects some eighty Arab recipes of both gastronomic and nutritional interest taken from a monumental Arabic treatise on gastronomy by Ibn Butlan, a physician who lived in Baghdad and died in 1100. Here we have the first description of a type of *ravioli* called *sambusaj,* a triangular pasta container filled with ground meat. Therefore, at its landing with the Muslims in Sicily, the *raviolo* was probably wrapped in pasta. This is supported by the now-famous remark of Salimbene da Parma, who, in his thirteenth-century chronicle, refers to a *raviolus sine crusta de pasta,*[9] that is, just the filling with no wrapping, and the word *raviolo* evidently, like Salimbene, came from the north. But if such a dish was served to the good Salimbene, it means that a bite-sized food, made with diverse ingredients from bread to cheese and variously spiced and sauced, must have been circulating at the same time.[10] In fact, the works over the next centuries mention the *raviolo* as we know it today in its double guise, wrapped and unwrapped *(ravioli gnudi)*. Thus, it seems the *raviolo* arrived with its pasta mantle, but then lost it and became confused with the *gnocco*.

In 1612, with the first dictionary published by the Accademia della Crusca, we finally have a first precious definition: under *raviolo* we read, "delicate food in small pieces, made of cheese, eggs, herbs, and spices"; and under *tortello*, "a kind of *raviolo* with pasta wrapping." The subsequent editions of the *Vocabolario della Crusca*[11] repeat these definitions, and the same holds for the various eighteenth- and nineteenth-century Italian dictionaries.

For the very few able to read and write, then, the *tortello* was a *raviolo* covered with pasta, a distinction still made in Tuscany. Attestations to this effect follow in the *Libretto di cucina* of Gio Batta Magi, who lived in Arezzo between 1842 and 1885;[12] Fanfani's *Vocabolario dell'uso toscano;*[13] the anonymous *Cuoco sapiente,* published in Florence in 1881; and finally in the work of Pellegrino Artusi, of Florence, who published the first of countless editions of his own invaluable book, *La scienza in cucina o l'Arte del mangiar bene,* in 1891.

Meanwhile, additional terms emerged from other locations to reopen the confusion. In 1934, in the Marche, Vincenzo Agnoletti defines *raviolo alla romana* as a modern *raviolo di ricotta e spinaci* wrapped in pasta and shaped like a half-moon, and he introduces an *agnolotto piemontese,* which for him is a *gnocco* cooked in broth. He alludes to *tortellini* and *cappelletti* as small *ravioli* wrapped in pasta, variously filled.[14] Moving southward, Ippolito Cavalcanti, duke of Buonvicino,[15] in his amusing 1846 work in Neapolitan dialect, explains the *raviolo* as wrapped in pasta, stuffed with meat and ricotta, and as big as a Neapolitan *tarì* or a Tuscan *paolo*, both coins. Caterina Prato, whose *Manuale di cucina* was published in Trieste in 1906, describes the *raviolo* as wrapped in pasta and illustrates a half-moon *raviolo* alongside a wheel-type pasta cutter.[16] The Roman authors Adolfo Giaquinto[17] and his famous niece, Ada Boni,[18] never speak of *tortelli*, but their works always contain the typical Roman *ravioli*, a filling of ricotta wrapped in pasta. *Il vero re dei cucinieri*, in the Milanese edition of 1933, distinguishes the *raviolo alla milanese* (a *gnocco* of boiled meat) from the *agnolotto alla toscana*, whose filling is wrapped in pasta, and from the classic *tortellino alla bolognese*.[19] *Agnolotti* and *tortellini* are both cooked in broth. Finally, the very popular recipes of Petronilla[20] evoke Christmas *ravioli*: ". . . remember the superlative *minestra*, the one that is the Christmas classic, the one that requires an ultra-delicious filling; the one that is called *ravioli*, or *tortellini*, or *agnolotti*, or *cappelletti*." We have thus arrived at the modern term, which does not distinguish between *tortello* and *raviolo*, and this is confirmed by the numerous Italian-language dictionaries published since just after World War II.

If next we have a look at the great cookbooks published since the 1960s, we see now that Luigi Carnacina considers *tortelli* and *ravioli* synonyms:[21] he uses *tortelli* for the squash-filled ones found in Lombardy and *ravioli* for the ricotta-filled ones of Genoa, but they are essentially the same thing, a filling wrapped in pasta. The seventh edition of the famous *Il cucchiaio d'argento*[22] moves along the same line. We can conclude the topic by consulting Battaglia's dictionary:[23] in this monumental work, we find confirmation of the modern version of the *raviolo* wrapped in pasta, but also the specification that it can be found without pasta in the old terminology.

The modern regional stuffed pastas are more likely to vary the fillings than the ingredients of the dough, though olive oil may be added in the south. The sizes and shapes are usually specified, and the most important ones have their own entries in this book.

Homemade Pasta

By what mysterious channels the various homemade formats spread throughout Italy is difficult to say, though one thing is certain: conquest played a role. For example, the presence of *orecchiette* can be traced to the domination of Puglia by the Angevin lords of Provence in the thirteenth century. They resemble the *crosets* of Provence, which are still made in Piedmont with the same name. Migrations have also been an influence, such as the successive waves of Albanians who settled in various parts of the peninsula starting in the 1400s. They brought the extra-long *spaghetti* called *shtridhëlat*, which, with little variation, became the *maccheroni a fezze* of northern Lazio and the *maccheroni alla molenara* typical of Abruzzo, the latter probably introduced by the Albanian communities of nearby Molise. The same pasta is known as *manare* in the areas of Basilicata where a number of Albanian communities reside. Fairs and markets, some of which lasted for months at a time—the fair held from March to October at the Abbey of Farfa in Sabina, in northern Lazio, is a good example—likely contributed in no small measure to the diffusion of recipes and foods. Workers who migrated for seasonal labor or transhumance also carried knowledge of new foods back and forth. Finally, equal importance must be ascribed to specialist artisans[24] who frequently took their work here and there in the service of this or that *signore*.

On the other hand, some types of pasta took the opposite path: they were typical of a particular territory, yet were unknown only a few miles away. Often this was because the two territories once belonged to different estates, though sometimes the reason lay in chauvinistic hostilities between two nearby towns. Or the two towns, close by as the crow flies, were separated for centuries by lack of roads, many of which date in Italy only to the 1960s.[25]

The advent of the modern pasta industry, facilitated by large-scale retail chains, has fostered maximum diffusion of shapes that were once limited to their place of origin.

From Homemade Pasta to the *Maccheronaio*

Homemade pasta moved early from family kitchens into the workshops of the mills. There the town women, used to preparing pasta in their own kitchen, continued in the workplace to make creative shapes, at first always by hand. With the arrival of the early machines, the small formats—*gnocchetti, strascinati,* and *farfalline,* to name a few—remained the province of the women.[26]

At the beginning of the sixteenth century, the hills that frame the Bay of Naples were punctuated by myriad so-called *cirmoli,* the old mills powered by the precious waters of the river Sarno, or by donkeys, horses, or even men. Much later, with the development of hydraulic mills, these small, family-run industries were not replaced by the nascent industry, but have continued operation up to our own day.[27]

The mills scattered through the Campanian hinterland, and especially those of Torre Annunziata and Gragnano, on the Bay of Naples, were already working with such special grains as the precious *saragolle* of the Capitanata area. Making pasta was highly specialized labor, slow, difficult, and exhausting: the dough was made in the *martora,* a sort of large *madia,* in which the worker kneaded it with his feet, exactly like crushing grapes, while gripping a hanging cord. It could take two to three hours to stomp a batch of *semola* with cold water. The dough was then transferred onto the rolling pin, in those days called a *schianaturo* (or sometimes *laganaturo*), with which the women made the various shapes of *fusilli, tufoli, vermicelli,* and the like by hand. Every day, these pastas were duly dried, packed into large baskets, and carried by mule down remote mountain paths to Naples, the populous capital of the kingdom, as in a religious procession.[28]

The breakthrough in working methods came in the sixteenth century, with the appearance of the first *ingegni*. They made the work faster and easier, and at the same time increased production to meet an ever-more-pressing demand.

These were simple machines that multiplied rapidly thanks to skilled woodworkers: the historical archive of the Banco di Napoli contains a receipt for payment for an *'ngegno da maccaruni*, dated 1596. Also in Naples, in 1579, the Capitolazioni dell'Arte, the registry of guilds, distinguished between *maccaruni* (which were *bucati,* pierced) and *vermicelli,* and the *vermicellari,* now members of a prestigious political structure, launched their Statuto dell'Arte dei Vermicellari on October 16, 1699, establishing a chapel in the church of the Carmine Maggiore (one of the largest churches in Naples).[29] This was the moment when the price of pasta dropped significantly, making pasta available even to the poorest citizens. It was more or less beginning in this period that the Grand Tour travelers to Naples watched with amusement the daily meal of the so-called *lazzari,*[30] at the street corners, who, with a deft movement of the fingers, slid *maccheroni* dressed with cheese into their mouths. The *maccheronaio* was often willing to extend credit to those too poor to pay cash. But this ready supply of pasta was an urban, a Neapolitan, phenomenon. Throughout the region, the rural poor ate mostly "green."

The miraculous *'ngegno da maccaruni* consisted of a wooden cylinder made from a single piece of oak, lined with copper on the inside and held fast by bolts. It had a sort of screw piston that pushed the hard dough through the die, from which emerged the first *maccheroni,* the hole perfectly centered. Now dough could be made with hot water, which gave better results. But the dough had to be kneaded quickly, as it fermented easily: the difficulty for the operator did not decrease; it merely shifted. With time, the work was facilitated by the first shafted mixers for kneading, and other improvements were to follow.

The Difficult Process of Drying

A batch of pasta began its long march when the workman called *'o spannatore* grabbed it with a rapid movement as it emerged from the machine and hung it on long sticks. From there it was taken immediately into the sun or warm open air, with due attention to drafts. Thus began the difficult process of drying. Fresh pastas are hygroscopic and sensitive to weather, which is why the early pasta makers of the coast were almost always magicians. They scrutinized the sky, questioned the stars, and examined the phases of the moon and the winds to establish how to set the pasta to dry because the pasta, they said, "has to dry with its own air": humid air at the beginning and then dry air in the days that follow. There is a saying, "Make the *maccheroni* with the *scirocco,* dry them with the *tramontana,*" referring to the warm, moist wind from the south and the cold, dry wind from over the Alps. The old chief *pastaio* (pasta maker) knew that the winds usually changed at noon and midnight along the coast, and that his drying racks would need attention at those hours. Toward April and October, if the *scirocco* blew, it turned into a *tramontana* at around one or two in the morning, and it was necessary to hurry and move the pasta to the large drying areas. The back streets echoed with the voice of *u chiammatore* (the caller), who awakened the workers for their shift.

The old streets of Torre Annunziata and Gragnano became immense open-air drying racks,[31] under the vigilant nose of the *pastaio,* who kept track of the changing winds. This was where what is technically called *incartamento* took place. It was the first drying, and the faster the better. Then the precious product was brought to *rinvenire,* that is, to rest in cool, damp rooms, preferably underground, with absolutely no drafts. The *pastaio* had no thermometer, but knew how to gauge when the temperature was just right, that is, about 59°F (15°C), cooler than for the *incartamento.*[32]

Next, the long sticks were taken to special two-story buildings called *stenditoi,* where they were carefully hung in two or more tiers and positioned so the tips of the pasta hanging from the sticks just touched the pasta on the tier just beneath it. The tips of the pasta of the lowest tier had to be at least 4 inches (10 cm) from the ground. The sticks were positioned next to one another, and the closer they were, the better the drying.[33] Here the pasta rested for a day, allowing the internal moisture to come slowly to the surface, making the pasta seem fresh again. The last operation was the transfer of the pasta to its final drying place, another two-story structure, as for the *rinvenimento.* Here the sticks were arranged again in several tiers, but this time the important distance was from the ceiling: the topmost row of hanging pasta had to be about a meter (about a yard) from it. Again the sticks were set so that the tips of the pasta above just touched the tops of that beneath, which helped keep them from drying out too fast. The head *pastaio* checked the doors and windows to provide the slow final drying with the needed air, a little at a time. In summer, the whole operation took eight days, but in winter, it took nearly three weeks, or more in damp weather. Breaking a piece of *maccherone* near his ear, the pasta magus could hear whether it had dried perfectly and could survive the long sea voyage under the Pulcinella trademark that took the pasta of Naples around the world.

The march of industrialization has been long and tortuous throughout Italy, which at the beginning of the twentieth century still lacked electricity and channels of communication. For example, in 1913, the electric mill built by the Swiss at Monteroduni, in Molise, produced pasta day and night and provided electricity to light the town.[34]

From the *Ingegno* to the Modern Machines

Meanwhile, further improvements led to faster and more numerous machines and greatly improved the quality of production. The *pastaio* was still needed, however, to dose out the water, the quantity of which was his secret: he made the dough harder for the largest sizes; softer for *fettuccine, vermicellini,* and *capellini;* and softer still for *spaghetti* and *bucatini.* If the pasta came out defective, the *pastaio* would eliminate it as *munnezzaglia* (trash). The shapes multiplied with the invention of new dies, now made not only with bronze but also with nickel and other noncorrosive materials. Local scholars have estimated that the number of formats grew from about one hundred fifty to eight hundred or more.[35] This was also when new folding and cutting machines produced special formats—long pastas diversified in length, width, and thickness—which were more in demand in the south. The *Esposizione nazionale illustrata di Palermo 1891–92,*[36] in summing up the advanced Sicilian pasta industry as represented at the exposition, pointed out that the new technologies allowed Sicilian producers to offer a catalog of more than one hundred pasta formats.

In the north, thinner, nested pastas or tiny *pastine* were preferred. A particular type of pasta with ruffled edge and variously folded, such as *farfalle,* was catalogued as *pasta tipo Bologna.*[37] Many of these formats disappeared long ago, but pasta makers today still vie to invent imaginative types, and some innovative formats are even suggested by important designers. The national archive in Rome contains documents detailing the patents granted by the Kingdom of Sardinia, and later of Italy, beginning in 1855, including a notable quantity on projects on various aspects of food, in particular increasingly sophisticated machines for the production of pastas. This was the dawn of the modern pasta industry, with pastas nowadays dried in about five hours at 176°F (80°C), 212°F (100°C), and higher.[38]

Pastasciutta, Our Daily Dish

The spread of pasta on Italian tables, as we understand the term today, is relatively modern. Until the years just before and just after World War II, four-fifths of the population of Italy living in the countryside had a diet generically based on plants. Pasta was reserved for feast days, often served in a legume soup. With the economic boom that began in the early 1960s, pasta began to be made daily in rural homes, and these are the formats codified by tradition. At the same time, the emerging urban bourgeoisie were eating pasta every day. On Sunday, they served special pastas, perhaps stuffed, with even more special condiments.

In the gastronomic-cultural enclaves of the south, on the other hand, housewives were making *strascinati:* rolled with one finger, with two, with four, even with eight, to make different sizes. Every little town, almost every family, called these pastas something different, and they served them on feast days enveloped in flavorful sauces of pork, lamb, or vegetables, all linked by the obligatory tomato and parmigiano.

Consumerism and prosperity, evident in the proliferation of packaged prepared foods, are obfuscating the ancient roots of our gastronomic culture. With this book, well aware of the inevitable limits of my research, I have aimed to open the way to more profound research on the difficult subject of the world of pasta. In other words, this is a first, hesitant attempt to catalog an inalienable heritage that belongs to all Italians. Perhaps there are some courageous and willing souls to carry it on.

Notes

1. L. Sada, *Spaghetti e compagni* (Bari, 1982).
2. G. Pitré, *Usi, costumi, credenze e pregiudizi del popolo siciliano* (Palermo: Pedone-Lauriel, 1889).
3. G. Perez, *Vocabolario siciliano-italiano* (Palermo, 1870).
4. R. Rovetta, *Industria del pastificio o dei maccheroni* (Milano: Hoepli, 1951), 270.
5. The full name of pasta. The Italian word *pasta* covers a great deal of ground, including almost anything for which the English word *paste* is used.
6. See E. Medagliani and F. Gosetti, *Pastario ovvero atlante delle paste alimenari italiane* (Milano: Bibliotheca culinaria, 1997); also S. Cirillo, *Belle, tipiche e famose, 240 formati di pasta italiana* (Perugia: ali&no editrice, 2002).
7. G. Battista Rossetti, *Dello scalco* (Ferrara, 1584).
8. Ms. Lat. 9328, Bibliothèque Nationale, Paris, brought to light by Anna Martellotti, *Il Liber de ferculis di Giambonino da Cremona. La gastronomia araba in Occidente nella trattatistica dietetica* (Fasano: Schiena, 2001).
9. Salimbene de Adam, *Cronica* (Bari: Laterza, 1966), 2:797.
10. See the entries on *gnocco* and *ravioli*.
11. Nevertheless, these dictionaries are fundamentally literary and are not absolutely reliable in matters of arts and trades.

12. *Libretto di cucina di Gio Batta Magi, Aretino, 1842–1885*, ed. P. Zoi (Arezzo, 1989).

13. Pietro Fanfani, *Vocabolario dell'uso toscano* (Firenze: Barbera, 1863).

14. V. Agnoletti, *Manuale del cuoco e del pasticcere* (Pesaro: Nobili, 1834).

15. "La vera cucina casereccia del cavalier Ippolito Cavalcanti duca di Buonvicino," in *Cucina teorico-pratica divisa in quattro sezioni* (Milano, 1904).

16. C. Prato, *Manuale di cucina* (Verona and Padova: Fratelli Drucker, 1906).

17. A. Giaquinto, *La cucina di famiglia* (Roma, 1922).

18. A. Boni, *La cucina romana* (Roma, 1924). There is not a trace of *tortelli* or *ravioli* in this edition, while the last Roman edition, 1992, contains the typical Roman *ravioli* with ricotta, but does not mention *tortelli*.

19. G. Belloni, *Il vero re dei cucinieri* (Milano: Madella, 1933).

20. A. Moretti Foggia Della Rovere, *Altre ricette di Petronilla* (Milano: Sonzogno, 1937), 76.

21. L. Carnacina, *Il Carnacina* (Garzanti, 1961).

22. A. Monti Tedeschi, *Il cucchiaio d'argento* (Milano: Domus, 1950–86).

23. S. Battaglia, *Grande dizionario della lingua italiana* (Trento: UTET, 1990, reprint of 1961 edition), vol. 15, s.v.

24. See G. Filangieri, *Indice degli artefici delle arti maggiori e minori, la più parte ignoti o poco noti sì napoletani e siciliani, sì delle altre Regioni d'Italia o stranieri . . .* (Napoli, 1891).

25. The single town of Guidonia Montecelio, in the province of Rome, was once divided into two different municipalities about half a mile (800 meters) apart. In Guidonia, *pingiarelle* are not yet found, while they are typical of Montecelio.

26. This stage of development between home pasta making and industrial manufacturing was short-lived, especially for the middle classes, whose kitchens commonly included a small *torchio*, which permitted different pasta formats to be made. These small devices for home use are documented in all the regions and survived even into the 1950s, with the *bigolaro* in Veneto.

27. In 1789, the municipality of Torre Annunziata authorized a private citizen, Don Salvatore Montello, to make and sell *maccaroni* "of good quality and a single kind"; two years later, in 1791, this concession was also granted to Pasquale Sabatino, and then in 1792 to Vincenzo Coda, in 1795 to Gaetano de' Liguoro, and in 1796 to Francesco Izzo. The French occupation at the end of the eighteenth century completely upset the long-standing pasta factories so severely that much of the equipment was used as firewood for a particularly bitter winter. Between 1900 and 1920, associations of mills and pasta makers formed, but the serious crisis came in 1935 (*Quaderni culturali – Biblioteca comunale di Gragnano – Gragnano dei macaroni*, 1983).

28. Complete set of equipment for a pasta workshop in the 1600s is listed in G. Pratesi, *L'industria della pasta alimentare* (Molini d'Italia, 1957). See also A. Abenante, *Maccaronari* (Napoli: Novus Campus, 2002).

29. Archivio di Stato di Napoli, Cappellano maggiore—statuti di Corporazioni, Congregazioni ed altri enti civili ed ecclesiastici (1483–1808), fascio 1201/3.

30. In southern Italy, especially Naples, the word means a rag-clad beggar, after the Lazarus of the Gospel of Saint Luke (16:19–31). The Spanish in Naples used the term

disparagingly to indicate the common people of the Mercato quarter who had participated in the revolt of Masaniello in 1647.

31. A fine collection of photographs of pasta production is kept in the town archive of
Gragnano (Naples Province).

32. For the complex production of the first industrial pastas, see also Rovetta, *Industria*,
and L. Lirici, *Manuale del capo pastaio* (1983).

33. A. Giordano, *L'arte bianca di Torre Annunziata* (n.d.).

34. For the situation of the pasta factories in Molise in the first years of the twentieth
century, see G. Masciotta, *Il Molise dalle origini ai nostri giorni* (Napoli, 1915).

35. This thesis is supported by, among others, Abenante, *Maccaronari*.

36. Unbound pages, private collection, Rome.

37. Rovetta, *Industria*, 270.

38. But drying the pasta at low temperature still remains the best course. Even if this
road is not likely to be followed by the large industrial pasta makers, there are still
small niche producers, such as Martelli, in Lari (Pisa), who produce very few types
and dry them at 91.4° to 95°F (33° to 35°C).

INTRODUCTION TO THE FIRST ITALIAN EDITION

[CORRADO BARBERIS, PRESIDENT

OF THE ITALIAN INSTITUTE OF RURAL SOCIOLOGY]

In the beginning was the *gnocco*. Our ancestors learned that by adding water to flour and subjecting the mixture to intense pressure, the resulting mass could yield both what we call pasta and what we call bread. The difference was only in the addition of a little yeast or salt. The mother of all the pastas is thus represented by an enormous *gnocco*. If allowed to ferment, it begins to become bread dough. If not, it can be worked into fresh noodles and dried. Or it can be formed into the true *gnocchi* of our gastronomic treatises. German best expresses this intuition: from the massive corpulence of the dumpling (*Knödel, gnocco* in Italian) derives the airy lightness of the noodle *(Nudel).*[1]

Maurizio, a Polish botanist clearly of Italian ancestry, active in the period between the two world wars, wrote that the history of pasta should be written in parallel with the consumption of cereals.[2] There would thus be four stages. In the first, the cereal is consumed like any other fruit. In the second, it is transformed by toasting (see *cajubi* entry) or by boiling, of which *cuccía,* the traditional Siracusan dish in honor of Saint Lucy, is an excellent example. The third is represented by milling to make flour that can be made into a polenta. In the fourth, the flour is kneaded with water, kept hard but elastic, producing a mass that can be made into bread or pasta, which is exactly the case of the *gnocco*.

The simplest use is the cut grain gathered in the field. The grains are chewed like berries or other wild fruits. The most authoritative testimony on this stage is in the Gospel of Saint Mark (2:23–24): "And it came to pass, that he went through the cornfields on the Sabbath day; and his disciples began, as they went, to pluck the ears of corn. And the Pharisees said unto him, Behold, why do they on the Sabbath day that which is not lawful?" Note that the Pharisees do not contest the taking of food by hungry people. Their objection is to an otherwise legitimate activity taking place on the Sabbath.

Jesus's disciples were behind the times, adopting styles of life still allowed but out of date. The practice of swallowing grains, not green or semigreen but toasted, is attested in Leviticus (2:14), datable around the fifteenth century B.C., and in the book of Ruth, in the eleventh century B.C. But were they toasted grains or polenta? Modern translations favor the first, the older ones the second—a sign of a certain interchangeability of terms and of a contemporary practice of two types of consumption. The second and third phases of cereal use, toasted grains and polenta, thus occurred at the same time.

Pliny the Elder tells us that the diet of the ancient Romans was based not on bread but on mushes, pottages, or porridges,[3] which was true not only of the future *caput mundi* but also of Mediterranean civilization in general. In fact, if bread came before mushes, the order of appearance would no longer be unleavened bread followed by leavened bread, but exactly the opposite. Cooking the fermented mushes before they went bad, thereby transforming them into bread, was the simplest way to placate the Hebrew concerns about the purity of food. This is why—maintains Gaetano Forni, who gets credit for the reversal of the commonplace—unleavened bread preceded leavened only if the toasted immature sheaf is considered bread, at least in embryo. Otherwise, it was the feared degeneration of the polenta of grain, with its own yeasts, that created bread.[4]

As for pasta, it is a descendant not of bread but of the other form of the *gnocco,* which belongs to Maurizio's fourth stage in the history of grains. Gottschalk was probably the first to deny this lineage, observing that in pasta making, "any sort of fermentation is carefully avoided, which is what suggests that pastas came before bread."[5] Not yet illuminated by Forni's thinking, Gottschalk departed from the historical primacy of unleavened bread, though for the wrong reason. But it is significant that one of the greatest and first historians of food had overturned the assumption that bread precedes pasta. This opened the way to Prosdocimi, who put forth the exquisitely philological argument that bread did not become pasta but the reverse.[6]

This is a minefield. The word *pasta* does not exist in Latin, or, better, it is useless to seek it in scholastic dictionaries, even the most famous. It belongs to what Prosdocimi calls "submerged" Latin. However, it appears fleetingly in the *Lexicon totius latinitatis* by Egidio Forcellini, defined as *"farina aqua subacta et in massam conversa."*[7] And it appears, much more broadly, in its two diminutives of *pastillum,* "small bread," and *pastillus,* also a small bread (*panino* in Italian) but also a pastille (*pastiglia* in Italian). The hypothesis brought up by Prosdocimi, that it belonged to a submerged Latin, is supported by the fact that Rocci's monumental Greek-Italian dictionary defines τὰ παστὰ as a sort of *farinata* (another possible confusion with *pappe,* or "mushes") and attributes its paternity to a rather obscure second-century A.D. author, Aelius Dionysius, as though after some three hundred years of Roman domination the word was still not comfortable in Greek.

If the generic concept of pasta is submerged in Latin culture, a concrete expression of it—*pasta sfoglia*—is certainly explicit in the literature. Cato thus presents the recipe for *placenta:* "Make a lower crust with two pounds of durum-wheat flour and make a sheet with four pounds of soft-wheat flour and two of durum, adding little by little the first to the rolled dough."[8]

This dough is called *tracta,* from the verb *trahere,* "to draw."[9] And the word reappears exactly in the Greek τράκτα, used by Athenaeus in the second century A.D., which suggests a certain Italic initiative at the international level. It is also on the agenda in Apicius: no fewer than seven recipes for fricassees end with "when it boils, break the *tracta* into it to bind, and stir."[10] This perplexing particular presupposes a regression from pasta to something else.

The importance of Cato's text, even more than the later references in Apicius, derives from three factors:

a. It documents the presence of two types of flour, soft wheat and true durum wheat, as ingredients for making pasta.

b. It emphasizes fresh pasta as the basis for pasta that can be stored.

c. It puts an end to the dispute about the objects depicted in the so-called Tomb of the Reliefs, or Tomba Bella, in Cerveteri, where some have seen a rolling pin, a pasta cutter, and even a board. The identification is certainly not universally accepted. Indeed, it is contested by the author of a semiofficial monograph on the diet of the Etruscans.[11] Rolling pin or no rolling pin, cutter or no cutter, board or no board, Cato's recipe tells us that these utensils could be found, if not on the walls of a wealthy tomb, at least in the kitchens of Etruscan-Roman families. Without them, no *tracta.*

Certainly, the pastas did not have the same importance on the tables of the Italian peninsula as they would later. They are absent from the three colossal banquets whose menus have been preserved by Horace (*Satires* 2.8), Petronius (*Satyricon* 49), and Juvenal (*Satires* 1.5), and also from the two rustic meals described by Horace (*Satires* 2.2) and Juvenal (*Satires* 4.2). And since *salumi* are likewise absent, we must deduce that the Italian diet has changed significantly.

The only mention of a plate of pasta—if, of course, pasta it was—is in Horace. The poet, tired of wandering through the Forum evening after evening, announces he is going back home where *"porri et ciceris laganique catinum"* (a bowl of leeks, chickpeas, and *lagane*) awaits him.[12] This combination is truly worthy of a son of Puglia, where still today *orecchiette* are served mixed with greens. And—given

Horace's ostentatiously simple tastes—this is also a first testimony of pasta as a common food.[13]

Bread or *lasagna*? To take the word toward its original meaning of bread we turn to the Bible, in the Vulgate of Saint Jerome, according to the reading, at least, given it by Bruno Laurioux.[14] And bread is also the *láganum* described by Isidorus of Seville, "wide and thin, cooked first in water, then fried in oil,"[15] even though the exegetes see this as an early *lasagna* because of the boiling.[16]

Lagane would probably never have become *lasagne* if it were not for the *lasanum,* the pot for boiling slices of bread or toast or fresh *tractae.* It was thus the container that transformed the contents, to make its definitive version, playing on consonants. Calepino in the fifteenth century has already pointed out that "soft" is within the word *lagana,* by its kinship with *laxus.* And Forcellini's *Lexicon totius latinitatis* gives us "thin strips made with flour and water which are cooked with fat broth, pepper, saffron, and cinnamon. It is certain that this is a very soft food that can be eaten without difficulty."[17] A splendid future—yet transitive—participle, *laganaturo,* tells us that a rolling pin is used much more often on a sheet of pasta than on a block of bread and that therefore *lagane,* for all intents and purposes, can be considered *lasagne.*

The Bible, Aristophanes, Horace, Cato, the appendix of Saint Isidorus of Seville—all the Mediterranean is present at this debate on what constitutes *lasagna.* And the same goes for dry pasta, with the necessary point of departure the Arab geographer al-Idrisi, who lived in Sicily at the time of the Norman king Roger II, between 1100 and 1165: "In Sicily there is a town called Trabia, an enchanted place endowed with perennial waters and mills. In this town they make a food of flour in the form of strings in quantities such as to supply in addition to the towns of Calabria, those of the Muslim and Christian territories."[18]

According to al-Idrisi, then, dry pasta, or what he called *itriya,* was of Sicilian origin and was carried elsewhere by Arab ships. Yet it is important to look at the whole Mediterranean. Emilio Sereni has documented, in a fundamental essay, that "by the ninth century we find in Syriac the word *itriya* being used to designate a sort of pasta," and that similar terms with much the same meaning already appeared in the Babylonian Talmud, in the Jerusalem Talmud, and in Aramaic.[19]

More recently, Silvano Serventi and Françoise Sabban have stated that:

· In the Jerusalem Talmud exists a trace of a pasta called *itrium,* known in Palestine between the third and fourth centuries of our era.

· Two terms have been identified in the glosses to the Babylonian Talmud, which complete the commentaries of Rachi (1040–1105, who lived at Troyes in Champagne): *trijes* and *vermishels,* assimilable respectively to the Italian *tri* and *vermicelli.*

· In the western Yiddish spoken by German Jews, the word *vrimzlisch* appears
as early as the twelfth century, that is, the time of al-Idrisi or shortly before.[20]
A Jewish candidacy for a product that, by virtue of the Diaspora, would have
reached northern Europe across the continent, not the Mediterranean? That
does not mean that Arab caravans did not also find it convenient to carry a little dry pasta, against the desert. *Itrion,* then, is a word found not only in
Galen, where it means generically doughs of flour and water, but also in the
Greek classics, from Anacreon (sixth century B.C.) on. Athenaeus (14.646 D),
in fact, refers to Anacreon to evoke a sweet made with sesame and honey,
something like those Carnival fritters that in various regions of Italy are
called *galani, chiacchiere,* and *frappe,* as noted by the wise commentator Leo
Citelli.

In other words, many diverse ethnicities have cooperated in obtaining the result.
We can conclude that the origin of pasta is not Italian, not Greek, not Jewish, not
Arab. It spread throughout the whole Mediterranean area at a stage that could be
defined as endemic, with probability of contagion along the Silk Road, seeing that
the Chinese have also been called in as possible progenitors, albeit erroneously.

Whatever may be its complicated origins, it is clear that pasta has served as a
sometimes opulent substitute for bread. This role has been illuminated by Emilio
Sereni, who reports that the count of Ripa Cursia, viceroy of the kingdom, is-
sued an edict in Naples on January 25, 1509, decreeing that "when the price of
flour rises because of war, or famine, or bad weather by five *carlini* or more per
tomolo, taralli, susamelli, ceppule, maccarune, trii, vermicelli, or other things of pasta
must not be made except in case of need for the sick."[21]

Thus relegated, together with various sweets, among foods that can be done
without in time of famine, *maccheroni* assumed secondary importance to the pri-
mordial one of bread. And so they would remain for a long time, if it is true, as
Fusco points out, that in 1755, the needs of the *maccheronari* for the city of Naples
were estimated at one hundred fifty thousand *tomoli* of wheat, against two mil-
lion of total consumption, putting their share at only 7.5 percent,[22] although Giacomo Casanova, exiled in a Bohemian castle, was said to get cranky if he was not
given his daily dish of *maccheroni.*[23] And Casanova was Venetian, not Neapolitan,
a sign that, especially among the upper classes, pasta had spread further than the
statistics suggest.

Casanova notwithstanding, consumption of pasta is relatively recent. What is
more, even today in Italy the official figure for pasta consumption is 25 to 28 kilograms (55 to 61.6 pounds) per person per year (the figure refers to factory-made
pasta; homemade defies quantification), while that of bread totals 60 to 65 kilograms (132 to 143 pounds).

The emergence of pasta as an important item on the shopping list had repercussions on the organization of the labor force. In Naples in 1546, the *vermicellari,* or pasta makers, broke away from the bakers' guild to found their own independent Arte dei Vermicellari. (Later, in 1699, its members were called *maccaronari.*[24]) Also, in Genoa, the *fidelari,* producers of very thin *spaghetti* still called *fedelini,* founded their own guild in 1574. They, too, had broken off from a larger body, not without discord, establishing a cohesive new entity. The chapters of the Arte dei Fidelari forbade any *maestro* of said art to ". . . go in an English ship, or in any other navigable vessel, to buy wheat or flour under penalty of five lire . . . , it is lawful only to buy them on land and it is obligatory to share said wheat or flour among the men of said art, that is, two-thirds and the other third remains to the buyer. . . ." In this way, no *pastaio* was able to monopolize the purchases. Furthermore, the whole guild had access to the same flours.[25]

This schism of the producers of new things from older and more authoritative organizations extended to more than pasta. The fight between the butchers and sausage makers of Modena dates to 1538, and it would take until early 1599 for the statutes of the new guild of the *lardaroli e salcicciari* (lard and sausage makers) to be approved by the duke Cesare d'Este.[26]

Economic specialization and technical progress are solidly joined. Between the sixteenth and eighteenth centuries, the appearance of new juridical bodies accompanied the first mechanical discoveries. The Brazilian sugar refineries made the word *engenho (ingegno)* fashionable to describe every device inspired by science. *Gramola* (kneading machine) and *torchio* are cited in a poem by Francesco Lemene in 1654.[27] But Messisbugo had already mentioned an *ingiegno per li maccheroni* in the first half of the sixteenth century.[28] Even earlier, none other than Leonardo da Vinci had attempted to industrialize pasta making, an aspect of his genius not as well known as it should be. The Atlantic Codex (foglio 51 R) contains the design of a gigantic machine for making *lasagne,* which could be reduced into "edible string," more like noodles than *spaghetti.* Unfortunately, the enormous wall of pasta, subjected to pressure to attain the desired thinness, broke before it could be cut. Faced with failure, Leonardo, who preferred to be thought of as a cook rather than a painter or even a military engineer (early in his career, while he was still at the workshop of Verrocchio, he managed a restaurant part-time), stubbornly did not give up. Again, the Atlantic Codex (2 v.a, 2 v.b) illustrates how to measure the tension sustainable by the *tagliarini,* or *spaghetti* as the case may be.[29] At the end of the eighteenth century, Goethe ate *maccheroni* of high class—but rather more manual than mechanical—at Agrigento.[30] Finally, in 1827, at Borgo Sansepolcro, as noted in the *Enciclopedia Treccani* under *pasta alimentare,* the Buitoni family opened "the oldest mechanical *pastificio* in Italy and therefore the world." Even after that date, however, the procedures often remained primitive, as evidenced by the famous episode of Ferdinand II, who was upset at seeing workmen kneading with their bare feet—without even a cloth to protect it—the dough that was to be transformed into various kinds of *maccheroni*.[31]

The introduction of dies for extrusion meant there were no longer any limits on the number of possible pastas, whose shapes had very much to do with taste and enjoyment. Cesare Marchi stresses the importance of the various shapes: "Try to drink a *spumante* first in a crystal glass and then in a coffee cup. . . ."[32] And the industrial proliferation, programmable at will, led the same author to ask: "How can we wonder at the many currents that fragment a political party if the same dough of eggs and flour can give rise to so many different children?"[33]

No matter how many different dies there are, they have never matched the creative fantasy of the Italian peasants. Rovetta estimated that industry had invented six hundred different types of pasta.[34] But in this book, which also includes many factory-made shapes, more than thirteen hundred products are cited. That number is in part the result of an undeniable creative imagination and in part the result of the same shape being given a different name. Italo Arieti has documented how within a single province, Viterbo, the same product, *lombrichelli,* is known by twenty-eight names.

We could choose from among the various nicknames in use in other towns in the province. Colorful but impolite is *culitonni,* used in Vignanello and Canepina; Bagnaia's *ghighi* is amusing; *scifulati* (or *schifulati?*—"slippery"), at Bomarzo, is curious; Grotte di Castro's *lilleri* likely brings happiness; and so on, with the *torcolacci* of Tessennano, the *tortorelli* of Ronciglione, the *filarelli* of Marta; the *chicarelli* of Bolsena; the *bighi* of Acquapendente; the *bichi* of Latera, San Lorenzo Nuovo, and Valentano; the *brigoli* of Carbognano; the *pici* of Latera and Caprarola; the *piciolelli* of Bassano Romano; the *pisciarelli* of Bagnoregio; the *visciarelli* of Orte; the *ceriole* (eels) of Monterosi; the *cechi* (hatchling eels) of Capranica; the *vermicotti* (worms) of Grotte Santo Stefano; the *ciuci* of Corchiano; the *spuntafusi* of Nepi; the *stratte* of Blera; and the *strangoli* of Farnese. At Tuscania, the elimination of the article transformed *lombrichelli* into *ombrichelli;* at Canino, we have *l'ombricoli,* and at Castiglione in Teverina, *l'umbrichelli.* At Vitorchiano, they are called *cavatelli,* attributing to this pasta, through an error now too late to correct, the name of the typical Puglian pasta of a different shape, namely, *cavatelli.*[35]

Twenty-eight names for a single food, only a few miles apart—what fun Nicolò Tommaseo, who was already smiling at the multiplication of pasta types in the middle of the nineteenth century, would have had with this litany. At this point arises the question brought up not only—and with greater force—by Roberto

SIMMS LIBRARY
ALBUQUERQUE ACADEMY

Fusco, but also by Ariel Toaff: Should homemade pasta be considered rich and factory made poor?[36]

Why is homemade rich? According to Fusco and Toaff, it is because it often contains eggs and it presupposes gentle hands—of a woman—to do the work. To
measure pasta with our yardstick, handmade pasta is unquestionably rich. Behind it
is a lady who has sacrificed a more profitable occupation to give her family an
exceptional product. Or she is a working specialist—a *sfoglina* as they call her in
Bologna—whose services have been acquired at their weight in gold. But it was not
always thus, and to relieve us of such hasty generalizations is the *Enciclopedia Treccani,* reflecting the national culture at the middle of the nineteenth century, which
states that "for the Italians of the Mezzogiorno, of Liguria, and of some other Italian regions, pasta already constituted the main dish and one of the two daily meals.
However, for much of that time, the southern peasants looked on it almost as a luxury food because it was factory made and had to be bought with cash," while
women's work in the home was calculated at zero cost because God gives time for
free (it took the industrial revolution of the 1950s to show that time is money, even
in Italy) and because the domestic pasta was also generally without eggs. The *Enciclopedia* continues, apropos of consumption of factory-made pasta, "by now it is
general among the less well-off classes of all Italy, while it is falling off among the
wealthier."

Emilio Sereni—as will be repeated in the entries that follow—documented the
decline of the Neapolitan diet during the years of Spanish rule: the invaders
found the Neapolitans *mangiafoglia* (with a fine fat broth made with plenty of
meat) and left them *mangiamaccheroni,* with these carbohydrates their only resource. The north, too, had had its culinary ups and downs, which had to do with
the mother of all the pastas and all the breads, the *gnocco.* The regression of the
Neapolitans from meat to wheat was matched, at the beginning of the nineteenth
century, by that of the Veronesi, and of the Po Valley in general, from wheat to
potato. Every reference to the French Revolution and to the advent of the bourgeoisie as the weight-bearing structure of the industrial society is purely by
chance. The old kings, to trick their subjects, plated bronze coins with silver. The
new powers gave their people potatoes disguised as wheat.

Outwardly, nothing had changed. The rolls of sieved potatoes, to which cooks
continued to add some flour, an egg, and a glass of milk, were still cut in rectangles with a knife lightly greased with butter. The rectangles were then pressed
against the back of a cheese grater and allowed to drop, perfectly ridged on one
side. They were then arranged in a pan and covered with sauce, just like their
wheaten predecessors.

Did the Veronesi notice that their *gnocchi* were no longer the same? If so, it did
not bother them very much. Every year they still celebrated the "bacchanal of

the *gnocco*," crowned by the election of its pope. And as long as it still had plenty of cheese, the product was extremely tasty. Just as a general euphoria occurs in certain times of economic inflation, the joyousness of the condiments concealed the worsening of the nutritional value, the devaluation of the coin.

Italy was the leader in the Mediterranean of the revaluation of the gastronomic currency. With *fregula*, Cagliari, in fact, created an Italian *cuscus*. *Fregula* is the counterreformation of the *semolini*. It is to *cuscus* what the Council of Trent was to Martin Luther. It grants its opponents a pinch of truth, in our case, the raw material of the *semolino*. It is pointless to be overly proud of Italy's primacy in pasta if it is of *flor di farina*, or soft wheat, which is merely a pastification of bread, as that great expert on mills, Pasquale Barracano, liked to repeat. It would be to refuse the dialogue, to close ourselves in a delusion of omnipotence. Both *sa fregula* and *cuscus* reduce the *semolino* to tiny balls, but the difference is that *cuscus* remains—exquisitely—a *semolino,* while *sa fregula* is a true pasta. It makes a leap in quality analogous to that which, for the faithful of the Holy Roman Church, separates the Catholic from the Lutheran—or, seeing that *cuscus* is Arab, the Christian from the Muslim. Technically, to be sure, even *cuscus* is a pasta, and as such it is included in this book.

In the beginning, there is the same receptacle: the shallow bowl that in Tunis is called *djefna* and in Sardinia *scivedda*. The *semolino* is arranged on its wall in each case. But here begin the differences: In the flat bottom of the *scivedda* are beaten eggs (two yolks), three tablespoons of lightly salted water, a good pinch of saffron to provide color, and sometimes also pecorino. Against such luxury the *djefna* seems desperately poor since into it go only a few drops of water. The parallel resumes with the work. A highly agile touch of fingers turned on the palm of the hand reduces the moistened *semolino* to tiny balls the size of a peppercorn in each case, though the Trapanese variant of *cuscus* cited by Ada Boni is the size of a tiny ball of shot and that of the Jewish tradition as tiny as a grain of sand. Both examples display a predilection for the small that has no equivalents in *fregula,* which tends, if anything, to heartier versions, as large as chickpeas, for eating as *pastasciutta*. With slight exaggeration we would say that *cuscus* is to *fregula* as plankton is to the smallest of tiny fish, the hatchlings, known as *neonata, gianchetti,* or *bianchetti,* on the coasts of Italy. These you chew; the others you swallow. And the definitive difference lies in the cooking, which for *cuscus* is steaming, and for *fregula,* to earn the name and be cookable, is to be dried in the oven (back when nobody worried about sanitation, the sun did the job, flies or no flies).

Only after this beginning, which makes it the smallest pasta in the world, but still an Italian pasta, is *fregula* worthy of being gently shipwrecked in its usual broth of *arselle* (tiny clams).

Notes

1. F. Kluge, *Etymologisches Wörterbuch der deutschen Sprache* (Berlin and New York, 1999), 593.

2. A. Maurizio, *Histoire de l'alimentation végétale depuis la préhistoire jusqu'à nos jours* (Paris, 1932), 482. Apropos of Italy and pasta he had just stated (p. 478): "if it is possible that they were born there as industrial product, it is nevertheless not their country of origin."

3. Pliny the Elder, *Naturalis historia* 18.83: "Pulte autem, non pane, vixisse longo tempore Romanos manifestum."

4. G. Forni, "L'agricoltura: coltivazione ed allevamento," in *Accademia dei Georgofili. Storia dell'agricoltura italiana* (Firenze, 2001), 54. On the derivation of *pane,* "bread," from *pappa,* "mush," Forni brings to bear an illuminating glottological documentation. It is sufficient to note, in German—therefore in a non-Mediterranean language—the affinity between *brot* = bread and *brei* = mush, similarly in the Slavic languages to that between *chleb* and *pochlebka* (p. 55). The occasion is propitious to recall that according to Maurizio (*Histoire,* p. 508), the Babylonians called beer "a bread that is drunk," while bread was called "a beer that is eaten." And the great Liebig also defined beer as "a liquid bread." See, on this entire topic, the valuable document of an Italo-Brazilian scholar, A. Barghini, *Did man once live by beer alone?* (São Paulo: Laboratorio de estudios evolutivos humanos, Cidade universitaria).

5. A. Gottschalk, *Histoire de l'alimentation et de la gastronomie depuis le préhistoire jusqu'à nos jours* (Paris, 1948), vol. I, 29.

6. A. Prosdocimi, "Sul nome del pane ecc.," in *Homo edens* IV (Regione autonoma Trentino–Alto Adige, Atti del Convegno tenutosi a Bolzano nei giorni 3/6 giugno 1993), 41–45.

7. *Lexicon totius latinitatis, Patavii,* 1940/41. It is equally worthwhile to point out that, according to the Touring Club Italiano, *L'Italia della pasta* (Milano, 2003), p. 8, the word *pasta* appears for the first time in Italian in a 1244 document in the Genoa State Archive. It is a recipe in which a physician of Bergamo, Ruggero di Bruca, forbids a patient to eat *pasta lissa* (Italian *liscia,* or "smooth").

8. Cato, *De agricultura* 76. "Farinae siligneae L. II, unde solum facias, in tracta farinae L. IIII et alicae primae L. II. Alicam in aquam infundito. Ubi bene mollis erit, in mortarium purum indito siccatoque bene. Deinde manibus deposito. Ubi bene subactum erit, farinae L. IIII paulatim addito. Id utrumque tracta facito. In qualo, ubi arescant, conponito."

   I have supplied the Latin, but the English is translated from Barberis's Italian interpretation of Cato's Latin.—MBF

9. In Italian, *tirare,* which means both "to draw," as, say, a wagon, and "to roll out" the dough. *Tractus, -a, -um,* the past participle of *trahere,* gives us, for example, the English word *traction.*—MBF

10. E.g., Apicius, *De re coquinaria* 4.3.1, *minutal marinum.*

11. H. Black, "La Tomba dei Rilievi di Cerveteri" in Ministero per i Beni Culturali e Ambientali, *L'alimentazione nel mondo antico: gli Etruschi* (Roma, 1987), 115: "In the large rec-

tangular panel represented on the right-hand pillar and in the sort of nightstick on the opposite pillar a noted archaeologist (Mingazzini 1954) saw the proof that the ancient Etruscans already knew *maccheroni*. But just as the stick, with its noncylindrical shape, cannot be a rolling pin, the board could not be for rolling dough, because it is clearly a game board for dice." The reference is to P. Mingazzini, "Gli antichi conoscevano i maccheroni?" in *Archeologia classica* 6 (1954), 292 ff.

12. *Satires* 1.6.115.

13. The *láganon*, whence the Latin *lagánum*, is already present at the beginning of the fifth century B.C., in Aristophanes' comedy *Lysistrata*. According to Athenaeus, writing, however, in the second century A.D., six hundred years later, it is a light and not very nutritious bread (III, 110 a). A bit further on (III, 110 b), Athenaeus mentions an other bread cooked over coals but softer: a sign that the lightness attributed to the *láganon* did not keep it from being crisp. Still further on (XIV, 647 e), he describes a Roman dish, the *catillus ornatus*, which the worthy commentator on Athenaeus Leo Citelli defines as a *pasticcio di lasagne verdi*, although the word *láganon* does not appear. What appears rather is *trákta*, more like the Italian *sfoglia*. And it is *trákta* that is soaked in the sauce of vegetables *(lasagne verdi)*, as opposed to what happened in Horace's bowl, which was just a juxtaposition of *lagani* and vegetables. Also, at the end of the book we can glimpse an idea of pasta: "take the *lagane* and put them in a bowl, put pieces of chicken on top and serve" (XIV, 663 e).

14. B. Laurioux, *Des lasagnes romaines aux vermicelles arabes* (Paris, 1995), 195–215.

15. Laurioux, *Des lasagnes romaines,* 204.

16. S. Serventi and F. Sabban, *La pasta* (Bari: Laterza, 2000), 23.

17. See R. Fusco, *Pagine di storia viste dalla parte degli sconfitti ovvero la pasta, evoluzione di una lotta* (Massa Lubrense: Edizioni Lubrensi, 1989), 38. In reality, among the types of pasta in the Roman period should be mentioned also the *lixulae,* which Varro talks about in book 5 of *De lingua latina.* These, according to Calepino, would be "disks made with flour, cheese, and water, which used to be considered among the cheapest foods." According to Fusco (p. 44), however, "the lack of a precise attestation regarding the cooking of *lixulae* . . . makes it impossible to assign them with certainty to the category of pasta."

18. Quoted in M. Amari and C. Schiapparelli, eds., *L'Italia descritta nel "libro di re Ruggero"* compilato da Edrisi* (Roma: Salvucci, 1883).

19. E. Sereni, "I napoletani da mangiafoglia a mangiamaccheroni," in *Terra nuova e buoi rossi* (Torino: Einaudi, 1981), 329.

20. Serventi and Sabban, *La pasta,* 23, 41, 42.

21. Sereni, "I napoletani," 321.

22. Fusco, *Pagine di storia,* 111. One *tomolo* was equal to 55.5 liters (about 58.6 quarts).

23. I. Montanelli, *Storia d'Italia,* vol. III (1600/1789), 811: "The prince of Ligne has left us a splendid portrait of Casanova during this period. The day did not go by that the Venetian did not complain either about the coffee or the milk or the plate of *maccheroni* that he demanded at every meal."

24. Fusco, *Pagine di storia,* 107.

25. Fusco, *Pagine di storia*, 76.

26. Assessorato alla Cultura e Beni culturali, *Modena capitale dell'arte salumiera: gli statuti dei salcicciai e lardaroli* (Modena, 1995), 53.

27. F. Lemene, *Della discendenza e della nobiltà de' maccheroni* (Modena, 1654).

28. C. di Messisbugo, *Libro novo* (Venezia, 1557), 6, where kitchen utensils are listed; reprint of the previous edition.

29. S. and J. Routh, eds., *Notas de cocina de Leonardo da Vinci* (Madrid, 1996), 84–88.

30. J. W. von Goethe, *Italian Journey [1786–1787]*, translated by W. H. Auden and Elizabeth Mayer (London: Penguin, 1970), 266: "A green curtain separated us and our baggage from the members of the household, who were manufacturing macaroni of the finest, whitest and smallest kind, which fetches the highest price. The dough is first moulded into the shape of a pencil as long as a finger; the girls then twist this once with their fingertips into a spiral shape like a snail's. We sat down beside the pretty children and got them to explain the whole process to us. The flour is made from the best and hardest wheat, known as *grano forte*. The work calls for much greater manual dexterity than macaroni made by machinery or in forms." Goethe's experiences with pasta continued in Naples (p. 324): "The macaroni, the dough of which is made from a very fine flour, kneaded into various shapes and then boiled, can be bought every-where and in all the shops for very little money. As a rule, it is simply cooked in water and seasoned with grated cheese."

31. Fusco, *Pagine di storia*, 128.

32. C. Marchi, *Quando siamo a tavola* (Milano: Rizzoli, 1990), 28.

33. Marchi, *Quando siamo a tavola*, 119.

34. R. Rovetta, *Industria del pastificio o dei maccheroni* (Milano: Hoepli, 1951), 3. The first edition was published in 1908. According to *L'Italia della pasta* (Milano, 2003), 42, the excellent food-and-wine guide of the Touring Club Italiano, "the pasta catalogs today count more than three hundred different shapes, almost all invented at the end of the 1800s."

35. I. Arieti, *Tuscia a tavola* (Viterbo: Quatrini Archimede, 2000), 69.

36. Fusco, *Pagine di storia*, 47 ff. A. Toaff, *Mangiare alla giudia* (Bologna, 2000), 92.

TRADITIONAL
ITALIAN PASTA SHAPES
A TO Z

1. ABBOTTA PEZZIENDE

Pasta corta

INGREDIENTS: Durum-wheat flour, water, and salt.

HOW MADE: The flour is sifted onto a wooden board and kneaded for a long time with water and a pinch of salt. When the dough is firm and smooth, it is rubbed with oil and left to rest. It is then rolled into a sheet about ¹⁄₁₆ inch (2 mm) thick, which is wrapped around a rolling pin and cut lengthwise into two strips, each about 1½ inches (4 cm) wide, depending on the diameter of the rolling pin. One strip is placed on top of the other, and together they are cut on the bias into lozenges. The pasta is boiled in plenty of salted water.

ALSO KNOWN AS: *Sagne a pezze.*

HOW SERVED: As *pastasciutta,* with a simple tomato sauce and pecorino, or in a soup of beans, *cicerchie,* or lentils.

WHERE FOUND: Abruzzo.

REMARKS: *Abbotta pezziende* is Abruzzese dialect for "feed the beggar," and already the translation tells us that this is a pasta of the poor, with a name that suggests more wishful thinking than actual consumption. In vast stretches of Abruzzo until World War II and after, the peasant's meal was limited to a pie of corn flour and cabbage leaves, and even a simple pasta like this was a luxury. Indeed, pasta appeared on rural tables only once or twice a year, and the middle classes ate it only on important feast days.

2. AGNELLOTTI TOSCANI

Pasta ripiena

INGREDIENTS: Wheat flour and eggs. The classic filling contains veal, brains, chard or spinach, and ricotta.

HOW MADE: The flour is sifted onto a wooden board, kneaded long and vigorously with eggs, and then left to rest. It is rolled out into a thin sheet with a rolling pin, and small rectangles measuring about 1¼ by 1 inch (3 by 2.5 cm) are cut from it. A teaspoon of filling is placed in the center of half of the rectangles, the remaining rectangles are placed on top, and the edges are carefully sealed. The *agnellotti* are boiled a few at a time in plenty of salted water.

ALSO KNOWN AS: *Tordelli, tortelli,* and *ravioli.*

HOW SERVED: As *pastasciutta,* traditionally with a hearty meat *ragù* and a dusting of grated cheese, today usually parmigiano.

WHERE FOUND: The Maremma, in both Lazio and Tuscany.

REMARKS: The name is a venerable Florentine synonym for *ravioli,* which are of age-old tradition in Tuscany. With a different filling and sweet wrapping, they appear as *calcioni* as early as the fourteenth century, when we find them in Siena, in *Corte bandita per cavalieri,* in December 1326.[1] *Torte* (pies) and *tortelli* were popular throughout the prosperous Medici period. Luigi Pulci says:

> . . . *e credo nella torta e nel tortello*
> *l'uno è la madre e l'altro è il suo figliolo.*[2]

> [. . . and I believe in the *torta* and in the *tortello*
> the one is the mother and the other is her child.]

Grand Tour travelers spoke of having tasted *agnellotti* on their stops in Florence, and *tortelli* are still the standard dish for feast days, with different fillings typical of different areas: The classic *agnellotti,* found in the Casentino, are made with ricotta and spinach, but some are filled with nettles and served with a walnut sauce. Also typical of the Casentino are *ravioli* with a filling of chicken livers flavored with Vin Santo, served *in bianco.* The filling of Arezzo's tiny *cappelletti* is softened with bone marrow.

Around Siena, *tortelli* are served in broth. In Florence and in the Mugello, *tortelli di San Lorenzo,* with a potato filling, are served on August 10, the feast day of Saint Lawrence, sometimes with a *sugo finto.* Lucca's *tortelli* filling has the unmistakable fragrance of ricotta from mountain pastures. In the Maremma of southern Tuscany and northern Lazio, ricotta-filled *tortelli* are served with melted butter, sugar, and cinnamon. In Lazio, in the Tiber valley, spring brings two types of *tortelli:* filled with nettles and served with a mushroom sauce, and filled with traveler's joy[3] and served with a meat sauce.

No other region has the variety that Tuscany has. Every town, almost every family, has its own recipe for *ravioli* and its special sauce.

3. AGNOLI DI MOSTARDELE

Pasta ripiena

INGREDIENTS: Wheat flour, bran, buckwheat flour, walnut oil, and eggs. For the filling, leeks and *mostardele* (a salami made from pork offal cooked in red wine and seasoned).

HOW MADE: The flours are sifted onto a wooden board and kneaded long and vigorously with eggs and walnut oil. When the dough is firm and smooth, it is left to rest, and then rolled out into a very thin sheet. Well-spaced spoonfuls of filling are placed on half of the sheet. The other half is folded over, and the pasta is pressed around the filling to seal. Then a round pasta cutter is used to make *ravioli* of variable size. The *agnoli* are boiled lightly in plenty of salted water.

ALSO KNOWN AS: *Agnoli delle Valli Valdesi.*

HOW SERVED: As *pastasciutta*, traditionally with a leek sauce.

WHERE FOUND: Piedmont, in the Valli Valdesi.[4]

REMARKS: Fresh pasta made with eggs, such as these *agnoli*, were once reserved only for feast days. These *ravioli* are made in winter, when the pig was traditionally slaughtered to provide meat for the coming months, which is also when the *mostardele* are made. In the past, the leeks for the *mostardele* were stored in large tubs or buried in the cellar under a layer of sand.

The eldest family member made the seasoning for the *mostardele* by marinating leeks in spices, herbs, and red wine. The children had the job of stirring the blood poured into the marinade, to keep it from coagulating. This was done with a long stick, with leeks attached to the tip to add their flavor to the mix. Next came cooking, stuffing, and drying the *mostardele* as for a normal salami.[5]

4. AGNOLINI MANTOVANI

Pasta ripiena

INGREDIENTS: Soft- and durum-wheat flours, eggs, and water or milk. For the filling, beef *stracotto*, pork *salamella*, pancetta, and parmigiano.

HOW MADE: The flours are sifted together onto a wooden board and kneaded long and vigorously with eggs and water or milk. When the dough is firm and smooth, it is left to rest, and then rolled out into a thin sheet with a rolling pin. The sheet is cut into pieces about 2½ inches (6 cm) square, a teaspoon of filling is placed in the center of each square, the *agnolino* is closed into a triangle, and the edges are carefully sealed. The two corners on the longest side are then folded back and placed one on top of the other. The *agnolini* are boiled gently in broth.

ALSO KNOWN AS: No alternative names.

HOW SERVED: In broth.

WHERE FOUND: Lombardy, in Mantova and surrounding province.

REMARKS: *Agnolini* similar to these are said to have been made for the Gonzaga court at Mantova. What is certain is that the court, sensitive to a policy of careful exploitation of the territory, almost always used local cooks. The exception was Bartolomeo Stefani, the Bolognese author of *L'arte di ben cucinare et instruire i men periti in questa lodeuole professione* . . . , published in Mantova in 1662. But he knew how to apply his knowledge to Mantova's products. A century earlier, Duchess Isabella d'Este had at her service—the story goes—a certain Libussa, a woman of the Mantuan countryside. Every Mantuan gourmet attributes to Libussa the invention of the *agnolino,* which, with almost the same filling, was also made then. A certain, similarly named Libista, inventress of the *raviolo* (see entry) at Cernusco, was mentioned by Ortensio Lando in his *Commentario delle più notabili, et mostruose cose d'Italia et altri luoghi,* first published in 1548.[6]

The *agnolini* of Mantova, including their name, are often confused with their cousins in Parma and Bologna, which they resemble in shape and preparation.

Great importance is attached to establishing who were the inventors of certain popular food traditions, typically with disputes that cannot have winners or losers. The Mantuan *agnolino,* as opposed to the Emilian *anolino* or *tortellino,* is among the most heated topics of discussion. In reality, dishes are almost always the fruit of slow transformations over time and space, dictated by the need to perfect drying techniques or cooking systems, or even simply to obtain a tastier or more visually appealing result. What is more important is to evaluate the place in which a certain preparation is attested until it has become a truly typical product, as in the case of this *agnolino.*

It is worthwhile to clarify the differences between the Mantuan *agnolino* and the Bolognese *tortellino.* The *agnolino* is generally larger than the *tortellino,* but the shape is the same. The main distinction is the filling: the *tortellino* is stuffed with a combination of prosciutto, mortadella, and lightly browned white meats mixed with parmigiano, bone marrow, and spices; the *agnolino* is filled with a mixture of beef, *salamella,* pancetta, parmigiano, spices, and herbs that has been stewed for a long time with wine. Both are served in broth (see also *ravioli* and *tortelli*).

5. AGNOLOTTI

Pasta ripiena

INGREDIENTS: Wheat flour and eggs. The classic filling of this Piedmontese pasta calls for mixed meats, usually veal and pork or occasionally donkey meat, and other ingredients that vary from place to place. The meats are braised and flavored with wine and herbs. Numerous local variants exist, including the addition of vegetables, such as artichokes, and often cheese fondue. Fontina cheese is another typical filling.

HOW MADE: The flour is sifted onto a wooden board and kneaded with eggs, then allowed to rest. The dough is rolled out with a rolling pin into a thin sheet, and cut into 2-inch (5-cm) squares with a smooth or toothed wheeled cutter. A small amount of filling is placed in the center of each square, and the *agnolotto piemontese* is folded and closed to form a rectangle. Sometimes a small amount of spinach is added to the dough, which colors it pale green. Shapes and different types of closings characterize *agnolotti* in other regions of Italy. They are gently boiled in plenty of salted water.

ALSO KNOWN AS: Formerly *agnelotti; agnulot, agnolotti col plin, langaroli,* and *langheroli* in the Langhe; in Tuscany, *agnellotti* (see entry).

HOW SERVED: As *pastasciutta,* with meat juices or sauces, which vary from place to place, and dusted with parmigiano.

WHERE FOUND: Piedmont, but also other parts of Italy.

REMARKS: The terms *agnolotti, tortelli,* and *ravioli* (see entries for latter two) are used almost everywhere for stuffed pasta made with locally available resources. But the *agnolotto* is above all a typical Piedmontese pasta, and the region, which is rich in alpine pastures and boasts excellent meats, is home to countless variations of form and filling. In the area of Tortona, where the influence of Ligurian cooking is felt, the *agnolotti* are small and formed by sealing an herb-based filling between two sheets of pasta. Around Novara, they are filled with borage. Cooks in Alessandria serve them with a hearty sauce flavored with Barbera wine. In the

Marengo area, the filling contains brains and sweetbreads, and in the Monferrato area, special *agnolotti* are stuffed with donkey meat. The so-called three-meat *agnolotti*, with three different roasts in the filling, are found around Asti, and a meat filling enriched with Savoy cabbage is made in the Langhe. Also typical of the Langhe are the tiny *agnolotti col plin*, filled with the same three-meat mixture and sealed with a pinch, which is what the word *plin* means in the local dialect. Less well-known are the *agnolotti* filled with fondue called *fagottini della Bella Rosina*, in honor of Rosa Vercellana, morganatic wife of the Savoy king Victor Emanuel II.

Camillo Cavour[7] was a frequent guest at Il Cambio, a venerable Turin restaurant across from Carignano, once seat of the Savoy Parliament. The chef seems to have dedicated a particular type of *agnolotti*, served with a sumptuous *finanziera*, to the great man, which passed into history as *agnolotti alla Cavour*.

It is hard to say when *agnolotti* took hold in Piedmontese cooking. *Il cuoco piemontese perfezionato a Parigi*,[8] published in Turin in 1766, does not mention them, but before the end of the century, *agnolotti all'italiana* had found their way into *La cuciniera piemontese*.[9] Before the middle of the 1800s, the dish did not exist on bourgeois tables; it did, however, figure in François Chapusot's 1846 *La cucina sana, economica ed elegante*. The second (1851) edition of the book, titled *La cucina sana, economica e dilicata*[10] (that is, no longer "elegant" but "delicate") includes *agnolotti* in soup, now called *zuppa di raviuoli alla villereccia*, a name that gives a rustic connotation to a dish that only a few years before had been served only on upper-class tables. In *Trattato di cucina pasticceria moderna credenza e relativa confettureria* and in the subsequent *Cucina borghese* (in the 1854 and 1901 editions), both by Giovanni Vialardi,[11] *agnelotti* are already much as they are today. The great cook files *agnelotti* under "economical, simple, *signorile*, and bourgeois" cooking, suitable for the emergent, but also thrifty, bourgeoisie that had learned quickly to use Russian service at table and to appreciate simple dishes, made with local products. The Russian service, consecrated by Urbain Dubois and introduced by the Russian prince Kurakin in 1860, called for, as today, serving hot dishes one at a time according to an order established by the lady of the house. This broke with French service, which called for putting everything on the table before the guests entered the dining room.

In time, the old practice of serving *agnolotti* in broth was replaced by the custom of adding a glass of red wine to the drained, but not yet served, *agnolotti*, which is still occasionally done today.

In the Marche, the term *agnolotto* is usually applied to a pasta lavishly stuffed with meats, as we learn from a *Ricettario della famiglia Franchi di Ascoli Piceno*,[12] drafted in the 1920s, which calls for *semolino* and only the egg yolks.

In Puglia, *agnolotti* are stuffed with turnip greens and pecorino and served with fish-based sauces.

6. ALFABETO

Pastina

INGREDIENTS: Durum-wheat flour and water.

HOW MADE: Factory-made tiny pasta in the shape of letters of the alphabet, sometimes pierced with a small hole.

ALSO KNOWN AS: No alternative names.

HOW SERVED: In broth.

WHERE FOUND: Widespread.

REMARKS: Literally "alphabet," the *alfabeto* was surely invented to amuse children, the usual consumers of *pappe* and *minestrine*, as were *stelline* (little stars), *cuoricini* (little hearts), and a whole variety of other tiny shapes that evoke the world of childhood. In fact, in Carena's *Vocabolario domestico*,[13] published in 1859, the *stellina* already appears alongside *campanelline* (little bells), *lentine* (little lenses), *semini* (little seeds), *puntine* (little dots), and more. The *pastina* called *doppio zero*, of variable size and with a tiny hole in the middle, can be placed in the same series.

7. ALISANZAS

Pasta lunga

INGREDIENTS: Durum-wheat flour, water, and lard.

HOW MADE: The flour is sifted onto a wooden board, kneaded long and vigorously with lukewarm water and melted lard, and left to rest. It is then rolled into a sheet, cut into irregular shapes with a toothed wheel *(s'arrodanza)*, and hung over a thin reed to air dry. The pasta is usually boiled in abundant salted water or in broth.

ALSO KNOWN AS: *Sas lisanzas.*

HOW SERVED: As *pastasciutta*, generally with a *ragù* of mixed meats, usually pork, mutton, and veal; also traditionally cooked in lamb broth.

WHERE FOUND: Sardinia, where it is a specialty of the Oristano area, especially the town of Bosa.

REMARKS: In the Logudoro and Gallura, this type of pasta is served with both regular meat-based sauces and *ozu-casu,* or "oil-cheese," which is butter that has been clarified with a handful of semolina. As the clarified butter solidifies, the semolina draws all of its impurities downward. The butter remains transparent and keeps for a long time.

8. ANELLETTI, ANELLINI

Pastina

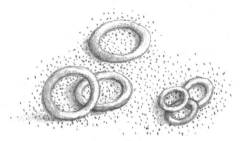

INGREDIENTS: Durum-wheat flour and water.

HOW MADE: Factory-made pasta in the shape of tiny rings, both with and without ridges. In Sicily, the rings are much thinner and are round, rather than square, in section. The Sicilian version is boiled in salted water, but *anellini* are usually cooked in broth.

ALSO KNOWN AS: *Anelline* and *anellette;* in Ruvo di Puglia, *cerchionetti;* in Lecce, *taraddhuzzi;* in Sicily, *anidduzzi;* and factory labels according to size, including *anelloni d'Africa, anelli,* and *anelletti,* which may have serrated edges.

HOW SERVED: *Anellini* in broth, and *annelletti* in a *timballo.*

WHERE FOUND: Throughout Italy, but especially in Puglia and in Sicily.

REMARKS: The name means literally "little rings." Until at least the 1930s, southern pasta makers produced various forms of *anellini,* including thick and thin, ridged and smooth, and some of these variations are still sold in the south. *Anelloni d'Africa,*[14] now quite rare, were probably inspired by the large hoop earrings worn by African women, which must have struck the fancy of Italian soldiers during the African campaigns.

In Puglia, *anellini* are known as *cerchionetti,* from the earrings called *cerchietti a campanella* (bell-shaped hoops). *Cuddhurite,* yet another Puglian *anellini,* are ring shaped and take their name from the *cuddhura,* an Easter *ciambellina* (doughnut) made with bread dough that conceals hard-boiled eggs.

In Sicily, this pasta is traditionally used to make a sumptuous *timballo.* The *timballo di anelletti* is usually large enough for several portions, but individual *sformati* (molds) are also made. In general, these are a *pasticcio in crosta,* with a crust of rustic bread dough made with lard or of classic *pâte brisée,* often enriched with eggs. The sumptuous stuffing includes pork, vegetables such as peas, sausages, and local cheeses, primarily *caciocavallo.*

In Palermo, until recently, cooks made a large *timballo* for Ferragosto (Assumption Day, August 15) because it could be prepared in advance and is excellent at room temperature. For a long time, this type of pasta dish was taken to the beach, and around the port of Siracusa, it is called *pasta ro bagnu,* or "pasta for *i bagni.*" In this version, it can also be stuffed with fried eggplant and is sometimes made with other types of pasta.

9. ANOLINI

Pasta ripiena

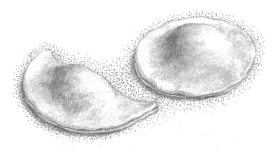

INGREDIENTS: Type 0 wheat flour and eggs. The filling is meat, typically *stracotto,* and parmigiano. In the Arda valley, the filling is made of parmigiano and dry bread crumbs, and in Piacenza, with variations on *stracotto.*

HOW MADE: The flour is sifted onto a wooden board, kneaded with eggs for a long time until smooth and firm, and left to rest. It is then rolled out with a rolling pin into a thin sheet, and a round pasta cutter or inverted liqueur glass is used to cut out disks about 2 inches (5 cm) in diameter. The filling is placed in the center of a disk and topped with another disk. In the past, the *anolino* was folded into a semi-circle, but today the traditional form is a disk. *Anolini* are gently boiled in broth, a few at a time, until they bob to the surface and float.

ALSO KNOWN AS: *Annolini* and *caplett;* around Piacenza, *anvein* and *marubei;* see also *ravioli* and *tortelli.*

HOW SERVED: In meat broth.

WHERE FOUND: Emilia-Romagna, but typical of Parma, with numerous variants in the surrounding territory; also in the Arda valley and elsewhere in the province of Piacenza, where they are distinguished by a simpler closing. The term *anolino* is also found in the popular gastronomy of the Marche.

REMARKS: The *anolino*—already present in the work of Scappi, who also spells it *annolino*—is attested at the court of Parma at least from the middle of the sixteenth century, when Carlo Nascia (or Nassi), of Palermo, was hired as cook for Ranuccio II Farnese, duke of Parma, on exactly August 4, 1659.[15] At *carta* 29 of his *Li quattro banchetti destinati per le quattro stagioni dell'anno,*[16] he describes *anolini* prepared with a very modern recipe: paper-thin pasta sheet of flour and eggs. Scappi[17] himself gives a recipe "for making *tortelletti* with pork belly and other ingredients that the common people call *annolini*." They start from a small disk or square of pasta and their form is similar to that of *cappelletti* (see entry), which, he specifies, must be "as small as beans or chickpeas and their points joined to form little hats."

The spread of this pasta in the Duchy of Parma is also documented by an eighteenth-century manuscript of the Augustinian nuns whose convent was attached to the church of Ognissanti. The sister cook tells how they made the stuffed pastas, which they cooked in capon broth and served on New Year's Day. Today, *anolini* are still served as a first course at Christmas and New Year's luncheons.

The method of closing the pasta has varied over time and from place to place: the classic closing calls for sealing the filling between two small pasta disks. Artusi,[18] however, speaks of one disk 2 inches (5 cm) in diameter, without specifying whether the edge is serrated or smooth, closed into a half-moon. The edge was probably smooth, either because our grandmothers and great-grandmothers at home usually used an inverted liqueur glass as a pasta cutter, or because the boxwood molds used to cut the pasta were the size of a silver *scudo* (coin) of the Duchy of Parma in the time of Maria Luigia.[19]

The *anolini* of Parma are the emblem of a gastronomic civility, a harmonious marriage between popular cooking and bourgeois cuisine that was able to exploit and transform the genuine quality products of its bountiful land. In 27 B.C., the Greek geographer Strabo described it as "a very fertile plain, adorned with fruit-bearing hills."[20]

As with all the dishes of ancient tradition, there are many debates on how to prepare the filling. Cooks in the past insisted the *stracotto* must cook slowly for sixteen to thirty-six hours, so the meat would come apart completely, at which point, all that was needed was enough parmigiano to give the filing the right consistency. Housewives, then and now, use a specific terra-cotta pan with a concave lid, into which they pour hot red wine, which is added to the sauce gradually as it evaporates. To sweeten the filling, some cooks slip in a small piece of donkey meat, and others a spoonful of tomato sauce. Usually this princely dish, albeit with small variations, is cooked in the ritual *brodo in terza*, a broth made with at least three different meats, including beef, capon, and *salame da cottura,* the latter today often replaced with easier-to-find pork ribs.

The *anolini* of Piacenza differ from those of Parma in the type of *stracotto* in the filling, in their slightly different shape, and in the use of fewer eggs in the dough. Even if *anvein piacentini* are served as *pastasciutta,* they must first be cooked in broth. One typical preparation has them *pasticciati,* layered with a sumptuous meat *ragù,* chicken giblets, and mushrooms.

The *anolini* of the Arda valley, in particular those typical of Castell'Arquato, are characterized by a very poor filling of parmigiano and dry bread crumbs and no meat. These, too, are supposed to be cooked in *brodo in terza*. The word *marubei* is used for *anolini* along the banks of the Po, in the towns of San Lazzaro, Monticelli d'Ongina, Castelvetro, Cortemaggiore, Besenzone, and Fiorenzuola, all in the province of Piacenza. In Cremona, the name becomes *marubini* (see entry).

It is worthwhile here to be precise about the differences between *anolino* and *tortellino*. First, there is the shape: The *tortellino* of Bologna starts from a small square of pasta, which is folded into a triangle and wrapped around a fingertip. The *anolino* of Parma starts from a disk, which is folded into a half-moon that some people also wrap around a fingertip. But the main difference is the filling: The filling of the *tortellino bolognese* (see entry for *tortellini*) combines prosciutto, mortadella, lightly cooked white meats, bone marrow, parmigiano, and spices. The filling of the *anolino* mixes beef, pancetta, parmigiano, and various *odori* and cooks them slowly with wine and tomatoes. It also used to include *enula* roots. "*Se tu voy fare torteleti de enula con brodo . . .*" (If you want to make *tortelletti* of elecampane with broth . . .) proposes recipe XCVI of *Libro di cucina del secolo XIV*, dusted off by Ludovico Frati in 1899.[21] The word *anolini* could derive from *enulini*, instead of from *anello*, meaning "ring," as is commonly believed. However, *enula* roots, which until a few decades ago were candied and used mostly for sweetmeats, could have been introduced into the filling as small pieces of candied fruit.

10. ASSABESI

Pastina

INGREDIENTS: Durum-wheat flour and water.

HOW MADE: Factory-made small pasta of various sizes, generally cooked in broth.

ALSO KNOWN AS: *Bengasini*, *tripolini*, and *abissini* (referring to the Libyan cities of Benghazi and Tripoli and to Abyssinia).

HOW SERVED: In broth.

WHERE FOUND: Widespread.

REMARKS: Between the end of the nineteenth century and the first decades of the twentieth century, many requests for patents on machines for the factory production of dry pastas were deposited at the Ministry of Agriculture, Industry, and Commerce. Today, these patents are kept in the Italian State Archives. This was also the time when the pasta dies in imaginative shapes were proliferating.

The names of one group of shapes—*assabesi, bengasini, abissini,* and *tripolini*—reflect Italy's military exploits in Africa at the time of their production. For example, the name *assabesi* alludes to the 1869 purchase of the port of Assab on the Red Sea (Eritrea) by the Genoese Rubattino Shipping Company. The various shapes are unrelated to one another: *assabesi* look like a small ovoid with ruffles; *bengasini* are shaped like small bow ties; *abissini* are little shells; and *tripolini* are tiny hats or narrow, flat noodles ruffled on one side and often sold in nests. The shapes vary from producer to producer, according to the type of die used.

11. AVEMARIE

Pastina

INGREDIENTS: Durum-wheat flour and water.

HOW MADE: Factory-made tiny pasta of various forms, cooked in broth.

ALSO KNOWN AS: *Ditaletti* and *ditalini* (diminutives of "thimbles"), *tubettini* (little tubes), *paternoster* (Our Father), *gnocchetti,* and *barbe di cappuccino* (monk's beard); in Sicily, *iritaleddi;* in Calabria, *padrenostri* and *padrenostreddi.*

HOW SERVED: Generally in broth.

WHERE FOUND: Widespread.

REMARKS: The name means literally "Hail Marys." The custom of reciting prayers to measure the cooking time of foods is extremely old. The most common was the Ave Maria (Hail Mary), followed by the Pater Noster (Our Father) and Gloria Patri (Gloria), the three prayers that make up the rosary. Until a few decades ago, it was common for families—and not only peasant families—to say the rosary together in the evening while the food was being prepared. These tiny pastas, suitable especially for broth-based soups that served as dinner, were fully cooked in just the time it took to say one Hail Mary. The shapes are various and range from tiny pastas pierced with a hole to compact forms.

In Sicily, *avemarie* are a sort of *bucatini* made with a *torchio;* those made with a larger die are called *patrinnostri.*

12. BARBAGIUAI

Pasta ripiena

INGREDIENTS: Wheat flour, extra-virgin olive oil, white wine, and water. The filling mixes winter squash, *quagliata,*[22] eggs, parmigiano, and pecorino, with fragrance of marjoram. Sometimes chard is used instead of squash.

HOW MADE: The flour is sifted onto a wooden board and kneaded with wine, oil, and water until a firm, smooth dough forms. After the dough rests, it is rolled out into a thin sheet with a rolling pin, which is cut into strips about 3 inches (8 cm) wide. Small amounts of filling are placed lengthwise, well spaced, on one-half of each strip. The other half of the strip is folded over to cover the filling and sealed carefully, and square *ravioloni* are cut with a pasta cutter. The *barbagiuai* are deep-fried in oil.

ALSO KNOWN AS: No alternative names.

HOW SERVED: As *pastasciutta* or deep-fried and served hot.

WHERE FOUND: Liguria, particularly the area of Apricale, Camporosso, and Dolceacqua.

REMARKS: *Barbagiuai,* dialect for "Zio [Uncle] Giovannis," are specific to the feast of Our Lady of Sorrow, on September 15, celebrated with a *sagra* in the main piazza in the towns of Apricale, Camporosso, and Dolceacqua, during which the *barbagiuai* are deep-fried in an enormous skillet filled to the brim with fragrant Ligurian oil.

These small stuffed pastas, which are often served as an antipasto, cannot be called a poor food. The filling varies from town to town, and includes one that uses *brussu,* a slightly sharp goat's milk ricotta. Naturally, the most important ingredient is the squash, a common garden harvest because it keeps for a long time in the pantry.

13. BARDELE COI MORAI

Pasta lunga

INGREDIENTS: Wheat flour, borage leaves, eggs, and salt. For factory made, durum-wheat flour and water.

HOW MADE: The flour is sifted onto a wooden board and kneaded with borage leaves *(morai)* that have been boiled and finely chopped or sieved, eggs, and a pinch of salt. When the dough is firm and smooth, it must rest, covered, for an hour. It is then rolled out into a sheet with a rolling pin and cut into flat noodles about ⅜ inch (1 cm) wide. The noodles are boiled like regular *tagliatelle,* in salted water.

There is also a factory-made version without the greens, used especially for *pasticci.*

ALSO KNOWN AS: *Lasagne* and *lasagnoni.*

HOW SERVED: As *pastasciutta,* with butter, parmigiano, and sage leaves; in *pasticci.*

WHERE FOUND: The fresh pasta is found in Lombardy (province of Bergamo) and the Veneto. The factory-made form is available throughout Italy.

REMARKS: Because borage adds considerably less liquid to the dough than spinach does, *bardéle* (literally, "ribbons"), a type of *tagliatelle,* require less flour than is needed when making green pasta from sieved spinach. Borage leaves are slightly hairy, and so must be washed very carefully. They are then dropped into boiling water (just enough to cover) for a few minutes before they are chopped or sieved.

14. BASTARDUI

Pasta corta

INGREDIENTS: Wheat flour, water, and wild herbs.

HOW MADE: The flour is sifted onto a wooden board and kneaded long and vigorously with water and finely minced herbs until a firm, smooth dough forms, which is left to rest. Either tiny pieces of dough are pinched off and formed into *gnocchetti,* or the dough is rolled out into a sheet with a rolling pin and cut into lozenges. Both shapes are dropped into plenty of boiling salted water to cook.

ALSO KNOWN AS: *Lasagne bastarde.*

HOW SERVED: As *pastasciutta,* traditionally with a sauce of leeks and cream made in a *malga.*

WHERE FOUND: Liguria, in some valleys of the Maritime Alps.

REMARKS: The small towns that dot the valleys of the Maritime Alps, which are situated on the transhumance routes toward the Occitan[23] valleys of Cuneo Province, have developed *la cucina bianca,* so named because it relies on such white ingredients as milk, flour, fresh cheeses, tightly closed Savoy cabbages that mature in the bracing winter weather, and vegetables that grow underground without benefit of sunlight, including leeks and onions. In the past, the housewives of these valleys had nothing else with which to make and dress their *bastardui,* today the pride of the local cuisine.

15. BATTOLLI

Pasta lunga

INGREDIENTS: Wheat flour, chestnut flour, water, and often a few eggs.

HOW MADE: The flours are sifted onto a wooden board, kneaded long and vigorously with water and sometimes eggs, and left to rest. It is rolled out with a rolling pin into a thickish sheet, which is cut into flat noodles about 1½ inches (4 cm) wide. The noodles are boiled in water or milk.

ALSO KNOWN AS: No alternative names.

HOW SERVED: As *pastasciutta,* traditionally with *pesto alla genovese.*

WHERE FOUND: Liguria, especially the town of Uscio, in the province of Genoa.

REMARKS: Chestnut flour was once commonly used for making pasta in the region, and is still popular today for some traditional shapes, such as *trofie* (see entry). These special *tagliatelle* are boiled together with potatoes and a local type of white turnip, called *naun* in dialect.

16. BAVETTE

Pasta lunga

INGREDIENTS: Durum-wheat flour and water.

HOW MADE: Factory-made pasta shaped like thin *tagliatelle,* but usually convex. The name varies according to width and place. The noodles are boiled in abundant salted water or in broth.

ALSO KNOWN AS: The thinnest are *bavettine, linguine* (small tongues), *lingue di passero* (sparrow's tongues), *linguettine,* and *tagliatelline.* Wider examples include *trenette* and *trinette.* Wider still are *fettucce romane, fettuccelle, fresine, tagliarelli,* and *tagliatelle.* And finally, there are *fettucce, fettuccine, lasagnette,* and *pappardelle.* In Sicily, they are called *lasagneddi.*

HOW SERVED: Primarily as *pastasciutta,* with specific local sauces, but also in broth.

WHERE FOUND: Throughout Italy, with *bavette* and *trenette* used especially in Liguria and the wider cuts more common to central and southern Italy.

REMARKS: *Bavetta* is an early term, possibly from the French, attested already in the thirteenth century as a derivative of *baba* or *bava,* or "drool." In any case, Fanfani's 1863 dictionary[24] contains a reference to a pasta of this name (*specie di paste da minestra in file lunghe e sottili,* or "a sort of pasta for soup that comes in long, thin threads"), also called *baverine.*

This type of pasta is best served with herb-based sauces, such as the famous *pesto alla genovese,* but today is also paired with fish-based sauces. For example, on Lipari and on the islands of the Sicilian archipelago, *bavette* are served with tuna and capers. The buds of a wild bush, and long a common condiment on these islands, capers are gathered on the first warm days of spring, when they are small and fragrant, and used as an herb.

17. BERTÙ

Pasta ripiena

INGREDIENTS: Wheat flour, salt, and eggs. For the filling, *cotechino,* parmigiano, and eggs.

HOW MADE: The flour is sifted with a pinch of salt onto a wooden board and kneaded long and energetically with eggs until the dough is smooth and firm. The dough is wrapped in a dish towel and left to rest, then rolled out into a thin sheet. A pasta cutter is used to cut disks 2½ to 3¼ inches (6 to 8 cm) in diameter, and a teaspoon of filling is placed in the center of each disk. The disks are closed in a half-moon and the edges carefully sealed. They are boiled in plenty of salted water.

ALSO KNOWN AS: *Gai* (*orecchie d'asino*, "donkey's ears").

HOW SERVED: As *pastasciutta*, generally with a condiment *in bianco* of butter and pancetta.

WHERE FOUND: Lombardy, throughout the Bergamo area, in particular San Lorenzo di Ravetta.

REMARKS: This typical dish used to be made on October 7, for the feast of Our Lady of the Rosary, instituted by Pope Pius V to thank the Blessed Virgin for protecting the Christian armies against the Turks in the Battle of Lepanto (1571). The half-moon shape probably was inspired by the crescent moon on the Turkish banners captured on the battlefield. The pastas are also called *gai* ("donkey" in dialect) because the shape resembles a donkey's ear. The name *bertù* is likely from *bertulina*, a word used in Lombardy for a variety of popular cakes and *focacce*.

18. BIAVETTA

Pastina

INGREDIENTS: Wheat flour and water in the past, and today wheat flour and eggs.

HOW MADE: The flour is sifted and kneaded long and vigorously with water or, today, eggs, and left to rest. Tiny pieces, each one the size of a grain of rice, are pulled off the dough and worked between the thumb and forefinger to give them a slightly flattened shape. The *pastina* is cooked in meat broth.

ALSO KNOWN AS: No alternative names.

HOW SERVED: In meat broth.

WHERE FOUND: Piedmont, typical of Asti.

REMARKS: This handmade *pastina*, which is made with infinite patience and considerable dexterity, used to be prepared especially for *la minestra del battere il grano,*[25] a tasty soup of meat broth that also contains chicken giblets. It was served to the men during the harvest.

19. BIGOLI
Pasta lunga

INGREDIENTS: Generally whole-wheat flour made from durum wheat, but sometimes soft-wheat flour, water, and salt, and often duck or hen eggs.

HOW MADE: The flour is sifted onto a wooden board and kneaded with water and a pinch of salt until a very hard and uniform dough forms, then the dough is allowed to rest. It is cut into pieces and fed into a *torchio da bigoli.* As the handle is turned, long, thick *spaghettoni* come out the bottom. These strands are cut to a length of about 12 inches (30 cm) and boiled in plenty of salted water.

ALSO KNOWN AS: In Friuli–Venezia Giulia, a slightly thicker version is called *fusarioi.*

HOW SERVED: Traditionally as *pastasciutta,* with a sauce of onion, tuna, and anchovies, or with *aole*[26] or crab, but also in duck broth or with vegetable- or meat-based sauces. In Padova, they are traditionally served with *rovinassi* (chicken giblets). In Istria, *fusarioi* used to be served with a chicken sauce.

WHERE FOUND: Around Mantova (Castel d'Ario) and in the Veneto, especially around Vicenza and Verona, but also in Friuli–Venezia Giulia, Istria in particular. Today, *bigoli* are the most common local pasta in Venice, too.

REMARKS: In the early sixteenth century,[27] M. Savonarola is already speaking of *menuei, menudei,* or *minutelli,* variations on a local term for a type of string pasta that was widespread throughout the Veneto, and was initially made by hand and then with a device. Later, the dialect word *bigolo* was used to indicate this type of pasta, which was always dark until not long ago because the peasant women made it from whole-wheat flour. The term alludes to its resemblance to worms or, as the Latin root might suggest—*(bom)byculus* means "cockroach"—to poor, squalid food. A feather in the cap of the Veneto's homemade pastas, these long, thick strings are often confused with *spaghetti,* from which they differ substantially in composition and thickness. The most common *bigoli* are made from whole-wheat flour and water, but today are also made with white flour and sometimes even with eggs.

The preparation used to call for a small utensil, the *scolabigoli* (bigoli drainer), almost always made of copper or brass, and for a *tola da tajadèle,*[28] a perfectly smooth, rectangular board of neutral wood on which any type of dough was kneaded. The *torchio da bigoli*—also called a *bigolaro*—was attached to the table. A metal utensil with a compression chamber, it was produced around Vicenza, es-

pecially at Thiene, in the Colli Berici, and in Valle di Chiampo, but also around Verona. To use the *torchio,* a piece of very hard dough is inserted into the chamber, an action that requires two strong arms, and then a crank that operates a threaded shaft is turned and the *bigolo* emerges from a die pierced in the shape of a thick *spaghetto.* As the *bigoli* materialize from the *torchio,* they are sprinkled with corn flour to keep them from sticking to one another. Then they are cut with a knife and put to dry on the board.

In the past, *bigoli* were always made at home, and each family had several dies for different thicknesses. Among the various typical sauces worth mentioning is *pocio,* a hearty meat concoction named for the earthenware pot in which it was traditionally made.

Castel d'Ario (Mantova) holds a *sagra* called *bigolada* each February. In Vicenza, *bigoli* in duck broth was the traditional dish of the feast of Our Lady of the Rosary (October 7), and it was brought to the table with the duck used to make the broth. And in Istria, *fusarioi* take their name from the spindle (*fuso*) used to roll out the pasta.

20. BLECS

Pasta corta

INGREDIENTS: Buckwheat and wheat flours, salt, eggs, water, and sometimes also a little butter.

HOW MADE: The flours are sifted together onto a wooden board and kneaded with salt, eggs, and water. The dough is left to rest, then rolled out with a rolling pin into a very thin sheet, and triangles about 2 inches (5 cm) on a side are cut from it. The pasta is boiled in salted water.

ALSO KNOWN AS: *Bleki, biechi,* and *maltagliati.*

HOW SERVED: Generally as *pastasciutta,* with butter and grated local cheese.

WHERE FOUND: Friuli–Venezia Giulia, in particular Carnia (Prato Carnico, Treppo Carnico, and Ovaro) and the valleys of the Natisone.

REMARKS: The dialect word *blecs* literally means "patch, piece of cloth for patching, odd cutting." It is therefore likely that *blecs* were a type of *maltagliati* of different sizes. The proximity of Friuli to areas of Slavic language explains the term, which derives from the Slovenian *bleck,* "piece of cloth," which in turn was borrowed from the Middle High German *vleck.* Today, *blecs* are also made with a pinked edge.

    Pastasciutta, as we understand the term today, did not become common in Friuli until after World War II. Indeed, pasta never appeared in any form, not even on the tables of some girls' boarding schools of a certain station whose archives have been studied by L. Cargnelutt,[29] and the work of Perusini Antonini[30] agrees with this observation.

21. BLUTNUDELN

Pasta lunga

INGREDIENTS: Rye flour, wheat flour, eggs, and pig's blood.

HOW MADE: The flours are sifted together and kneaded with only a few eggs and with pig's blood until a firm, smooth dough forms. The dough is covered and left to rest, then rolled out into a thin sheet, and flat noodles about ⅜ inch (1 cm) wide are cut from it. The noodles are boiled in plenty of salted water.

ALSO KNOWN AS: *Pasta al sangue.*

HOW SERVED: As *pastasciutta,* with melted butter, sage, and *Graukäse,* the typical local gray cheese.

WHERE FOUND: Trentino, especially Bolzano, and the Pusteria in particular.

REMARKS: Today, some people still observe the tradition of making *Blutnudeln,* literally "blood noodles," when the hog is slaughtered. These tasty noodles could be dried and stored for several days. Nowadays, they are a niche dish in many restaurants of the Pusteria.

22. BRICCHETTI

Pasta corta

INGREDIENTS: Durum-wheat flour and water.

HOW MADE: Factory-made short *spaghetti.* The pasta is cooked in soup.

ALSO KNOWN AS: No alternative names.

HOW SERVED: In broth, especially vegetable or fish. The classic way to serve *bricchetti* is in minestrone.

WHERE FOUND: Liguria.

REMARKS: In Genoese dialect, *bricchetto* means *bastoncino,* or "little stick." The pasta was typically cooked in vegetable minestrone the day before it was served, so that when the soup was eaten cold, usually as a hearty breakfast before laborers headed out to work in the fields, it was dense and robust.

23. BRINGOLI

Pasta lunga

INGREDIENTS: Wheat flour, sometimes mixed with corn flour, and water.

HOW MADE: The flour is sifted and kneaded long and vigorously with water. When the dough is firm and smooth, it is left to rest for a half hour. Walnut-sized pieces are torn from the dough and rolled on a wooden board by hand into thick *spaghetti* about 8 inches (20 cm) long. An alternative method calls for rolling the pasta into a thick sheet, which is cut into strips ⅜ inch (1 cm) wide and about 4 inches (10 cm) long. The strips are then rolled on a wooden board with hands into thick *spaghetti.* The pasta is boiled in abundant salted water.

ALSO KNOWN AS: *Bringolo, brigonzolo,* and *bringuili;* around Terni, *biche;* and in the Val di Pierle, *bringuli.*

HOW SERVED: As *pastasciutta,* with various local sauces.

WHERE FOUND: The Marche; Tuscany, in particular around Arezzo but also in the Val di Pierle near Cortona; and Umbria, around Terni (Ficulle) and in the province of Perugia.

REMARKS: This is a peasant food typical of the Tiber valley, in the area between Tuscany, the Marche, and Umbria. Flour-and-water pastas were the rule in the rural world of the poor: Eggs were a precious commodity of exchange in an economy where cash was rarely seen. They could buy what could not be grown, from utensils to salt and shoes, from salt cod to clothing. The housewife's imagination made up for the poverty of the dough, her skilled hands creating small sculptures or simple shapes so regular they seemed machine made.

Around Arezzo, the dough for *bringoli* was made from a mixture of wheat and corn flours, rolled out, and cut into narrow, flat noodles. The intramural rivalries in Arezzo maintain that this pasta was copied by the Sienese to create *pici* (see entry).

The term *bringuli*, in the dialect of the Val di Pierle, means something twisted, which is exactly how these rustic *spaghetti* look when drained.

Today, *bringoli* are made in summer at town *sagre* to introduce tourists to a traditional specialty. One of the most famous of these festivals is held in August at Lisciano Niccone, in Umbria, at which *bringoli* made from bread dough are prepared.

24. BRODOSINI

Pasta corta

INGREDIENTS: Wheat flour, eggs, and water.

HOW MADE: The flour is sifted and kneaded with eggs and water long and vigorously until a smooth, firm dough forms. It is left to rest, then rolled into a sheet, not too thin, from which short, flat noodles are cut. The noodles are cooked in broth.

ALSO KNOWN AS: No alternative names.

HOW SERVED: Generally in broth.

WHERE FOUND: Abruzzo, especially around Chieti.

REMARKS: The name means literally "watery." The practice of serving *tagliatelle* in broth is very old. It was de rigueur during the Renaissance, when it was particularly given to new mothers because the broth was thought to favor the production of milk, a belief found in almost all of the Italian regions. But, in fact, its value rested in the additional nutrients it contributed to a diet that was otherwise, especially among the poor, quite meager.

25. BUCATINI

Pasta lunga

INGREDIENTS: Durum-wheat flour and water.

HOW MADE: Factory-made long string pierced through its length, with the diameter of the hole varying. The pasta is boiled in abundant salted water.

ALSO KNOWN AS: *Boccolotti, candele,* and *fidelini bucati; perciatelli, perciatellini,* and *perciatelloni; regine* and *ziti* or *zite* (see entry), according to diameter, but also *mezzani* and *scaloppi;* in Sicily, *filatu cu lu pirtusu* and *maccarruncinu,* but also *agoni bucati* and *spilloni bucati.*

HOW SERVED: Generally as *pastasciutta,* with various traditional local sauces; the larger sizes are also broken and added to soups or cooked in the oven.

WHERE FOUND: Liguria *(fidelini bucati)* and in central and southern Italy; *bucatini* are typical of Lazio, famously Amatrice in the province of Rieti, but they are also found in Campania as *perciatelli,* and farther south, particularly in Sicily, they are called *ziti* or *zite.*

REMARKS: Today, the term *bucatini,* literally "pierced," is used for a factory-made dry pasta. But the early fresh *bucatino,* made by rolling a small piece of dough on a *ferretto,* a rush, or a smooth stick, is still found in various sizes (see *busiata* and *fusilli*), especially in the south. Some scholars, citing Platina, maintain that the long *maccherone* was first made and then perforated through its entire length, an operation that, performed on a *spaghetto* as thin as a straw, we consider impossible even for expert hands. But Platina[31] misinterpreted his maestro, Martino da Como, who in his *Libro de arte coquinaria,* around the middle of the 1400s, writes under the entry *maccaroni siciliani:* "Take some very white flour and make a dough using egg whites and . . . water . . . and make sure that the pasta is very firm, then shape it into long, thin sticks, the size of your palm, and as thin as hay. Then take an iron rod as long as your palm or longer, and as thin as string, and place it on top of each stick, and then roll with both hands over a table; then remove the iron rod and the *macaroni* will be perforated in the middle."[32] Which is exactly how *fusilli* have been made for centuries and still are today.

The term *perciatelli* probably derives from the French verb *percer,* "to pierce," to indicate a pasta with a hole. The word, common especially in Campania, could have come out of the kitchen of the famous *monsù,* the French chefs who found work after the French Revolution with the families of the Kingdom of the Two Sicilies.

The first *spaghetto* to come through the dies of the *ingegno,* "device," the first pasta machine—fueled by human or animal force—was pierced. The *ingegno* made it possible to produce a pasta of regular shape with a perfectly centered hole, which is quite difficult if the dough is worked by hand.

Bucatini belong to that subgroup of pastas that upholders of gastronomic tradition demand always be served with certain sauces: in Abruzzo, at Giulianova, *bucatini* are dressed with a sauce made with *suri* (mackerel); in the Marche, tradition pairs them with a sauce of red mullet. The *boccolotti* of the Marche are also used to make the traditional *pasticcio di maccheroni* and to make its cousin, *pasticcio romagnolo,* for which our good Artusi preferred *maccheroni all'uso napoletano,* "a superfine pasta with thick walls and a narrow hole that stands up well to the cooking and absorbs more condiment."

Amatrice, a charming medieval town in an area of northern Lazio that was once part of Abruzzo, is home to the famous dish known as *bucatini all'amatriciana.* And the inhabitants are very possessive of their gastronomic monument, now known throughout the world. Even though today many cooks in Amatrice add tomato to the sauce, purists still make it *in bianco,* sometimes called *alla gricia,* with only *guanciale,* as they did before the farmers were familiar with tomatoes. The dish recalls the life of the shepherds and the transhumance in the valley of Amatrice, when the flocks were driven toward the Tyrrhenian Sea to avoid the cold mountain winter.

26. BUDELLETTI

Pasta corta

INGREDIENTS: Wheat flour, yeast, salt, and lukewarm water.

HOW MADE: First, the yeast is crumbled, dissolved in a little lukewarm water, and left to rest, covered, until it foams. The flour is then sifted with a pinch of salt onto a wooden board and kneaded with the proofed yeast until the dough is smooth and soft. The dough is covered and left to rise until it has doubled in volume. It is then rolled out with a rolling pin into a sheet about ⅛ inch (3 mm) thick, and strips 2¾ to 4 inches (7 to 10 cm) wide are cut from it. The strips are cut crosswise into thick, flat noodles. They are boiled in plenty of salted water and drained as soon as they float.

ALSO KNOWN AS: No alternative names.

HOW SERVED: As *pastasciutta,* served according to local practices.

WHERE FOUND: The Marche, in the province of Ascoli Piceno.

REMARKS: The name means literally "very thin intestines." Typical of Picene gastronomy, this pleasant pasta shape is traditionally served with sauces based on pancetta or pork fat. In the province of Ascoli Piceno, however, a tuna sauce is typical.

27. BUSA

Pasta corta

INGREDIENTS: Durum-wheat flour and water.

HOW MADE: The flour is sifted onto a wooden board and kneaded long and force-fully with water until a firm, smooth dough forms. It is left to rest, then rolled out into a sheet, not too thin, and cut into strips. The strips are wrapped around *fer-retti,* and then slid off and left to dry. According to another tradition, the dough is rolled into a pencil-thick rope and small pieces are cut off. The pieces are flat-tened on top of the *ferretto,* which is rolled on a wooden board, and the *ferretto* is slid out. The pasta is boiled directly in soup.

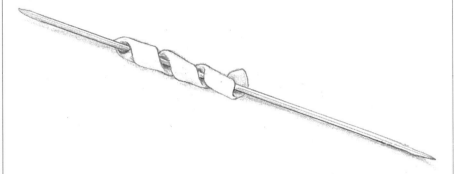

ALSO KNOWN AS: *Maccarones de busa.*

HOW SERVED: In mutton broth or with a rich sauce of boar, lamb, or veal, with a final dusting of the inevitable local pecorino.

WHERE FOUND: Sardinia.

REMARKS: This shape is typical of central-western Sardinia, but today is found all over the island. Contacts with Arab civilization, which began actively in the Mid-dle Ages, have left long trails in the language, in the folklore, and in the food habits, as this pasta illustrates. The word *busa* derives from the Arabic *bus,* the name of a plant *(Arundo aegyptiaca)* whose stem, or reed, was used for both pasta making and knitting. The term is still used for the pasta utensils that later re-placed the stems and, because of the similarity, for the pasta itself. See also *fusilli.*

28. BUSIATA

Pasta lunga

INGREDIENTS: Durum-wheat flour, salt, and water.

HOW MADE: The flour is sifted onto a wooden board and kneaded for a long time with salt and water until a firm, smooth dough forms. After the dough has rested, covered, for a half hour, walnut-sized pieces are pinched from it. Each piece is rolled into a rope 4 to 5 inches (10 to 13 cm) long or longer. The rope is then laid on a *ferretto* and the *ferretto* is rolled on a wooden board to make a thick *spaghettone* with a hole down its length. The pasta is slid off the needle with a rap of the hand, and boiled in abundant salted water.

ALSO KNOWN AS: *Maccarruna di casa* and *pirciati* or *filatu cu lu pirtusu;* on Pantelleria, *busiati ribusiati.*

HOW SERVED: As *pastasciutta,* with traditional local condiments.

WHERE FOUND: Sicily.

REMARKS: The *busiata* has become a queen of Sicilian gastronomy: formerly served with meats, especially pork, today it is more likely to be served with a fish-based sauce, and the fresh pasta can be cut to any desired length.

Historically, *busiata* belongs to the large *fusilli* family and was made in Sicily long before Marco Polo returned from China. Local historians consider it the oldest Sicilian homemade pasta and place its birth date at around the year 1000. Lucie Bolens,[33] who has studied Arabic manuscripts of the tenth and eleventh centuries, reports the presence of dry pierced pastas in Sicily already in that period.

The name, like that of *busa* (see entry), derives from *bus.* Both pastas were rolled on the same type of reed, which has a direction because the rolled pasta could be pulled off only from one side. Much later, the name was used for *la busa di ferru* or *di quasetta,* that is, the knitting needle.

Evidence that the pasta was widespread by the mid-1400s is found in Maestro Martino's *Libro de arte coquinaria,* where it is called *maccaroni siciliani* and is described in very modern and exacting language: "Take very fine flour and knead it with egg white and rosewater or plain water . . . and make a firm dough, then form sticks a palm long and thin as a straw. And take a wire a palm or more long and thin as a string, put it on top of the above-mentioned stick, and give it a turn with both hands on top of a board. Then remove the wire and pull off the pasta pierced down the middle."[34]

The manuscript languished in the Library of Congress until 1927, when it was discovered by Dommers Vehling; it was finally published in 1966 by the eminent Italian food historian Emilio Faccioli.[35] Martino also specifies that if these *maccheroni* were dried well and with the August moon, they could last for two or three years. The long shelf life made *busiata* an extremely valuable pasta and explains its rapid diffusion around the entire Mediterranean area.

With the advent of this pasta on ships, sailors' diets also changed significantly because they could now eat starches other than unappetizing moistened bread.

29. CADUNSEI

Pasta ripiena

INGREDIENTS: Wheat flour and water, and today also eggs. The old-style filling includes chicken innards, *odori*, and peach pits; the modern filling combines mixed meats, salami, amaretti, *odori,* and grated cheese.

HOW MADE: The flour is sifted onto a wooden board and kneaded long and vigorously with water until a smooth, firm dough forms. After resting, the dough is rolled out into a thin sheet, from which disks about 2½ inches (6 cm) in diameter are cut. Filling is placed in the center of each disk, and the disk is folded into a half-moon. The edges are pressed with the tines of a fork, then pinched at intervals around the seam to create a decorative motif. The *cadunsei* are gently boiled in plenty of salted water.

ALSO KNOWN AS: *Cahunhei.*

HOW SERVED: As *pastasciutta,* with melted butter.

WHERE FOUND: Lombardy, in particular the Val Camonica and the town of Artogne.

REMARKS: Pride of the cuisine of the Val Camonica, *cadunsei* are great protagonists of the alpine valley's summer feasts. In the local valleys, in particular at Fucine, they are made for the feast of Saint Anne, on July 14. At the end of August, they are on every table in the village of Erbanno, near the town of Darfo Boario Terme. The use of the peach kernel (also called *magnole*) says much about the simplicity and poverty of alpine valleys, where everything edible communities could produce and preserve was used. With today's prosperity, the peach kernel is replaced by amaretti, though the result is different.

The addition of peppermint to the filling is a summer variant.

30. CAICC

Pasta ripiena

INGREDIENTS: Wheat flour, water, and eggs. The filling includes various meats, amaretti, chard, seasonings, and grated local cheese.

HOW MADE: The flour is sifted onto a wooden board and kneaded with water and eggs. After the dough is left to rest, it is rolled out with a rolling pin into a thin sheet, and disks 4 to 5 inches (10 to 13 cm) in diameter are cut from it. The disks are generously filled and folded into half-moons. They are gently boiled in plenty of salted water.

ALSO KNOWN AS: No alternative names.

HOW SERVED: As *pastasciutta,* with butter, sage, and grated local cheese.

WHERE FOUND: Lombardy, in particular Breno, in the Val Camonica.

REMARKS: The curious name, pronounced ca-EECH, is dialect for *cuneo* (wedge) and certainly refers to the shape of this large *raviolo,* which, in the old days, was flavored with peach pits or bitter almonds in place of the amaretti. To make the filling, chicken giblets are sautéed with corn flour and vinegar, chopped, and then cooked in butter with onion.

In the town of Breno, a large annual fair is held on the feast of Saint Valentine, February 14, and *caicc* are traditionally served, in the past accompanied by polenta.

31. CAJUBI
Pasta corta

INGREDIENTS: Durum-wheat and whole-wheat flours, salt, and water; often a bit of *grano arso* was added.

HOW MADE: The flours are sifted together on a wooden board and kneaded long and forcefully with a pinch of salt and water until a firm, smooth dough forms. It is left to rest, then pieces of dough are rolled with hands into ropes about ⅜ inch (1 cm) in diameter, and the ropes are cut into pieces about ⅝ inch (1.5 cm) long. The pieces are rolled on a *ferretto,* which is then slipped out, and the pasta is left to dry. The pasta is boiled in plenty of salted water or in broth.

ALSO KNOWN AS: *Cagghjubbi* (Mesagne and Squinzano), *cajubbi, ditalini, minchiareddhi* (Salento), and *tubettini.*

HOW SERVED: Generally as *pastasciutta,* typically with *ricotta salata,* but also in broth, with local vegetables.

WHERE FOUND: Puglia.

REMARKS: *Cajubi* are the pride of the gastronomy of the towns of Lequile and Matino, where they are almost always made with whole-wheat flour, often with a small amount of *grano arso,* and served in a tasty soup of dried peas.

In the past in Puglia, and in other regions as well, gleaners went into the fields after the grain was threshed to glean whatever meager amount remained on the ground. The fields were then burned to fertilize the land. Some grain always escaped the expert eye of the gleaners, so the poor gathered the burnt grain and milled it. They added the black, smoky-flavored flour to other flours for making bread and pasta—the flour a symbol of the boundless poverty that gripped the people of the south for centuries.

Today, the food of the poor has become fashionable, and *cajubi* are served in Puglia's best restaurants. But nobody has to glean the scorched fields for the *grano arso*. Now it is made on purpose by small local producers.

32. CALCIONI

Pasta ripiena

INGREDIENTS: Wheat flour and eggs. The filling calls for sheep's milk ricotta, cheeses, and various herbs, always including marjoram.

HOW MADE: The flour is sifted onto a wooden board, kneaded long and vigorously with eggs to form a smooth, firm dough, and allowed to rest. It is then rolled out into a thin sheet and cut into disks 3 to 4 inches (7.5 to 10 cm) in diameter. A teaspoon of filling is placed in the center of each disk, the disk is folded into a half-moon, and the edges are pressed closed with the tines of a fork. The *ravioli* are boiled, a few at a time, in plenty of gently boiling salted water.

ALSO KNOWN AS: *Calcione col sugo, carciù, cacui,* and *raviolo*.

HOW SERVED: As *pastasciutta*, with rich meat *ragù*.

WHERE FOUND: The Marche, a specialty of Treia.

REMARKS: The name of this typical stuffed pasta recalls the old *calcione dolce*, a sweet *raviolo* made under various names in all regions of Italy. Today in Treia, where there is a *sagra* in its honor, the sweet version has been revived: the filling is sweetened and moistened with liqueur and the *calcione* is fried. Savory *calcioni*, or *carciù*, are generally a springtime dish.

In the Marche, deep-fried *ravioli* dusted with sugar are quite common. They are considered pastries because their filling is usually ricotta flavored with lemon peel or cinnamon.

33. CALHÙ

Pasta ripiena

INGREDIENTS: Wheat flour, water, and very few eggs. For the filling, potatoes, salami, *odori*, and spices.

HOW MADE: The flour is sifted onto a wooden board, kneaded long and vigorously with water and eggs until the dough is firm and smooth, and left to rest. It is then rolled out into a thin sheet and small disks are cut from it. A teaspoon of filling is placed on each disk, the disk is folded into a half-moon, and the edges are sealed with the tines of a fork. The pastas are gently boiled in salted water.

ALSO KNOWN AS: No alternative names.

HOW SERVED: As *pastasciutta,* traditionally with foaming butter and sage leaves.

WHERE FOUND: Lombardy, in particular the upper Val Camonica.

REMARKS: The name refers to the traditional costume of the towns of the valley. *Calhù* are the baggy trousers worn by the men. This dish, typical of a peasant civilization accustomed to a strict autarky, used to be made only for feast days, but today it is a specialty of the restaurants in this alpine valley.

34. CALZONCELLI

Pasta ripiena

INGREDIENTS: Durum-wheat flour, water, and sometimes eggs. For the filling, ricotta and eggs or ground meat and eggs.

HOW MADE: The flour is sifted onto a wooden board and kneaded for a long time with water and sometimes eggs until a firm, smooth dough forms, then allowed to rest. It is rolled out into a thin sheet, and disks about 2 inches (5 cm) in diameter are cut from it. Filling is put on the disks, and the disks are either folded into half-moons or topped with a second disk, and the edges are well sealed. The stuffed disks are deep-fried in oil or lard, or boiled in plenty of salted water.

ALSO KNOWN AS: *Agnolotti baresi, calzoncieddi,* and *calzoncini;* around Taranto and Foggia (Manfredonia), *cazune.*

HOW SERVED: Fried, as is, or as *pastasciutta,* with a meat sauce.

WHERE FOUND: Puglia, in the provinces of Bari, Foggia, and Taranto.

REMARKS: These *calzoncelli* (a diminutive of *calzoni,* literally "pants") are a variant of the better-known and more common sweet ones found not only in Puglia but also in Campania. A venerable food typical of feast days, *calzoncelli* were considered particularly versatile because they could be made and deep-fried in advance and then served cold to visiting friends and relatives. They qualify for inclusion here only because they can also be a *primo piatto.* Pastas, especially stuffed pastas, that can cross the line between the sweet and the savory, ancient heritage of when sweet and savory courses were served in alternation, are not rare.

35. CALZONICCHI

Pasta ripiena

INGREDIENTS: Wheat flour and eggs. For the filling, brains, onion, and spices.

HOW MADE: The flour is sifted onto a wooden board and kneaded long and vigorously with eggs until a firm, smooth dough forms, then left to rest. It is rolled out with a rolling pin into a thin sheet and cut with a toothed pasta cutter into roughly 1¼-inch (3-cm) squares. A teaspoon of filling is placed in the center of each square and the square is folded into a triangle. The *calzonicchi* are cooked in broth.

ALSO KNOWN AS: *Tortellini di cervello.*

HOW SERVED: Usually in broth, but often also as *pastasciutta,* with meat *ragù.*

WHERE FOUND: Typical of the Jewish cuisine of Rome.

REMARKS: These extremely delicate *ravioli,* a classic of the Roman Jewish kitchen, are served for the Jewish new year (Rosh Hashanah), which is celebrated on 1 and 2 Tishri, at the beginning of autumn. This is the holiday that opens the ten days of penitence that precede Yom Kippur. The traditional menu of the Italian Jewish community on these two days consists of, in addition to the *calzonicchi,* a dish of *triglie* (red mullets) *alla mosaica* and one of turkey meat loaf, which follow deep-fried yellow squash or other deep-fried seasonal vegetables. The menu concludes with a sweet made with honey or with the famous *sfratti*[36] followed by fresh fruit.[37]

36. CANDELE

Pasta lunga

INGREDIENTS: Durum-wheat flour and water.

HOW MADE: Factory-made long strands pierced with a hole measuring from ⅛ to ⅜ inch (3 mm to 1 cm) in diameter for the larger strands. The term *candela* usually refers to the latter. The pasta is boiled in abundant salted water.

ALSO KNOWN AS: In Lazio (Ariccia), but also in the Marche, *cannacce;* small sizes are *bucatini, fidelini bucati, foratini,* and *perciatellini;* medium sizes are *bucatini, maccheroncelli, mezzanelli, mezzani,* and *perciatelli;* and the largest sizes are *boccolotti, ziti* or *zite* (see entry), *zitoni,* and *zituane.*

HOW SERVED: Generally as *pastasciutta,* with traditional local sauces.

WHERE FOUND: Liguria for the smallest sizes, and especially southern Italy for the larger sizes.

REMARKS: The name means literally "candles," and it refers to the long, thin candles used in liturgical processions. Today in small towns, especially in the south, the processions have become less frequent, but during the important ones, such as Corpus Domini or some feasts of the Madonna, long, white lit candles are still carried, their profile and color resembling the pasta once sold unpackaged in grocery shops.

Nowadays, *candele* is considered more or less synonymous with *ziti* or *zite* (see entry) because the latter is the term most frequently adopted by the modern pasta factories. In reality, *ziti* are slightly thinner. *Candele* are broken up for the preparation of some typical dishes, such as *timballi* or *pasticci* with a crust.

In Umbria, a similar pasta whose name also means "candles," *moccolotti,* is used to make the famous *sbombata,* a kind of *pasticcio.* A baking dish is lined with a sheet of pasta, filled with *moccolotti* heavily sauced with giblets, sprinkled with local pecorino, and then closed, sealed, and baked.

Cannacce aricine, often served with mushroom sauce, are usually made for the feast of Saint Apollonia, in memory of a fire in 1622 that destroyed the church of Ariccia. Both the faithful and the altar dedicated to the saint emerged miraculously unharmed. The term probably derives from *canne* (reeds), which, according to tradition, were the material on which the saint was burned when he was martyred in Africa, and with which roofs, not only of the churches, used to be made.

The term *cannacce* or *pezzole* in the Marche, especially in the valleys of the Esino and Misa, indicates little irregular squares of flour-and-water pasta, 4 to 6 inches (10 to 15 cm) wide, which are traditionally served with a sauce of lamb *coratella* (see *pasta strappata*).

37. CANEDERLI

Gnocchi / gnocchetti

INGREDIENTS: Stale bread, wheat flour, milk, eggs, bits of prosciutto or *speck,* parsley, and parmigiano or other local grated cheese, with ingredients varying depending on area of production.

HOW MADE: Large *gnocchi* are made with stale bread softened in milk and bound with eggs, often with the addition of herbs or *salumi.* Or stale bread is softened in water, squeezed dry, and mixed with eggs, sifted flour, grated cheese, minced parsley, and finely minced odd pieces of *speck* or prosciutto to form a dough. The dough is shaped into rather large *gnocchi,* which are generously dredged in flour, then boiled, one at a time, in abundant salted water and drained as soon as they float. They can also be cooked in broth.

ALSO KNOWN AS: *Knödel,* but also *gnocchi di pane, canedeli,* and in the Chiavenna valley area of Lombardy, *gnocchetti chiavennaschi.*

HOW SERVED: In broth, but also as *pastasciutta,* served as an accompaniment, usually topped with dry bread crumbs browned in butter, to typical regional main dishes.

WHERE FOUND: Lombardy and the Veneto Alps, Trentino–Alto Adige, and Friuli–Venezia Giulia.

REMARKS: Literally "bread dumplings," these large Tridentine *gnocchi* inhabit south-central Europe and are also known by the German-derived name *canederli* and the German word *Knödel*. *Canederli* are enjoyed, variously made with liver, fruit, or only bread, in Germany, in Austria, and in the former Czechoslovakia.

This is not a true pasta: the old *calison* were sweets made of almond paste wrapped in hosts and fashioned in a wide variety of shapes. Young men offered heart-shaped ones to their sweethearts. But they are always mentioned as a pasta in the early family recipe collections that document the food culture of the Trentino. In no other Italian region is the tradition of handing down family cookbooks from mother to daughter so firmly rooted. A. Bertoluzza[38] has explored the cultural contribution of these family recipe collections, examining some such preparations as, among others, *cannedoli di magro* (meatless), made with the usual bread but bound with eel fat. In a recipe book of the late 1700s, the author highlights *cuscinetti di nudeln:* flour-and-water *gnocchetti* boiled in milk and curiously used as the filling for a square *raviolo*, which was then dipped in beaten egg and fried. Felice Libera[39] lists some fifteen recipes for *canederli*, which attests how popular this food was among the alpine populations, even the wealthier people.

The use of stale bread was once common in traditional Italian cooking, especially when bread was not baked every day at home. Nor did city families buy bread every day; often it stayed in home pantries even for several days. In the countryside—where most people lived—bread was baked weekly, fortnightly, or even monthly. Stale bread, when it was very hard, was softened in soups, of which it constituted an important element; was grated and added to dishes; or was grated and kneaded as if it were a flour. This made it possible to make a pasta dough with a small addition of wheat or other flour, a considerable economy for the typically troubled finances of peasants. Today, bread constitutes the most important ingredient of this large *gnocco*, which is found primarily in mountainous areas where the winter isolation and meager land often impose a subsistence economy.

Almost no dish in Italian cooking manages to fully exploit, as do *canederli*, the products of a difficult territory, of *masi chiusi*,[40] where everything has long been recycled and used, from the bread, cheeses, and alpine greens to the cured meats and forest products, such as mushrooms. In the high-mountain *masi*, bread was made only four times a year and kept in special racks; then, when it was stale and hard, it was moistened or crumbled and added to recipes as an ingredient, or it was turned into large *canederli*. In the high mountains where buckwheat is grown, *canederli* are made with dark buckwheat bread lightened with potatoes; lower down, where the climate is milder, spinach is added to the dough.

Every valley, every small town, almost every family still jealously guards its recipes: in the Val d'Ultimo, the *canederlo* is enriched with ricotta and brains, made and consumed shortly after the animals are slaughtered; around Cortina d'Ampezzo, one type of *canederlo* is kneaded with liver in addition to the bread, and another type has a fresh plum, with sugar in place of the stone, which creates a pleasant sweet-and-sour contrast. Almost everywhere *speck* enriches the dough, and prosciutto fat is often added to provide some protein and flavor to the poor but tasty soups as well. In the past in the Tyrol, *canederli di luccio* were made using the fat flesh of pike easily caught in the local mountain lakes and streams. Their form, which recalls that of a cannonball, is linked to a popular legend: a female innkeeper, awakened in the middle of the night by German soldiers asking for food, whipped up large and anonymous *gnocchi* from stale bread to serve them.

Canederli, enriched with *casera* (a hard cow's milk cheese typical of the Valtellina), are a specialty of Lombardy, too, of Bormio in the Valtellina. This valley is, in fact, a communications link between the lands of Lombardy and the Tyrol that traders and armies necessarily passed through. The *gnocchetti* of the Chiavenna valley are much smaller than normal *canederli*.

Around Mantova, *mariconda* is a soup in which small bread *gnocchi* made in the style of *canederli* are cooked in broth. A soup called *mericonda* also appears in the recipe book of B. Stefani, who was a cook at the Gonzaga court in the seventeenth century, evidence of the broad diffusion of refined bread *gnocchetti*, even in court kitchens.[41]

38. CANNELLONI

Pasta ripiena

INGREDIENTS: For homemade, wheat flour, eggs, and often olive oil. The filling varies from meats to fish to cheeses, according to local traditions. For factory made, durum-wheat flour and water.

HOW MADE: The flour is sifted onto a wooden board and kneaded with eggs and usually a spoonful of olive oil for a long time, then the dough is left to rest. It is rolled out with a rolling pin into a thin sheet, and 5-inch (13-cm) squares are cut from it. The squares are boiled in salted water, drained, and spread out on a dish towel to dry. Filling is placed in the center of each square, and the square is rolled into a tube. Factory-made tubular *cannelloni* exist under various names in large and small sizes, both smooth and ridged.

ALSO KNOWN AS: From the term *canna* (tube), known as *cannaciotti, canneroncini,* and *canneroni;* in the Valtellina, as *manfriguli* or *manfrigoli;* in Naples, as *cannerone* or *cannarone,* with reference to the shape of an animal's esophagus; in Puglia, as *cannarune* and *cannarunciedde,* and Lecce, as *cannaroni;* and in Sicily, as *cannoli* and *crusetti.*

HOW SERVED: The *cannelloni* are arranged in an ovenproof dish, covered with béchamel or or other sauce according to local practice, dusted with grated cheese, generally parmigiano, and baked.

WHERE FOUND: Throughout Italy, but especially in central Italy. Variants exist in Piedmont, in Valle d'Aosta, in the Valtellina in Lombardy, and in Rome, Naples, and Sicily.

REMARKS: The name means literally "big tubes." This is without doubt among the youngest of the wealth of centuries-old recipes that make up Italian gastronomy. In fact, there are only rare mentions of *cannelloni* in the dictionaries beginning in the mid-1800s, where they are typically described as a type of large pasta to be filled. We find a recipe for a *timballo* of *cannelloni* in a manuscript on the cuisine of Arezzo by Gio Batta Magi, a local cook who lived between 1842 and 1885. We also find *maccheroni ripieni* in Vincenzo Corrado's *Cuoco galante,*[42] though they seem to be not what we call classic *cannelloni,* but rather a large stuffed pasta, as found in Naples.

It is only with the recipe books of the twentieth century that the *cannellone* makes its appearance as we know it today, stuffed with meat and often covered with béchamel, and then gratinéed in the oven. After World War II, the *cannellone* for filling, both fresh and dried, became common in regional gastronomy, not least for the practicality of its preparation, which can be done several hours before baking. Since then it has been considered the feast-day dish par excellence.

The many recipes are split among meat filled, fish filled, and cheese and/or wild greens filled. For example, *manfriguli,* typical of the Valtellina, are wide buckwheat crepes filled with *filante* (stringy when melted) cheese and baked; in Calabria, *schiaffettoni* (see entry) are stuffed with meats; and Sicilian *crusetti,* a specialty of the area around Monreale, are small *cannelloni* with a filling often based on zucchini.

39. CANNOLICCHI

Pasta corta

INGREDIENTS: Durum-wheat flour and water.

HOW MADE: Factory made in the shape of a tiny tube, either smooth or ridged. They are boiled in abundant salted water or in broth.

ALSO KNOWN AS: *Sciviottini, svuotini,* and *tubettini.*

HOW SERVED: As *pastasciutta* or in broth, depending on size and place.

WHERE FOUND: Widespread.

REMARKS: Small *cannolicchi*—literally "little tubes"—are used in the south, especially in legume soups, where their presence represents a true tradition. In fact, no southern housewife would think of making *pasta e fagioli* with any other pasta shape. In Campania, but also in Lazio and other regions, the *cannolicchio* must be just the right size so the bean will fit comfortably into the hole. When this happens, the Neapolitans say that the *"ciccillo è 'ncruvattato."*[43] *Cannolicchi* exist in various diameters, even large, and are both smooth and ridged.

40. CAPELLI D'ANGELO

Pasta lunga

INGREDIENTS: For homemade, wheat flour and eggs, but also wheat flour and water. For factory made, durum-wheat flour and eggs, but also flour and water.

HOW MADE: The flour is sifted onto a wooden board and kneaded with eggs for a long time, then left to rest. The dough is rolled out into a very thin sheet, which is cut into very thin *tagliolini* (see entry for *tagliatelle, tagliolini*). In some areas, the dough is colored with chard or spinach. The factory-made shape is thinner than a *spaghettino,* generally long, round, and about 1/32 inch (1 mm) in diameter. The pasta is cooked in broth.

ALSO KNOWN AS: *Capelvenere;* in Lazio, *maccaruni ciociari* in Ciociaria and *gramigna* or *ramiccia* in the province of Latina and in the Monti Lepini; in Calabria, *capiddi d'angilu;* in Sicily, *capiddi d'ancilu* and *vrimicieddi.*

HOW SERVED: Generally in broth, according to local traditions, but also as *pastasciutta.*

WHERE FOUND: Found throughout Italy, but in particular in Liguria and also in Lazio.

REMARKS: Literally "angel hair," *capelli d'angelo* were cited in Rome as early as the seventeenth century, where they were described as an extremely thin egg pasta. They were the specialty of some convents in the city, and the nuns used to send them to new mothers or to ailing members of important families with a curious ceremony. The historian Alessandro Moroni describes the distinguished personages charged with delivering these precious gifts, preceded by the servants of the noble houses, ramrod straight in their livery: ". . . and immediately afterward, brought in by numerous bearers, one saw the towering 'pavilion of the new mothers,' that is, a grandiose machine with bizarre designs, entirely covered with long threads of *tagliolini* or other egg pasta, the whole surrounded by a swarm of capons and hens for the use of the illustrious patient."[44]

In Naples, *capelli d'angelo* are used to make a special *pasticcio*. The same pasta is used in some regions to make a sweet dish. In Calabria, *capiddi d'angilu* was once a specialty of the nuns known as the Poor Clares.

41. CAPPELLACCI DEI BRIGANTI

Pasta corta

INGREDIENTS: Durum-wheat flour, eggs, water, and salt.

HOW MADE: The flour is sifted onto a wooden board and kneaded long and vigorously with a few eggs, water, and salt. The dough, which should be firm and smooth, is left to rest, then rolled out with a rolling pin into a very thin sheet. An inverted liqueur glass is used to cut small disks from the sheet. Each disk is wrapped into a cone around the tip of an index finger and the edge sealed, then one side is folded back like the brim of a hat. They are air dried and then boiled in plenty of salted water.

ALSO KNOWN AS: No alternative names.

HOW SERVED: As *pastasciutta*, typically with lamb *ragù*.

WHERE FOUND: Molise and Lazio (Formello).

REMARKS: The name, literally "brigands' hats," refers to the conical hat with upturned brim that was part of the everyday uniform of the *briganti*, from *brigantaggio*, a bloody and disorderly social and political movement active in the Mezzogiorno during the Unification of Italy and the first decade of the Kingdom of Italy. It is not known who invented this particular shape, but it has been made in Molise for more than a century.

In Jelsi, in Molise, in the province of Campobasso, the most prominent families used to order a small tin cone on which to shape the *cappellacci*.

In Formello, a town in the province of Rome along the Tiber valley, the name *cappellacci* is used for a sort of *crespella* (crepe) with different fillings.

42. CAPPELLACCI DI ZUCCA

Pasta ripiena

INGREDIENTS: Wheat flour and eggs. For the filling, winter squash, parmigiano, sugar, *savor*, nutmeg, and often *mostarda*. The mildly sweet yellow squash of the Po Valley, known as *zucca barucca* in the Veneto, is used.

HOW MADE: The flour is sifted onto a wooden board and kneaded long and vigorously with eggs until a firm, smooth dough forms, which is wrapped in a dish towel and left to rest. Then the dough is rolled out into a thin sheet, and 2¾-inch (7 cm) squares are cut from it. A spoonful of filling is placed in the center of each square, the square is closed into a triangle, and the edges are carefully sealed to form a large *raviolo*. They are boiled, a few at a time, in salted water.

ALSO KNOWN AS: No alternative names.

HOW SERVED: As *pastasciutta*, generally with a sumptuous meat *ragù*, dusted generously with parmigiano.

WHERE FOUND: Emilia-Romagna, especially Ferrara, Reggio Emilia, and surrounding areas.

REMARKS: The Ferraresi have long relied on the produce of the Veneto plain, including the special sweet squash called *barucca*, mentioned in Goldoni's *Baruffe Chiozzotte* (act I, scene II), when Canocchia offers Toffolo a *zucca barucca* just out of the oven. However, the vegetable's etymological root could also be *verruca*, for the wartlike bumps on its peel. By the 1700s, the squash was already being prepared correctly: baked first to dry it completely. The typical *cappellacci*, or "squash hats," of Ferrara can be made only with this type of squash; less flavorful varieties invariably yield a result that does not resemble the typical Ferrarese product.

The sweet-and-sour filling is a legacy of the sumptuous court cuisine. The Este family made Renaissance Ferrara a center of culture, including gastronomic, an accomplishment that was regarded as a shining example by all the courts of Europe.

Ferrara's important Jewish community also counts *cappellacci di zucca* among its ritual dishes.

43. CAPPELLETTI

Pasta ripiena

INGREDIENTS: Type 0 wheat flour and eggs. For the meat filling, generally mixed meats and spices, according to local customs. For the meatless filling, soft cheese, generally ricotta, *cacio raviggiolo, cassatella, stracchino,* or other; grated lemon rind; and nutmeg. Often spinach, parsley, or other seasonal greens are added. In Cesena, a provincial capital in Romagna, candied citron is added to both meat and meatless fillings.

HOW MADE: The flour is sifted onto a wooden board and kneaded long and vigorously with eggs. After resting, to give the gluten time to develop and make the dough elastic, the dough is rolled out into a thin sheet, and 1 ¼- to 2-inch (3- to 5-cm) squares are cut from it. A teaspoon of filling is placed on each square, and the pasta is folded in a special way to resemble a small hat. The filled pastas are cooked in meat broth.

ALSO KNOWN AS: *Caplet.*

HOW SERVED: Traditionally in capon or other meat broth.

WHERE FOUND: Emilia-Romagna, in particular Reggio Emilia, but also in Lazio, the Marche, and Umbria.

REMARKS: Kissing—and much larger—cousin of the more famous *tortellino* (see entry) of Bologna, and distinguished by a different filling, the *cappelletto romagnolo* has the same characteristic shape of a medieval hat, hence the name. In the Middle Ages, with the variegated world of stuffed pastas already delighting the palate of the more fortunate, meatless *cappelletti,* as they were made in Romagna, were likely helping to fill the void that Lent and numerous holy days left in the stomach of the privileged.

Filled with a sumptuous *squaquarone,*[45] *raviggiolo,*[46] or even simply ricotta, *cappelletti* were always on the table for the feast of the Ascension, when nettle tips or other wild greens replaced the spinach or chard in the filling. The already-famous meatless version—but with the addition of kidney fat and beef marrow—was made for the bishop of Imola, Barnaba Chiaramonti, the future Pope Pius VII.

And perhaps exactly for this infraction of the rules for vigils, the recipe drafted by the cook Alvisi dubbed them *cappelletti alla bolognese,* inaugurating a series of terminological confusions among fairly similar products.[47]

One old tradition called for making a special *cappelletto,* much larger than the rest. Dubbed *e' caplitaz* and filled only with pepper, it was served as a joke to the biggest glutton.

The Napoleonic inquests into the traditions of the Kingdom of Italy[48] attest to the extreme poverty of the rural areas, where the consumption of *cappelletti* was typically limited to no more than three times a year, on feast days. Often, they were on the table only once, for Christmas lunch, when even the poorest peasants made the effort to serve *cappelletti* filled with ricotta. Those who absolutely could not afford to make them were given them by their neighbors. The prefect of the department of the Rubicon, an area around the river, in Emilia-Romagna, gives an account of a curious practice of the locale: "On Christmas day, each family makes a soup of pasta with ricotta filling called *cappelletti.* The greed for this dish is so general that *everyone,* especially the priests, places bets on who can eat the largest number, with some reaching four hundred or five hundred, and each year this custom leads to the death of some individual, who succumbs to grave indigestion." This might be what the poet Giacomo Leopardi was talking about when, on December 19, 1825, he wrote from Bologna to his brother Pierfrancesco: "Wish Don Vincenzo a merry Christmas and tell him not to eat too many *cappelletti.*"[49]

During the summer, when everyone—men and women—worked in the fields, the *cappelletto* also appeared during the *seganda,* the difficult operations of reaping, raking, and baling. The day, which began at three or four in the morning, included five meals. The first was the *panetto* at 7 A.M., which consisted of salami, cheese, and shallots. There followed, at 10 A.M., the *colazione grossa,* or "big breakfast," based on *maccheroni* and *tagliatelle,* and at noon, the *desinare,* with a hearty broth containing *cappelletti* or *tagliolini* and accompanied by boiled meat. At 4 P.M. came the *merenda,* or "afternoon snack," which was the leftover boiled meat or roast, or salami and eggs. When the day's work was done, *cena,* or "dinner," was eaten, with fried *piadine* (flat bread), *tortelli, ciambelle* (savory ring cakes), and salad. Each meal was washed down with the local wine.

But times change, and with the postwar boom came the initiative of the Faenza section of the Accademia Italiana della Cucina, founders of the Accademia del Cappelletto, which conducted blind tastings. These tests were followed by a decree, registered with a notarial act, that stated that the true *cappelletto romagnolo* is filled with cheese.

Well beyond Romagna, *cappelletti* have become the typical Christmas dish throughout central Italy. In Rome, beginning at least in the early 1900s, the women and children gathered around the table on Christmas Eve day to make the *cappelletti* for the Christmas Day meal. Meanwhile, the men ate roasted chestnuts and drank hot Sangiovese wine with sugar, cinnamon, and cloves, until it was time to go to Mass.

Cucina di famiglia, a cookbook written by a Roman, Adolfo Giaquinto, and published in 1903 and again in 1922, speaks only of *tortellini alla bolognese.* However, Ada Boni, Giaquinto's niece, in her famous *Talismano della felicità,* published in 1925 by the magazine *La Preziosa,* which she herself directed, already makes a distinction between *cappelletto alla romana* and *tortellino bolognese,* specifying that the Roman is slightly larger and that the filling is made with raw, not cooked, meat.

Naturally, each locality adds its own specialties: in Umbria, *cappelletti* are sauced like *pastasciutta,* with garlic, oil, and a good grating of local truffles, and in the Marche, they are redolent with the famous truffle of Acqualagna. Here, too, the *cappelletto* is associated with Christmas dinner and the custom of gathering the whole family the day before to prepare the pasta by hand. Today, however, they are bought from small-scale pasta makers, who prepare them fresh for the occasion. The shaping is varied and left to the imagination of the maker.

In Puglia, *cappelletti* shaped to include a point are also called *cappelli del prete* (priest's hats).

44. CAPPIEDDI 'I PRIEVITI

Pasta ripiena

INGREDIENTS: Durum-wheat flour, salt, and eggs and / or water. For the filling, eggs, *soppressata* salami, *provola,* and seasonings.

HOW MADE: The flour is sifted onto a wooden board and kneaded long and vigorously with salt and eggs or water until a firm, smooth dough forms. After the dough has rested, it is rolled out into a thin sheet and cut into squares of variable size. A teaspoon of filling is placed at the center of each square, and the square is folded into a triangle, to simulate a three-cornered hat. The *ravioli* are boiled, a few at a time, in plenty of salted water.

ALSO KNOWN AS: *Cappelli del prete* and *tricorni.*

HOW SERVED: As *pastasciutta,* with tomato sauce.

WHERE FOUND: Calabria.

REMARKS: Although rare today in Calabria, this traditionally shaped *raviolo,* whose name translates as "priest's hat," was documented in the first *Guida gastronomica d'Italia.*[50] A pasta for feast days and holidays, it is distinguished by its filling, which calls for the typical local products.

45. CAPPUCCILLI

Pasta corta

INGREDIENTS: Durum-wheat flour and water.

HOW MADE: The flour is sifted onto a wooden board and kneaded long and energetically with water to create a smooth, firm dough, which is left to rest before it is rolled out into a very thin sheet. A toothed wheel is used to cut the sheet into 2-inch (5-cm) squares. The edges of each are pressed together to form small tubes. The tubes are boiled in plenty of salted water.

ALSO KNOWN AS: In Calabria, a smaller form is known as *calandreddi*.

HOW SERVED: As *pastasciutta*, with meat sauce.

WHERE FOUND: Basilicata, in the Agri valley, in particular the area around Viggiano.

REMARKS: This refined pasta was once made from an equally refined flour called *farina di cappella* (chapel flour). In winter, especially in January and February, the pork-based sauce is enriched with horseradish, which is grown in quantity in the area.

In Calabria, slightly smaller tubes are called *calandreddi*, named for the traditional reversed goatskin shoes worn by shepherds and peasants. The shoes, customarily worn with white woolen hose, were laced up the legs with leather thongs.

46. CASONSEI

Pasta ripiena

INGREDIENTS: Wheat flour, eggs, salt, and sometimes a little olive oil. For the filling, housewives in Brescia use various meats flavored with nutmeg, and those in the Val Camonica generally combine potatoes, garlicky salami, sausage, spinach, and the local *cacio*. The *ciaroncié* of Moena are filled with wild spinach, and around Cortina d'Ampezzo, they are usually filled with beets, grated local cheese, and smoked ricotta. Formerly *spersada,* an aged and smoked cheese of the Cadore, was used.

HOW MADE: The flour is sifted onto a wooden board and kneaded with eggs, sometimes a little oil, and a pinch of salt. The dough, worked long and vigorously, is then left to rest to give the gluten time to develop. Next, it is rolled out into a thin sheet with a rolling pin, and small disks, whose diameter varies from place to place, are cut. A teaspoon of filling is placed on each disk, and the disks are closed into half-moons and their edges carefully sealed.

Around Cortina d'Ampezzo, the disks are cut with a toothed wheel and, once closed, are lightly flattened in the center of the filling, giving each *raviolo* the look of a coxcomb. In the Val Camonica, *casonsei* are similar to *pi.fasacc* (see entry). The factory-made *ravioli* sometimes have distinctive decorative closings.

The half-moons are boiled, a few at a time, in abundant lightly salted boiling water.

ALSO KNOWN AS: *Casonziei, casunziei,* and *ciaroncié* in Moena, in Trentino.

HOW SERVED: As *pastasciutta,* in general with butter and local cheese; in Cortina d'Ampezzo, they are also served sprinkled with poppy seeds. The typical condiment was once minced *lardo.*

WHERE FOUND: Lombardy, especially in the valleys around Bergamo and Brescia and in the Val Camonica; and in the Veneto, around Cortina d'Ampezzo.

REMARKS: This very old stuffed pasta was already delighting diners at the end of the fourteenth century, when it was filled with cheese, pears, and spices. In the first half of the 1500s, Teofilo Folengo invented the macaronic *casoncellis* in his *Baldus.*[51] They have undergone many metamorphoses in their long life, with nineteenth-century recipe books describing them as filled with amaretti and candied fruit. Not surprisingly, fillings and condiments vary from town to town, from valley to valley, but definitely these *ravioli* are never absent from the table on important feast days. Around Brescia, they are also on the menu for family celebrations and civic occasions.

In *Scalco alla moderna,* a book on gastronomic training, Antonio Latini refers to these *ravioli* as *cappelletti alla lombarda.*[52] Latini, who moved from the Marche to Rome, attests to the fact that this stuffed pasta native to Lombardy was broadly known.

What is certain is that the differences among *casoncelli, ravioli, tortelli, agnolini,* and so forth are not immediately obvious. A great connoisseur of Italian food, Luigi Messedaglia,[53] echoes a joke of Folengo when he says that the same, or nearly the same, products could be called *tortelli graece, casocelli latine,* or *rafioli herbaice.*

47. CASSULLI

Gnocchi/gnocchetti

INGREDIENTS: Wheat flour, durum-wheat flour, water, and today eggs.

HOW MADE: The flours are sifted onto a wooden board and kneaded with water or with eggs until a firm, smooth dough forms. The dough is left to rest, then rolled out into sticks about ⅝ inch (1.5 cm) in diameter, which are in turn cut into ⅜-inch (1-cm) lengths. Each piece is rolled on a wooden board to make a sort of concave *gnocchetto,* and the finished pasta is boiled in abundant salted water.

ALSO KNOWN AS: No alternative names.

HOW SERVED: As *pastasciutta,* in general with a sauce of tuna, tomatoes, and herbs.

WHERE FOUND: Sardinia, in particular Isola San Pietro; the dish is typical of Carloforte.

REMARKS: When the Ligurians of Pegli found they were no longer welcomed by the Barbary kings to fish for tuna and coral near Tabarka Island, off Tunisia, they accepted the invitation of Carlo Emanuele III of Savoy, who installed them in Carloforte, on Isola San Pietro. A pure Ligurian dialect is still spoken there today, and this pasta, which resembles Ligurian *corzetti* (see entry), is still made.

48. CAVATELLI

Pasta corta

INGREDIENTS: Durum-wheat flour and water. In the south, was also formerly made with flour milled from fava beans, and in Puglia, with *grano arso.* The *pincinelle* of Pesaro are made with a dough of flour, eggs, oil, and salt.

HOW MADE: The flour is sifted and kneaded with cold water, energetically and for a long time, until a firm, smooth dough forms. After it has rested, cylinders about as thick as a pencil are rolled from pieces of the dough. These cylinders are cut into ⅜-inch (1-cm) lengths. With a blunt-tipped knife *(sferre),* each piece of dough is drawn across the board, leaving it with an indentation. The pieces are sometimes indented *(cavato)* with a finger. Factory-made *cavatelli* are also available. Both homemade and factory made are boiled in plenty of salted water.

ALSO KNOWN AS: In the Marche, around Pesaro, *pincinelle.* In Molise, *cazzarille, ciufele,* and also *cavatielle 'ncatenate* (chained) because they are rolled with two fingers. In Campania and in Puglia, they appear with other roots: in Campania, *cecatelli;* in Puglia, *cantaroggni, cavatieddi, cavatielli, mignuicchi, strascenate,* and *strascinati chiusi;* in the Puglian town of Molfetta, *tagghjunghele,* and near Foggia, in the area of Monte Sant'Angelo, *cecatidde, cecatielle,* and *cicatelli.*

In Basilicata, *capunti*, but also *capuntini, cingule, minuich, raskatelli*, and *zinne-zinne*. In Calabria, *cavateddri* and *rascatielli*. In Sicily, *gnocculi*, but also *gnucchitti* and *cavatuneddi*; around Ragusa, *cavasuneddi*; and in Modica, *lolli*.

Cavatelli also appear generically as *gnocchetti, manatelle, orecchie di prete, strascinari*, and *truoccoli*.

HOW SERVED: As *pastasciutta*, variously served with meat or vegetable sauces, always made with chili and finished with a dusting of local cheese, usually *cacioricotta*. The most typical sauce is *in bianco*, with turnip greens or *friarielli*.[54] However, in general, whatever vegetables are abundant in the area are used.

WHERE FOUND: Southern Italy, in particular Molise, Puglia, Campania, Basilicata, Calabria, and Sicily.

REMARKS: These small masterpieces of pasta sculpture, which resemble little hats, immediately evoke Puglia, even if now they are typical of all the regions of the south, where they have acquired different names and are treated to different sauces. Their name derives from the curious shape obtained with skilled hands from a dough always made from durum wheat. The shape is just one of the many that evolved from the flour-and-water *gnocco* common in the medieval Italian kitchen.

Nowadays, in addition to the factory-made dry production, a myriad of small artisanal producers, especially in the south, are marketing excellent vacuum-packed fresh *cavatelli*.

In Molise, both *cecatelli*, hollowed out with one finger, and *cavatelli*, hollowed out with two fingers, are found. The latter, which often include a small quantity of boiled potatoes in the dough, are the traditional devotional dish for the feast of Saint Anthony. Again in Molise, *vredocchie*, a sort of *gnocchetto* indented with two fingers and typical of Santa Croce di Magliano, are made. They were once used in a tasty one-dish meal with broccoli, oil, and chili.

In Puglia, but also in Basilicata and in Calabria, *cavatelli* are often served with turnip greens, which are particularly good, and a vivid green, in the Tavoliere.[55] But also common are a condiment with *rucola* and ricotta *marzotica* (from the month of March), another with wild turnips known as *lassini*, one made of mushrooms, and yet another with cabbage. The Puglian *cavatello* assumes different shapes from place to place: it can be larger or smaller, and more or less open. Those served in the towns of the Dauno Apennines, for example, are so tight that they could be *fusilli*, just as the *minchjaleddi* of Alessano and Castro are tiny *cavatelli* closed very tightly. At Taranto and Brindisi, *pizzicarieddi* are somewhat more cylindrical *cavatelli*, while the *pizzidieddi* of Brindisi are the same shape but made with *grano arso*.

In Campania, in the Vallo di Diano, a large *cavatello* is called a *parmarieddo* because it is rolled across the palm of the hand, instead of a wooden board.

Cavatelli are at the center of popular *sagre* in many towns in southern Italy during the August holiday season. For example, on August 1, in Cesinali, in the province of Avellino in Campania, a *sagra del cecatiello* is celebrated. It is repeated on August 14 at Sant'Angelo a Cupolo, in the nearby province of Benevento.

In Basilicata, another large area of diffusion, *cavatelli* are also called *orecchie di prete* (priest's ears) and are shaped by rolling the dough over a *cavarola*, a small, grooved wooden board. At one time, different types of flours were used, including, in times of famine, flour milled from acorns. This practice must have been common, both for pasta and for bread, because a statute in the town of Ruoti, dated August 3, 1621, prohibited the gathering of acorns on a certain estate for making bread. Also in Basilicata, in the area of Senise, tiny *cavatelli* called *zinnezinne* are cooked in soup with beans.

The Calabrian *cavateddri* are hollowed on a basket called a *crivu*. *Rascatieddri*, slightly longer, are indented with the index and middle fingers. In general, the sauce that accompanied these Calabrian pastas was simple and not very thick, though sometimes they were served with a lamb sauce.

49. CAZZAREGLI

Pasta corta

INGREDIENTS: Durum-wheat flour but also corn flour and lukewarm water.

HOW MADE: The flours are sifted together onto a wooden board and then kneaded long and vigorously with water until the dough is firm and smooth. After resting, the dough is cut into small pieces. These are rolled by hand into *spaghetti* the thickness of a matchstick, which are then cut into pieces about 3 inches (7.5 cm) long. In some towns, the dough is rolled into a sheet and cut into short, flat noodles about ¾ inch (2 cm) wide and 3 to 4 inches (7.5 to 10 cm) long, and then each noodle is rolled briefly with a hand to give it a little twist. The pasta is boiled in plenty of salted water.

ALSO KNOWN AS: *Cazzarieglie, cazzareji* (in Anticoli Corrado), and *strozzapreti*.

HOW SERVED: As *pastasciutta,* with simple local sauces.

WHERE FOUND: Molise, especially Vastogirard, and Lazio, around Subiaco (Anticoli Corrado).

REMARKS: In the peasant world, this type of small-format pasta has traditionally been served with beans, "the meat of the poor," and is thus found in all the regional cuisines. As Artusi (see note 18) says, beans stay in the stomach for a long time, calming the hunger pangs. In Molise, the pasta is paired with a special variety of red bean cultivated in the area, and at Vastogirardi in August, a *sagra dei cazzaregli con i fagioli* (with beans) is held. But today, this pasta is usually served with a meat- or fish-based sauce.

50. CAZZELLITTI

Pastina

INGREDIENTS: Durum-wheat and often also simple wheat flour, water, salt, and sometimes eggs.

HOW MADE: The flour is sifted onto a wooden board and kneaded with water and a pinch of salt to form a firm, smooth dough. After the dough has rested, pea-sized pieces are pinched off and carefully rolled across the board to make tiny *fusilli*. They are boiled in abundant salted water.

ALSO KNOWN AS: *Cavatille* and *cazzarille.*

HOW SERVED: As *pastasciutta*, with local vegetables, but also with a mutton sauce.

WHERE FOUND: Abruzzo, in Scanno and surrounding areas and around Vasto.

REMARKS: Perched on hilltops and in mountain forests, most towns in Abruzzo were far from the lines of communication in the past, and their residents traditionally relied on what they could grow and gather. The isolation of the region, a land of transhumance and sheep rearing, lasted almost through the 1960s. *Cazzellitti* used to be sauced with the vegetables grown by the shepherds near the mountain sheep pens, but also with such greens as wild spinach, zucchini shoots, and the like. The transhumance toward Puglia later introduced, through the shepherds, the knowledge and use of typical vegetables of that region, such as turnip greens, which are also used on this pasta. Around Vasto, on the Adriatic, fish sauces are common today.

51. CECAMARITI

Pasta corta

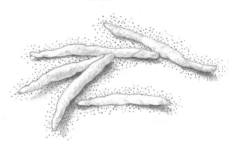

INGREDIENTS: Wheat flour, natural yeast, and water.

HOW MADE: Chickpea-sized pieces of raised bread dough are pinched off and rubbed between hands into the shape of a small spindle. As they are made, the *cecamariti* are laid out on a floured dish towel. They are boiled in salted water.

ALSO KNOWN AS: *Cicelieviti* in Abruzzo.

HOW SERVED: As *pastasciutta,* generally with a garlic- or tomato-based sauce, varying according to local customs.

WHERE FOUND: Lazio, in the Sabine country of the province of Rieti and the area of the Monti Lepini, and also in Molise (Poggio Sannita).

REMARKS: The Sabina, or Sabine country, of Lazio and extensive areas of Abruzzo are isolated lands of olive trees and castles, and their cooking has remained miraculously young because of this natural separation. Myriad homemade pastas are still made today in the towns and villages, but *cecamariti* may well be the oddest. When the bread dough was removed from the *madia* to bake it in the home oven, the dough that had collected on the walls and bottom of the box was used to make the famous *cecamariti,* or "husband blinders." They were so delicious that husbands, returning tired and hungry from work in the fields, were blinded (or at least dazzled). Often the term *cecamariti* is used instead of *strozzapreti,* with both terms always used for a particularly delicious dish.

The typical condiment for this pasta in Orvinio (province of Rieti) is a curious garlic sauce made by crushing a great deal of raw garlic in a wooden mortar with coarse salt and chili, then adding the excellent olive oil of the Sabina. At Rocca Canterano (province of Rome), *cecamariti* are shaped like normal *fusilli,* but from a mix of corn and wheat flours.

The term *cecamariti* can also be used for other handmade shapes: for example, around Rieti, *ciacamarini* are strips of egg pasta individually rolled between hands to make a sort of thin *spaghetto.*

52. CECATELLI

Pasta corta

INGREDIENTS: Durum-wheat flour, water, and salt, and also often whole-wheat flour or *grano arso.*

HOW MADE: The flour is sifted onto a wooden board, kneaded with water and salt long and vigorously, and then left to rest. Pieces of dough are pinched off and rolled into cylinders the size of a pencil. These in turn are cut into ¾-inch (2-cm) lengths and indented with a finger. They are boiled in plenty of salted water.

ALSO KNOWN AS: *Cicatilli.*

HOW SERVED: As *pastasciutta,* with typical local condiments.

WHERE FOUND: Campania and Puglia.

REMARKS: The name means literally "little blind ones." From the Latin *caeca* (blind), we get the Late Latin *caecula,* that is, a just-metamorphosed eel that looks like an almost-transparent thread, similar to the small eels called *ciriole*[56] (see entry). In the popular imagination, the *cecatello* has become similar to two or three small eyes that can be blinded with fingers. *Cecatelli* are typical of Lucera, in Puglia, where they are served with a sauce of rocket and tomato. They used to be made with alternative flours, especially in Puglia, including whole wheat, or in times of famine or in areas of severe poverty, with barley flour or flour from other minor grains. Sometimes *grano arso* was also used. Today, *cecatelli* are served in fashionable restaurants, and *grano arso* is marketed as a specialty product.

53. CENCIONI DI FAVE

Pasta corta

INGREDIENTS: Wheat flour, fava bean flour, and eggs.

HOW MADE: The flours are sifted together and kneaded long and vigorously with eggs until the dough is firm and well blended. The dough is left to rest, then rolled out with a rolling pin into a sheet, not too thin. It is cut into short, thick strips or into 1½- to 2-inch (4- to 5-cm) squares. They are boiled in plenty of salted water.

ALSO KNOWN AS: In the Marche, *cloncloni* and *concioni*.

HOW SERVED: As *pastasciutta,* in the Marche typically with a sausage-based sauce but also a *sugo finto*. It is also used in soup with beans, typically in the area of Pergola.

WHERE FOUND: The Marche (Pesaro and Macerata).

REMARKS: The name means literally "fava rags." It derives from *cencio,* or "rag," but the etymology is uncertain. The first vernacular attestation of *cencioni* goes back to the thirteenth century, but not for food. Food names inspired by humble everyday objects are common. The rag used to mop the floor or dust the furniture must have inspired a housewife making the daily pasta, and thus *cencioni* were invented.

In the old peasant world, where wheat flour was not always available, pasta was often made from a mix of various flours. Gluten-free fava flour still needed to be mixed with wheat flour to make a dough that could be rolled out. Today, fava *cencioni* have become a specialty dish, sought not just by gourmets, but also by inveterate lovers of traditional foods.

54. CHIANCAREDDE

Strascinati

INGREDIENTS: Durum-wheat flour, or sometimes whole-wheat flour, salt, and water.

HOW MADE: The flour is sifted with a pinch of salt onto a wooden board and kneaded long and vigorously with water. The dough is left to rest, then pieces are pinched off and formed into *strascinati* about 1½ inches (4 cm) long, thick, flat, and slightly rounded. They are boiled in abundant salted water.

ALSO KNOWN AS: *Recchietedde.*

HOW SERVED: As *pastasciutta,* with traditional local sauces, typically cabbage and pancetta.

WHERE FOUND: Puglia, especially in the areas of Taranto, Massafra, and Manduria.

REMARKS: The name means literally "paving stones." The allusion is to *chianche,* large, flat stones used for paving roads and gardens and to carpet the streets in every town in Puglia. The not-perfectly-smooth surface of the stone is similar to that of the pasta. The use of dark flours, both whole-wheat flour and, in areas of extreme poverty, *grano arso,* used to be quite common in Puglia. Often flours made from other grains, such as barley, or from legumes, in particular fava beans, were mixed with wheat flour to make pasta as well as bread.

55. CHIFFERI

Pasta corta

INGREDIENTS: Durum-wheat flour and water.

HOW MADE: Factory made in the form of a small, curved tube, imitating the Austrian sweet called *Kipfel;* may be smooth or ridged. *Chifferi* are boiled in plenty of salted water or in broth.

ALSO KNOWN AS: If small, *chiocciole, lumachine, lumachette, lumachelle* (the last three, all snails), *chifferini, cirillini, genovesini, gobbini* (humps), *gomitini* (elbows), *gozzini, pipette,* and *stortini.* If large, *chifferoni, gobboni, gomiti, mezzi gomiti, gozzettoni,* and *stortoni.*

HOW SERVED: The smaller ones are cooked in broth or soups; the larger ones are eaten as *pastasciutta,* with traditional local sauces.

WHERE FOUND: Widespread.

REMARKS: The name derives from *Kipfel,* a typical Austrian sweet of similar shape, common in the Grand Duchy of Parma in the day of Maria Luigia, in the early nineteenth century. The pastry chefs she brought with her to Parma from Vienna introduced the famous crescent-shaped pastry made to commemorate the Austrian victory over the Turks, who reached the gates of Vienna in 1683.

For a long time, the manufacture of fresh and dry pastas was the prerogative of bakers, making it likely that the shape of this pasta originated in a bread bakery where small, crescent-shaped sweets were also made.

56. CICIONES

Pasta corta

INGREDIENTS: Durum-wheat flour, saffron, and water.

HOW MADE: The flour is sifted and kneaded with water in which saffron has been dissolved. The dough is worked long and energetically until it is firm and smooth, then left to rest. Pieces of dough are pinched off and rolled between hands into sticks as thick as a pencil, which are cut into chickpea-sized pieces. There is also a factory-made version. Both are boiled in abundant salted water.

ALSO KNOWN AS: *Pizzottis* and *ciuccionis;* around Nuoro, *cravaus;* in the Logudoro, *macarones coidos;* and around Sassari, *cigiones* and *zizzones.*

HOW SERVED: As *pastasciutta,* with various local sauces, but usually with meat sauce and local pecorino.

WHERE FOUND: Sardinia, typical of Sassari.

REMARKS: The coloring of pasta with saffron is very old in Sardinia. That practice meant that poor flour-and-water pastas took on a beautiful golden hue that made them look as though they were prepared with eggs. The cultivation of the native crocus is widespread in the Campidano area, especially around the towns of San Gavino Monreale and Turri. The flowers used to grow wild among the limestone rocks. A crocus is depicted on the pediment carved at the entrance to the ancient Roman tomb of Attila Pompilia, today known as the Grotta della Vipera, near Cagliari.

The presence of saffron on the island was reported by Martin Carrillo, sent to Sardinia in 1610 by Philip III of Spain to draft a report on the living conditions of the population oppressed by bad administrators. On a visit to Mamojada in 1612, he was offered a Pantagruelian banquet for which was needed, among other items, "50 *libbre* of pepper, cloves, cinnamon, and saffron." Saffron is still used in many traditional Sardinian dishes, and an old adage of the Barbagia area says, "Only donkeys don't eat saffron."

Around Sassari, *ciciones* are prepared for the "dinner of the dead" (All Souls' Day, November 2): tradition has it that loved ones return during the night to eat the food they enjoyed in life, which is why the tables are set all night long.

57. CIRIOLE

Pasta lunga

INGREDIENTS: For homemade, soft-wheat flour, sometimes mixed with durum-wheat flour, and water. For factory made, durum-wheat flour and water.

HOW MADE: The flour or flours are sifted onto a wooden board and kneaded long and vigorously with water until the dough is firm and smooth. The dough is left to rest, then rolled out with a rolling pin into a sheet about ⅛ inch (3 mm) thick. The sheet is rolled up into a cylinder and cut crosswise into strips about ⅛ inch (3 mm) wide. The strips are rolled with hands on a wooden board to make long, irregular *spaghettoni*. The factory-made version is a long, flattish pasta, similar to *trenette* (see entry). Both types are boiled in abundant salted water.

ALSO KNOWN AS: In the Val di Chiana and around Siena, *ceriole;* in Sangemini in Umbria, *picchiarelli.*

HOW SERVED: As *pastasciutta,* with traditional local sauces. The *picchiarelli* of Sangemini are served with a typical horsemeat *ragù.*

WHERE FOUND: Tuscany and Umbria, especially the province of Terni.

REMARKS: *Ciriole* is an old name for a small, thin white eel, from which it is easy to imagine the association with the form and color of this pasta. The origin of the term is, again for similarity of shape, the Latin *cereolus* and then *ciriolus,* diminutives of *cereus,* meaning "candle." The term *ciriole* is used in the countryside on the border of Umbria and Tuscany, and it is also at home in the areas of the Crete Senesi, the Casentino, and the Maremma.

In Umbria, *ciriole* are the same as *stringozzi* (see entry). In Sangemini, they are called *picchiatelli* because of the custom of patting *(picchiettare)* the dough with fingers. In Terni, in addition to the traditional local sauces, *ciriole* are served with a sauce of *pioppo*[57] mushrooms.

58. CJALSONS

Pasta ripiena

INGREDIENTS: Wheat flour, sometimes boiled potatoes, and eggs. The fillings vary from place to place.

HOW MADE: The flour is sifted onto a wooden board and kneaded long and vigorously with eggs, and sometimes also with riced boiled potatoes, until a firm, smooth dough forms. The dough is left to rest, then rolled out into a sheet. Disks of various sizes are cut with a toothed pasta cutter. The disks are topped with filling, and then folded and sealed in a half-moon. Or a second disk is placed on top and the edges are sealed to form a round *raviolo*. In the town of Timau, the dough is shaped into a cylinder and then cut into round slices that are flattened into disks beneath the bottom of a glass. The filling is placed on the disk, and the *cjalson* is completed by placing a second disk on top. The *ravioli* are boiled in abundant salted water.

ALSO KNOWN AS: *Agnolotti, cialcions, cjarsons, cialzons,* and *ciargnei.*

HOW SERVED: As *pastasciutta,* traditionally with melted butter, smoked ricotta, and local aged cheese.

WHERE FOUND: Friuli–Venezia Giulia, especially in the Carnia area.

REMARKS: The name means literally "pants," like *calzoni.* These ancient and special *ravioli* are redolent of the woods and wild herbs of Carnia, and have as many spellings as they have fillings. The pasta dough can vary, too: made with flour and potatoes, or with potatoes only. In the past, the pasta sheet for this ritual dish must have been extremely thin: the women of the Degano valley were known to believe that the thinner the pasta was rolled, the higher the precious hemp would grow the next year.

Traditionally, these *ravioli* are eaten on Christmas Eve, before *madijnis,* the religious function of December 24. In some areas, as in the Canale d'Incarojo, north of Tolmezzo, they are eaten also on the last Thursday in January. But the eating of *cjalsons* is not limited to these days, especially in the mountains of Carnia, where they have always been offered to guests on feast days, the filling a mix of sweet and savory—raisins, candied citron, spinach, smoked ricotta. The different fillings indicate where the *cjalsons* were made. For example, potato is favored for the *cjalsons de planure (di pianura,* "lowlands") in the plain of Friuli. These were the ritual Easter lunch, both in homes and convents—*Pasche de cjalsons* was the popular name for the occasion—and were considered rich enough to be a one-dish meal.

The preparation of these special *ravioli* is very old: the *Liber de ferculis* of Giambonino da Cremona, which includes about eighty Arab recipes of both gastronomic and dietetic interest, drawn from a monumental Arabic work by a Baghdad physician who died in 1100,[58] contains a recipe for a stuffed pasta, *calizon panis,* a term that passed into medieval Italian as *calisone.* It must have been a sweet. The presence of a sweet of Arab origin in the mountains of the Italian north should not be surprising, however, since Frederick II and his court had enormous influence on habits and customs even in northern Germany. Remember, too, the Saracens dominated Provence throughout the tenth century, and today, marzipan *ravioli,* called *calissons,* are a specialty of Aix.[59]

A fifteenth-century expense note of the convent of Santa Maria in Valle di Cividale attests to the custom of preparing *cjalsons* for the feast of the Resurrection. Made by the nuns to celebrate various religious holidays, these, too, are sweet *ravioli*, variously filled and often dipped in honey.

Times have changed and so has the filling for these *ravioli*. Variants exist at Soandri and in the valleys of the Chiarso, the Tagliamento, and so on. Indeed, every valley has its typical fillings. At Zuglio, in the province of Udine, at the end of the age-old ceremony of the "kiss of the crocuses," it is customary to eat sweet *cjalsons* filled with ricotta and herbs. In Gorto, in the Degano valley, the filling is made from roasted onion, polenta, and raisins. At Cercivento, in Val Calda, herbs, smoked ricotta, dried figs, and raisins are used, and in Val del But, hard rye bread and often apples are found. In Timau, the *cjalsons* are filled with potatoes scented with mint and cinnamon; and in Val Pesarina, a filling of smoked ricotta, *montasio* cheese, lemon, and *pan di sòrc* (rye and corn bread) is assembled. At Ovaro, the filling is the old *pastum,* made from cheese, raisins, cinnamon, biscotti, and chocolate. In the 1970s, a famous Tolmezzo chef, Gianni Cosetti, organized a competition among the women of Carnia to define the typical recipe for *cjarcions*. Forty contestants participated; forty different recipes were presented.[60]

Cheese is omnipresent in the fillings and the sauces, because the people of Carnia have always had a strong culture of products *di malga.* Toward mid-June, with the melting of the winter snow, the herds leave for the mountain pastures, where they remain until it is time to return for the feast of the Nativity of the Blessed Virgin Mary on September 8. In the high-mountain huts, or *malghe,* smoked ricottas and other cheeses are made, long and patient work that will take all summer and will yield products that will make their way into numerous characteristic *cialsons.* On the way out and the way back, as the herds travel through the streets of small towns, a festive ringing of cowbells is heard, accompanied by the rhythms of the ancient *ciùculis (zoccoli),* the rough and worn wooden clogs of the cowmen.

59. CODE DI TOPO

Pasta corta

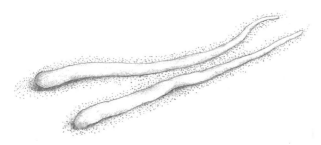

INGREDIENTS: Wheat flour and water.

HOW MADE: The flour is sifted and kneaded long and vigorously with lukewarm water. The dough is left to rest, then walnut-sized pieces are pinched off and rolled on a wooden board into little strings of various sizes, tapered at one end. They are left to dry slightly on a dish towel, then boiled in salted water.

ALSO KNOWN AS: In Lazio, around Palestrina and Frosinone, *coda de soreca* and *gnocchetti a coda de soreca*. Lazio is also home to *ciuci*, a modern, longer shape made from dough that includes porcini flour. In Abruzzo, in Rovere, *surgilli*, dialect for *topini*, "little mice."

HOW SERVED: As *pastasciutta*, traditionally with potatoes; but at Rovere (L'Aquila), they are served with a simple *soffritto* of garlic, oil, chili, and chopped walnuts.

WHERE FOUND: Lazio and Abruzzo.

REMARKS: The name means literally "mouse tails." From the acts of the Commissione parlamentare di inchiesta sulla miseria in Italia,[61] which was instituted immediately after World War II and finished its work in 1953, emerge conditions of life throughout rural Italy not easily grasped today. The houses were almost always *tuguri* (shacks), in which the family lived alongside its animals: the pig, the donkey, the hens—all precious because they meant survival. In what are now unimaginable nonhygienic circumstances—conditions that found mice and other vermin running free in the house—a housewife-wag likely created this pasta shape, with its tapered end, inspired by the tails of scurrying mice.

60. COJËTTE

Gnocchi/gnocchetti

INGREDIENTS: Wheat flour, stale bread, sometimes potatoes, milk, and herbs.

HOW MADE: The flour is sifted onto a wooden board and kneaded with bread that has been soaked in milk and squeezed dry. Minced herbs are added to the dough. To cook the pasta, teaspoonfuls of dough are dropped in boiling salted water. When they bob to the surface, they are ready.

ALSO KNOWN AS: *Caiettes.*

HOW SERVED: As *pastasciutta,* with butter and local cheese and gratinéed in the oven.

WHERE FOUND: Piedmont, in the Occitan valleys of Cuneo Province.

REMARKS: This pasta is typical of the Occitan cuisine found in the valleys of Cuneo Province. The same cuisine is eaten in Liguria, in the small town of Olivetta San Michele, and even in faraway Calabria, in the old town center of Guardia Piemontese. The latter was founded by the Piedmontese of Val Pellice, who took refuge there to escape the religious persecutions that lasted from the thirteenth to the sixteenth century—persecutions that followed them even to their new home.

The populations of Piedmontese Occitan language and tradition are very much alive today, and they cultivate their ancient gastronomic traditions and their folklore with manifestations that draw tourists to the valleys. The old Occitan cuisine has become the pride of all the small valley towns, and the name of flavorful dumplings called *cojëtte* is derived from an Occitan dialect term. They can be tasted on the Feast of the Immaculate Conception, December 8, called here Madona d'le Cojëtte, which is especially celebrated in the Gesso and Colla valleys.

61. CONCHIGLIE

Pasta corta

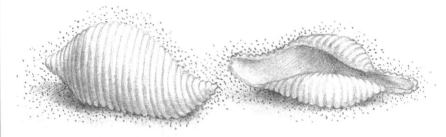

INGREDIENTS: Durum-wheat flour and water.

HOW MADE: Factory made, in the shape of a shell, or *conchiglia,* smooth or ridged. They come in various sizes and are boiled in abundant salted water.

ALSO KNOWN AS: *Abissini, arselle, cinesini, coccioline, cocciolette, conchigliette, tofarelle,* and *tofettine;* the larger sizes are called *conchiglioni.*

HOW SERVED: The smallest sizes are used in broth-based soups, and the largest are served as *pastasciutta,* with typical local sauces.

WHERE FOUND: Throughout Italy, though the large ones are most common in Campania.

REMARKS: Many master pasta makers have exercised their imagination on this shape, which literally means "shells." Some are almost photographically the shape of a seashell. Others are simpler and larger and are the favorites in some areas, such as Campania, where it is customary to fill them with meat, cover them with a sumptuous *ragù,* and brown them in the oven.

62. CORALLI

Pastina

INGREDIENTS: Durum-wheat flour and water.

HOW MADE: Factory made, tiny tubes pierced with a small hole. They are boiled in broth.

ALSO KNOWN AS: *Corallina, corallini, ditaletti,* and *tubettini;* in Sicily, *coradduzza.*

HOW SERVED: Usually in broth.

WHERE FOUND: Widespread.

REMARKS: The name, which literally means "corals," refers to a typical female ornament, once common among the populations of the Mediterranean coast, where coral fishing was widely practiced. The simplest coral bead was a tiny tube, exactly like the pasta tubes, which were cut very short as they emerged from the *torchio*.

63. CORDELLE CALABRESI

Pasta lunga

INGREDIENTS: Rye flour, eggs, and milk.

HOW MADE: Rye flour is sifted and kneaded with eggs and milk long and vigorously to make a firm, smooth dough. After resting, the dough is rolled with hands into a single, long *spaghettone,* which is wound into the characteristic coil and left to dry on a wooden board, then cut into two or three lengths. The pasta is boiled in abundant salted water.

ALSO KNOWN AS: No alternative names.

HOW SERVED: As *pastasciutta,* usually with a simple tomatoless sauce that always includes chili and grated local cheese.

WHERE FOUND: Calabria.

REMARKS: This extremely long *spaghetto* resembles the *shtridhëlat* (see entry) of the ethnic Albanian communities that began settling in Calabria in the sixteenth century. Given the difficulty both of making it and of finding rye flour—called *jermanu* in Calabria—this type of pasta is gradually disappearing.

64. CORDELLE SABINE

Pasta lunga

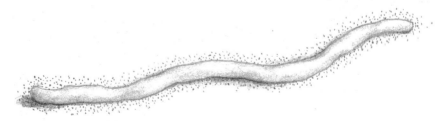

INGREDIENTS: Wheat flour, natural yeast, and water.

HOW MADE: This pasta is made with raised bread dough. A walnut-sized piece is pinched off and rolled with hands on a wooden board into a narrow rope 8 to 12 inches (20 to 30 cm) long. The *cordelle* are laid out to dry on a floured dish towel, and then boiled in salted water.

ALSO KNOWN AS: No alternative names.

HOW SERVED: As *pastasciutta,* with a simple tomato sauce and the local pecorino.

WHERE FOUND: Lazio, in the Sabine hills in the province of Rieti, notably the town of Rivodutri.

REMARKS: The common use of raised bread dough to make this sort of large *spaghettone* says a great deal about the once-poor Italian rural economy, where nothing, not even crumbs or odd bits, was wasted. After the household bread was made once every week or two, pasta was made with what could be scraped out of the *madia.* In the province of Rieti, in the Sabine hills, this pasta—and *cecamariti* (see entry)—is an example of that tradition.

65. CORONETTE

Pasta ripiena

INGREDIENTS: Wheat flour and eggs. For the filling, ricotta and parsley.

HOW MADE: The flour is sifted onto a wooden board and kneaded long and vigorously with eggs. The dough is left to rest, then rolled into a thin sheet, and small disks are cut with a fluted pasta cutter. A teaspoon of filling is placed in the center of each disk, the disk is folded into a half-moon, and the edge is sealed well. To make a larger pasta, the sheet is cut into roughly 2-inch (5-cm) squares, and each square is filled and folded into a triangle. Both shapes are boiled in plenty of salted water.

ALSO KNOWN AS: No alternative names.

HOW SERVED: As *pastasciutta,* with traditional local condiments.

WHERE FOUND: Campania, in the Vallo di Diano, in particular around Teggiano and Padula.

REMARKS: Literally "little wreaths," these small, curly-edged *ravioli* resemble their namesake. Tradition associates *coronette* with the marriage of Costanza di Montefeltro, daughter of Federico da Montefeltro, duke of Urbino (1422–82), to Antonello Sanseverino, prince of Salerno and lord of Diano (1458–99). In remembrance of this wedding, a historical reenactment is staged every year at Teggiano, and *coronette* are made for the celebration.

66. CORZETTI

Pasta corta/strascinati

INGREDIENTS: Wheat flour, eggs, and water. Piedmontese *croset* also contain a little oil, and the *crosit* of the town of Biella are made with flour, stale bread, and milk.

HOW MADE: The flour is sifted onto a wooden board and kneaded for a long time with a few eggs and some lukewarm water until a rather solid, smooth dough forms. Boiled borage is sometimes kneaded into the dough to color it green. Piedmontese *croset* also contain a little oil, and the *crosit* of the town of Biella are made with flour, stale bread, and milk.

To make modern *corzetti*, chickpea-sized pieces of dough are pinched off, placed on a wooden board, and pressed at the ends with the tips of the index fingers to produce an 8 shape. These are *corzetti tiae co-e die* (or *tirati con le dita* in standard Italian, meaning "rolled with the fingers"). For the traditional *corzetto stampato*, the dough is pressed between two wooden molds.

The pasta is boiled in abundant salted water; the wrinkles help the pasta absorb the condiment.

ALSO KNOWN AS: In Piedmont, variants appear under the name *croset, crosit,* and *torsellini*. In Emilia-Romagna, *crosetti* and *croxetti*.

HOW SERVED: As *pastasciutta,* traditionally with a tomatoless sauce flavored with marjoram, or with the classic Ligurian pesto, but also with different local sauces. The Piedmontese *croset* require a condiment based on Piedmontese *toma; crosit* are served usually with just butter.

WHERE FOUND: Throughout Liguria, but most typical of the Val Polcevera. Variants are found in Piedmont, in particular in Biella, Asti, and Alessandria.

REMARKS: This very old pasta is documented as early as the thirteenth century in Liguria and in Provence, where they are called *crosets.*[62] The text in medieval Latin, which dates to the fourteenth century, explains clearly how they are made: small pieces of pasta that are as thick as a thumb "... *cum digito sunt concauati*" (...

are hollowed with the finger). They are served with a large quantity of grated cheese.

Today, the same term is used for a similar pasta in Piedmont. The Piedmontese *croset* are indented like a *cavatello,* and the *crosit,* also found in Piedmont and made from moistened bread and flour, look like the classic modern *gnocco,* slid over the tines of a fork. *Torsellini,* very small and indented *gnocchetti,* exist in Piedmont as well, where they are a specialty of the middle Belbo valley.

The popular version of this thick pasta was—and is—indented with fingers. Since it could be dried easily, it constituted a good food resource both for sailors away for long periods and for everyone during the not infrequent periods of famine.

The little wooden molds with which the Ligurian *corzetti* were stamped were already common at the Renaissance courts and often bore an incised coat of arms. Alternatively, they bore a little stylized cross, from which the *crosetti* probably take their name. Other molds were incised with geometric and vegetal motifs, or with references to the celebration for which they were made. The molds needed to be fashioned of a neutral wood, such as apple, pear, maple, or beech, so the sap would not transfer an unpleasant taste to the pasta.

The molds are made of two separate pieces of wood: The first is in the shape of a small concave stamp, which cuts the pasta. The second is a tiny cylinder incised on one side. Until a few decades ago, the Ligurian town of Chiavari was the most famous home of *corzetto* molds. In the first decades of the twentieth century, some industrially produced incised molds were made with special cutter-folders; one type had the image of a coat of arms with a rampant lion.

During the sixteenth century, the silver *scudo* used in the Republic of Genoa was commonly called a *croset,* for its resemblance to the pasta.

One of the classic condiments for *corzetti* is pesto (see *picagge*), which has a long and venerable tradition in Liguria.

67. CRESC'TAJAT

Pasta corta

INGREDIENTS: Wheat flour, corn flour, and lukewarm water; sometimes just corn flour and water, or leftover polenta, flour, and water.

HOW MADE: The flours are sifted together onto a wooden board and kneaded long and vigorously with lukewarm water. The dough is left to rest, then it is rolled out with a rolling pin into a sheet—not too thin—from which large squares or rhombuses are cut. The pasta is boiled in plenty of salted water.

ALSO KNOWN AS: *Maltagliati, cresc'tajet,* and in the Montefeltro, *patacuc.*

HOW SERVED: As *pastasciutta,* with *lardo* and wild herbs in the past, and today usually with tomato and sausage sauce, but also often with beans.

WHERE FOUND: The Marche, area of Pesaro and Fano.

REMARKS: In testimony of the extreme poverty that once plagued parts of Italy, this pasta was even made with the crust that stuck to the walls of the *paiolo*[63] in which polenta had been cooked. The leftover polenta was kneaded with wheat flour and served with *lardo* in which wild herbs had been fried. In the area of Pesaro, especially in the towns of Piobbico and Cagli, *cresc'tajat* is still served for the feast of Saint Constantius, September 23.

68. CRESPELLE

Crepes

INGREDIENTS: In Valle d'Aosta, wheat flour, eggs, butter, and milk; in Tuscany and in Abruzzo, flour and water, sometimes with a very little oil. For the filling, in Valle d'Aosta, smoked prosciutto and *fontina valdostana* cheese; in Tuscany, usually ricotta and spinach; and in Abruzzo and Molise, a dusting of parmigiano.

HOW MADE: The flour is sifted and mixed with the other ingredients to make a batter, which is left to rest for a long time. It is then dropped in small quantities into a small iron pan and browned on both sides.

ALSO KNOWN AS: In Tuscany, *pezzole,* and in Abruzzo, *scrippelle.*

HOW SERVED: Covered with béchamel and baked. For the *scrippelle* of Abruzzo, in turkey broth.

WHERE FOUND: Valle d'Aosta, Tuscany, Abruzzo (typical of L'Aquila and around Teramo, but also around Scanno), and today throughout Italy under different names.

REMARKS: *Crespelle,* or "crepes," are generally extraneous to Italian regional pastas, but are firmly part of Abruzzese gastronomy. Originally, the *scrippella* followed a precise recipe and its manufacture was, and still is, entrusted to the eye and hand of the housewife, in a careful balance of eggs and flour, because, according to an old saying in Abruzzo and Molise, *la scrippella non è una frittata and nemmeno una frittella*—"the *scripella* is neither a frittata nor a pancake." Traditionally, *scrippelle* are cooked over a wood fire.

To make *scrippelle 'mbusse,* which remain firmly rooted in the Abruzzese and Molisan kitchen, the crepes are dusted with parmigiano, rolled into a tube, and immersed in broth. Still served on special occasions, these *scrippelle* absorb the broth and swell up, melting the cheese slightly to make a true delicacy. A sumptuous *timballo* of *scrippelle* is also made throughout both regions today.

In the Abruzzese area of Scanno, *scrippelle* have long been eaten plain, sometimes cut into strips and tossed in broth, and only recently have been transformed into *cannelloni.* But elsewhere in Italy, filled *crespelle* commonly appear as a hearty *primo piatto,* especially for feast days.

In an early recipe book from Trentino, we find *pasta scardelata,* from the verb *lardar,* in the sense of *lardellare* (to lard). A pasta sheet made from flour and eggs is covered with fried *lardo,* sprinkled with sugar (today, a little tomato would replace the sugar), folded into quarters, and cooked in a well-greased frying pan.

Going down the Boot, in the town of Nicastro, in Calabria, *crispelli* or *grispelli,* elongated *frittelle* (pancakes) stuffed with salted anchovies or sardines, are served for Christmas. In Bronte, in Sicily, *crispelle* are deep-fried anchovy-stuffed bundles. Also worth mentioning in Sicily is *'nfigghiulata,* a pasta sheet filled with ricotta and *insaccati,* folded into quarters, and baked.

69. CRESTE DI GALLO

Pasta ripiena

INGREDIENTS: For homemade, durum-wheat flour and eggs. For the filling, chicken, bread, and cinnamon. For factory made, durum-wheat flour and water.

HOW MADE: The flour is sifted onto a wooden board and kneaded long and vigorously with eggs until a firm, smooth dough forms. The dough is covered and left to rest, then rolled out into a thin sheet and cut into strips about 4 inches (10 cm) wide. Well-spaced spoonfuls of the filling are placed lengthwise on half of each strip. The other half of the strip is folded over the filling to cover, and the dough is sealed well around the filling with fingertips. Finally, the folded strips are cut into half-moons, forming large *ravioli* in the shape of a coxcomb. They are boiled in plenty of salted water.

Factory-made *creste di gallo* are rounded and convex. Large versions are boiled in abundant salted water, and small versions are cooked in broth.

ALSO KNOWN AS: *Griù*.

HOW SERVED: Generally as *pastasciutta,* with typical local sauces; the small factory-made sizes, in broth.

WHERE FOUND: The fresh version in the Marche, especially around Ascoli Piceno; the factory-made version, throughout Italy.

REMARKS: The name means literally "coxcombs." References to barnyard animals are common in pasta terminology. The shapes are varied, and the animals and insects of peasant life are extensively represented: there are *creste di gallo,* but also *galletti* (young cocks), *corna di bue* (ox horns), *denti di cavallo* (horse teeth), *denti di pecora* (sheep teeth), *lucciole* (fireflies), and *farfalline* (little butterflies).[64]

The large *raviolo* of the Marche is a dish for feast days. In the past, it was served with *sapa,* made by reducing grape must over heat until it forms a sweet syrup.

70. CULINGIONIS

Pasta ripiena

INGREDIENTS: Durum-wheat flour, type 00 flour, salt, lard, and lukewarm water. The filling can vary, including fresh *pecorino sardo* mixed with chard and flavored with saffron, sometimes replaced by mint-scented ricotta; mixed meats, but always including lamb; potatoes and pecorino; or eggplant, chard, and walnuts.

HOW MADE: The flours are sifted together onto a wooden board and kneaded with lard, lukewarm water, and salt. The dough must be worked long and vigorously until firm and smooth. It is left to rest, then rolled out into a thin sheet. Half of the sheet is topped with walnut-sized balls of filling arranged 2 inches (5 cm) apart. The uncovered half is folded over the filling, and the dough is sealed firmly around the filling with fingers. The *ravioli* are cut apart in the shape of half-moons. They are boiled in salted water, a few at a time.

The shape of *culingionis* can vary from area to area. They can be small squares, have ridges that recall fishbones, look like a flattened fig, or even, as around Ogliastra, be fashioned into a little bundle and tied with a small sheaf of wheat. Some cooks pierce the bundle twice with a needle to keep it from swelling up too much during cooking.

ALSO KNOWN AS: *Culurzones, kulurjones, culurjones, angiolottus, culurzones,* and *spighitti.*

HOW SERVED: As *pastasciutta,* with hearty meat *ragù* that vary according to the filling, but also with a simple sauce of tomato and basil. They are always sprinkled with local pecorino.

WHERE FOUND: Sardinia.

REMARKS: The skill of the Sardinian women in working flour, especially in bread making, is unrivaled in Italy. The nuptial breads they make are true works of art, and many of the island's sweets are precious small sculptures. The pastas, too, must be added to the list, recognized as tiny, extraordinary edible sculptures. They are simpler in shape than the breads because they must be boiled in water. However, eating them is like a dive into the fragrances and flavors of a fortunate island.

Each area of Sardinia has its *ravioli:* In Ogliastra, the filling is potatoes flavored with mint. In the small town of Armungia, potato *culingionis* are served for Ferragosto and All Saints' Day. At Ussassai, they make a different type of *raviolo,* filled with potatoes, acidic cheese, and caul fat from sheep and calves. Around Cagliari, they are filled with pecorino and chard, and the local housewives are particularly skillful in closing the *raviolo* in a half-moon: the edge comes out looking like a sort of little cord in the shape of a wheat sheaf, which terminates in a pointed horn.

71. CUSCUS
Unusual shape

INGREDIENTS: Durum-wheat flour and water.

HOW MADE: Large-grained *semola* is put into a special terra-cotta bowl, known as a *mafaradda* in Sicily. The grains are sprinkled with lightly salted water while fingers work the mixture in a rotary movement to form tiny lumps, in an operation called *incocciata.* The little lumps are spread to dry on a dish towel.

The *cuscus* is then steamed for a long time in a *pignata,* a specially designed terra-cotta pot with a bottom perforated with holes like a colander. This pot is placed on top of a second pot of the same diameter, and the join is sealed with a flour-and-water dough called *cuddura,* to keep steam from escaping. Liquid is boiled in the lower pot and the steam swells and cooks the *cuscus* in the upper pot. Today, a modern metal *cuscussiera,* or *couscousière,* is used, with two parts that fit together perfectly, so no sealing dough is needed.

ALSO KNOWN AS: *Cascà* or *cashcà* in Sardinia, *cuscussù* in Tuscany, and *cuscusu* in Sicily.

HOW SERVED: With fish or meat, depending on the place.

WHERE FOUND: Tuscany, in Livorno; Sardinia, especially in Calasetta and Carloforte; and Sicily, especially around Trapani.

REMARKS: According to the earliest citations, *semola* cooked in soup, a sort of *polentina* simmered in milk or broth, was considered a luxury dish. In fact, at the beginning of the fifteenth century, it was served at the table of Amedeo VIII, duke of Savoy, by his chef, Maistre Chiquart.[65] A short time later, the preparation of a *cemolella ciciliana* appears in the recipe book of Maestro Martino. It, too, must have been a soft *polenta,* because the *cuscus* is not dried completely. The same author speaks of *coscossone* in a dated manuscript[66] titled *Apparecchi diversi da mangiare et rimedii,* held in the Biblioteca Nazionale of Naples. Later, in Scappi,[67] we find a description of *succusu* in surprisingly modern terms; the author calls it "Moorish food."

Aside from these interesting memories, mention of *semola* or *cuscus* in cooking manuals is rare. Indeed, it is almost absent from such records until the middle of the twentieth century, and when *cuscus* does appear, it is filed under Arab recipes. The dish clearly originated in the Maghreb of North Africa and spread throughout the Mediterranean. The French call it *cuisine des pieds-noirs,* after their colonists in Algeria.

A link with Jewish cooking is clear in the Tuscan *cuscussù,* very probably brought to Livorno by Jews fleeing persecution in Spain during the sixteenth century. In Sicily, it was already consumed at the time of the flourishing Muslim colonization and remained unchanged in some areas.

In Sardinia, preparation of *cuscus* is linked to the colonization by the Ligurians. In the thirteenth century, trade wars to control the island raged between Pisa and Genoa, with both sides taking advantage of the internal struggles among the different *giudicati.*[68] The two republics divided the areas of influence among their militarily and commercially dominant families. Typical is the example of the Doria family of Genoa,[69] who had extensive holdings in the Logudoro and in vast areas in the north of the island, where they obtained houses, churches, cemeteries, and large warehouses.

In 1541, Ligurians, mostly from the area of Pegli, colonized the island of Tabarka, off Tunisia, to exploit it for tuna and coral fishing. At the beginning of the eighteenth century, beset by pirates, the people of Tabarka accepted the invitation of Carlo Emanuele III of Savoy, Piedmontese king of Sardinia (1701–73), to move to the then-uninhabited Isola San Pietro, just off the west coast of Sardinia. They named the port Carloforte in his honor. Here they pursued their fishing, and from here spread their Maghrebian couscous, an essential part of their cuisine. The tradition of Ligurian Tabarka is still alive today in the form of *fregula* (see entry), which resembles the earlier couscous only in the method of preparation. Every August, a *sagra* dedicated to Tabarkan cooking is held at Carloforte.

Commercial exchanges and immigration carried this dish to the rest of the peninsula, where each area simplified it by abandoning the use of durum-wheat flour in favor of regular flour and by cooking the little lumps directly in broth instead of steaming them in the *cuscussiera*. Thus, we find in Trentino and the Veneto, *fregolotti;* in Romagna, *manfricoli;* in Umbria, the Marche, and Lazio, *frascarelli;* and in many Italian regions, *pasta grattata* (see entry). What is important in all these preparations is the shape rather than the source or principal ingredients, which could vary.

Three typical Italian versions are characterized by what accompanies them: the Jews of Livorno use vegetables garnished with small meatballs and eat the dish for Tu Bishvat, the New Year of the Trees; in Sardinia, more in line with earlier Maghrebian practices, lamb or just vegetables are served with the *cuscus;* and in Trapani, fish is traditional.

Finally, there is a sweet *cuscus,* an old Sicilian recipe that is the pride of the Benedictine nuns of a convent in Agrigento.

72. CUTANEI

Gnocchi/gnocchetti

INGREDIENTS: Flour, a few eggs, boiling water, and salt.

HOW MADE: The flour is sifted onto a wooden board and kneaded long and vigorously with a few eggs and some lightly salted boiling water. The dough is left to rest, then long cylinders, about ¾ inch (2 cm) in diameter, are formed with hands by rolling pieces of the dough on the wooden board. These cylinders are cut into small pieces about ¾ inch (2 cm) long and boiled in plenty of salted water.

ALSO KNOWN AS: *Gnucchit de farina.*

HOW SERVED: As *pastasciutta,* generally with meat *ragù* and a grating of local cheese.

WHERE FOUND: The Marche, in particular Senigallia, but also Macerata.

REMARKS: *Cutanei* are a type of *gnocchetto*. The meaning of the word is unknown, and so is the origin of the food itself. In the Marche, as elsewhere, *gnocchi* are nowadays made with potatoes, but the sauces for both are usually based on mixed meats, often including duck (here called *papera*), rabbit, and *castrato*.

There is an old, popular saying: *L'amore è fatto come i cutanei, un giorno è bono, il giorno dopo è mei* (Love is like *cutanèi,* one day it's good, the next day it's better).

73. CUZZETIELLE

Pasta corta

INGREDIENTS: Durum-wheat flour and lukewarm water.

HOW MADE: The flour is sifted onto a wooden board and kneaded long and vigorously with lukewarm water until a smooth, hard dough forms. The dough is left to rest, then rolled out into a rather thick sheet, which is cut into flat noodles ⅜ inch (1 cm) wide. These noodles are in turn cut into ¾-inch (2-cm) lengths and indented with the pressure of two fingertips. The pasta is boiled in plenty of salted water.

ALSO KNOWN AS: No alternative names.

HOW SERVED: As *pastasciutta,* generally with meat *ragù* and a dusting of local pecorino.

WHERE FOUND: Molise.

REMARKS: *Cuzzetielle* are tiny squares of pasta transformed into rather open *strascinati* (see entry), whose curvature varies with the thickness of the pasta sheet.

74. CUZZI

Pasta corta

INGREDIENTS: Type 0 wheat flour, type 00 wheat flour, corn flour, and lukewarm water.

HOW MADE: The flours are sifted together onto a wooden board and kneaded long and vigorously with water until a firm, smooth dough forms. The dough is left to rest, then cut into small pieces, which are rolled and elongated with hands into *spaghetti* as thick as matchsticks. These are then cut into 3-inch (7.5-cm) lengths and boiled in plenty of salted water.

ALSO KNOWN AS: *Cellitti* (at Lariano).

HOW SERVED: As *pastasciutta,* with a simple sauce of garlic, oil, and tomato; today the sauce may also contain mushrooms.

WHERE FOUND: Lazio, around Subiaco, in particular Roviano and Anticoli Corrado; and in the Castelli Romani, at Lariano.

REMARKS: The use of corn flour for making pasta, here and elsewhere in Italy, is evidence of the extreme poverty of those who could not afford to use wheat flour alone. An old woman interviewed in Roviano recalled that the *signori* *"magneanu de biancu"* (ate white), the subordinates yellow. In other words, those who could had a cuisine rich in the more noble grains, and in meats as well. Wage earners had to make do with corn and only rarely ate the meat of the hog that each family raised along with chickens and rabbits, reserving it for feast days.

Today, *cuzzi* constitute a delicacy for tourists. Roviano even holds a popular *sagra* in their honor every July.

75. DIAVOLINI

Pastina

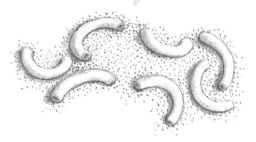

INGREDIENTS: Durum-wheat flour and water.

HOW MADE: Factory-made semicircular *pastina*. They are cooked in broth.

ALSO KNOWN AS: *Capricciose.*

HOW SERVED: Generally in broth.

WHERE FOUND: Widespread.

REMARKS: The name means literally "little devils." In the nineteenth century, *diavolini* was the name for hair curlers, and their curved shape may have inspired the name of this pasta.

76. DONDERET

Gnocchi/gnocchetti

INGREDIENTS: Flour, milk, eggs, salt, and often also boiled potatoes.

HOW MADE: The flour is sifted into a bowl and kneaded with milk, a pinch of salt, and eggs to make a dense and gluey batter, which is then left to rest for two hours. The batter is scooped out with a wet spoon, the spoon is placed against the inside top of a pot of boiling water, and the batter is allowed to spill gently from the spoon into the water, falling against the side of the pot and forming an elongated, narrow dumpling, or *gnocchetto,* which is removed from the water as soon as it floats to the surface.

ALSO KNOWN AS: *Dandarini* and *strangolapreti piemontesi.*

HOW SERVED: Traditionally with butter, especially *di malga,* and grated local cheese.

WHERE FOUND: Piedmont, especially the province of Cuneo, where it is an old preparation of the Valle Colla.

REMARKS: The housewife's skill lies in the long mixing needed to make a batter of the right consistency and in the making of *gnocchetti* of more or less uniform size and shape.

One of the very few Italian recipes cited in *Cuoco piemontese perfezionato a Parigi,* published in Turin in 1766, is for *dandarini,* a sort of pea-sized dumpling cooked in broth. In the Valle del Chisone, also in Piedmont, potato *gnocchi* called *tondoret* or *tunduret* are made. It is possible that before the arrival of the potato, these *gnocchi* were made with only flour and water.

In the old cuisine of Trentino, we find a curious recipe under the name *maccheroni:* a batter of milk and flour is dropped by the spoonful into boiling water to cook and then served with sugar and cinnamon, which is exactly how pasta was generally served in this region before the advent of the tomato.

Gnocchi similar to *donderet* are also made in the *malghe* of the Lessinia, in the Veronese alps. Called *gnochi sbatui,* and made from a soft dough of milk and flour, they are dropped into boiling water from a spoon to cook and then served with *puina fumà,* a local smoked ricotta. But in Ravello, in Campania, the term *dunderi* is used for large *gnocchi* made of ricotta, eggs, and parmigiano.

77. FAINELLE

Strascinati

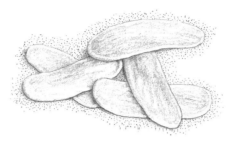

INGREDIENTS: Durum-wheat flour, water, salt, and often also whole-wheat flour or *grano arso.*

HOW MADE: The flour is sifted with a pinch of salt onto a wooden board and kneaded for a long time with water. When the dough is firm and smooth, it is left to rest. Then small pieces are pinched off and hand rolled into ropes the thickness of a pencil, which are in turn cut into 1½- to 2-inch (4- to 5-cm) lengths. These pieces are rolled with a *sferre* to make a sort of wide *strascinato* (see entry) about 4 inches (10 cm) long or a bit longer. They are boiled in plenty of salted water.

ALSO KNOWN AS: No alternative names.

HOW SERVED: As *pastasciutta,* but they are boiled with potatoes and rocket and then sauced with a *soffritto* of anchovies or pancetta.

WHERE FOUND: Puglia, typical of Foggia.

REMARKS: This rare and unusual pasta takes its name from its vague resemblance to carob, called *fainella* in dialect.

The use of dark flours in areas of extreme poverty for both pasta and bread was once common in Puglia. In addition to whole-wheat flour and *grano arso,* cooks used flours milled from other grains, such as barley, or from legumes, in particular fava beans.

78. FALLONI

Pasta ripiena

INGREDIENTS: Wheat flour, water, oil, and salt. For the filling, local vegetables.

HOW MADE: The flour is sifted onto a wooden board and kneaded rapidly and forcefully with water, a pinch of salt, and olive oil. The dough is left to rest, then rolled out with a rolling pin into a thin sheet, and disks or rectangles are cut from it. The cutouts are generously filled with vegetables, rolled, and pinched like a bonbon. They are then baked.

ALSO KNOWN AS: No alternative names.

HOW SERVED: As *pastasciutta,* with local sauces.

WHERE FOUND: Lazio, province of Rieti, especially Torri in Sabina, Selci Sabino, and Forano Sabino.

REMARKS: In the Middle Ages, a marshy lake extending from Terni to Rieti covered what today is the immense, fertile Rieti plain—the pride of Sabine agriculture. The area was a source of malaria and was cultivated with great difficulty by the peasants, who came down in the summer from the mountain towns that surrounded it. Now, the only relics that remain from those days are the wild greens that have always been the basis of the peasant diet and the dishes that are made from them.

These *falloni* ("big phalluses"), typical food of the hill towns that once surrounded the lake, have no precise recipe: each housewife made them with whatever greens grew in the countryside and along the streams. The practice is still alive today, though some cooks add cultivated vegetables to the filling.

79. FARFALLE

Pasta corta

INGREDIENTS: For homemade, wheat flour, eggs, and sometimes water. For factory made, durum-wheat flour, eggs, and water.

HOW MADE: The flour is sifted onto a wooden board and kneaded long and forcefully with eggs and sometimes with a small amount of water until a smooth, firm dough forms. The dough is covered and left to rest, then rolled out into a sheet, not too thin. A toothed pasta cutter is used to cut wide, flat noodles, which are in turn cut into pieces about 1½ inches (4 cm) long. Each piece is pinched in the middle to make a little bow or butterfly shape. The factory-made form, which comes in various sizes, usually has scalloped edges. The *farfalle* are boiled in plenty of salted water.

ALSO KNOWN AS: *Fiocchetti* (bows) and *stricchetti*. In Piedmont, around Cuneo, *sciancon;* in Umbria, *fiocchetti;* in Abruzzo and Puglia, *nocchette;* and in Calabria, *nocheredde.*

The names for the factory-made versions vary according to the size of pasta. The small ones are *canestri, canestrini, galani, nastrini, nodini, stricchetti, stricchetti bolognesi,* and *tripolini.* The larger ones are *farfalle genovesi, farfalloni, francesine,* and *galani.*

HOW SERVED: The small shapes are generally cooked in broth, and the larger ones are served as *pastasciutta,* with sauces typical of the area.

WHERE FOUND: Widespread.

REMARKS: The name means literally "butterflies."[70] The names of many factory-made pastas refer to the animal kingdom, including tiny *chiocciolette, mezze chiocciolette,* and *lumachine* (all meaning "little snails"); *coralli* and *corallini* (coral); and *fischioni* and *fischiotti* (wigeons, a type of duck), both smooth and ridged. Even *vermicelli* (worms) fall in this category. The shapes are various and often differ from maker to maker in happy confusion.

The anonymous author of the *Cuoco perfetto marchigiano,* published in Loreto in 1891, cites a soup called *a scacchette:* pasta ribbons, half a finger wide, cooked in broth. At the beginning of the twentieth century, Rovetta[71] classified a series of pasta shapes, all of them derived from the *farfalla* and cut with a toothed pasta cutter, as *"pasta a mano uso Bologna."* And thus we have *galle,* which are large *farfalle; cuffiette,* made with a special fold; the *canestrino lungo,* in the shape of a tiny *garganello* (see entry), smooth but with ruffled edges; and the *canestrino,* which resembles an *orecchietta* with ruffled edges. Some of these shapes went on to be produced with special cutting-and-folding machines.

In Puglia, we find *nocchette,* which are rectangles of fresh pasta pinched in the middle, just like *farfalle,* to form small bows or knots, thus their name.

80. FARFEL

Pastina

INGREDIENTS: Wheat flour and eggs.

HOW MADE: The flour is sifted onto a wooden board and kneaded long and vigorously with eggs. The dough is rolled out into a thin sheet, and cut into tiny, irregular pieces, which are dried in a hot oven.

ALSO KNOWN AS: No alternative names.

HOW SERVED: Generally in chicken or goose broth, but also in vegetable broth.

WHERE FOUND: Italy *(cucina ebraica).*

REMARKS: According to Jewish dietary law, the whole process of kneading and making this tiny *pastina*, especially good in broth, must be completed in no more than eighteen minutes, that is, before the flour begins to ferment.[72]

81. FATTISÙ

Pasta ripiena

INGREDIENTS: Wheat flour, eggs, and water. For the filling, Savoy cabbage, local cheese, and *insaccati*.

HOW MADE: The flour is sifted onto a wooden board and kneaded with eggs and water long and vigorously until the dough is smooth and firm. The dough is left to rest, then a thin sheet is rolled out with a rolling pin and disks are cut from it. A teaspoon of filling is placed on each disk, and the ends are twisted like a candy wrapper, encasing the filling. The pastas are boiled, a few at a time, in plenty of salted water.

ALSO KNOWN AS: No alternative names.

HOW SERVED: As *pastasciutta,* with traditional local sauces.

WHERE FOUND: Emilia-Romagna, in particular Piacenza.

REMARKS: The name comes from *fare su* and refers to the action of twisting the pasta closed. This is typically a winter dish that was once made only on feast days. The filling is based on Savoy cabbage, which goes particularly well with the local cheeses and *insaccati* that are mixed with it. Ideally harvested when the days are cold, Savoy cabbage is an essential ingredient in the cooking of the lower Emilian plain, where the thin fog that envelops the crops in winter makes the head close its leaves, the best time to pick it for its many uses.

82. FERRAZZUOLI

Pasta lunga

INGREDIENTS: Durum-wheat flour and water.

HOW MADE: Factory made, about 12 inches (30 cm) long, similar to a thin *bucatino* open down the side (called a *spaccato*). The pasta is boiled in abundant salted water.

ALSO KNOWN AS: *Cannucce,* when smaller in diameter.

HOW SERVED: As *pastasciutta,* with local sauces.

WHERE FOUND: Throughout Italy, but especially in Calabria.

REMARKS: The peculiarity of this pasta is the cleft running its entire length. This facilitates cooking and collects the sauce.

83. FETTUCCE

Pasta lunga

INGREDIENTS: Durum-wheat flour and water.

HOW MADE: Factory made, in the shape of a flat ribbon (*fettuccia*), generally about 10 inches (25 cm) long and of varying thickness. The pasta is boiled in abundant salted water.

ALSO KNOWN AS: Depending on size, *fettucce ricce, fettuccelle, fettuccine, fresine, lasagnette, nastrini, pappardelle, reginelle,* and *reginette.* The *lasagnette ricce* have both edges curled. In Sicily, *filateddi.*

HOW SERVED: Generally as *pastasciutta,* with sauces typical of the area.

WHERE FOUND: Central and southern Italy.

REMARKS: In the seventeenth century, the term *fettuccia* (ribbon) was already well established as a synonym of *tagliatelli, tagliolini, lasagnette,* and so on, all flat noodles. G. Aleandri, in his *La difesa dell'Adone* (Venice, 1630), writes:

> *Giuocando alcuni gentilhuomini a sbaraglino in casa del marchese Pepoli, fu da uno di loro detto all'altro per burla, ch'egli era briaco di tagliatelli, cioè di quella minestra di minute fettucce di sfoglia di pasta, che in molti luoghi di Lombardia si dicono lasagnette e a Roma—se male non mi ricordo—tagliolini.*

> [Some gentlemen were playing *sbaraglino*[73] in the house of the Marchese Pepoli. One of them teased another that he was drunk on *tagliatelli,* that is, that dish of tiny ribbons of pasta that in many parts of Lombardy are called *lasagnette* and in Rome—if I remember correctly—*tagliolini.*]

Antonio Latini, in his *Scalco alla moderna,*[74] gives advice on how to make *fettucce,* also called *zagarelle.*

In the Marche, *fettucce al fior di latte,* which is mentioned in the anonymous *Cuoco perfetto marchigiano,*[75] are made. *Fiore di latte* was dairy cream, and these *fettuccine,* which would not be out of place on an important menu even today, were coated with butter and tossed in the pan with cream, parmigiano, and spices.

Some southern pasta makers used to catalog the long pasta forms from the longest to the shortest in this order: *lasagne, fettuccelle, fresine, tagliatelle, lingue di passero, linguine, linguettine,* and *cardelline.*

The various shapes, in the various regions, are often served in particular ways for religious holidays. In Sicily, for example, *filateddi* are cooked in a tasty soup of chickpeas for the feast of Saint Joseph (March 19).

84. FETTUCCINE

Pasta lunga

INGREDIENTS: For homemade, wheat flour, but also often alternative flours, salt, eggs, and sometimes a little water. For factory made, durum-wheat flour, eggs, and sometimes water.

HOW MADE: The flour is sifted with a pinch of salt and kneaded long and vigorously with eggs and sometimes a little water until the dough is firm and smooth. It is covered and left to rest for at least 30 minutes, then rolled out into a sheet, not too thin, from which noodles about ⅜ inch (1 cm) wide are cut with a knife. The factory-made kind, both fresh and dried, also exists, often packaged in nests. The pasta is boiled briefly in abundant salted water.

ALSO KNOWN AS: *Gnocche pelose, lane, lane pelose, ramicce,* and *sagne.* In Umbria, thick *fettuccine* are called *maccheroni;* in Abruzzo, *tajarelloni;* in the Marche, *strenghe;* and in Sicily, *lasagne.*

HOW SERVED: As *pastasciutta,* preferably with various meat *ragù* and giblets, often with mushrooms. The sauce is topped with grated cheese.

WHERE FOUND: Central and southern Italy, in particular Lazio. Factory-made versions are found throughout Italy.

REMARKS: The name means literally "little ribbons." A feather in the cap of the gastronomy of Rome and Lazio, egg *fettuccine,* which are of very old tradition (see also *tagliatelle*), are made in every small town. The collective memory may have forgotten their ancient origin: the famous, extremely thin *capelli d'angelo* (see entry) of the Renaissance, made by nuns in Roman convents and sent to new mothers in the belief they would aid the production of milk.

Today, *fettuccine* are found, fresh and dried, in supermarkets, though city dwellers still consider them a somewhat special dish. But urban *fettuccine* have lost that precious aura they still have in the countryside and in small towns, where making this type of pasta at home, especially on Sunday, remains common. Particular attention is given to the cooking, which is always done in a great deal of water, and the *fettuccine* are dropped in a few at a time so the water returns almost immediately to the boil. Otherwise, "the pasta gets sick," as they say in Sabine country.

Until a few decades ago, Roman *fettuccine,* thicker than their Bolognese sisters, were the pride of the city's avant-garde restaurants. How can we forget the famous *fettuccine al triplo burro* that the legendary Alfredo, owner of the Roman restaurant of the same name, used to make for Hollywood royalty on their visits to Rome? He tossed them with a gold fork and spoon given him as a gift by Mary Pickford and Douglas Fairbanks during their 1927 visit. Everyone remembers the pictures of Tyrone Power and Ava Gardner photographed in front of a dish of sparkling white and buttery *fettuccine*. Aldo Fabrizi, sensitive poet and great actor, as well as brother of Sora Lella, owner of the famous restaurant that bears her name, interpreted in verses and songs the kitchen of the capital, especially its flavorful pastas. His enjoyable rhymes remain an important reference point in the history of the evolution of Roman cooking in the 1950s and 1960s. For example:

La sposa ormai se deve da convince
che ne le beghe de la vita a due
si cià er fornello facile pò vince.

[The bride now had better be convinced
that in the quarrels of life as a couple
she'll win if she's a good cook.]

The high-end tourism of the day opened the way to mass tourism, which meant that the city's visitors, in addition to seeing the Colosseum, crowded its trattorias in the evening to taste the typical dishes, with the sumptuous *fettuccine* with a sauce of giblets at the top of the list.

Today, many variants exist, each typical of a different place in the region. For example, *fettuccine* made with flour and bran in Capranica Prenestina are called *lane pelose* (hairy wools); very thin *fettuccine* made in Casapè, Roviano, and Percile are dubbed *ramicce;* and *sagne co jaju pistatu* (*con l'aglio pestato,* "with pounded garlic") served in San Gregorio da Sassola are *fettuccine* with an uncooked garlic sauce. At San Vito Romano, very thin *fettuccine* are called *lane* (wools), but it is uncertain whether the term is a contraction of *lagane* (see entry) or refers to wool (*lana*) threads that the pasta is thought to resemble.

Fettuccine is a synonym, mainly but not only in the center-south, for *tagliatelle,* the handmade flat noodles served at Sunday dinner and elsewhere.

In Umbria, *fettuccine,* called *maccheroni* and tossed with honey and walnuts, are served on Christmas Eve. Around Orvieto, *fettuccine* with goose *ragù* was once served at the threshing lunch. In Abruzzo, *tajarelloni* are served with *sottaceti* (pickled vegetables), minced and sautéed. In Sardinia, *fettuccine* called *busaki* are made for Easter and for important guests. They are also made for wedding luncheons to symbolize the wish for prosperity for the new family.

Among the common alternative flours, especially in the mountainous areas, was—and still is—chestnut flour: *Fettuccine* made of chestnut flour are traditional in the Apennines around Parma and in the Val Camonica. Chestnut *fettuccine* are also served in the Lunigiana, in northwestern Tuscany, and in Valle d'Aosta, at San Vincenzo, they are sauced with Savoy cabbage and pork ribs.

85. FETTUCCINE DI AZZIME

Pasta lunga

INGREDIENTS: Matzo meal and eggs.

HOW MADE: Matzos are crushed to a fine flour, which is kneaded with eggs to form a dough. The dough is rolled out into a sheet—not too thin—and short, flat noodles are cut from it.

ALSO KNOWN AS: No alternative names.

HOW SERVED: In broth, usually chicken or goose, but sometimes vegetable.

WHERE FOUND: Italy in general, but in particular in Ferrara.

REMARKS: This dish is prepared for Passover, or Pesach, when leavened or fermented food is prohibited for several days, hence the use of matzos crushed into flour. The same dough is used to make small *maltagliati,* which are also served in broth, usually chicken or goose but sometimes vegetable. The use of matzo flour is ancient and is already present in the book of Exodus.[76]

86. FIDELINI

Pasta lunga

INGREDIENTS: Durum-wheat flour and water.

HOW MADE: Factory made, in the form of a thin, round *spaghetto.* The pasta is boiled in abundant salted water or in broth.

ALSO KNOWN AS: *Fedelini, fideli,* and *fidelli,* but also *capelli d'angelo* (angel hair) or *capelvenere* (Venus's hair). In southern Italy, also known as *capellini* and *sopra-capellini,* in both cases very thin.

HOW SERVED: The thinnest in broth, with condiments typical of the Ligurian Riviera; the others as *pastasciutta.*

WHERE FOUND: Liguria, but also by other names in southern Italy.

REMARKS: The trade in dry pastas is documented in Genoa as early as the twelfth century, though no documents exist from the period relating to local pasta production. The most-often cited source of the Genoese *miles*[77] (an important personage) Ponzio Bastone, who left a legacy of a *"barixella plena de macharoni"* (a barrel full of *macaroni*), does not assure us this pasta was actually made in Genoa. Certainly, the powerful maritime republic imported dry pasta from Sicily or Sardinia.[78] Notarial acts studied by Luigi Sada attest to intense trade exchanges between Norman Sicily and the Republic of Genoa, with the importation of grains and pasta prominent. It is not until the beginning of the fourteenth century that we see the manufacture of *macharoni* and *tria,* also called *fidej* or *fideus,* along the Ligurian coast, and especially at Savona. These new products were very thin, a characteristic that continues to distinguish *fidelini* from *spaghetti* today.

The merchants of Genoa, above all, were responsible for the spread of pasta from the Mediterranean into Europe, and the pasta produced in Liguria quickly became one of the most sought after in international markets, in part because of the quality of the wheat used in its manufacture.

The Arte dei Fidelari of Genoa, an association constituted in 1574, has always paid a great deal of attention to the quality of the durum wheat used in the local manufacture of dry pastas. Again, toward the middle of the seventeenth century, the grain orders made by the Genoese consuls always emphasized top-quality durum wheat. And no less attention was given to how pastas were dried and marketed. In fact, around the same time, an ordinance enforced by Genoa's city censors required *rerbaioli* (traders of various goods, including pasta made with chestnut flour and second-grade wheat flour) to operate at a suitable distance from the *fidelari,* and imposed on them, in case they marketed the same types of pasta, the following restriction: "cannot and must not practice said art in the same shop, but in another shop thirty paces away from where they practice said art of *fidelaro.*"[79] The first documents attesting to the presence of *fideli* in the diet of sailors—at first only for the higher ranks—in service on Genoese *galere*[80] date to the middle of the sixteenth century. By the end of the eighteenth century, the pasta was regularly supplied to everyone on the *galere:* fine *fideli* for the sick, ordinary pasta for the rest.[81]

Although present earlier, pasta manufacturing in Liguria really got going between the 1600s and the 1800s, with the creation of factory clusters all along the coast—San Remo, Imperia, Savona, Porto Maurizio, and Oneglia. By exploiting the unique climate and by painstakingly choosing only the best raw materials, manufacturers were able to establish one of the great concentrations of Italian pasta production. Father J. B. Labat, a Dominican priest who, while traveling through Italy at the beginning of the eighteenth century, carefully recorded the gastronomic habits and customs of the country, provides us with information on the vast and flourishing diffusion of the pasta industry in Liguria.

The 1766 edition of *Il cuoco Piemontese perfezionato a Parigi* states that the best *vermicelli* were made in Genoa. The book calls for extremely long cooking times and the pasta is always cooked in broth. The author also informs us on the size of the pasta, describing what was available as being very thick. Meanwhile, the production of excellent pastas was spreading into other regions and abroad, so that the next edition of *Il cuoco,* dated 1775, maintained that the *vermicelli* of Rivoli outclassed in quality those of Genoa. But because Rivoli lies within the Piedmontese cultural area, we suspect this statement smacks a bit of *campanilismo.* What we can state with certainty, however, is that at this moment the *maccheroni* of Naples and the pasta of Genoa were present in all the European markets. In London, where pasta had appeared as early as the sixteenth century, there was even a Club Macaroni that was regularly mentioned in local periodicals, and the term *macaroni* was snobbish.[82]

87. FIENO DI CANEPINA

Pasta lunga

INGREDIENTS: Wheat flour and eggs.

HOW MADE: The flour is sifted onto a wooden board and kneaded for a long time with eggs until a smooth, firm dough forms. The dough is left to rest, then rolled out into a very thin sheet, which is cut into flat noodles about ¹⁄₁₆ inch (2 mm) thick. The cooking method is unique: the pasta is cooked al dente in boiling salted water, drained, immersed in almost cold salted water, drained again, and dried with a dish towel, after which it is ready for the sauce.

ALSO KNOWN AS: No alternative names.

HOW SERVED: As *pastasciutta,* with a local sauce made of chicken giblets or even meat.

WHERE FOUND: Lazio, in Canepina, in the province of Viterbo.

REMARKS: *Fieno* means "hay." Cutting these extremely thin, flat noodles requires great manual dexterity on the part of the housewife, which Italo Arieti talks about in his *Tuscia a tavola.*[83] A special knife, with a very long blade and a handle running its length to allow faster cutting, is used.

88. FILATI

Pasta lunga

INGREDIENTS: Durum-wheat flour, water, and a few eggs.

HOW MADE: The flour is sifted onto a wooden board and kneaded long and vigorously with water and a few eggs. The dough is left to rest, then walnut-sized pieces are pinched off and rolled back and forth on a wooden board into *spaghetti* 8 to 10 inches (20 to 25 cm) long. They are boiled in abundant salted water.

ALSO KNOWN AS: No alternative names.

HOW SERVED: As *pastasciutta,* with chickpeas.

WHERE FOUND: Campania, in the Vallo di Diano, in particular around Teggiano and Padula, where the wooden board for making pasta is called a *quadro.*

REMARKS: After the Italian Unification, and until the 1920s, the emerging bourgeoisie, especially in the south, abhorred all the foods they associated with the common people. For important luncheons and banquets, they preferred fashionable foods from the north. Nevertheless, legumes and vegetables were often seen on the everyday tables, perhaps also because the official press of the day promoted chickpeas, anchovies, and *pesce azzurro*, foods that lower—the today feared—cholesterol, and together invited a return to the old ways, using as an example the dried legume instead of the fresh. These *filati*, but also *lagane* (see entry), were thus prepared as *pastasciutta*, with a condiment of chickpeas sautéed with garlic, oil, and chili. A dusting of the precious local cheese was always the finishing touch.

89. FILEJA

Pasta lunga

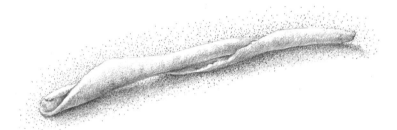

INGREDIENTS: Durum-wheat flour and water.

HOW MADE: Durum-wheat flour is sifted onto a wooden board and kneaded with water for a long time until a firm, smooth dough forms, which is left to rest. It is rolled with hands into pencil-thick ropes, which are cut into pieces about 1¼ inches (3 cm) long or more. One at a time, a specific *ferretto* or a thin reed is placed on a length of dough and pressed, forcing the dough to roll around the *ferretto* until it becomes a spiral about 8 inches (20 cm) long. The pasta is then slid off the *ferretto*. The spirals are boiled in plenty of salted water.

ALSO KNOWN AS: *Filateddhi, filatelli, fusilli, maccaruni aru ferru, maccaruni 'i casa,* and *ricci di donna* (woman's curls).

HOW SERVED: Traditionally as *pastasciutta*, tossed with *'nduja* and *ricotta salata*, but also with a hearty pork or lamb *ragù*.

WHERE FOUND: Calabria, typical of the area where *'nduja* (a soft, very spicy salami) is produced, around Vibo Valentia and Tropea.

REMARKS: The use of hearty meat sauces was common on Sundays and feast days among the wealthier classes. In small and large towns throughout Calabria, each day had its specific foods: for example, on Monday, there was vegetable soup, and on Sunday, *ragù*, always with homemade pasta. In the afternoon, after the midday meal, people went for a stroll and then to a pharmacy for a chat. The pharmacies had become clubs of a sort. At one pharmacy, everyone talked about hunting; at another, the subject was cooking; at another, farming was discussed; and at yet another, the subject was crime. Only politics was off limits, because the authorities "had long ears and would have made [us] close up shop without thinking twice about it."[84]

90. FILINDEU

Unusual shape

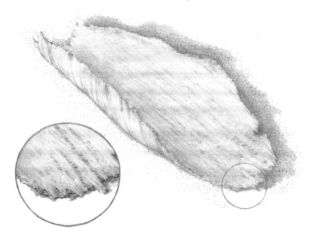

INGREDIENTS: Durum-wheat flour and water.

HOW MADE: The flour is sifted onto a wooden board, kneaded long and vigorously with water, and left to rest. Expert hands weave unimaginably fine threads of dough into thin, gauzelike sheets, which are laid out to dry and stiffen in the sun. The sheets of "gauze" are broken into pieces and boiled in broth.

   To make the woven sheets, a small amount of dough is pinched off and rolled with hands until long and thin. It is then folded in half eight times. During this process, the hands are moistened with salted water. With the last fold completed, the result is a skein of 256 very thin threads. These threads are laid on a wooden disk called a *fondo* (bottom), and then cut around the edge. The operation is repeated with additional layers of pasta threads and, with each layer, the *fondo* is turned ninety degrees. When the *fondo* is completely covered, a second layer of fine threads is placed at right angles to the first layer. Finally, a third layer made the same way is placed atop the other threads at oblique angles. The *fondo* is set on a special trestle and placed in the sun, where the pasta is left to dry, forming a sort of thin gauze. It is broken into seven large pieces, and the pieces are kept well wrapped in special paper. Just before cooking, each piece is broken into small pieces.

ALSO KNOWN AS: No alternative names.

HOW SERVED: Cooked in mutton broth with sharp cheese.

WHERE FOUND: Sardinia, typical of Nuoro.

REMARKS: *Filindeu* means "veil of God," for the pasta's extreme thinness. But the term could also derive from the ancient *fideus,* for *fidelini* or *fedelini,* with interference from the Sardinian word *filu* (the Italian *filo*), or "thread." It is a pasta typical of the Barbagia area, where it is made for the feast of Saint Francis of Lula. It is served as a welcoming and restorative dish in the sanctuary enclosure where the faithful from all over the island gather and sleep for the first week of May, which is how long the celebration for the saint lasts. The *filindeu* is miraculous food and woe betide anyone who refuses it. It is cooked in mutton broth, enriched with *odori* and potatoes, that is made every day in the sanctuary's open-air kitchens. Boiled meat and potatoes are the main course.

For the celebration of Santu Frantziscu de Luvula, fights and feuds between families and between towns are suspended, and the Mother Goddess and the god called Babai are replaced by Saint Francis as symbols of health and prosperity.

Legend has it that the sanctuary was built in the 1600s by a famous brigand who obtained salvation from prison from Saint Francis in exchange for the promise of building him a church. If the story about the source of the construction funds is true and this church in the heart of the Barbagia was built to provide a refuge and fool the police, it must not have been a bad investment.

In Sardinia, the festivals in these rustic sanctuaries used to be extremely lively, especially around Nuoro, and are described by Grazia Deledda.[85] The great writer, a devotee of the saint, often participated in the pilgrimages to the sanctuary in the Barbagia. These festivals were related not only to religious holidays but also to the agricultural cycle of the year, whose roots go to back to the ancient world of the Punic and nuragic,[86] traces of which are still visible in Sardinia. Celebrated especially at Valverde, San Sebastiano, and Sant'Agata, these festivities were preceded by the collection of grain from local families, who were asked *se volevano accudire,* literally "if they wanted to participate," that is, in the making of the *filindeu* with a donation of grain.

The sanctuaries where people traveled to spend the nine days of a novena are located in beautiful but remote areas of the Sardinian hinterland. They were reached on foot, after a long walk amid unspoiled and magical nature, and were generally built near a spring. Over time, a complex of porticos and little houses called *lollas, cunbessinas,* or *muristenes* developed around them for lodging the pilgrims. The families brought with them furnishings and provisions for their daily meals. It was customary for the prior of the sanctuary to offer the faithful *su filindeu* and *su zurrette,* or *sanguinaccio* (blood pudding), of sheep's blood cooked in the sheep's own stomach, boiled or grilled over coals. Other playful rites took place during the hours of rest, and on the ninth day, a great open-air meal was served.

91. FIORONI

Pasta ripiena

INGREDIENTS: Wheat flour, water, lard, eggs, and salt. For the filling, *salame napoletano,* young and aged pecorino, and eggs.

HOW MADE: The flour is sifted onto a wooden board and kneaded long and vigorously with a few eggs, lard, lukewarm water, and a pinch of salt. The dough is left to rest, then rolled out with a rolling pin into disks about 8 inches (20 cm) in diameter. Filling is placed on each disk, which is folded into a half-moon and the edges sealed. The *fioroni* are baked.

ALSO KNOWN AS: No alternative names.

HOW SERVED: As *pastasciutta,* drizzled with oil and cooked in the oven.

WHERE FOUND: Campania, in particular Morcone and hinterland.

REMARKS: Not far from Benevento, nestled among the gentle hills of the Fortore, the Alto Tammaro, the Tiferno, the Taburno, and the Partenio, is the heart of the Sannio, or Samnite country. A mysterious land of ancient magic, it offers visitors uncontaminated landscape and a rich artistic and cultural heritage that includes food specialties almost unknown even to the most inveterate seekers. One of these is this large *raviolo,* whose particularity comes from the combination of grated (that is, aged) and fresh pecorino in the filling. Some towns also make it in a smaller size, in which case it is fried in the local olive oil and served as an antipasto. The abundant filling makes it resemble a large *fiorone* fig, whence probably its name.

92. FISCKARIEDD'

Pasta corta

INGREDIENTS: Durum-wheat flour and eggs.

HOW MADE: A kind of irregular, geometric *maltagliati,* these are the odd cuttings that remain after disks for *ravioli* have been cut from a pasta sheet with an inverted glass. They are usually cooked in soup.

ALSO KNOWN AS: No alternative names.

HOW SERVED: Especially in legume soup.

WHERE FOUND: Basilicata, typically Acerenza.

REMARKS: At least until the early 1960s, the Basilicata region had a subsistence economy, where it would have been inconceivable not to use the odd leftover bits of a rich flour-and-egg dough. This amusing pasta was cooked in soups made with legumes, the only abundant products of a poor land where woods and pastures occupied about 770 square miles (2,000 square kilometers) out of a total area of about 965 square miles (2,500 square kilometers). What little cultivatable land remained was planted primarily with cereals, but also with olive trees and vines. As has been noted elsewhere, pasta with legumes was always reserved for feast days, especially if the pasta contained eggs.

93. FOGLIETTI

Pasta lunga

INGREDIENTS: Wheat flour and eggs.

HOW MADE: The flour is sifted onto a wooden board and kneaded long and vigorously with eggs. The dough, which must be very firm, is rolled out into a sheet, and long, flat noodles of unspecified width are cut from it. The noodles are popped right into a very hot oven and toasted, and then are boiled in broth or water.

ALSO KNOWN AS: No alternative names.

HOW SERVED: In broth or as *pastasciutta*.

WHERE FOUND: The Marche, in the Ancona area.

REMARKS: The name means literally "little leaves." This is a Jewish dish, and the toasting of the pasta in a very hot oven stops it from rising, even minimally.

Vincenzo Lancellotti, in his treatise *Lo scalco prattico*,[87] tells of a banquet on January 1, 1610, given by Cardinal Aldobrandini for the *"monsignori auditori di Rota,"* at which was served a *minestrina di fogliette,* made with flour, egg yolks, and pine-nut milk.

94. FOJADE
Pasta corta

INGREDIENTS: Flour, salt, eggs, and oil.

HOW MADE: The flour is sifted with a pinch of salt onto a wooden board and kneaded long and vigorously with eggs and a little oil. When the dough is firm and smooth, it is left to rest, covered, for at least thirty minutes. It is then rolled out into a sheet, not too thin, from which wide noodles are cut. They are boiled in salted water.

ALSO KNOWN AS: No alternative names.

HOW SERVED: As *pastasciutta,* usually with mushrooms and local cheeses.

WHERE FOUND: Lombardy, the Val Brembana in particular, but also around Mantova and Bergamo.

REMARKS: The park of the Orobian Alps, which contains the Val Brembana, has been inhabited for centuries by cowherds and shepherds. They populated the woods and peaks of the highest altitudes with sheep pens and shelters, where they spent the summer preparing their special cheeses, from *formai de mut*[88] to *taleggio* to *branzi,*[89] that were always present in many of the area's recipes. The long periods spent in the woods with the grazing animals made them expert gatherers of mushrooms, still abundant in the park. The dense network of paths, many of which were already of strategic importance in the sixteenth and seventeenth centuries as routes to Venice and Central Europe, made it possible for the inhabitants to trade and export not only their precious cheeses but also mushrooms. In fact, today, when numerous kinds of mushrooms are gathered in the woods and along the banks of the Adda River in autumn, almost all the towns of the Val Brembana put on a *sagra delle fojade* to celebrate the typical combination of local products.

The word *fojade* is used as a synonym for *tagliatelle* at least as early as the *Baldus* of Teofilo Folengo.[90]

95. FRASCARELLI

Pastina

INGREDIENTS: Durum-wheat flour and water. In Trentino, they are also made with buckwheat. In Tuscany, in the Valdarno, flour and eggs are used. In the Marche and Puglia, eggs are added, or *cruschello* is used instead of flour.

HOW MADE: The flour is sifted into a large bowl and then mixed with fingers in a circular motion while hot water is sprinkled from above. The small lumps that form, called *frascarelli*, are sifted to separate them from the flour, and then put to dry in a basket. Work continues like this until the flour is used up. The technique of preparation can vary from place to place. The *frascarelli* are boiled in broth or in plenty of salted water.

ALSO KNOWN AS: *'Nsaccaragatti*. In Trentino–Alto Adige, *Milchfrigelen*. In Tuscany, around Livorno, *briciolelli*, and in the Valdarno, *spruzzoli*. In the Marche, *frascarielli*, *piccicasanti*, and *tritoli*; and in the area of Carpegna, in the Montefeltro, *granetti*. In Abruzzo and Lazio, *frascareji*, and in the province of Latina, *infrascatiei*. In Naples, *fiscarielli*; and in Molise, *frascarielle* and *frascatielle*. In Puglia, *'ntrisi* and *frascatelli*; in Serracapriola, *frascatellene*; and around Taranto, in the areas of Grottaglie and Massafra, *'ndromese* or *'ndromise*. In Basilicata, an Arbëreshë preparation is called *drömsat*; in Calabria and in Sicily, *frascatole* or *frascatuli*, but also *'ncucciatieddi*; and in Modica, the term *piciocia* is used.

HOW SERVED: Generally in broth, but also as *pastasciutta*. The *Milchfrigelen* of Trentino are cooked in milk. In the Marche, they are used in a tasty soup with fava beans.

WHERE FOUND: Central and southern Italy.

REMARKS: The making of *frascarelli* sometimes involves special equipment. In the Marche, the flour is stirred with a wooden stick with three wires attached to the end. In Abruzzo, it is stirred with a sorghum *granarella*, a small broom used only for this purpose.

In the Arbëreshë kitchen, *drömsat* are made by sprinkling a wooden board with a layer of flour about ¼ inch (6 mm) thick. This is "baptized" by dipping a sprig of oregano into water and then mixing the flour with the sprig until tiny balls form. The typical sauce is made with onion and tomato.

To make this type of tiny pasta perfectly, the quality of the durum-wheat flour is important, and the small lumps must be left to dry, or they will disintegrate during cooking and turn the soup into a sort of *polentina*.[91] This is why, to avoid the inconvenience of having to wait for the pasta to dry, and to give the sensation of the presence of the small lumps, some recipes call for the addition of rice during cooking. In some areas, including Matelica in the Marche and in Tuscany, especially in the Valdarno, where this tiny pasta is called *spruzzoli,* eggs are added to the dough. Tuscan housewives put the small grains through a sieve (called a *crivello* or *buratto*) with mesh wide enough to let the flour and tiniest lumps pass through.

The unresolved problem of the drying has meant that the term *frascarelli* is also used for a thick polenta made of flour or *semola* and water, usually served with a tomato sauce and grated cheese, in some areas, including the Marche, around Fabriano, and Umbria, around Orvieto.[92] Hard and properly dried, *fras carelli* will keep their shape and texture in cooking. At Montorio nei Frentani, in Molise, where this type of pasta is said to have originated, there is an old saying about people who always complain: *Pare ru chellare d'i frascatielle*—"He looks like the pot where the *frascarelli* are boiling"—because when hard, dry *frascarelli* boil, they can seem to sputter.

In Puglia, in the province of Taranto, the *'ndromese,* from the Albanian *drömsat,* are made the same way as *frascarelli.* Often this preparation is classified as a polenta. In Calabria, in Cosenza, *frascatola* is known as a polenta. Sada[93] cites *'ndromisi,* another Pugliese variant (San Pancrazio, San Pietro Vernotico, Lizzano, Sava, Massafra, Grottaglie, Montemesola, Taranto, Veglie) as a type of pasta made from an irregularly cut sheet. The root of this curious name might derive from the Byzantine Greek word *endrósisma,* meaning "sprinkle," but this would lead us back to the lumps of flour, more than to a cut shape, however tiny.

Small lumps of flour and water, common in many regions of Italy and variously named, were once boiled, topped with grated cheese, and served rather watery to new mothers, to help them produce abundant milk. Today, as in the past, the condiments obviously depend on local custom: At Campobasso, the pasta is served with garlic and chili fried in oil. In Tuscany and in Sicily, they are sometimes made for children, but *'ncucciatieddi siciliani* are also served in a tasty soup with squash and fresh ricotta. *Piccicasanti,* which are made in the Marche, in particular in the countryside around Fermo, but also at Montefano and Recanati, owe their name to the almost-gluey consistency they develop while cooking—a consistency so sticky the pasta could be used to hang holy cards on the wall.

The precious durum wheat with which *frascarelli* are made was partly sold and partly milled to make pasta, but, more important, to make the bread loaves branded S A, that is, Sant'Antonio (Saint Anthony), which were blessed and distributed to the faithful. These rites, associated with the sacrality of the wheat, used to be found in almost every corner of rural Italy.

96. FREGNACCE

Pasta corta

INGREDIENTS: For homemade, formerly durum-wheat flour and water and today durum-wheat flour and eggs. For factory made, durum-wheat flour and eggs or water.

HOW MADE: The flour is sifted, combined with eggs, and kneaded long and vigorously until a smooth, firm dough forms. The dough is left to rest, then rolled into a thin sheet, and squares or lozenges of variable size are cut from it. Factory-made *pantacce* have ruffled edges. The pasta is boiled in plenty of salted water.

ALSO KNOWN AS: *Frescacce, paciocche,* and *pantacce.*

HOW SERVED: As *pastasciutta,* with different, usually piquant sauces based on various meats—pork, beef, lamb—but also vegetables, always with a dusting of local pecorino.

WHERE FOUND: Northern Lazio (Sabine country of the province of Rieti and the Subiaco area), Abruzzo, and the Marche.

REMARKS: The term *fregnaccia* in the dialect of Rome and Lazio means "pack of lies, silliness, trifle" and emphasizes the simplicity of the preparation. It comes from the dialect word *fregna,* meaning "female genitals." It is curious to note how often popular terminology for pasta, an important dish in the everyday diet, makes reference to sexual organs: along with *fregnacce,* there are *cazzellitti* (see entry), *pisarei* (see entry), and others. All of them are in addition to the many pasta terms that refer to things, animals, or general words of disparagement.

In Acquapendente, on the border between Lazio and Tuscany, the term *fregnaccia* is used for a type of fritter for Carnival.

97. FREGULA

Pastina

INGREDIENTS: Durum-wheat flour and water; saffron is sometimes added for color.

HOW MADE: Water is sprinkled, a little at a time, over the flour, which is stirred with a rotary movement until tiny balls no bigger than a peppercorn form. The *fregula* is gradually sifted from the rest of the flour and left to dry in the sun on a special sieve made of horsehair and covered with a dish towel. When dry, it is cooked in broth.

ALSO KNOWN AS: No alternative names.

HOW SERVED: Always in broth-based soups with varied additions, from fish to vegetables, or in plain meat broth.

WHERE FOUND: Sardinia.

REMARKS: The production of durum-wheat flour dates to the Middle Ages in Sardinia. According to the fourteenth-century statute of the millers of Tempio Pausania, the mills could produce pasta from Monday to Friday, but on Saturday and Sunday the water had to be used for watering the gardens. This tells us that *fregula* was already not merely a home preparation, but could be bought from millers, who were the first to make pasta to sell. The various governments that have ruled the island have always been aware of the excellent quality of the durum wheat used to make the local pasta: it was even prohibited to mix old grain with new, a rule reiterated by the Spanish governors until the island was handed over to the House of Savoy.[94]

The word derives from the Latin *ferculum,* which came into the vulgate as *fregolo* (in Italian, *briciolo* or *minuzzolo,* "crumb"), to indicate the tiny size of the pasta. Or, more vulgarly, it came from the verb *fricare,* "to rub." *Fregula* is also known as *cascà* around Calasetta and Carloforte. The technique for making it is the same as is used for North African couscous (see *cuscus*), but how it is cooked and served differs. In fact, like *cuscus,* this very old, still popular dish was, and is, made in a terra-cotta or wooden bowl with a wide, flat bottom called a *scivedda.* The operation requires great skill. An old Sardinian proverb goes, *Koiaimi ca sciu fai frégula* (Give me a husband, because I know how to make *fregula*). And it was the first and most important dowry required of a wife.

98. FRIGULOZZI

Pasta lunga

INGREDIENTS: Flour, yeast starter *(biga),* and water.

HOW MADE: Raised bread dough is kneaded a second time, then walnut-sized pieces are pinched off and rolled out into *spaghettoni* 10 to 12 inches (25 to 30 cm) long. They are laid out on a dish towel to dry, then boiled in plenty of salted water.

ALSO KNOWN AS: No alternative names.

HOW SERVED: As *pastasciutta,* generally with a homemade tomato sauce and local pecorino.

WHERE FOUND: Lazio, in the Sabine country of the province of Rieti, in particular Montopoli Sabina.

REMARKS: Extending from the Sabine country down toward the Tiber valley, the soft hills lined with neat rows of olive trees are populated with villages and towns where pasta, especially *fettuccine,* is of primary importance. Other shapes, such as these *frigulozzi,* with slight variants in method, dough, or sauce, used to be the daily food after the return from the fields. Today, they are specialties served by local restaurants to tourists in search of new gastronomic experiences.

99. FUSI ISTRIANI

Pasta corta

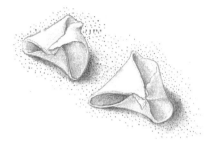

INGREDIENTS: Wheat flour and eggs, and sometimes pork blood, which makes them dark.

HOW MADE: The flour is sifted onto a wooden board and kneaded long and vigorously with many eggs. The dough, which must be firm and smooth, is left to rest, then rolled out with a rolling pin into a sheet. Small triangles are cut from it, and two points of each triangle are pressed together. A variant calls for cutting small squares of pasta, wrapping them around the handle of a wooden spoon, and sealing them by pressing with fingers. Both kinds are boiled in plenty of salted water.

ALSO KNOWN AS: No alternative names.

HOW SERVED: Generally as *pastasciutta,* with typical *ragù* of hen or game, especially furred, very plentiful in the area.

WHERE FOUND: Friuli–Venezia Giulia, in particular Istria.

REMARKS: The name means literally "Istrian spindles." Father Dante used to say: "*Si com' a Pola, presso del Carnaro / ch'Italia chiude e suoi termini bagna . . .*"[95] (Or as at Pola, near Quarnaro's gulf / That closes Italy and bathes her bounds . . .)—in other words, a pasta made in Istria must certainly be considered Italian. The part of present-day Istria that lies across the border in Croatia is still a land whose "Venetianness" is expressed in both the language and especially the cooking.[96]

Fusi, considered a one-dish meal because they are usually served with plenty of hearty *ragù,* are a photograph of the resources of the vast mountain and forest area between Trieste and the border. And on both sides of the border *fusi* are served for Easter.

100. FUSILLI

Pasta corta

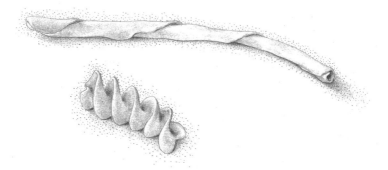

INGREDIENTS: For homemade, durum-wheat flour or type 00 wheat flour and water. Sometimes the two flours are mixed, and eggs are often added. *Maccheroni bobbiesi* are made by mixing the flour with *semolino*. For factory made, durum-wheat flour and water.

HOW MADE: The flour is sifted and kneaded with water. When the dough is firm, it is left to rest, wrapped in a dish towel. Then, a piece of the dough is pinched off—the size depending on the length of the *fusillo* desired—and flattened on a special square *ferretto*. With a quick movement, the dough is rolled on a wooden board and, with a sharp rap, slid off the *ferretto*. Depending on the area, *fusilli* can range in length from 2 to 6 inches (5 to 15 cm). Factory-made *fusilli* have a different shape. They are a single or double spiral of varying width, length, and thickness. The pasta is boiled in abundant salted water.

ALSO KNOWN AS: In Piedmont, *macaron dell'Alta Langa*. In the Veneto, *subioti* and, with a different shape, *fusarioi;* around Piacenza, *maccheroni bobbiesi*. In Abruzzo, Molise, and northern Lazio, *ciufolitti*, but also *sfusellati, zufoletti,* and *gnocchi col ferro*. In Puglia, *fenescecchie, ferricieddi, fricelli, lombrichelli,* and *maccheroni a ferrittus;* but also *code di topo* and *fusidde* (in Bari), *fusille,* and *maccarune a fierre* and *pizzarieddhi* (around Foggia). In Basilicata, *firzuli* and *maccheroni chi fir*—"with the *ferro*" (Matera). In Calabria, *fischietti, fillil, fusiddri,* and *filatelli,* and around Crotone, *scilatielli*. In Sardinia, *maccarones inferrettati* and *maccarones a ferrittus;* one special shape is called *berriasa*.

For factory made, *fusilli ad alette, fusilloni, gemelli, riccioli, spirali,* and *tortiglioni*.

HOW SERVED: Generally as *pastasciutta*, with a piquant *ragù* especially of lamb or pork, but also with vegetable-based sauces, and plenty of grated local pecorino.

WHERE FOUND: The fresh pasta is eaten throughout the center and south of Italy and in Sardinia. The factory-made form is common throughout Italy.

REMARKS: When the nascent pasta industry appropriated this particular shape, it had to think about how to differentiate it from the normal *bucatino* or *perciatello:* the women workers would take just-made *perciatelli,* wrap them around a *ferretto* (a tool something like a knitting needle) in a spiral, and then withdraw the tool. But this method resulted in a product of irregular lengths and thicknesses, which were a problem for uniform cooking. Many dies were tried without success, until the world of factory-made pasta was forced to think that the *fusillo* simply could not be made by machine. It was two Italians living in New York, the brothers Guido and Aurelio Tanzi, who in 1924 perfected their machine called the *fusilla.* It made it possible to produce *fusilli* of uniform size with a perfectly centered hole running their length, and today this spiral-shaped pasta is found throughout Italy.

The *fusillo* is of Arab derivation: it is known as *busiata* in Sicily and *busa* in Sardinia, the two Italian regions where Muslim civilization first penetrated. Both *busiata* and *busa* come from the Arabic word *bus,* which is the thin reed (*Arundo aegyptiaca,* commonly called *canna egiziana,* "Egyptian reed") around which the dough was traditionally wound to make the pasta. This technique is already documented in the fifteenth century, when it appears as *strangolapreti* (see entry). It soon spread to southern and central Italy, and then throughout the rest of the peninsula.

The shape and dimensions vary from place to place: in some areas, the small piece of pasta is replaced by a strip as long as the *ferretto,* to make a long, thick *spaghetto* pierced down the middle. But what links this type of pasta to a particular place is, above all, how it is served, as the wealth of alternative terminology shows. For example, in Sicily, *busiata* is served with *pesto alla trapanese* (which contains tomato), and instead of the *ferretto,* a well-sanded stick of dry wood is used. In the Sicilian high country of the Madonie, the *fusiddi di Madunii* are served with meat *ragù* flavored with saffron. The general Abruzzese term *ciufolitti* and the L'Aquila dialect term *ciufele* derive from the word *zufolo* (Pan pipe) and refer to the elongated shape of the pasta, which makes it resemble a rustic *zufolo.* The same goes for the *fischietto pugliese,* typical of Taranto and Roseto Valfortore. Here, but also in Lazio and in general in highly pastoral areas, the favorite condiment is lamb. In Puglia, *lombrichelli* are typical of the province of Foggia, especially the towns of Cerignola and San Severo.

Fusillo is a Neapolitan dialect term, and the old pasta makers of the Amalfi and Sorrentine coasts probably used it for this curious pasta shape, which had landed there many centuries earlier. It was made with a type of spindle-shaped *ferretto* called a *fuso* (spindle), which the Gypsies also used to use to make pasta: the long tool was tapered at the ends to make it easy to slide the *fusillo* off. In our grandmothers' day, the *ferretto* had to be ordered from a blacksmith, who made it square in section. Every southern kitchen had one. It was replaced by a knitting needle, a stalk of sorghum, or a rib of an umbrella.

Fusilli were handmade products and were widespread especially in Naples and in the provinces of the kingdom when the millers, in addition to milling the grain, used female labor to make the various pasta shapes. They were the everyday pasta among the wealthier classes. Also called *maccheroni fatti in casa* (homemade macaroni), *fusilli* appeared on the rural tables only on special occasions. In Basilicata, for example, it was customary to eat *fusilli* during Carnival with rich *ragù* and *cacioricotta,* made piquant with horseradish grown especially in the Agri valley. A popular song went, *"Carnival mio chien' d'uogl / stassera maccaron e crai fuogl' "* (. . . this evening macaroni and tomorrow leaves), and that "tomorrow" lasted beyond Lent to cover almost all the remaining days of the year.

The regional menu punctuated the feast days: on the last Sunday of Carnival, the dish was *orecchiette* with a sauce of *salame* and kid accompanied by *rafanata,* a mixture of eggs, horseradish, and sausages; on the following Monday evening, it was a vegetable soup with pork bones, *calzone* filled with eggs and sausages, and cheese cooked on the *brace* (grill); on Shrove Tuesday, it was *fusilli* with *salame* and the ever-present horseradish, but in some towns *cavatelli* replaced the *fusilli.* Shrove Tuesday brought an orgy of *fusilli* and *cavatelli* throughout the region: in Matera, there were also *ravioli dolci* filled with ricotta and cinnamon and served with pork sauce; in Potenza, *fusilli* and *orecchiette* were served *in bianco* with horseradish and sausage; in Roccanova, *pallott,* little balls of cheese soaked in sauce, were added to the horseradish and pork sauce. At midnight, before the bell announced the death of Carnival, the last dish of *fusilli* was brought to the table, and then gloomy Lent knocked at the door.

Also in Basilicata, at Viggiano in the Agri valley, it is still customary to toss a long *fusillo* in boiling water to tell the sex of a baby: if it stands up straight, it will be a boy, if it takes a horizontal position, a girl.

In Calabria, special *fusiddri* are made on a wooden board called a *timpagno.* A little piece of dough is rubbed between the hands until it becomes a *vermicello* about 3 inches (7.5 cm) thick, which is cut into pieces 4 inches (10 cm) long. Only then is each piece placed on the *ferretto* and rolled on the *timpagno* until it becomes a *fusillo* 8 to 10 inches (20 to 25 cm) long.

The towns of Arbëreshë tradition, which are found in lower Molise and in Puglia, Basilicata, Calabria, and Sicily, maintain that this type of pasta has Slavic origins and resembles something that is made in the Italian territory that lies within the Slavic countries, such as Istria. Curiously, in fact, in the areas of Fiume and Capodistria, which are no longer in Italy, cooks make *subioti,* a pasta wrapped around a large sock-knitting needle and cut into 2-inch (5-cm) lengths. The name derives from the Veneto dialect term *aguglie* (garfish), which the pasta is supposed to resemble. It used to be eaten with sauce on the last day of Carnival.

In Piedmont, in the Langhe, cooks make the so-called *macaron dell'Alta Langa* by kneading water, flour, and dry bread crumbs and wrapping a teaspoon of dough on a sock-knitting needle. The canonical sauce is a *ragù* of lamb offal.

An old recipe book of Trentino cites *pasta a migné*, a noodle of flour, milk, and eggs that is wrapped around a spoon handle for shaping and then fried in butter.

And finally, in Lazio, around Viterbo, especially in the Monti Cimini, a type of *gnocchi col ferro* is made.

101. GARGANELLI

Pasta corta

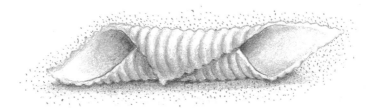

INGREDIENTS: For homemade, wheat flour and eggs; variants may include a little parmigiano and a dash of nutmeg in the dough. For factory made, durum-wheat flour and eggs or water.

HOW MADE: The flour is sifted and kneaded long and vigorously with eggs. The dough is left to rest, then rolled out into a thin sheet, and 1¼-inch (3-cm) squares (though they may be as large as 2¾ inches/7 cm) are cut from it. These are rolled obliquely on a wooden stick, and then drawn across a special utensil to make the characteristic ridging.

Both factory and homemade versions are often colored. *Garganelli* are boiled in plenty of salted water.

ALSO KNOWN AS: In the Marche, *maccheroni al pettine* and *fischioni*. For the factory made, *paglia e fieno* (straw and hay).

HOW SERVED: They used to be cooked only in broth, especially of capon, but to-day they are traditionally served as *pastasciutta*, dressed with a hearty meat *ragù*.

WHERE FOUND: Emilia-Romagna (a specialty of Lugo di Romagna), but also in the Marche and Umbria.

REMARKS: The name derives from the dialect word *garganel*, meaning "chicken's gullet," which the ridged *garganello* resembles. The ridges, made with a *pettine*, hold the sauce better than a smooth surface.

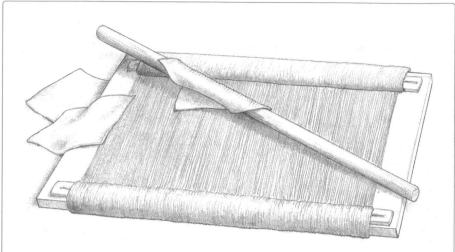

This shape is now quite common, both fresh and factory made. Its appearance as *pastasciutta* is relatively modern. *Garganelli* used to be served in capon broth, and the dough was scented with nutmeg and often enriched with a little local cheese. Similar to *garganelli,* but not ridged, are *scifuloti*, also from Romagna. Another variant is the *fischioni* of the Marche, made with flour and fine durum-wheat bran. They are typical of the towns in the Esino valley.

Not surprisingly, there are many legends about the origin of this curious pasta, such as the one about the poor housewife whose cat ate all the filling for the *tortellini* she was making. The guests had already arrived, and she had already cut the pasta squares. In a moment of inspiration, she rolled the squares around a stick and then over the loom comb that every peasant household in Romagna possessed.

102. GARGATI

Pasta corta

INGREDIENTS: Wheat flour and eggs.

HOW MADE: The flour is sifted and then kneaded for a long time with eggs until the dough is smooth and hard. The dough is inserted by the piece into the *torchio da bigoli* (see *bigoli*), fitted with a die for ridged pasta. The *gargati*, about ¼ inch (6 mm) wide and ¾ to 1¼ inches (2 to 3 cm) long, resemble small *sedani rigati* (see *sedani*). They are boiled in plenty of salted water.

ALSO KNOWN AS: No alternative names.

HOW SERVED: As *pastasciutta,* traditionally with *consiero,*[97] an old-style *ragù* of mixed meats, or with *rovinassi,* a *ragù* made from chicken giblets. A pigeon sauce is also traditional.

WHERE FOUND: The Veneto, especially near Vicenza, in the foothills around the valleys of the Leogra, the Posina, and the Astico.

REMARKS: The name means literally "gullets." *Gargato* is the Veneto dialect for *gola*, or "throat," which in the popular imagination stands for the esophagus of the chicken. *Rovinassi*, or *rovinazzi*, means "plaster fragments" in the dialect of Pola (on the Istrian peninsula), an imaginative but precise comparison with the tiny pieces of chicken giblets that do not disintegrate in the cooking of the tasty *ragù* of the same name. *Consiero* is typical with *gargati* as well, and each family in the Leogra valley and the Schio area possesses the "true and authentic recipe" for it, naturally with small variants. The sauce used to be made only with tomato *conserva*, but now may be enriched with *durei* (chicken giblets).

103. GASSE

Pasta corta

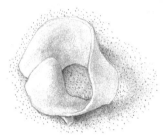

INGREDIENTS: Wheat flour, salt, eggs, and water.

HOW MADE: The flour is sifted with a pinch of salt and kneaded with a few eggs and as much water as needed to make a firm, smooth dough. The dough is left to rest, then rolled out into a sheet, not too thin. The sheet of dough is wound completely around a rolling pin, forming many layers, and then cut from one end to the other with a knife. The wide strips that result are placed on a wooden board, one on top of the other, and cut into narrower strips ⅝ to ¾ inch (1.5 to 2 cm) wide. The strips are picked up one at a time and the ends are pinched together to form a ring.

This pasta needs long drying, which helps it to hold together when boiled in abundant salted water.

ALSO KNOWN AS: No alternative names.

HOW SERVED: Generally as *pastasciutta*, traditionally *in bianco*, or else with a lamb *ragù*, but in general with typical local sauces.

WHERE FOUND: Liguria.

REMARKS: *Gasse* are already cited in 1893, in a book considered the bible of Ligurian cooking.[98] The text gives us no indications of how the pasta was served, however. It looks like small knots, or nooses, which Genoese sailors call *gasse*. In nautical terminology, they are knots for holding a ring at the end of a sheet or line. According to some, the term is of Spanish origin, but its use was already widespread as a reference for pasta in Liguria during the seventeenth century. This could be explained by the linguistic contaminations that resulted because of the lively trade exchanges that have always characterized the people of Liguria.

104. GATTAFIN

Pasta ripiena

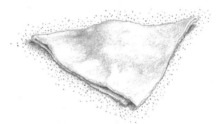

INGREDIENTS: Wheat flour, oil, lukewarm water, and salt. For the filling, chard, marjoram, eggs, and cheese.

HOW MADE: The flour is sifted and kneaded long and vigorously with oil, lukewarm water, and a pinch of salt. When the dough is firm and smooth, it is left to rest, then rolled out into a thin sheet, and 3-inch (7.5-cm) squares are cut from it. A spoonful of filling is placed on each square, the square is folded into a triangle, and the edges are sealed carefully. The *gattafin* are deep-fried in Ligurian olive oil and eaten piping hot.

ALSO KNOWN AS: *Gattafuin.*

HOW SERVED: Deep-fried in oil.

WHERE FOUND: Liguria, typical of the eastern half of the region, known as the Riviera del Levante.

REMARKS: The term derives from *gattafura,* a fourteenth-century word for *ravioli* (see entry) and also for cake. Scappi provides a detailed recipe, but so does Maestro Martino,[99] who gives a precise, very modern recipe for a *torta* with chard that is similar to the Ligurian *torta pasqualina*. The metamorphosis from large *torta* into small *raviolo* has occurred often in the history of pasta shapes. Like the early *ravioli*, the *gattafin* is deep-fried and served piping hot.

105. GIGLI

Pastina

INGREDIENTS: Durum-wheat flour and water.

HOW MADE: Tiny, ridged factory-made pasta, but variable, shaped like either a vine tendril or a small calla lily, with both shapes known by the same name. They are boiled in broth or abundant salted water.

ALSO KNOWN AS: *Cavatappi* and *cellentani*, and with only one turn of the screw, *amorosi*, *cornetti*, and *jolly*.

HOW SERVED: As *pastasciutta* or in broth, according to shape.

WHERE FOUND: Widespread.

REMARKS: The name means literally "lilies." Twisted like a lily in bloom, this unusually shaped factory-made pasta is an example of the pasta maker's imagination. The shape is both pleasing to the eye and functional: it must not break during cooking and, above all, must collect the sauce. If we leaf through one of the first illustrated catalogs of pasta shapes, we realize how far the machinery has come to satisfy an ever-more-demanding world of consumers.

106. GLORIA PATRI

Pastina

INGREDIENTS: Flour, eggs, and water.

HOW MADE: The flour is sifted and kneaded long and vigorously with eggs and water. When the dough is firm and smooth, it is left to rest, then rolled out into a sheet, not too thin. *Fettuccine* about ⅜ inch (1 cm) wide are cut from the sheet. These are wrapped around wooden sticks to form tiny rings, then the sticks are passed over a weaver's comb, to give the pasta ridges that will help trap the sauce. The pasta is cooked in broth.

ALSO KNOWN AS: *Fischioni;* in Umbria, in the town of Gubbio, *lumachine.*

HOW SERVED: Generally in soups, with local condiments.

WHERE FOUND: The Marche, around Ancona, in the area of Montefano, and in Umbria.

REMARKS: The name means literally "Glory be to the Father." Housewives in the kitchen used to recite prayers like the Our Father, or Pater Noster (see *paternoster*), and Hail Mary, or Ave Maria (see *avemarie*) to measure the time the pasta cooked. *Gloria patri* were reserved for feast days because they required a long and laborious procedure. The sticks used in the preparation were generally made of a neutral wood, such as beech. However, the peasants, who had their own fruit trees, preferred well-sanded fruitwood. They were kept and reused whenever the pasta was made, as was the *pettine* that created the ridges.

107. GNOC DE SCHELT

Gnocchi/gnocchetti

INGREDIENTS: Wheat flour, chestnut flour, buckwheat flour, eggs, milk, and salt.

HOW MADE: The flours are sifted together onto a wooden board and kneaded with milk, eggs, and a pinch of salt. The dough, which should not be too hard, is shaped into small dumplings, which are boiled in plenty of salted water.

ALSO KNOWN AS: No alternative names.

HOW SERVED: Generally as *pastasciutta*, with a simple tomato sauce.

WHERE FOUND: Lombardy, in the Val Camonica.

REMARKS: The use of flours other than wheat flour was once common in inaccessible mountain areas, where for centuries the rural economy was one of survival. Today, these special *gnocchi* are made only rarely. Some restaurants serve them as an artifact of the valley's cuisine.

108. GNOCCHETTI

Gnocchi / gnocchetti

INGREDIENTS: For homemade, type 00 wheat flour, durum-wheat flour, or *semola*, or a mixture, water, and sometimes salt. Often other kinds of flours, such as corn flour, are used, and the dough can also be enriched with dry bread crumbs. Richer *gnocchetti* contain eggs, sometimes with the addition of boiled potato, but also with ricotta. For factory made, durum-wheat flour and water.

HOW MADE: The flour is sifted onto a wooden board and kneaded long and vigorously with water and sometimes a pinch of salt until a firm, smooth dough forms. The dough is left to rest, then formed into sticks about ⅜ inch (1 cm) in diameter (the size can vary from region to region). The sticks are cut into irregular lengths of about ¾ inch (2 cm).

In the south, *gnocchetti* are usually made of durum-wheat flour, alone or mixed with soft-wheat flour. In the north, other flours, such as buckwheat or corn, are also used. *Gnocchetti* do not tolerate long drying and must be boiled soon after they are made, in plenty of salted water.

Factory-made *gnocchetti* of various shapes, both smooth and ridged, are available.

ALSO KNOWN AS: In Piedmont, in the Belbo valley, *torsellini*. In Friuli–Venezia Giulia, *gnocchetti de gris*, but in Istria, *sbirici* and *zlicnjaki*. In the Veneto, *pestarici*. In Emilia-Romagna, *gnuchét*, though the same *gnocchetti* when passed over the tines of a fork are also called *maccheroni matti*, *gnocchetti*, and *gnocchi al latte*. In the Tosco-Emilian Apennines, *battollo*. In Tuscany, *topini*, but in the Lunigiana, *gnocchetti* made with chestnut flour are called *gnochi mes'ci d'castagne*. In the Marche, *suricitti* and *gnocchetti alla dispreta*. In Umbria, *falchetti* are made with ricotta and spinach, and in Collescipoli (Terni), the dough also contains bread. In Lazio, in Guidonia Montecelio, *frascarelli;* in Leonessa, *gnucchitti pilusi;* and around Viterbo, *gnocchi 'ncotti*. In Abruzzo, at Castel del Monte, *cianfrachiglie*. In Campania, on Procida, *suricidde*. In Sicily, *gnucchetti* are small indented *gnocchi*.

HOW SERVED: Generally as *pastasciutta,* with various sauces based on meats, cheeses, or vegetables, with the latter frequently used in the dough as well. They are often added to legume soups, as in Abruzzo, where a soup with chickpeas is typical. In the Marche, in the town of Mogliano, in the province of Macerata, they are used in a vegetable soup. The factory-made pasta is served in broth or as *pastasciutta,* depending on its size.

WHERE FOUND: Widespread.

REMARKS: As the numerous alternative names and varied uses, both in broth and as *pastasciutta,* indicate, *gnocchetti* is a diminutive of the term *gnocco* (see entry). They merit a separate entry because innumerable different, but similar, small pastas found throughout Italy can all be considered forms of *gnocchetti.* The best known receive their own entries.

The *Inchiesta napoleonica sui consumi e le tradizioni nel Regno italico (1805–15)*[100] includes information on the dietary practices of the peasant families in Romagna: when a child was born, friends were invited to a great meal as soon as the new mother got out of bed. If the baby was a boy, *gnocchi*—called *maccheroni*—cooked in milk had to be served; if the baby was a girl, *lasagne.* And *maccheroni,* in this guise, were considered a ritual dish that was served also for the New Year's luncheon, which, with the addition of dried grapes,[101] was considered a propitiatory meal for future well-being and wealth. The small flour-and-water *gnocchi* were also made for the last day of Carnival, when it was the custom for young men to let off harquebus shots under the windows of their ladyloves. If this noisy courtship ritual was well received, the girl's family invited the young man in for a bowl of *maccheroni.*

Piedmontese *torsellini,* a specialty of the Belbo valley, are made with flour, eggs, and dry bread crumbs.

In the province of Viterbo, especially in the Latian Maremma, *gnocchi 'ncotti* are made by forming a well in the flour, pouring boiling water into the well, and kneading rapidly, trying not to burn the hands. Then *gnocchetti* are formed, about ¾ inch (2 cm) in diameter and length.

Made in the Marche, *gnocchetti alla dispreta,* that is, *alla disperata* (desperate woman), are eloquent testimony to the poverty of many rural families. Put together from leftover polenta and flour and no larger than a kernel of corn, they were served with just pork fat and onion.

109. GNOCCHETTI DI TRICARICO

Gnocchi/gnocchetti

INGREDIENTS: Durum-wheat flour and water.

HOW MADE: The flour is sifted onto a wooden board and kneaded long and vigorously with water. The dough is left to rest, then shaped into sticks about ⅜ inch (1 cm) in diameter and cut into roughly ¾-inch (2-cm) lengths. These pieces lengthen as they are rolled with hands on a wooden board into tiny coils. The *gnocchetti* are then boiled in plenty of salted water.

ALSO KNOWN AS: In the area of Potenza, around Montocchio, *cantarogn* (made with or without eggs); in Avigliano, *cantarogn* dough contains only flour and water.

HOW SERVED: As *pastasciutta,* with traditional local sauces, often with vegetables and *cacioricotta.*

WHERE FOUND: Basilicata, especially in the little town of Tricarico.

REMARKS: Different sauces are served with the *cantarogn* of Avigliano, depending on how open or closed the coils are. The closed *cantarogn* are best with vegetable sauces, particularly turnips; the more open versions, which are oval with the edges slightly upturned, are traditionally served with tomato and *cacioricotta,* sometimes with sausage.

110. GNOCCHI DI SEMOLINO

Gnocchi/gnocchetti

INGREDIENTS: *Semolino,* salt, eggs, milk, butter, and grated cheese (generally parmigiano).

HOW MADE: The *semolino* is cooked in boiling milk, then a pinch of salt, some eggs, and parmigiano are added. The mixture is spread out on a moistened marble surface to a thickness of about ⅜ inch (1 cm). When the mixture is cold, it is cut into rhombuses or squares, about 1½ inches (4 cm) on a side. The pieces are laid out, slightly overlapping, in the bottom of a buttered baking dish. Additional layers, interspersed with butter and parmigiano, are arranged on top, with the layers slightly stepped back to form a dome shape. The composition is browned in the oven.

ALSO KNOWN AS: *Gnocchi alla romana.* In Trentino, *canederli di gries,* and in Sardinia, *pillas.*

HOW SERVED: Browned in the oven with cheese and butter.

WHERE FOUND: Lazio, typical of *cucina romana*. With small variants, they are found in other regions, too, such as Sardinia, Trentino, Umbria, and Friuli–Venezia Giulia.

REMARKS: This is one of the few dishes in the Roman repertory worthy of an elegant and important meal, and is one of the most popular. Ada Boni, the great writer on *cucina romana*,[102] presents them as they used to be, in a dome. Today, it is more usual to spread them out in an ovenproof dish in equal layers to facilitate serving at the table.

In Trentino, *canederli di gries*—*gries* means durum-wheat flour—are small *gnocchetti* served in broth or with meat sauce. They are often found in the old family recipe collections that are jealously handed down from mother to daughter.[103]

Also in Sardinia, *gnocchi di semolino,* called *pillas,* are made. They are generously sauced with meat *ragù* and grated pecorino and browned in the oven.

III. GNOCCHI DI ZUCCA

Gnocchi / gnocchetti

INGREDIENTS: Wheat flour, squash, eggs, and sometimes also a small amount of grated parmigiano.

HOW MADE: The flour is sifted onto a wooden board and kneaded with baked, pureed squash and eggs. Teaspoonfuls of the soft dough are dropped in boiling salted water, and the *gnocchi* are lifted out one by one as they float to the surface.

ALSO KNOWN AS: No alternative names.

HOW SERVED: As *pastasciutta,* with traditional local condiments, usually melted butter and local cheese. In Valle d'Aosta, they are covered with fontina cheese and browned in the oven.

WHERE FOUND: Valle d'Aosta (Gressoney-Saint-Jean), the Veneto (around Belluno), and Friuli–Venezia Giulia (around Gorizia).

REMARKS: The name means literally "squash dumplings." Before potatoes became common, squash was typically used in the filling of certain pastas, and is one of the basic ingredients of these *gnocchi*. The hot, sunny summers of the northern Italian plains yielded excellent, sweet squashes, which kept well during the harsh winters when gardens were blanketed by snow. *Gnocchi, ravioli,* and savory pies made with them were a feast-day alternative to the more costly *ravioli* filled with meat.

This type of *gnocco* must once have been common along the northern Adriatic coast, since a detailed recipe appears in the *Cuoco maceratese*.[104]

112. GNOCCHI LONGHI

Pasta lunga

INGREDIENTS: Wheat flour, water, and some eggs.

HOW MADE: The flour is sifted onto a wooden board and kneaded long and vigorously with water and eggs, then covered and left to rest. Pieces of dough are pinched off and rolled with the hands on a board to form *spaghetti* up to a yard (a meter) or more in length. They are boiled in plenty of salted water.

ALSO KNOWN AS: In Sardinia, *maccheroni lunghi.*

HOW SERVED: As *pastasciutta,* typically with goat meat.

WHERE FOUND: Lazio (Monti Lepini), but also Sardinia.

REMARKS: Literally "long dumplings," these rustic *gnocchi* used to be made with the flour milled from special varieties of wheat, such as *romanella* and *frassineto,* which had very low yields and have now disappeared. The skill in making this pasta lay in pulling each piece of dough until it was so long it broke.

In Sardinia, *maccheroni lunghi* were a ritual food, cooked in soup and left out on the evening before All Souls' Day (November 2) for the souls of the departed, who returned home for the occasion to taste their favorite food. The same *maccheroni* were also prepared for harvest and *vendemmia* (grape harvest) lunches, with sauce and pecorino.

113. GNOCCHI OSSOLANI

Gnocchi/gnocchetti

INGREDIENTS: Wheat flour, chestnut flour, squash, potatoes, eggs, and spices.

HOW MADE: The flours are sifted together onto a wooden board and kneaded with eggs, squash, and potatoes (boiled and sieved), and the dough is flavored with spices. The classic *gnocchi* are formed and rolled on the tines of a fork or the back of a grater, then boiled in salted water and drained as soon as they float.

ALSO KNOWN AS: No alternative names.

HOW SERVED: As *pastasciutta,* generally with butter, sage, and grated local cheese.

WHERE FOUND: Piedmont and Lombardy, in particular the Val d'Ossola.

REMARKS: The name means literally "dumplings of Ossola." Between the Vallese and the Ticino, wedged into the mountains that face Switzerland, the Val d'Ossola is home to alpine pastures where milk from grazing cows is used to make fine butter and small quantities of truly special cheeses in summer. Simple *gnocchi* once made with chestnut flour, squash, and potato—ingredients traditionally

used by people living a subsistence existence—and enhanced with the local butter and cheeses are now sought-after niche products and the pride of the local
gastronomy.

From the sixteenth through the eighteenth century, the mountain people of
the Val d'Ossola would go down to Intra and Pallanza, two important market
towns on Lake Maggiore, where a large important market was held on alternate
Saturdays. Here, they would stock up on precious wheat and whatever else the
family needed.[105]

114. GNOCCHI RICCI

Gnocchi/gnocchetti

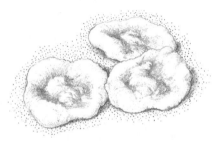

INGREDIENTS: Wheat flour, eggs, boiling water, and salt.

HOW MADE: Two doughs are prepared: one of flour and eggs, the other of flour,
boiling water, and salt. The two doughs are kneaded separately until each is firm
and smooth. After resting, they are kneaded together until well blended. Tiny
gnocchetti are pinched off, then flattened and curled against a wooden board with
the pressure of three fingers. The *gnocchi* are boiled in plenty of salted water.

ALSO KNOWN AS: No alternative names.

HOW SERVED: As *pastasciutta,* with *ragù* of mixed meats, prevalently lamb, sprinkled with local pecorino cheese.

WHERE FOUND: They are a specialty of Amatrice, in the province of Rieti, in
northeastern Lazio.

REMARKS: This endangered ancient pasta was once made in the wealthier homes
of Amatrice for feast days. Over time, everyone who knew how to make *gnocchi
ricci* (literally, "curly gnocchi") died off until only two old women were left. The
town decided to offer a training course so the technique would not be lost. The
class was held in 2004 for thirty participants, some housewives, some professionals, and was a great success. Today, the shape is widely used locally and even produced by small local artisanal pasta makers.

115. GNOCCO

Various shapes

INGREDIENTS: For homemade, wheat flour or durum-wheat flour and water; but also flour mixed with potatoes, sometimes eggs, and various other ingredients. For factory made, durum-wheat flour and water.

HOW MADE: Bite-sized dumpling formerly made of flour and water, and probably of irregular shape because it was torn. Stale bread was subsequently added to the original dough, and, much later, potatoes. The *gnocco* was then enriched with other ingredients, such as ricotta, different flours, vegetables, or often a mixture.

Gnocchi made with flour are kneaded for a long time and formed into various traditional shapes. They are boiled in plenty of salted water and removed as soon as they come to the surface.

A vast range of factory-made forms also exists.

ALSO KNOWN AS: See *gnocchetti* entry. For the factory-made types, *gnocchetti* or *mezzi gnocchetti*, in many different shapes and sizes.

HOW SERVED: Generally as *pastasciutta*, with traditional local sauces. They also used to be typical in legume soups. The smaller factory-made *gnocchetti* are cooked in broth.

WHERE FOUND: Widespread.

REMARKS: The word *gnocco* is not of Latin origin, but one of the many words that culinary Italian has taken from the immense pool of dialect terms, in this case probably from the Veneto, where we find the dialect word *gnoco*. The latter may go back to the time of the Longobard domination and the term *knohha*, which is *nocca* or *nodo* in Italian, or "knot." Thus, the old name probably referred to the irregular shape of tree knots. In support of this interpretation, we note that Slavonia, a region of Croatia around Zagreb, has a similar food, *noklice* (literally *gnocchetti*, because the suffix *ica* is a diminutive or term of endearment).

A recipe for *gnocchi* is found in a fragment of a fourteenth-century manuscript published in 1877.[106] The old term is subsequently cited by Teofilo Folengo (see *maccherone*), a passage that calls to mind Boccaccio's *maccherone* that slips on the mountain of parmigiano. Some centuries later, in 1774, the *gnocco* was celebrated in the satiric epic *La gnoccheide,* by Angonio Ferrero da Valdieri:

> *Imbalsamati che saranno i gnocchi*
> *con bianca toma e con butir gialletto*
> *un cibo resterà non da pitocchi*
> *ma per Colui che sortì regio letto. . . .*

> [The *gnocchi* will be enveloped in white cheese and yellow butter, one food will remain not for the poor but for Him who came out of the royal bed. . . .]

And "Him" must mean Vittorio Amedeo III of Savoy, who, on a visit to Cuneo on August 17, 1773, tasted *gnocchi* at lunch with the mayor, Count d'Andonno.

The *gnocco,* which has often also been called *maccherone,* can be considered the first basic pasta type. The term covers an infinity of originally handmade pasta shapes, both round and dumplinglike and long and *spaghetti*-like. They may be bite-sized pieces of dough dragged across a wooden board, sometimes hollowed by being dragged with the fingers, but more often by laying them on the back of a grater, on the tines of a fork, or on a special grooved wooden utensil. This shape can be recognized in the few visual images that have come down to us. The early *gnocco* was cooked in liquid or often fried, the latter still traditional today in some Italian regions.

Centuries in the history of the *gnocco* remain undocumented; we know that people made *gnocchi,* but we do not know their shape. In the *Vocabolario domestico,* printed in Parma in 1761, under *gnocco* we read "kind of *pastume,*"[107] meaning that its shape was undefined. At the beginning, it must have resembled a simple, irregular *boccone* (mouthful), then became perfected in diverse shapes that acquired different names in different places.

The *gnocco* is the ancestor of almost all the Italian pastas: it is the origin of *strozzapreti* (see entry for *strangolapreti, strozzapreti*), which can be simple *gnocchetti*—irregular, round, or concave—and also of thick *spaghettoni* of variable size, sometimes indented on the inside. *Gnocchi* can be subdivided into rolled with one finger *(cavatelli, orecchiette),* with two fingers (Lucanian *strascinari*), with three or four fingers (Lucanian *trigghiazz* and *cantaroggni*), and even with eight fingers *(strangulaprievete),* the latter a sort of thick *spaghettone.* In Basilicata, in the area of Pomarico and of Palazzo San Gervasio, this type of pasta is called *kapunda,* because it is made by dragging the dough on a *cavarola,*[108] or small board *(ca punta,* for *con la punta,* "with the point," that is, the tip, of the fingers).

They are all pastas typical of central and southern Italy, and today are always made with durum-wheat flour. In the north, where soft wheat is more common, pasta doughs have typically called for eggs, which made them easier to roll thin. But in the small mountain enclaves of the north, where the products of the plains filtered through with difficulty, pastas relied on flours made from local grasses or other sources: wheat but also emmer, chestnuts, barley, rye, and the like. *Gnocco* was often made with stale bread, grated or simply soaked (see *canederli*).

Poverty gave rise to the practice of making pastas that were not true pastas. The *gnocco* could be made with leftovers and crumbs of raised bread dough (see *cecamariti*) and the dough colored yellow with saffron (see *ciciones*), in imitation of the richer egg pastas. *Gnocchi* could also be made from a thick batter (see *donderet* and *gnoche de ciadin*), and an emollient, such as oil (see *menietti*), could be added to the ingredients.

Gnocchi alla veneziana, which are not Venetian, were made with only rice flour. They are cited in the seventeenth-century recipe book manuscript of the Bonaccorsi family of Macerata,[109] a century later reported by Nebbia, and, later still, by the anonymous author of *Il cuoco perfetto marchigiano,* who published his interesting little manual in Loreto in 1891. For the latter two authors, the *gnocchi alla veneziana* are made with rice flour or with wheat flour.

For the gradual introduction of the potato as an ingredient of *gnocchi,* we have to wait for the nineteenth century. In the domestic recipe collections, potato *gnocchi* rarely appear alongside those of flour, *semolino,* and corn, even as late as the beginning of the twentieth century. Farmers were not quick to accept this precious import. In V. Agnoletti's *Manuale del cuoco e del pasticciere* (Pesaro, 1834), potato *gnocchi* still contain only one-third potatoes and two-thirds flour. The recipe for *gnocchi alla marchigiana* given in *Il cuoco sapiente*[110] calls for half potatoes and half wheat flour; we find the same proportions in *Cucina borghese semplice ed economica.*[111] Caterina Prato, who published the fifth edition of her *Manuale di cucina* in Padova in 1906, does not speak of *gnocchi,* but gives a recipe called *pallottole di patate* (potato bullets), in which boiled potatoes are worked with dry bread crumbs or flour. In E. Baltzer's *Cucina vegetariana* (1910), potato is included in the ingredients lists of the numerous *gnocchi* recipes, but again in a proportion of one-third potato to two-thirds bread and/or flour. And, again, A. Giaquinto, who published *I quattro volumi riuniti della cucina di famiglia* in Rome in 1907, speaks of *gnocchi alla napoletana detti strangulaprievete* made with potatoes, as we make them today, using only a small amount of flour to bind. In the 1922 edition, we find them cited simply as *gnocchi di patate* and made the same way. The 1932 *Biblioteca di gastronomia*[112] still distinguishes between *gnocchi alla mantovana,* made with flour, and *gnocchi alla milanese,* made with potatoes, alongside those of *semolino,* bread, and so on. But by the 1930s, the recipes of Petronilla[113] teach the modern formula for *gnocchi,* where the amount of flour (300 grams/about 10 ounces for every 2 kilograms/scant 4½ pounds) serves only to bind.

Evidence of the broad diffusion of the *gnocco* in Italy is provided by the many fairs held to celebrate certain holidays or special occasions: at Castel Goffredo, near Mantova, the coronation of King Gnocco during Carnival; in Verona, the Friday of Shrovetide is also called *gnocolar,* and a huge *gnocolata* in honor of Saint Zeno is celebrated in the town square; and at Montalcino, in Tuscany, on the last Sunday of October, *donzelline,* small deep-fried *gnocchetti* of raised bread dough, are made during the centuries-old *sagra* of the thrush. In Umbria, around Foligno, rich *gnocchi dei preti* (of the priests) of flour, milk, and eggs are made, and at Sigillo and Costacciano, the same gnocchi are made from flour and ricotta. At the local festivals of many small towns in the *campagna romana,* tiny flour-and-water *gnocchetti* called *frascarelli* (see entry) or *reverelli* are served in a soup of pork rinds and beans.

In Abruzzo, these same *gnocchetti* are typically served with *cacio e uova* (cheese and eggs), a legacy of the frugal meals of the *carbonai*, "charcoal makers," who stayed out for long periods working in the woodland *carbonaie*. In Naples, certain *gnocchi* are made with choux pastry, but with lard instead of butter.

116. GNOCHE DE CIADIN

Gnocchi / gnocchetti

INGREDIENTS: Wheat flour, eggs, and milk.

HOW MADE: The flour is sifted into a bowl and mixed with eggs and milk to make a thick batter, which is beaten forcefully until bubbles form on the surface. It is dropped by spoonfuls into lightly boiling salted water and cooked for at least ten minutes.

ALSO KNOWN AS: No alternative names.

HOW SERVED: As *pastasciutta,* most often with butter and grated local cheese.

WHERE FOUND: The Veneto, especially Cortina d'Ampezzo.

REMARKS: The name means literally "basin *gnocchi"* and refers to a large bowl set into a washstand. The curious term derives from the fact that the batter was mixed in a wooden bowl, the *ciadin,* used specifically for this preparation. In the Veneto, in particular Cortina d'Ampezzo, but also in all the valleys of Trentino, there is a tradition of carving wooden pasta-making utensils, such as this bowl.

117. GNUDI

Gnocchi / gnocchetti

INGREDIENTS: Wheat flour; spinach, chard, or other greens; ricotta; grated cheese; sometimes eggs; and spices.

HOW MADE: Boiled greens, squeezed dry and finely chopped, are kneaded with flour, ricotta, grated cheese, spices, and eggs. Tiny dumplings are formed from the dough, then floured and dropped in boiling salted water and drained as soon as they float.

ALSO KNOWN AS: *Malfatti, ravioli gnudi,* and *strozzapreti* (see entry for *strangolapreti, strozzapreti*).

HOW SERVED: As *pastasciutta,* with both meat and meatless sauces.

WHERE FOUND: Tuscany, in the Val di Chiana, the Casentino, and in general in areas that were once very poor.

REMARKS: This very old term, which literally means "nudes," used to refer to a *raviolo* without pasta—that is, balls or patties of "nude" filling. Salimbene da Parma, who wrote his *Cronica* toward the end of the 1200s, speaks of them: the monk says he tasted *ravioli gnudi* for the feast of Saint Clare and considered them a true delicacy.[114] They must have been the same *"Rafioli . . . licaproprii,"* made with cheese and flour and deep-fried in lard, we read about in the *Libro di cucina del secolo XIV.*[115] Artusi, much closer to our own day, recommends them also as a *contorno,* or side dish, and *in bianco,* if they are served as a *primo piatto.*

This preparation, which is not, of course, a true pasta, was present in formerly depressed areas of Tuscany, where it was made with the products available in peasant homes. In the pastoral mountains, rich in *cacio raviggiolo,* ricotta, and fresh and aged *pecorino,* housewives made *malfatti* in spring with the season's special ricotta and added chard or spinach. In the Casentino, chard is preferred. In fact, at Papiano, on the mountain above Stia, great quantities of chard were cooked for making the *malfatti* for the feast of Saint Catherine. When the cooking water was poured out into the streams, the waterways turned greenish, and residents living downstream would say, "If the water is green when it reaches Stia, there's a feast at Papiano."

118. GRAMIGNA

Pastina

INGREDIENTS: For homemade, durum-wheat flour, type 00 flour, and eggs. For factory made, durum-wheat flour and eggs.

HOW MADE: The flours are sifted together and kneaded with eggs long and vigorously until a firm, smooth dough forms, which is left to rest. It was once grated with a large-holed grater and later with a specific utensil with a large-holed die. In one variation, spinach or saffron is added to color the pasta. The factory-made version varies from small to medium size, in the shape of a tiny worm, and is often found also in a *paglia e fieno* version. *Gramigna* is boiled in abundant salted water.

ALSO KNOWN AS: In the factory-made shape, *gramignoni* and *spaccatelle.*

HOW SERVED: As *pastasciutta,* usually with flavorful sauces with sausage, with a final dusting of parmigiano. In the summer variation, the pasta is cooked directly in a light tomato sauce.

WHERE FOUND: Emilia-Romagna, the Marche, and Friuli–Venezia Giulia.

REMARKS: The small seed of a weed grass probably suggested the shape of this pasta, which at one time must have been very tiny. Common in Emilia-Romagna, but also in some border areas, such as the Marche, it could be an interpretation of *cuscus* (see entry), imitated in many pasta shapes in many Italian regions because the correct preparation was unknown. Like all the tiny pastas, *gramigna* is now widely sold in factory-made versions. The peculiar shape, recalling tiny worms, probably derives from what resulted when homemade *gramigna* dough was too soft: what emerged from the grater looked like small worms.

119. GRANDINE

Pastina

INGREDIENTS: Durum-wheat flour and water.

HOW MADE: Tiny factory-made pasta that is cooked in broth.

ALSO KNOWN AS: In Tuscany, *grandinina,* and also a variation called *grandinina soda* (hard). In Sicily, *palline da schioppo* (musket balls) and *pirticuneddi.*

HOW SERVED: Generally in broth; *grandinina* in goose broth or as *pastasciutta* with peas.

WHERE FOUND: Throughout Italy; typical of Tuscany.

REMARKS: The name means literally "hailstones." The atmospheric agents, on which the fate of the harvest often depended, have regularly inspired the popular imagination, and thus some tiny pastas are called *grandine,* or the diminutive *grandinine* and *tempestine,* even though the shape is not always that of a hailstone.

In the area of Cortona, in Tuscany, *grandinina* was the soup that opened wedding luncheons; in the Casentino, it was always made for the threshing and grain-beating lunches. It was customary to cook the *grandinina* "hard" in goose broth. And because the dough was quite firm, this tiny product of the first professional pasta makers was also sold in a version with holes.

In Sicily, *pirticuneddi* are mentioned among the first pastas made with a special *torchio*, the so-called *paste d'arbitrio*.[116]

120. GRAVIUOLE MOLISANE

Pasta ripiena

INGREDIENTS: Durum-wheat flour, salt, and eggs. For the filling, ricotta, cheeses, vegetables, spices, and sometimes pork.

HOW MADE: The flour is sifted with a pinch of salt and kneaded long and vigorously with eggs. After the dough is left to rest, it is rolled out into two sheets. Small heaps of filling are placed on one sheet. The second sheet is placed on top and pressed around the filling. Then, a wheel-type pasta cutter is used to cut square *ravioli*. They are cooked, a few at a time, in lightly boiling salted water.

ALSO KNOWN AS: *Ravioli alla montanara.*

HOW SERVED: As *pastasciutta*, with the typical lamb *ragù*.

WHERE FOUND: Molise.

REMARKS: The gastronomic tradition of Molise does not have many stuffed pastas. *Graviuole*, which once were more often filled with wild greens than with the products of the garden, are an old mountain dish: shepherds would stop alongside the sheep pens and make their simple cheeses, while around them expert hands gathered the fragrant wild herbs, a memory nearly lost today.

121. GRUMI DI GRANO SARACENO

Pastina

INGREDIENTS: Buckwheat flour, type 00 flour, warm water, and today also milk.

HOW MADE: The flours are sifted into a very wide bowl. While warm water is sprinkled from above, the dough is mixed with open fingers working in a circle, creating very tiny lumps of dough. These lumps are then sieved to separate them from the flour. The work continues until the flour is used up. The lumps are cooked in milk soup.

ALSO KNOWN AS: No alternative names.

HOW SERVED: Most typically in milk soup.

WHERE FOUND: Trentino–Alto Adige.

REMARKS: The name means literally "buckwheat lumps." This *pastina* is served extensively in the high-mountain areas, where buckwheat, which is milled into a gluten-free, protein-poor flour, is grown. This is another tiny pasta that imitates the earlier *cuscus* (see entry) still made in Sicily and Sardinia. The people who made these *grumi* imitated couscous, without knowing how it was made.

In Trentino, soup prepared with *grumi di grano saraceno* is believed to have calmative properties, and, in fact, is usually served at the evening meal to promote sleep.

122. IMPANADAS

Pasta ripiena

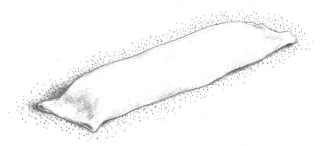

INGREDIENTS: Durum-wheat flour, lard, saffron, and salt. For the meat filling, various meats, pork *insaccati,* artichokes, peas, vegetables; for the meatless filling, salt- and freshwater fish and crustaceans. A filling of eel or cheese is also typical.

HOW MADE: The flour is sifted with saffron onto a wooden board and kneaded for a long time with lard and salt. When the dough is firm and smooth, it is left to rest, then rolled out into a sheet, not too thin. A wheel-type pasta cutter is used to cut rectangles of variable size from the sheet. A spoonful of filling is placed on the edge of each rectangle, and then the rectangles are rolled to make short, sealed tubes. Traditionally, the tubes are fried in hot oil. Modern *impanadas* resemble small two-crust pies and are baked.

ALSO KNOWN AS: No alternative names.

HOW SERVED: As *pastasciutta,* deep-fried in lard, but also baked.

WHERE FOUND: Sardinia.

REMARKS: *Impanadas,* made with a variety of fillings, are common throughout Sardinia. *Impanadas de pezza,* which look like small, round two-crust pies, are usually filled with meat. They also can be squares or disks, with the edges pinched and raised, echoing the shape of the island's elaborate sweets that only very experienced hands are able to make.

The practice of coloring the pasta with saffron is very old. The spice gave pallid flour-and-water dough a golden hue, as though it was rich in eggs, a legacy of the centuries when food decorated with gold was a sign of wealth and prestige.

"Panadas" (but especially *fideus,* of which Sardinia was a big exporter) were found on the tables of the wealthier classes in Barcelona in the fifteenth century,[117] a fact that invites the question of whether the recipe is of Catalan origin exported to Sardinia, rather than the reverse.

123. KNEIDLACH

Gnocchi / gnocchetti

INGREDIENTS: Matzo meal, eggs, oil (or chicken or goose fat), fried onion, parsley, ginger, salt, and pepper.

HOW MADE: Matzos are pulverized into a fine flour, which is kneaded with eggs, oil (or goose or chicken fat), fried onion, parsley, grated ginger, salt, and pepper. The dough, which is left to rest for a couple of hours before it is shaped, must be soft yet still firm enough to form *gnocchetti* the size of an olive.

ALSO KNOWN AS: No alternative names.

HOW SERVED: Generally in chicken or goose broth, but also in vegetable broth.

WHERE FOUND: Italy *(cucina ebraica).*

REMARKS: The difficulty of making these small *gnocchi* lies in making a soft dough that will hold its shape. The hands need to be oiled because the dough is a bit sticky.

124. KRAFI

Pasta ripiena

INGREDIENTS: Wheat flour, eggs, and oil. For the filling, *latteria* cheese, eggs, and sometimes a pinch of sugar.

HOW MADE: The flour is sifted onto a wooden board and kneaded with eggs and a little oil long and vigorously until the dough is firm and smooth. After resting, the dough is rolled out into a thin sheet, and small disks are cut from it with an inverted glass. A teaspoon of filling is placed on each disk, which is then folded into a half-moon and the edges carefully sealed with the tines of a fork. The *Krafi* are boiled in plenty of salted water.

ALSO KNOWN AS: *Crafi de Albona.*

HOW SERVED: As *pastasciutta,* with *sugo di arrosto* (pan juices from roast meat).

WHERE FOUND: Friuli–Venezia Giulia.

REMARKS: The small part of Istria (Muggia) within Italy has remained, like the Croatian side, a land whose "Venetianness" can be perceived in both the language and the cuisine. These *Krafi* reflect the resources found in the vast mountainous, wooded area between Trieste and the border, where the festivities are celebrated, today as yesterday, with this typical pasta.

The substantial mass presence of pasta on the tables of Friuli–Venezia Giulia dates to the period after World War II. Information on the manufacture of pastas in the region or their importation is practically unfindable. M. L. Iona does not mention *Krafi* in his study on the statutes of the region from the Middle Ages to the Napoleonic domination.[118] Meats and *biade*[119] were the basis of the diet, not wheat, and therefore not pasta. In contrast, wine and olive oil, produced along the coast from Trieste to Muggia and beyond, occupied much space in the statutes.

125. LADITTAS

Pasta corta

INGREDIENTS: Durum-wheat flour, lard, water, and salt.

HOW MADE: The flour is sifted onto a wooden board and kneaded for a long time with lard and water; as the work proceeds, hands are salted to incorporate the salt into the dough. The dough is left to rest, then walnut-sized pieces are flattened between palms to make thick disks that are indented in the center with the pad of a fingertip. The pasta is boiled in plenty of salted water.

ALSO KNOWN AS: No alternative names.

HOW SERVED: Generally as *pastasciutta,* with simple tomato sauce and local pecorino.

WHERE FOUND: Sardinia.

REMARKS: This curious pasta is usually layered with sauce and plenty of sheep's or goat's milk cheese. *Viscidu,* a sheep's or goat's milk cheese kept in brine and with a vaguely acidulous flavor, is also often used.

126. LAGANE

Pasta lunga

INGREDIENTS: Durum-wheat flour, sometimes type 0 wheat flour, water, and salt.

HOW MADE: The flour is sifted and kneaded long and vigorously with water and salt until a firm, smooth dough forms. The dough is left to rest, then rolled out into a sheet, not too thin, and *tagliatelle,* or a sort of regular *maltagliato,* are cut from it. Their width and length vary from place to place, as does the sauce. They are boiled in plenty of salted water or in broth.

ALSO KNOWN AS: In Lazio, *lacchene, laganelli,* and *lane;* in Campania, around Avellino, *lavane* and *lavanelle;* in Puglia: *laine* and *tria;* in Basilicata, *laane, laanedde, lahane,* and *piatto del brigante;* and in Calabria, *laganedde.*

HOW SERVED: As *pastasciutta* and in broth, served variously according to local customs. In Basilicata, they are traditionally used in legume soups.

WHERE FOUND: Central and southern Italy, in particular Lazio, Campania, Puglia, Basilicata, and Calabria.

REMARKS: The word is of Greek origin, and, in fact, something like this pasta was used in ancient Greece and Rome. Greeks consumed barely toasted grains that were ground into flour and used to make true *lasagne—laganon* in Greek, *laganum* in Latin, and *lagane* in Italian—which even then were accompanied by legumes.

An echo of these dishes survives in a Salentine[120] dish of pasta and chickpeas, *ciceri e tria,* in which half the flat noodles are boiled in water and the other half, like ancient *lagane,* are fried in oil. The custom of pairing boiled and fried pasta in broth is also found in Abruzzo (see *volarelle*).

As for the ancient Roman world, the poet Horace, born in Venosa in 65 B.C., tells in the *Satires* how he used to go home to eat his simple soup of "leeks, chickpeas, and *lagane.*"[121] But we cannot establish what kind of grain he used: it is likely that in addition to *Triticum dicoccum,* he might have used what was called *far* in Latin, spelt or *T. monococcum,* which was more resistant than *T. dicoccum* and extensively used in the Etruscan and Roman world.

The bucolic poem *Moretum,*[122] once attributed to Virgil, describes a sort of oven-baked pizza. The oft-cited text of Apicius, *De re coquinaria,* very late and extensively reworked, says a great deal about how *lagane* were served, but nothing of how they were made. Nevertheless, there is a reference (5.1) to dry pasta, called *tracta,* a term that suggests the dough was rolled out:[123] *"tres orbiculos trac-tae siccas et confringis, et partibus in lac summissis . . ."* (dry out three rounds of pasta, break them, and toss the pieces in milk).[124]

The medieval documentary sources are numerous, and the term *laganum* is often associated with the word *maccherone,* and at the beginning was used for a type of *gnocco* (also verifiable in some images), and later generically for pasta.

Today, the *lagana,* in the form of *tagliatella,* is present everywhere in the gastronomy of central and southern Italy. In Lazio, *lagane* are *maltagliati* or wide *tagliatelle,* typical of some towns in the Monti Lepini (Sezze and Bassiano). In Campania, particularly in the Sannio, thick *lavane* are used in a chickpea soup.

In Puglia, *lagane,* there called *laine,* are cut from a roll of fresh pasta called *lu lainàre* in dialect. In some towns, curly *lagane* are cut with a wheel-type pasta cutter that ruffles the edge. At Monteparano, in the province of Taranto, *laine* are made for a ritual "luncheon of the poor": First mussels are opened and the liquid reserved; then in the old *catare,*[125] water is put on to boil, with the liquid of the mussels providing the salt. When the water boils, all the *laine* are poured in until the *laganaturo,* or rolling pin, can stand up by itself in the *catara.* Then the "mass" of pasta is left to cook. The result is a dense soup. The *catare* are carried before the altar of the patron saint and the contents are turned out onto the *spunlatora* (a wooden board with raised edges) and served with raw mussels, oil, and abundant pepper. The *laganaturo,* a term today still used for rolling pin, was—and is—the old utensil for making *lagane.* In Lecce, the famous dish called *ciceri e tria* (see *tria*) contains *tria* cut into small lozenges, half of which are cooked directly in the soup and half of which are fried and then added to the soup before serving, on the feast of Saint Joseph (March 19).

The area known in antiquity as Lucania (today called Basilicata) was home to both indigenous peoples and, from about 700 B.C., Greek colonists. There must have been an intense exchange of food products with Bruttium (the area that corresponds roughly to the south of modern Calabria), certainly during the festivals in the rustic sanctuaries documented in the area as early as the sixth century B.C. In Late Antiquity, at the most important fair of the south, held at Padula, the interchange of products, especially food, among Campania, Puglia, and Calabria must have been greatly encouraged. This explains the survival of ancient food names and preparations in Lucanian territory.

In the Vulture area, *lagane* are also called "dish of the brigand," in memory of a famous brigand who lived in the eighteenth century and was nicknamed Scolalagane. The names given to the Lucanian *lagane* may change with the length and width of the flat noodles. In the Arbëreshë towns of Maschito and Ginestra, the short *tumaçë me drugën* are eaten on Palm Sunday; at Barile, they are on the table for the feast of Saint Joseph; and at Pisticci, they are made wider and longer and are called *tapparedd.* Still in the Vulture area, *lagana chiapputa* is served for

Christmas with soft bread crumbs fried with oil, sugar, and chopped walnuts. The differences are sometimes minimal and can be about the type of sauce: at Maschito, they put tomato sauce on the *lagane,* and at Barile they add anchovies, in an ancient mix of sour and sweet.

At Satriano di Lucania, Muro Lucano, Piperno, Bragiano, and Bella, special *lagane* cooked in goat's milk are made. At Brindisi Montagna, these flat noodles are about 2 inches (5 cm) long and are usually cooked with legumes or in broth. But on Saint Joseph's feast day, they are served with the characteristic bread crumbs, and on Ascension Day, they are cooked in milk. In Calabria, *lagane* and *ciciri* are prepared for All Souls' Day, November 2.

127. LAGANE INCANNULATE

Pasta lunga

INGREDIENTS: Durum-wheat flour, salt, and water.

HOW MADE: The flour is sifted with a pinch of salt onto a wooden board and kneaded for a long time with water until a firm, smooth dough forms. The dough is left to rest, then rolled out into a sheet, not too thin, and *fettuccine* about ⅜ inch (1 cm) wide are cut from it. They are rolled in a spiral on a round stick or tube about ⅜ inch (1 cm) in diameter, then slid off the tube and left to dry. They are boiled in plenty of salted water.

ALSO KNOWN AS: *Sagne incannulate* and *lasagne arrotolate.*

HOW SERVED: As *pastasciutta,* with traditional local sauces.

WHERE FOUND: Puglia.

REMARKS: Extensively picked up by the pasta industry and sometimes marketed under the old name of *fusilli* (see entry), this type of pasta, which requires great skill to make, used to be made by the girls in orphanages. The *lagane incannulate* made in the two orphanages in Foggia, the Orfane and the Maddalena, were particularly celebrated, and were also sold in neighboring Abruzzo. The preparation of the pasta was almost the only work that supported these pious institutions.

128. LAIANELLE

Pasta ripiena

INGREDIENTS: Durum-wheat flour, eggs, and salt. For the filling, sheep's milk ricotta, pepper, and nutmeg.

HOW MADE: The flour is sifted onto a wooden board and kneaded long and vigorously with eggs and a pinch of salt. The dough is left to rest, then rolled out into a very thin sheet, from which large squares are cut. A spoonful of filling is placed on each square, and the square is folded into a triangle and the edges carefully sealed. The *laianelle* are cooked, a few at a time, in lightly boiling salted water.

ALSO KNOWN AS: *Laganelle.*

HOW SERVED: As *pastasciutta,* with typical lamb *ragù.*

WHERE FOUND: Molise, specialty of Monteroduni and Montorio nei Frentani.

REMARKS: The pasta is named for the rolling pin with which it was made. In many parts of Molise, a rolling pin was called a *laganature* or *laianature,* from the Latin *laganum.*

129. LASAGNA
Various shapes

INGREDIENTS: For homemade, type 0 or 00 wheat flour and eggs; formerly, also just flour and water. In the south, durum-wheat flour and water. For factory made, durum-wheat flour and water, but also soft-wheat flour and eggs.

HOW MADE: The flour is sifted, combined with eggs or just water, and kneaded for a long time until a firm, smooth dough forms. The dough is left to rest, then rolled out into a relatively thin sheet from which various shapes are cut, according to the local custom. In Friuli–Venezia Giulia, the dough is wrapped in a damp dish towel and left to rest for a day before it is rolled out. The shape of factory-made versions varies from producer to producer. *Lasagne* are boiled in plenty of salted water, sauced, and baked.

ALSO KNOWN AS: In the Veneto, factory-made *lasagne* are called *bardele* or *lasagnoni.* In Liguria, a similar shape is often called *cappellasci.* In the Salento, *sagne;* and elsewhere in Puglia, *lagana.* The factory-made *lasagna* with ruffled edge is called *lasagna riccia* or *doppio festone,* but also *sciabò* or *sciablò.* The narrower *lasagne* are known as *mezze lasagne, mezze lasagne ricche,* and so on.

HOW SERVED: As *pastasciutta,* generally in a *timballo,* with traditional local sauces, but also in broth.

WHERE FOUND: Widespread.

REMARKS: The term *lasagna* is applied to one of the earliest Italian pastas. Its form, yesterday as today, varies from place to place, and ranges from a square of pasta to a wide noodle.

The word *lasagna* seems to derive from the Latin *lasanum,* or "kitchen pot," from the Greek *lasanon,* meaning "tripod" or "kitchen pot." *Lasanea* was probably what was cooked in the pot. We find a first occurrence of the term *lasagna* in vulgate in the *Memoriali bolognesi*, notarial documents important for the evidence they have left us of early written Italian: the notaries used to fill the spaces of the pages left blank with Latin *sententiae*, prose excerpts, or vernacular poems. And often there are cooking notes. The document, in the notarial archive of Bologna, bears the date 1282:

> *Giernosen le comadre trambedue a la festa,*
> *de gliocch'e de lasagne se fén sette menestra;*
> *e disse l'un a l'altra: "Non foss'altra tempesta,*
> *ch'eo non vollesse tessere, mai ordir né filare."*

Lasagna is, however, the protagonist in many medieval texts, including the famous verses of Jacopone da Todi:

> *Chi guarda a maggioranza spesse volte s'inganna: granel di pepe vince per virtù*
> *lasagna.*

> [He who looks at the majority is often deceived; a peppercorn beats *lasagna* for virtue.]

We do not know with certainty what pasta shape the medieval term referred to. The shape itself probably derives from the early *gnocco*, which evolved into a relatively thin form of *focaccia* that was boiled, fried, or cooked on a heated stone, as in ancient Rome.

An important testimony on the shape is found in the fourteenth-century *Liber de coquina:*[126]

> *De lasanis: ad lasanas, accipe pastam fermentatam et fac tortellum ita tenuem sicut poteris. Deinde diuide eum per partes quadratas ad quantitatem trium digitorum. Postea, habeas aquam bullientem salsatam, et pone ibi ad coquendum predictas lasanas. Et quando erunt fortiter decocte, accipe caseum grattatum. (III-10)*

> [On *lasanae:* take fermented dough and make a little cake as thin as you can. Then divide it in four parts of three fingers. Then have boiling salted water, and put the *lasanae* in it to cook. And when they are well cooked, add grated cheese.]

The centuries and local habits have altered the shapes and composition of the dough. For example, many regions abandoned the use of eggs. Elsewhere, water was added to the eggs for reasons of economy. The flour varied at different times and places, too. Nowadays, *lasagna* is made with wheat flour, but other flours were used in the past, such as emmer, rye, chestnut, and, from the end of the eighteenth century, corn. Other ingredients, such as saffron, spinach, or chard, were added for color.

In the principality of Trento, in the sixteenth century, wide, flat noodles cut with a toothed pastry wheel and fried were codified under the term *lasagne*.[127] Reserved for feast days, the Trento dish, composed of noodles arranged in layers with much and varied filling and sauce, was heated from above and below to form a crust, or, for those who had an oven, baked. Beginning in the 1800s, baked *lasagne* began to appear at important luncheons, especially in the south, where the dish spread more quickly. Pasta in general was supplied to the court of Naples, under Murat,[128] in the form of *"pasta fine, vermicelli, maccaroni, lasagne,* pastas of Cagliari, different pastas," and the custom continued on the tables of the Bourbons when they returned to the capital. Not by chance, the father of Francesco II, the last king of Naples, nicknamed him Lasa, from *lasagna,* for his passion for this particular type of pasta.

Today, *lasagne al forno* are typical of many regions, and both the filling and the shape vary. The cooking times vary, too, depending on whether the pasta is fresh or factory made. The most recent tradition calls for the *lasagna* to be rigorously rectangular and thin, though for some preparations a square cut is used. A long, narrow type is called *lasagna a nastro* or *pappardella.*

The most famous *lasagne* are the *bolognesi,* now available every day in almost every restaurant in Bologna, which has certainly not helped their image. For the dish to be any good, the pasta must not be store-bought, which is too thick and insipid. Instead, the dough must be homemade, rich in eggs, and rolled out paper-thin. Found in all the Italian regions, this *sfoglia* occupies a special place of honor in Emilia, and at home its preparation was once a true ritual. Until a few decades ago, the interpreters of this tradition were the *sfogline,* professionals who made such typical dishes as *lasagne, tagliatelle,* and *tortellini,* and who made the paper-thin sheets of pasta before their clients at home or in restaurants. But, with the advent of factory-made fresh pastas, this venerable craft is becoming rarer and rarer. Another essential ingredient is true Bolognese *ragù,* often manhandled by modern gastronomy. The béchamel—or *balsamella,* as the good Artusi renamed it—must be used sparingly, the time in the oven must be brief, because it serves only to bind the flavors, and the final product must be soft. Only then is the textbook dish obtained. Naturally, there are many variants: Some cooks add a porcini sauce between the layers of pasta, some add the béchamel only for the last layer, and still others alternate yellow and green pasta. There are even meatless *lasagne,* made only with béchamel and mushroom sauce. But these are small traditional variants and do not detract from the pleasure of bringing a fancy baroque dish to the table.

The journalist Paolo Monelli, in 1934, wrote in the *Gazzetta del popolo,* referring to the already famous *lasagne alla bolognese:*

> I have read books sacred and profane, I have sought certainties and consolations in a thousand volumes, but no book is worth this volume of *lasagne . . .* which the salacious Bolognese *osti* serve. Between the pages is a sticky resin of cheese, and a blink of truffles, teeming with precious giblets. Skim it, devour its pages: it is a little *Decameron,* a handbook of philosophy, a consoling poem that makes us happy to be alive.

This seems rather like the description of *"lagana cum caseo"* given by Salimbene da Parma in his *Cronica* (vol. II, 803).

Today, every Italian region has its *lasagne:* In the Dolomites, in the Valle del Biois, *lasagne da fornèl,* baked with apples, are served on Christmas Eve. In the Marche, already at the end of the 1800s, the anonymous author of *Il cuoco perfetto marchigiano* describes a *timballo di lasagne* and truffles worth pausing over. The author says that in the bottom of the pan, in place of the usual condiment, was a layer of "truffles with their butter." Does this mean the custom of preserving truffles in butter was already in use? It is possible.

The regional terms for this type of pasta are numerous: In Trieste, *lasagne* are normal *tagliatelle* and are often served with a *pesto* of sugar, butter, and poppy seeds, which resembles the Danubian *Möhnnudeln.* In Liguria, *lasagne tordellate* are small squares of egg pasta sauced like a normal *pastasciutta,* with *ragù* and chard. In Tuscany, they are *pappardelle,* but also pasta squares, and in Chiusi they are *pannicelli.* In Umbria, they have a bit of truffle. In Campania, dry pasta is preferred for *lasagna.* In Basilicata they are made with flour and water, and the filling consists of *ricotta salata,* mozzarella, *capocollo,* and tiny meatballs.

In general, in the south, the old term *lagane* is still used. In Basilicata and in Calabria, they are called *sagne,* too, a term also found in Abruzzo and in Lazio, in the province of Rieti, to indicate simple noodles or pasta squares, with the latter also known as *fregnacce* (see entry). In Molise, the *lasagna* is a strip of pasta about 3 inches (7.5 cm) wide, which is eaten in broth and which, especially in Riccia, is served at the *pranzo del consolo.*[129] The Calabrian stuffed *sagne,* called *sagne chjne* (see entry), often have a filling of meat, hard-boiled eggs, peas, and artichokes, and everything flavored with mushrooms from the Sila.[130]

In Sicily, *lasagne ricche* are wide *pappardelle* with curly edges, which at Caltanissetta are served with deep-fried broccoli. Around Palermo, where they are both smooth like normal *tagliatelle* and ruffled, the *lasagne* are traditional on Christmas Day, with a rich *ragù* and the special local ricotta. Also around Palermo, *lasagni cacati* are a delicious dish for New Year's; their unappetizing name refers to the large quantity of ricotta dropped from above, before the *lasagna* is put in the oven. An old Sicilian saying goes: *Lasagni cacati e vinu a cannata, bon sangu fannu pri tutta l'annata* (*Lasagne cacati* and plenty of wine make good blood for the whole year). But note: the broad *lasagne* with the wavy edge that are prepared for New Year's could not be made at home. *Lasagni d'arbitriu,* that is, made with a *torchio,* were purchased from the *pastaio.* Before the pasta was assembled and baked, the *lasagne* had to be boiled carefully because to tear them would bring bad luck. Around Modica and Ragusa, these *lasagne* were also served at weddings. In the area around Enna, *lasagne ricche,* again with *ragù,* are redolent of cinnamon and are slightly sweet. Ricotta is often used instead of the normal grated cheese.

In Sicily, the term *lasagna* is also associated with the old world of farmwork: *li lasagni* were cooked in a legume soup, or with tomato and *ricotta salata,* and consumed in front of the hut or in the courtyard of the farmhouse after the day's work. A *culaziuni,* one of the meals eaten by workers in the fields, was four *once*[131] of pasta and legumes, with the addition of wild greens. During harvesttime, seven meals were eaten,[132] one every two hours, with six of them consumed in the fields. They were (1) *muzzicani* (*boccone,* "mouthful"), a mouthful of bread at sunup; (2) *agghia* (garlic), bread with roasted garlic, cheese, and olives; (3) *a culaziuni* (for *colazione,* or "lunch"), which could be a salad of tomatoes, onion, cucumbers, and lettuce, instead of pasta; (4) *menzujuornu o suppa,* soup of cabbage or eggplant with *taglierini* or *cavatu;* (5) *mirenna* (*merenda,* "snack"), similar to (3); and (6) *arrifriscu* (for *rinfresco,* "refreshment"), a little snack. Then, finally, (7) *li lasagna* was eaten back at the house.

Every time the workers stopped to eat, at a signal from the foreman, there arose almost simultaneously from all the fields a long, melancholy chant of thanksgiving for the food: *Sia lodatu e ringraziatu, lu santissimu divinissimu Sacramentu* (May the most holy and divine sacrament be praised and thanked). Each man sang with his right hand open and raised toward heaven. The slow dirge echoed from one parcel of land to another, and those simple souls were thus sure their thanks could be heard in Paradise.

130. LASAGNE BASTARDE

Pasta corta

INGREDIENTS: Wheat flour, chestnut flour, salt, and water.

HOW MADE: The flours are sifted together with a pinch of salt onto a wooden board and kneaded with water for a long time until a firm, smooth dough forms. The dough is left to rest, then rolled out into a sheet, and 3-inch (7.5-cm) squares or lozenges are cut. The proportion of chestnut flour varies from 25 percent to 50 or 60 percent, according to the area. There is also a factory-made version. *Lasagne bastarde* are boiled in plenty of salted water, then baked.

ALSO KNOWN AS: *Lasagne matte* (crazy). In Lunigiana, *armelette.*

HOW SERVED: The boiled *lasagne* are layered in a baking dish with local ingredients, usually *lardo,* leeks, and tomato, with a grating of cow's milk cheese. In the Lunigiana, they are served with the classic *pesto alla genovese,* or with good local olive oil and pecorino cheese.

WHERE FOUND: Tuscany, in particular the Lunigiana area in the province of Massa Carrara.

REMARKS: Literally "bastard *lasagne,*" they take their name from their reliance on lesser flours, such as chestnut, the use of which helped to save on costly wheat flour, a luxury in rural homes. The woods of the Lunigiana have for centuries been an immense chestnut grove, and it seems that it was none other than Matilde di Canossa[133] who promoted the cultivation of chestnut trees in the region. Since then, the chestnut has fed generations, especially in the areas of greatest demographic pressure, and is still the main ingredient in many typical local products. Among them are the *panigacci*[134] of the Garfagnana, which attest the exchange in the past between the grain-producing valley areas and the chestnut-rich hill or mountain zones.

131. LENZOLERE E CUSCENERE

Pasta corta

INGREDIENTS: Durum-wheat flour, salt, and egg whites.

HOW MADE: The flour is sifted onto a wooden board and kneaded long and vigorously with a pinch of salt and egg whites. When the dough is firm and smooth, it is left to rest briefly, then rolled out into a thickish sheet, from which strips are cut crosswise at odd angles to create "sheets" *(lenzuola)* and "pillows" *(cuscini)*. The pasta is boiled in salted water.

ALSO KNOWN AS: No alternative names.

HOW SERVED: Generally as *pastasciutta,* with simple tomato-and-basil sauces.

WHERE FOUND: Molise, typical of Castelbottaccio.

REMARKS: The name means literally "sheets and pillows." Nothing was ever wasted in a household. This pasta was made when egg whites were left over from another recipe. Its white color—unlike the golden hue of pasta made with whole eggs—called to mind the pure white of bed linens.

132. LOMBRICHELLI

Pasta lunga

INGREDIENTS: Wheat flour, water, salt, and sometimes an egg.

HOW MADE: The flour is sifted onto a wooden board and kneaded for a long time with water and a pinch of salt. When the dough is firm and smooth, it is rubbed with oil and left to rest. Pieces of dough are then pinched off and hand rolled into thick *spaghetti* 8 to 10 inches (20 to 25 cm) long. These are air dried before being boiled in salted water.

ALSO KNOWN AS: In the province of Viterbo, *lombrichi* in Tuscania, Tarquinia, Canino, and Gradoli; *ghighi* in Bagnaia; *pici* in Viterbo; *pisciarelli* in Bagnoregio; *visciarelli* in Orte; *cechi* in Capranica; *torcolacci* in Tessennano; *brigoli* in Carbognano;

bighi in Acquapendente, San Lorenzo Nuovo, and Latera; *lilleri* in Grotte di Castro; *culitonni* in Vignanello; *schifulati* in Bomarzo; *filarelli* in Marta; and *tortorelli* elsewhere in the province.

HOW SERVED: As *pastasciutta,* with a simple sauce of tomato, garlic, oil, and chili.

WHERE FOUND: Lazio, in the province of Viterbo.

REMARKS: The name means literally "earthworms." This is the most common type of pasta in the Tuscia[135] area, as evidenced by its many names around Viterbo. In addition to being accompanied by the typical sauce, they are often served *all'amatriciana* or with a richer meat *ragù.*

133. LORIGHITTA

Pasta corta

INGREDIENTS: Durum-wheat flour, salt, water, and today eggs.

HOW MADE: Durum-wheat flour is sifted with a pinch of salt onto a wooden board and kneaded with water for a long time until a smooth, firm dough forms. The dough is left to rest, then pieces are pinched off and rolled into long *spaghetti.* Each piece is wrapped twice around three fingers of the right hand (index, middle, and ring), then the top is split and, with a rapid movement similar to winding a watch, the two cut strings are joined between the index finger and the thumb in such a way that the strings twist and take the shape of an elongated ring. The pasta is left to dry for three days in a special basket, then boiled in abundant salted water. The addition of eggs to the dough is a recent variation.

ALSO KNOWN AS: No alternative names.

HOW SERVED: As *pastasciutta,* generally with a simple tomato sauce or with *ragù* of *galletto* (young cock).

WHERE FOUND: Sardinia, only in the township of Morgongiori.

REMARKS: This unusual pasta is listed in the national registry of traditional food products.[136] It used to be made only for All Saints' Day, but today *sa lorighitta* are made year-round. Production, however, is very limited because the preparation is extremely time-consuming and the durum-wheat flour used in the dough is now hard to find.

The name refers to the shape of a long ring known as a *loriga* in Sardinian, from the Latin *lorum,* the leather ring placed under the yoke of oxen. *Lorighittes* are the vine tendrils whose coils resemble a row of rings.

134. LUMACHE

Pasta corta

INGREDIENTS: Durum-wheat flour and water.

HOW MADE: Factory made in the shape of small elbows, smooth or ridged. They are boiled in abundant salted water.

ALSO KNOWN AS: Smaller types are *chifferini, chiocciolette, lumachelle,* and *lumachine* (snails); *pipe* and *pipette* (pipes); and *cirillini, genovesini, gomitini* (elbows), *gozzini, tofarelle,* and *tortini.* The larger types are *chiocciole, lumache grandi* and *lumache medie,* and *lumaconi* (all words for snails).

HOW SERVED: Generally as *pastasciutta;* the smallest ones also in broth.

WHERE FOUND: Widespread.

REMARKS: The name means literally "snails." Allusions to the tiny animals of the garden and field are not rare in pasta shapes. The *lumachine* in the area of La Scheggia, in Umbria, are sauced with trout and are typical for Christmas Eve. The larger size, similar to *conchiglie* (see entry), is common especially in the south, where it goes well with the flavorful local *ragù;* they are often stuffed and finished in the oven.

135. LUMACHELLE

Pasta corta

INGREDIENTS: Wheat flour, eggs, and spices such as cinnamon and the grated rind of lemon that has not been sprayed with preservatives or wax.

HOW MADE: The flour is sifted and kneaded long and vigorously with eggs, sometimes also with cinnamon and grated lemon rind, until the dough is smooth and firm. The dough is left to rest, then rolled out into a sheet, not too thin, which is cut into ribbons about ⅜ inch (1 cm) wide. These ribbons are wrapped around a stick ½ to ¾ inch (12 mm to 2 cm) in diameter and sealed in a ring, and the rest of the noodle is cut away. The operation is repeated two or three times until the noodle is used up. The pasta rings are then rolled on a *pettine,* which gives them their characteristic striation. The stick is given a sharp rap with the hand and the pasta is slid off. The rings are boiled in plenty of salted water.

ALSO KNOWN AS: In Umbria, *lumachine.*

HOW SERVED: Often in hearty soups, especially a traditional one of cabbage and sausage.

WHERE FOUND: The Marche, especially the province of Pesaro and Urbino; also in Umbria.

REMARKS: Popular legend has it that *lumachelle,* literally "little snails," originated at the ducal court of Urbino[137] and were carried outside the palace by the duke's kitchen servants. But it was also, for a long time, a specialty of the convents of the Poor Clares and Benedictine nuns scattered throughout the Marche.

Lumachelle are typical of Urbania, the old Castel Durante, where the Montefeltro court went to hunt, but they can also be tasted in all the towns that look on the Metauro valley. A curious variant is found in Sassoferrato, where a *maccheroncino* called *con le battecche* (sticks) consists of a short ribbon of pasta wrapped around a *battecca,* a willow-wood stick the size of a pencil, then rolled over a typical comb, leaving the impression of the wires on the pasta.

The smaller size is found in neighboring Umbria. It is served with a tasty sauce of trout and truffles in the town of Scheggino. Around Gubbio, *lumachelle,* drawn across a *pettine* to make the classic ridges, are cooked in broth.

136. LUNAS

Pasta corta

INGREDIENTS: Durum-wheat flour, natural yeast, water, salt, and saffron.

HOW MADE: Raised bread dough is kneaded a second time with saffron to color it yellow. Very thin disks, about 4 inches (10 cm) in diameter, are formed by hand. *Lunas* are fried and then sauced.

ALSO KNOWN AS: No alternative names.

HOW SERVED: Fried, then served with tomato sauce and local pecorino.

WHERE FOUND: Sardinia.

REMARKS: The name means literally "moons." Round like a full moon, these delicate disks of dough are made by an ancient technique, like the Roman *tracta* described by Apicius, *"tres orbiculos tractae siccas et confringis, et partibus in lac submissis . . . ,"*[138] and still seen today in different regional preparations (see *volarelle*). In fact, the practice of frying, boiling, or cooking on stone a sort of thin *focaccia* runs through the history of Italian food to modern times. Even today, flour-and-water preparations that are not true pastas but are served like pasta are still found in many parts of Italy. Examples include *testaroli* (see entry), *tigelle, crescentine, piadine,* and—why not?—pizza with tomato sauce.

137. LUNGHETT

Pasta lunga

INGREDIENTS: Wheat flour and water.

HOW MADE: The flour is sifted onto a wooden board and kneaded long and vigorously with water. The dough is left to rest, then rolled out into a thick sheet, from which noodles are cut. Each noodle is then rubbed between floured hands to form a sort of *spaghetto*. The *lunghett* are boiled in salted water.

ALSO KNOWN AS: No alternative names.

HOW SERVED: As *pastasciutta*, traditionally served with oil and homemade cheese. After the 1930s, also with tomato sauce.

WHERE FOUND: Romagna.

REMARKS: The name means literally "longies." This peasant pasta was typically made in winter, in times when people were poor and eggs were hard to find in the cold months. Today, older people still recall *lunghett* served *in bianco;* the tomato version came much later. Children in the countryside liked the pasta very much, and for this reason there was an amusing variant: the *lunghett* were served with oil and sugar, but naturally only by the better-off peasants, who could afford the luxury of sugar for a childish caprice.

138. MACCARRUNI
Various shapes

INGREDIENTS: Durum-wheat flour and water, but can also be made with other flours.

HOW MADE: Fresh pasta made with a *torchio,* in various sizes and shapes depending on the die used. Produced with artisanal machines before the advent of the pasta industry. The pasta is boiled in plenty of salted water.

ALSO KNOWN AS: *Maccarrune 'e casa, maccarruni d'a zita,* and *paste d'arbitriu.*

HOW SERVED: As *pastasciutta,* with traditional local sauces, most commonly pork *ragù.*

WHERE FOUND: Calabria and Sicily.

REMARKS: In Sicily, *maccarruni* should be written with a capital M, as they were once synonymous with prosperity, achieved or only dreamed of by generations of rich and poor. They were made on a *sbria,* a wooden board supported by two trestles, and the durum-wheat flour was sifted several times to obtain a very fine flour, today known as *semola rimacinata,* or "twice-ground flour."

Maccarruni were served in *pasticcio* on the tables of Il Gattopardo, were present in homes on feast days, and were on the daily menus of taverns. At Bravasco, near Palermo, a tavern frequented by the abbot Meli and later also by Giuseppe Pitré,[139] everyone knew that *"lu garzuni cridava come un mattu: li maccarruna a due grana lu piattu"* (the waiter yelled like a lunatic: macaroni at two coins a plate). And at the end of the 1800s, it was a truly reasonable price.

In any manual on classic Sicilian cooking, the section on *pasticci di maccarruni* occupies a significant number of pages. The recipes describe dishes that vary according to the feast days for which they were made and according to the nature of their crusts. For example, the crust could be of bread, as in *pastizzu di Natali,* a specialty of Noto, or of sweet pasta, which concealed a filling of fish and wild *finocchietto* and was made in Palermo for the feast of Saint Joseph. There are also a *pastizzu di sustanza,* which we should not talk about since it contains no pasta at all—it was all a fragrant filling of various well-seasoned meats—and the modern *timballo di anelletti* (see entry for *anelletti*), which was enriched with eggplant and was slipped into picnic baskets for eating at the beach until the 1950s.

Many feasts have grain as a direct or indirect protagonist, yet we read in the 1676 *Maestranze dei cuochi e pasticceri di Palermo,* housed in the Palermo city archive, that making or selling "things of pasta" on the street to celebrate both the feast days of the patron saints Martha and Lawrence and Easter was prohibited. Also, popular tradition called for invoking Saints Philip and James on May 1 to protect the flour from cockroaches: on that day, *"non si abburatta"* (flour is not worked) because the pasta would go bad. And then from grain, beliefs whose roots lie in pre-Christian superstitions evolve into behaviors, which is why a local proverb warns that *la zita majulina nun si godi la curtina*—"the May bride doesn't enjoy the party." In other words, it is bad luck to marry in May. Grain is also the protagonist on June 2, the feast of the Madonna delle Grazie, a day on which the first sheaves of the harvest are tied in a bunch as an offering to the Virgin, to ensure abundance and grain of good quality.

But *maccarruni* were also the protagonists of the feasts themselves. Carnival lasted three days—Sunday, Monday, and Tuesday—to give the shepherds, far from their families tending their flocks, time to travel the long road home to sit at the table before a steaming dish of *maccarruni ca sasizza* (pasta with sausage).

In the ancient *contea* of Modica, *maccarruni di sdirrimarti* were served at the last meal at midnight before the beginning of Lent. Around Messina at Easter, farmers and sharecroppers presented the landlord with one of the three annual tributes (the other two were for Christmas and for their patron saint): homemade pasta and bread, cheeses, ricotta, eggs, and chickens. In return, the landlord gave them a real egg covered with sweet almond paste; *cuddura d'ovu* and *pupa cu l'ovu*, two sweets containing whole eggs; and so-called pasta *d'arbitrio*, that is, made with a *torchio*. Meat and some coins were added.

In Sicily, *maccarruni* are fresh pastas of various shapes made at home, but they were formerly also made by small commercial pasta makers equipped with an *ingegno*. Official documents, such as the registry of patents, classify these operations as "manufacturers of *maccheroni* with machine and warehouse," and they were distributed in all the island's towns.

Pitré, in his *Usi, costumi, credenze e pregiudizi del popolo siciliano*,[140] repeating the terms given in the *Vocabolario siciliano-italiano* of G. Perez,[141] makes a census of the various types of pastas in use on the island at the end of the 1800s, with a succinct description of the most important shapes. Many of these are surely pastas *d'ingegno*, that is, not strictly homemade:

> paste *d'arbitriu*, made with the *strettoio*;[142] *gnocculi; maccarunedda 'mpanati; turciunateddi; spizzieddu; attupateddi* or *maltagliati*, thick pasta cut short; *cannizzolu*, or *maccherone* as thick as a middle finger; *capiddi d'anciru; cavatuni*, or thick, wide rings, *campanelle; fidillini*, that is, *fedelini, vermicelli; filatu*, which are *vermicelli; filatu cu lu pirtusu*, or *vermicelli bucati; ganghi di vecchia*, or *pasta rotonda, ricurva*, ridged, *denti di cavallo; gnocculi*, that is, *cavatelli; jiritaledda*, similar to *vermicelli bucati*, made with the *torchio* and cut as they come out; *avemaria*, the largest are *patrinostri; lasagni*, that is, *lasagne; lingua di passaru* (sparrow tongue), like flat grains of rice; *punte d'ago* (needle points) used in soups; *maccarruncinu*, or *bucatino*, thinner than those of Naples; *maccaruni*, that is, *maccarruni napoletani; magghietti* or *maccaruni napoletani*, cut as they

come out of the *torchio*, a little curved, *gambe di donna* (woman's legs); *oricchi di judeu* (Jew's ears), that is, large *cavatello; pirticunedda*, a *pastina*-like shot, for soup; *sciabbò* or *scibbò, lasagne* wide and coiled, *pappardelle; spaghettu*, that is, *spaghetti; spizzieddu*, a round, tiny *pastina; stidduzzi*, small stars for soup; *tagghiarini*, or *tagliolini*, narrow *lasagne; tria bastarda*, a long pasta, thicker than *capellini; vampaciuscia, lasagne strette* (narrow); *virmiceddi*, in general, long, round, and thin pastas; *zitu* and *maccarruni d'a zitu*, or large *maccherone*, smaller than the *cannizzolu*.

In the province of Siracusa, in Modica to be exact, home to the greatest concentration of pasta production, Pitré continues, they also made:

ciazzisi, ciazzisuotti, maccarruna ô 'usu, maccarrunedda di zita, scivulietti, cavatieddi, gnucchitti, lasagni, taccuna, pizzulatieddi, 'ncucciatieddi, melinfanti, filatieddi, gnuocculi, pasta rattedda, vrimicieddii, alica, and very many others.

In Calabria, *maccarruni d'a zita*, but also *tagghiarelli* with mutton *ragù*, were always served at wedding luncheons. In the place of honor sat *a donna* and *lu patriu*, the parents of the bride; to the bride's right sat the best man, and at the lavish lunch was served the wine bottled at the birth of the bride. The long meal ended in the evening with distribution of *confetti*,[143] harquebus shots fired in the air, and music from the *organetto*. This tradition was still alive in the 1950s.[144]

139. MACCHERONCINI DI CAMPOFILONE

Pasta lunga

INGREDIENTS: Formerly wheat flour, today durum-wheat flour and egg yolks, but also whole eggs.

HOW MADE: The flour is sifted and then kneaded long and vigorously with yolks or whole eggs until a very firm, smooth dough forms. It is left to rest, then rolled out into a very thin sheet, and extremely thin *tagliolini* are cut from it. They are boiled in plenty of salted water, more than doubling their volume when cooked.

ALSO KNOWN AS: *Capellini di Campofilone* and *maccarini* (Ancona).

HOW SERVED: As *pastasciutta*, generally with various excellent meat *ragù*, but today with any number of sauces.

WHERE FOUND: The Marche, in Campofilone and surrounding areas.

REMARKS: How long these thin egg *tagliolini* have been made in the Marche is unknown. But town statutes of the Marca of Ancona from the fourteenth century do document particular attention to the quality of the wheats and their grinding, to the rigorous hygienic regulations for the mills, and to the careful checks the government authorities made daily.[145] This type of pasta is not yet mentioned; some centuries had to pass before the people of Ancona, in the 1600s, were able to enjoy a pasta whose bright yellow color came from the many eggs it contained, or from the use of saffron, which was far less costly than eggs. In the seventeenth-century price lists of Ancona, the significantly lower cost of the pastas is emphasized this way: *vermicelli* made with the device cost 11 *quattrini* the *libbra,* but if colored with saffron, they could be purchased for 9; the same difference is found for *maccheroni* and *taglierini,* which could cost 5 or 7 *bajocchi* (coins), depending on whether they contained saffron.[146]

Certainly, in times much nearer our own, in the period during and between the two world wars, these *maccheroncini* colored golden with eggs were being made in small-scale workshops and then packaged in cardboard boxes by the artisans. The boxes were loaded onto trains or buses, which carried them to cities, such as Rome, where the pasta was beginning to be appreciated. At first type 0 wheat flour was used for the dough, and only later the finer type 00 flour. For each kilo (2.2 pounds) of flour, 10 eggs, weighing about 55 grams (2 ounces) each, were used. The dough was left to rest for three hours, then it was rolled out by hand into a thin sheet with a rolling pin. The sheet was cut with a knife into fine *tagliolini,* which were lifted on the back of the knife and combed with fingers to separate the pieces, the most delicate operation in the preparation of the pasta. The *tagliolini* were then left to dry in a room heated by a terra-cotta stove.

Today, HACCP[147] no longer allows these archaic methods, and the small artisanal producers are equipped with machines and dryers. But the procedures used are more or less those of long ago. In the small shops around Campofilone, women can still be seen at work preparing *maccheroncini.* They use top-quality durum wheat and twice as many eggs, which means the producers can market *maccheroncini* only a millimeter (1/32 inch) thick. Further, according to the University of Ancona, the addition of sunflower oil to the diet of the chickens means the eggs are enriched significantly with vitamin E and omega-3 fats. That means the eggs give the *maccheroncini di Campofilone* excellent nutritional properties.

Thanks to its high protein content and superb taste, this pasta, with its particularly intense aroma and extraordinary texture, is considered one of the best fresh egg pastas in Italy, even though its national distribution dates only to the 1980s and 1990s.

140. MACCHERONE

Various shapes

INGREDIENTS: For homemade, soft- or durum-wheat flour, water, and often eggs and other ingredients. For factory made, durum-wheat flour and water or eggs.

HOW MADE: Generic term for various types of pasta, both fresh and dry, which are boiled in abundant salted water or in broth.

ALSO KNOWN AS: No alternative names.

HOW SERVED: As *pastasciutta* or in broth, depending on size.

WHERE FOUND: Widespread.

REMARKS: The story of *maccherone* on the Italian peninsula has followed tortuous paths that have not yet been fully charted. Today, the term generically indicates a dry pasta of various sizes made with durum-wheat flour and water. But in the south, the word *maccheroni* is used for some types of fresh pasta and, even more often, for any dry pasta, long or short, from *penne* or *spaghetti* to *bucatini*. In the north, once dominated by rice and polenta, the word *maccheroni* is the name of a specific type of pasta, usually tubular, short, and curvilinear, like *conchiglie* (see entry).

Numerous dictionaries of the Italian language confirm that the word *maccherone* (the singular) means pasta in general, not a specific shape. In mid-nineteenth-century Naples, Carena's dictionary[148] defines *maccherone* the southern way, as a long, flat pasta, like *bavette* or *pappardelle* (see entries). This is probably the meaning attributed by commercial documents of the same period: in 1838, Naples exported 48,600 kilograms (about 107,000 pounds) of *maccheroni*,[149] described as long, string-shaped pasta. Even today, in the very modern Garzanti dictionary,[150] long, narrow pasta is the first meaning.

The etymology of the word is uncertain. Popular theory explains it with a punning anecdote. A stingy sovereign, presented with a bowl of pasta and the cook's expenses, complained, *"molto buoni ma . . . caroni"* (very good but quite expensive). More scholarly is the origin proposed by some Hellenists, for whom *maccheroni* means "beatifiers of the palate" (*macarios* in the language of Homer means "blessed," and not for nothing was the name *macaria,* in the 1500s, given to the watery soup served at funerals). Maccus was, however, also the name of a stock character, a clown, in the Atellan farces of ancient Campania, who evolved into the Macco mask of the commedia dell'arte. And it is precisely with the meaning of stupid that Giuseppe Prezzolini records[151] the first mention of the word *maccherone* in a document dated 1041, from Cava dei Tirreni, in Campania. The meaning continues into such early dictionaries as the *Nuovo Vocabolario, ossia raccolta di vocaboli italiani e latini,*[152] where we read two meanings: a "kind of pasta" and a "silly man." But how could a silly soup beatify the palate?

A simpler source of the origin can be sought in the verb *ammaccare,* "to strike with force," which also makes it no coincidence that a fava-bean purée of Puglia is called *macco.*

In medieval documents, the word indicates generically both what we today call *gnocco* (see entry) and various types of dry pasta. The well-known 1279 inventory of the belongings of Ponzio Bastone (page 106) records *"una barixella plena de macharoni"* (a barrel full of macaroni), and probably any sort of dry pasta is meant.

The *maccheroni* mentioned by Boccaccio,[153] on the other hand, were probably fresh:

> . . . a *contrada* named Bengodi,[154] where the vines are tied up with sausages . . . and there was a mountain of grated parmigiano cheese, on top of which were people who did nothing but make *maccheroni* and *ravioli* and cook them in capon broth and then they threw them down, and whoever gathered the most, got to keep the most.[155]

They were eaten as soon as they were made, exactly like *gnocchi*—but what except *gnocchi* could Boccaccio's *maccheroni* have been? And here is Folengo's famous paraphrase (*Baldus* I, 48 / 51):[156]

> . . . *solicitant altrae [nymphae] teneros componete gnoccos*
> *qui per formaium rigolant in frotta tridatum*
> *seque revoltantes de zuffo montis abassum*
> *deventant veluti grosso ventramine buttae.*

> [. . . other nymphs are busy making soft *gnocchi* that roll down higgledy-piggledy into the grated cheese and from the top of the mountain go tumbling ever down until they are as fat as potbellied barrels.]

It is worth pointing out that in both works, the *maccherone* falls on the cheese, not the reverse. And so, it seems, it was for the whole of the sixteenth century, according to Giordano Bruno.[157]

The polymorphism of the *maccherone* is confirmed in 1577 by Costanzo Felici, from Piobbico in the Marche, who, in his *Lettera sulle insalate*,[158] enumerates, in praise of the good wheat, "*lasagne, macaroni de più sorte, tagliatelli, vermicelli, granetti, lassagnate sottili.*" The nomenclatural orgy explodes with Tommaso Garzoni:

> . . . *polente, gnocchi, maccheroni, lasagne, tagliatelle, vermicelli, sfogliate di più sorti, mantecate, tortelletti, ritortelli, truffoli, ravioli senza spoglia o con spoglia, cascose, casatelle, morselli, pasta tedesca, stelle, guanti, torte, reticelle, pasta finta, mariconda, pastadelle, castelletti, frittelle, levatelli.*[159]

And perhaps it was exactly this multiple meaning, sign of an irrepressible fantasy, that suggested the baptism of the singular poetic vein dubbed *maccheronica*, whose major exponent was Teofilo Folengo.

The cookbooks also attest to this polymorphism: we begin with Messisbugo, who explains in his *Banchetti compositioni di vivande, et apparecchio generale*[160] that *maccheroni* are large flour-and-water *gnocchi* rolled across the back of a grater. But he then distinguishes *maccheroni alla napoletana*, which are *spaghetti* cut from a thickish sheet, from the Roman variety, which are finger-width *tagliatelle*, rather fat and short. Platina[161] says something similar. For him, *minestra alla romana* consists of finger-width *tagliatelle*, but when he speaks of *minestra siciliana*, he specifies *spaghetti* that are thin straws and pierced their entire length with an iron stylus, an operation that we consider impossible even for the expert hands of a high-ranking *scalco*. But here Platina has misinterpreted his *maestro*, Martino da Como, who, in his *Libro de arte coquinaria*,[162] written in the mid-1400s, says the following under *maccaroni siciliani*: "Take very fine flour and knead it with egg white . . . ordinary water . . . make this dough hard, then make it into little sticks a palm long and thin as a straw. And take a wire a palm long, or longer, and thin as a string, place it on top of the above-mentioned stick [of dough], and give it a turn with the hands on a board. Then remove the wire and pull off the *maccherone* pierced in the middle."[163]

That was exactly how *fusilli* have always been made, and still are today. For *maccheroni romaneschi*, Martino speaks of a fine sheet, not too thin, which is wrapped around a stick and cut "as wide as a small finger," that is, like a thin, modern Roman *fettuccina*.

A commonplace traces the geographic origin of *maccheroni* to Naples. On the trail of the philosopher Benedetto Croce and of the play *La vedova* by Giovambattista Cini (1569), Emilio Sereni[164] has, however, documented that as late as the second half of the 1500s, the epithet *mangiamaccheroni*, "macaroni eaters" (so reminiscent of the *macaroni* with which the French have long mocked the Italians), was used by a Neapolitan for a Sicilian, who, answering him in rhyme, accused him of being a *mangiafoglia*, "leaf eater." But the Neapolitan would not be a *mangiafoglia* for long. The economic crisis brought by the Spanish induced the Neapolitans to abandon the *pignato maritato*, a broth containing a great many leaves and a few pieces of meat, for *maccheroni* and the consumption of carbohydrates.[165]

On the Sicilian paternity of *maccheroni*—homage to al-Idrisi[166]—not even Ortensio Lando had any doubt. In his *Commentario delle più notabili et mostruose cose d'Italia*,[167] he confessed, "Truly I am greatly envious of you because in a month, if the winds do not fail you, you will reach the rich island of Sicily, and you will eat those *macheroni*, which have taken their *name from beatifying*." Naples began to be associated with *maccheroni* in the 1600s, but this did not necessarily apply to the rest of the south, which was too poor to be able to afford anything so luxurious.

La Statistica del Regno di Napoli,[168] drafted in 1811, cites *maccheroni* rarely and only with reference to Basilicata, where, it says, "extensive use is made of *maccheroni*, which the people either make themselves or buy from the town *maccaronaro*." In other words, pasta was still reserved for feasts and feast days in Naples. But in reality, in the populous capital of the kingdom, pasta was common among the better-off classes by the middle of the 1600s.

Finally, Gioacchino Rossini—who considered himself a second-rate musician but the greatest cook in the world—bragged of his own *"maccheroni"* when he lived in Passy: they were actually *bucatini*, which he filled with goose liver using a special silver-handled syringe that he had made for the purpose by a Parisian silversmith.

141. MACCHERONI ALLA CHITARRA

Pasta lunga

INGREDIENTS: Durum-wheat flour and eggs and sometimes water.

HOW MADE: The flour is sifted and kneaded with eggs for a long time. Depending on the type of pasta desired, water may be added. When the dough is firm and smooth, it is covered and left to rest. It is then rolled out into a sheet, not too thin, which is laid on a special stringed instrument called a *chitarra* (guitar). Under the uniform pressure of a rolling pin, the strings cut the pasta to make the famous *maccheroni*, which are a sort of square *spaghetti* about 12 inches (30 cm) long. They are boiled in salted water.

ALSO KNOWN AS: *Caratelle; tonnarelli* in Lazio; *crioli* in Molise; *stringhetti* in the Marche.

HOW SERVED: As *pastasciutta*, traditionally with mutton *ragù*, but today also with other sauces.

WHERE FOUND: Lazio; Abruzzo, especially around Scanno; upper Molise; the Marche; and Puglia.

REMARKS: The *chitarra* consists of a wooden frame (beech or other neutral wood) strung with parallel steel wires. The space between the wires varies according to the type of pasta desired. For *maccheroni tutt'ova*, fine as angel's hair, the wires are

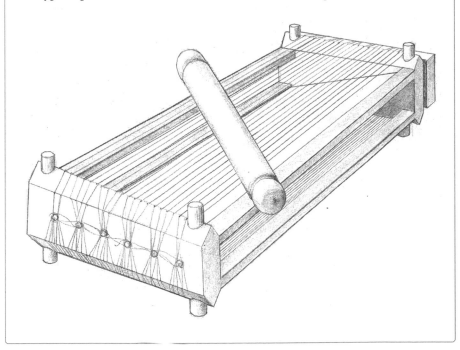

closer together. For *maccheroni mezz'ovo,* which are thicker, the wires are spaced farther apart.

The artisans of Secinaro and Pretoro, in the provinces of L'Aquila and Chieti, were specialists in making this utensil. Its ancestor is *lu rentrocelo,* which was once used around Pescara and L'Aquila.

Today, *maccheroni alla chitarra,* also called *tonnarelli,* are universally associated with Abruzzese and Molisan gastronomy and marketed both fresh and dry.

142. MACCHERONI ALLA PECORARA

Pasta corta

INGREDIENTS: Wheat flour, eggs, and water.

HOW MADE: The flour is sifted and kneaded long and strenuously with eggs and water until a smooth, firm dough forms. The dough is then shaped into thin strings, which are pressed closed in rings about 2 inches (5 cm) in diameter. The rings are boiled in salted water.

ALSO KNOWN AS: No alternative names.

HOW SERVED: As *pastasciutta,* with mutton *ragù,* but also with vegetable-based sauces, and always with a final dusting of local pecorino. A sauce of pancetta, eggs, and cheese is also common.

WHERE FOUND: Abruzzo.

REMARKS: Sheep are omnipresent in the gastronomy of Abruzzo, land of pastures and of transhumance. Flavorful sheep's milk cheeses are always on hand for the pasta.

The sauce of pancetta, cheese, and eggs was typical of the *carbonai,* "charcoal workers," who stayed in the mountains—the Apennines of central Italy—for long periods making charcoal. Eggs, cheese, and pancetta kept well and could be carried easily on mule back, together with dry homemade pasta. Today, this preparation, now called *alla carbonara,* has circled the globe.

143. MACCHERONI CON LU CEPPE
Pasta lunga

INGREDIENTS: Durum-wheat flour, eggs, oil, and water. At one time, no eggs were used.

HOW MADE: The flour is sifted, combined with eggs, oil, and water, and kneaded for a long time. When the dough is firm and smooth, it is covered and left to rest. It is then rolled out with a rolling pin into a sheet, not too thin, and cut into strips about ⅝ inch (1.5 cm) wide and about 6 inches (15 cm) long. These strips are wound around a smooth, thin stick to make thick *bucatini*. They are boiled in plenty of salted water.

ALSO KNOWN AS: *Ciufulitti;* at Magliano dei Marsi, *torcinelli.*

HOW SERVED: As *pastasciutta,* generally with hearty meat *ragù.*

WHERE FOUND: Abruzzo, a specialty of Civitella del Tronto.

REMARKS: The term *ceppe* indicates the wooden stick used for making this pasta. In its absence, women used a number 4 sock-knitting needle or a knitting needle without the head. The sock needle is still used in all regions where similar pastas are made. But in reality, each housewife uses, in addition to the *ferretto* found in every house, less practical pieces of wood shaped for the purpose called *ceppe,* or reeds like *busa* in Sardinia and in Sicily. Even the ribs of an old umbrella can be used, the custom of the Arbëreshë.

144. MACCHERONI DI CIACCIO
Pasta corta

INGREDIENTS: Wheat flour, chestnut flour, salt, eggs, oil, and water.

HOW MADE: The flours are sifted together with a pinch of salt and kneaded long and vigorously with a few eggs, a spoonful of oil, and water until a firm, smooth dough forms. The dough is left to rest, then rolled out into a thin sheet and rhombuses about 1¼ inches (3 cm) long are cut from it. They are boiled in plenty of salted water.

ALSO KNOWN AS: No alternative names.

HOW SERVED: As *pastasciutta,* with hearty meat *ragù.*

WHERE FOUND: Tuscany, in particular Upper Versilia and around Lucca.

REMARKS: The economy of the Upper Versilia and part of the province of Lucca has long revolved around the chestnut. The main towns involved in the processing of the chestnuts used to be Cardoso, Capezzano Monte, and Camaiore, where, toward the end of summer, the *rimondatura* took place, the cleaning of the ground beneath the venerable chestnut trees to facilitate the harvest of the precious fruits. The *ruspa*, or free gathering of the chestnuts, is documented in a statute of 1553 in the community of Farnocchia, which stated that no person of said town or living in it must go *"a ruspare per le selve che sono in sul comunale né su quello di particolari persone per insino a Sant'Andrea,"* that is, they could not go to the woods and gather chestnuts before September 30.

Maccheroni di ciaccio are similar to the *lasagne bastarde* (see entry) made in the Lunigiana, on the border with Liguria.

145. MAFALDE

Pasta lunga

INGREDIENTS: Durum-wheat flour and water.

HOW MADE: Factory-made ribbons with one or both edges curled. They are boiled in abundant salted water.

ALSO KNOWN AS: *Mafaldine, signorine, trinette, ricciarelle,* and *sfresatine.*

HOW SERVED: Generally as *pastasciutta,* with traditional local sauces.

WHERE FOUND: Widespread.

REMARKS: The name means literally "[Princess] Mafalda." At the beginning of the twentieth century, a small group of pastas was dedicated to the House of Savoy, the new monarchs of Italy. Thus, we have *regine,* "queens," and their diminutives, *reginelle* and *reginette,* but also *mafalde* and *mafaldine.* The latter shape could have been produced for the first time in 1902, birth year of Princess Mafalda, daughter of Victor Emanuel III, who was then on the throne.

Signorine (young ladies), *trinette, ricciarelle,* and *sfresatine* (curlies) are the same type of shape.

146. MALFATTINI

Pasta corta

INGREDIENTS: Wheat flour and eggs.

HOW MADE: The flour is sifted, combined with eggs, and kneaded for a long time. When the dough is firm and smooth, it is covered and left to rest. Then pieces of dough are pinched off and rolled on a wooden board into a small salami shape. These are cut into thick slices, which are in turn cut up into small, irregular pieces. They are boiled in broth or salted water.

ALSO KNOWN AS: *Manfrigne*. In Lombardy, they are *gnocchetti verdi* (flour, spinach, and ricotta).

HOW SERVED: In broth, traditionally in soup with beans, but also as *pastasciutta*. In the Marche, in a typical soup of lentils and pork rinds. In Lombardy, *gnocchetti* are served with melted butter.

WHERE FOUND: Lombardy, Emilia-Romagna, and the Marche.

REMARKS: Hemp was once the main crop in some areas of Romagna. Harvest-time brought many young arms to the fields, and in the moments of rest from the heavy labor, loves and friendships blossomed. At the end of the workday, everyone sat around a rustic table for the restorative meal, which was accompanied by lively popular songs and easy-drinking wine. The menu included *malfattini*, with a *ragù* with peas (see also *manfricoli*). Peas generally begin to mature in May, and the hemp was cut at the end of August, so we can assume the peas had been picked and dried, or preserved in a salt brine. The work of the hemp then passed to the able *cordai*, who braided and twisted the fibers into sturdy ropes and twines.

147. MALLOREDDUS

Pasta corta

INGREDIENTS: Durum-wheat flour, saffron, water, and salt, and formerly also barley flour.

HOW MADE: The flour, sifted with saffron and a pinch of salt, is kneaded with water into a firm, smooth dough, which is left to rest. Small pieces of dough are pinched off and rolled with hands into ropes as thick as a pencil. These are cut at intervals of about ¾ inch (2 cm) into *gnocchetti,* which are flattened with the pad of the thumb against the bottom of a wicker basket called a *ciurili.* The final shape is like a little shell with ridges on the back. There is also a type of factory-made *malloreddus,* usually without saffron. The pasta is boiled in abundant salted water.

ALSO KNOWN AS: In the Logudoro area, *macarones caidos,* and around Nuoro, *macarones cravaos.* One variation, made with barley *(orzo),* is called *maccarronis de orgiu.* Factory-made versions are *gnocchetti sardi.*

HOW SERVED: Generally as *pastasciutta,* with hearty sauces based on meats or sausage and finished with a dusting of local pecorino. But also with light sauces of fresh tomato and basil.

WHERE FOUND: Sardinia, especially in the Campidano and Logudoro. The factory-made shape is generally common throughout Italy.

REMARKS: The term *malleolus* was already used in Latin for a type of *gnocco.* In the Sardinian language, it is preserved in the diminutive *malloreddu,* literally, "small *gnocco.*" The present-day term *malloreddus* also means "calves" or "young bulls."

    Malloreddus can rightly be considered the Sardinian dish par excellence. The *Triticum durum* grown in Sardinia since Roman times is still today considered the best wheat for pasta. The pasta is found throughout the island and is also factory made. At Tempio Pausania, a more closed *gnocchetto* is made called *chiusone,* which used to be rolled on glass with embedded wire and one grainy surface, on the back of a grater, or, the best method, in the bottom of an asphodel basket.

The practice of coloring pasta with saffron is very old; it turned the pale flour-and-water dough golden, as though it were rich in eggs, a heritage of the centuries in which food was decorated with real gold. Almost all the saffron grown in Sardinia is concentrated around the small town of San Gavino Monreale, but it is used throughout the island for pasta and also for the preparation of liquors and traditional sweets. In many towns, for All Souls' Day, November 2, the ritual food is saffron yellow *maccheroni* with a *ragù* of meat cut into small pieces.

The raising of sheep, still widespread today on the island, has profoundly affected the local cooking. For example, precious pecorino is melted in a bain-marie and poured over the *gnocchi* for *malloreddus a casu furriau*, and *malloreddus a mazza frissa* are served with a sauce of dairy cream. *Maccarronis de orgiu* (*maccheroni d'orzo*, "of barley") were traditionally served simply with a dusting of grated sheep's milk *ricotta secca*. And the same recipe varies from area to area, with the flavor of the pecorino varying from pasture to pasture.

Maccheroni, food for feasts, play an important role in weddings: At Ollolai, the engagement luncheon is customarily held in the home of the future groom, and traditionally the fiancée would have to bring *maccheroni* she had made herself. According to the ritual, the evening of the feast, the bride-to-be, wearing the typical costume and exquisite filigree jewelry, would cross the town carrying a large basket of *maccheroni* in her arms, followed by her parents and closest relatives. When she reached her fiancé's house, she was warmly welcomed at the door by numerous rifle shots into the air, and then during dinner, the betrothed couple would eat from the same plate. The same *maccheroni* would appear at the wedding lunch, when they were also made for all the town poor.

148. MALTAGLIATI

Pasta corta

INGREDIENTS: Wheat flour and eggs, or sometimes flour and water. In Lombardy, some parmigiano is added. In Carnia (Friuli), buckwheat and butter; in some areas of the Marche, only fine bran.

HOW MADE: The flour is sifted and kneaded long and vigorously with eggs or just with water. The dough is left to rest, then rolled out with a rolling pin into a sheet, not too thin, and irregular lozenge shapes of variable size are cut from it.

The *maltagliati* of Puglia begin as a very thin pasta sheet, which is cut into long strips 1½ or 2½ inches (4 or 6 cm) wide. These strips are then cut on the short side into small, flat noodles. Both shapes are boiled in plenty of salted water or in broth.

ALSO KNOWN AS: *Malmaritati*. In Friuli–Venezia Giulia—in particular in the Carnia area, at Prato Carnico, Treppo, and Ovaro—they are called *blecs* (see entry). In the Valtellina, tiny *maltagliati* are called *pizzocherini*. In Mantova, they are known as *straciamus (spruzzamusi)*. In Liguria, they are *martaliai*, but in eastern Liguria, the part known as the Riviera del Levante, they are *preagge*. In Emilia-Romagna, they are *bagnamusi, sguazzabarbuz,* and *malintaià,* and in the Marche, *strengozze*. In Lazio, in Camerata Nuova, irregular rhombuses of pasta are called *sagne 'mpezze*. In Puglia, rhombus-shaped *pizzelle* are made.

HOW SERVED: In broth or as *pastasciutta*. In the Veneto, they are used in *pasta e fasioi (fagioli,* in Italian); in Puglia, they are served with chickpeas; in Emilia-Romagna, they are flavored with *lardo* and *conserva;* and in a typical recipe of the Marche, they are served with a duck sauce.

WHERE FOUND: Throughout Italy, but especially in Lombardy, the Veneto, Emilia-Romagna, the Marche, and Puglia.

REMARKS: The name means literally "badly cut." Dough rolled out into a sheet is the first pasta shape of which we have a record: from the *tracta* of ancient Rome, which were cut or torn and then fried or cooked on a hot stone and drizzled with honey. This sheet, or *sfoglia,* of pasta has traveled a long path down the centuries, variously enriched with eggs, made thinner, made thicker, cut and sectioned in myriad shapes, up to our own day.

Irregularly shaped *maltagliati* were once made from the odd bits of *sfoglia* left over after *tagliatelle* were cut. They could even be large enough to earn the nickname *spruzzamusi* (face sprayers) because of the consequence of eating them too enthusiastically in soup. The tiny *maltagliati* of the Valtellina are made from the dough used for *pizzoccheri* (see entry) and are called *pizzoccherini,* and the Ligurian *martaliai* often have cheese in the dough. In Piedmont, small lozenge-shaped *lasagnette,* called *foglie di salice* (willow leaves), are used especially in bean soup. In Emilia-Romagna, they are usually the result of making a series of irregular cuts on a pasta sheet: cut straight, on the bias, at odd angles—these little pieces are true *mal tagliati,* "badly cut." In Tuscany, especially Arezzo, they are made by rekneading the cuttings left over from making *ravioli*. Traditionally, they were arranged in layers in individual bowls and served with only oil and pecorino.

149. MANATE

Pasta lunga

INGREDIENTS: Durum-wheat flour, salt, and water, and today also eggs, oil, or lard.

HOW MADE: The flour is sifted with a pinch of salt onto a wooden board and kneaded long and vigorously until a firm, smooth dough forms. The dough is left to rest, then divided into little loaves whose size depends on the housewife's skill and strength. A hole is made in the center of each loaf and, with oiled hands, the loaf is pulled and stretched into a long loop—as long as the length of the maker's arms permits. The loop is folded over twice to form a sort of skein of four threads, which is folded again and again, with the threads of pasta becoming thinner and thinner. They are dusted with flour from a sieve every so often to keep them from sticking. The skein is then opened and cut at two equally spaced points to make *spaghetti*, which are separated, dusted with flour, and left to dry. They are boiled in plenty of salted water.

ALSO KNOWN AS: *Manatelle, manare,* and *tratti.* In Abruzzo, they are called *maccheroni alla molenara.*

HOW SERVED: As *pastasciutta*, with traditional local sauces.

WHERE FOUND: Abruzzo and Basilicata, where they are typical of Potenza, especially around Vaglio di Basilicata.

REMARKS: This very unusual pasta, whose method of preparation somewhat resembles that of the *shtridhëlat* (see entry) of the Arbëreshë community of San Paolo Albanese, used to be made in the flour mills. It was tedious work, and only the strong arms of the millers managed to make skeins of very thin threads. In fact, it survives only in Vaglio di Basilicata, where it reportedly originated. The sauce, also used for other homemade pastas, is a meat *ragù* with *'ntruppicc,* a finely diced mix of lamb and pork. At the table, diners add their own crumbled chili or a drop of *santo* (olive oil in which hot chili has macerated).

   In Abruzzo, this pasta has been known since the Middle Ages, having been introduced, according to local tradition, in the twelfth century by the soldiers following Roger the Norman, in conquest of the region.

150. MANDILI 'NVERSOI

Pasta ripiena

INGREDIENTS: Durum-wheat flour, water, and salt. For the filling, sausage, sweet-breads, chard or borage, and cheese.

HOW MADE: The flour is sifted onto a wooden board and kneaded long and vigorously with water and salt until a firm, smooth dough forms. The dough is left to rest, then rolled out into a sheet, and small squares of pasta of unspecified size are cut from it. A spoonful of filling is placed on each square, which is folded in half or into a triangle, and the edges are sealed. They are boiled in plenty of salted water.

ALSO KNOWN AS: No alternative names.

HOW SERVED: As *pastasciutta,* with traditional local sauces.

WHERE FOUND: Piedmont, in the province of Alessandria, toward Liguria.

REMARKS: The name means literally "reversed handkerchiefs." This tasty stuffed pasta, documented in the vast hilly area of the province of Alessandria that looks south toward Liguria, has almost disappeared today. It takes its name from an old Ligurian pasta, *mandilli de sea* (see entry), meaning "silk handkerchiefs." In the popular imagination, these small squares of pasta, stuffed like a *tortello* (see entry), are small silk handkerchiefs, reversed, folded in two, and closed.

151. MANDILLI DE SEA

Unusual shape

INGREDIENTS: Wheat flour, salt, eggs, and lukewarm water.

HOW MADE: The flour is sifted with a pinch of salt and kneaded long and vigorously with eggs and with a little lukewarm water, to increase the yield. When the dough is firm and smooth, it is left to rest, then rolled out with a rolling pin into a very thin sheet. The sheet is cut into 6-inch (15-cm) squares, which are boiled briefly in salted water.

ALSO KNOWN AS: No alternative names.

HOW SERVED: As *pastasciutta,* with the classic Ligurian pesto.

WHERE FOUND: Liguria.

REMARKS: The Ligurian dialect term for this pasta translates as "silk handkerchiefs," which emphasizes how thin, almost transparent, the pasta must be. Curiously, Piedmont also invokes silk for a rather less delicate specialty of the Valli Valdesi, namely, *batsoà,* from the French *bas de soie,* or "silk stocking." The dish consists of pig's feet, first boiled and then coated with a thin veil of dry bread crumbs or flour and deep-fried. The result is crisp on the outside and tender on the inside. Extreme thinness traditionally characterized the dishes of Italian kitchens in close contact with the sophisticated cuisine of France. Indeed, in the Renaissance, the *capelli d'angelo* were of a thinness almost unachievable today, and the *tortellini* were the size of a chickpea. In fact, the more difficult a dish was to make, the more it matched the ideals of perfection of the cooks of Italy's great houses—cooks in whose kitchens arrived the echoes, not even too faint, of the Renaissance philosophy of life.

152. MANEGHI

Pasta corta

INGREDIENTS: Flour, bread, eggs, milk, almond paste, and raisins.

HOW MADE: The flour is sifted onto a wooden board and kneaded with the bread, which has been moistened with milk, eggs, almond paste, and raisins. Walnut-sized *gnocchi* are formed, though sometimes they are rolled into sticks. They are boiled in salted water.

ALSO KNOWN AS: *Strangolapreti*.

HOW SERVED: As *pastasciutta*, with butter and grated cheese.

WHERE FOUND: The Veneto, in the province of Padova in particular.

REMARKS: This dish was served for the vigils of holy days during fall and winter. In the Polesine, the part of the Veneto at the mouth of the Po, it is traditional to serve *maneghi* with butter, sugar, and cinnamon, a custom inherited from the aristocracy's abundant use of sweeteners and spices during the Renaissance.

153. MANFRICOLI

Pastina

INGREDIENTS: Durum-wheat flour, but also soft-wheat flour, eggs, and water.

HOW MADE: The flour is sifted and then kneaded with eggs and water for a long time until a firm, smooth dough forms. The dough is left to rest, before it is rolled out into a sheet about $\frac{1}{16}$ (2 mm) thick. Then, before it dries, the sheet is rolled around a rolling pin and cut from one end to the other with a very sharp knife into a number of wide strips. These strips are then cut again into thin strips 1 to 2 inches (2.5 to 5 cm) long and about $\frac{1}{16}$ inch (2 mm) wide, or the same thickness as the sheet, which means they come out square. But the process differs from area to area. For example, in Emilia-Romagna, *manfricoli* resemble *passatelli* (see entry). They are boiled in plenty of salted water or in broth.

ALSO KNOWN AS: In Emilia-Romagna, *battutini* and *manfrigul;* in the Marche, *pencenelle, pincinelle,* and *pingiarelle;* in Tuscany, *manifregoli.* In northern Lazio, *picchiettini* and, specifically in Viterbo, *manfrigoli.*

HOW SERVED: In broth or as *pastasciutta,* with traditional local condiments. In Emilia, they are served with *conserva* and *lardo,* or sometimes with beans.

WHERE FOUND: Central and northern Italy, including Liguria; Emilia-Romagna, in particular around Forlì; the Marche; Tuscany; Umbria; and Lazio.

REMARKS: The term is ancient, from the Latin *manus* and *fricare,* and in Italian is *sfregare,* or "knead." We find it cited as *manfrigo* in the *Libro de arte coquinaria* of Maestro Martino, who catalogs it as a pasta for soup, made with grated stale bread, eggs, and *"farina bella"*—what today we would call *fior di farina,* the top grade of flour. The great cook's precise description would not be out of place in a modern recipe book.

The 1811 Napoleonic inquest on customs and traditions of the Kingdom of Italy gives us an account of a custom in Romagna, especially Forlì: relatives and friends gathered at the home of the deceased, after accompanying the coffin to the cemetery, to consume the so-called lunch of the dead, which was *manfrigoli.* But the deceased had to be an adult: no *manfrigoli* was served if a child died.

In Emilia, it was the main ingredient of a poor peasant soup: In winter, the housewife, *arzdora* in dialect, made this simple, quick *pastina* with only flour and water; there were no eggs because the hens do not lay in the cold months. The hard dough was then beaten and minced with a knife, or it was grated on a large-holed grater (see also *pasta grattata*). The cooking required great attention because, without eggs, if the pasta is not perfectly dried, it comes apart in the boiling water. It had to be drained quickly for it to stay al dente. When possible, it was enriched with beans.

In the province of Forlì, *manfrigul* also used to have cheese, spices, or lemon rind in the dough, and the broth in which it was cooked was made with "tired pork bones," meaning previously used. This description says a great deal about the extreme poverty of the peasant table. *Piadine* left over from the previous day were also added to the soup.

In other regions, the category *manfricoli* covers similar pastas made with varying techniques. In the Marche, they are *pingiarelle* (see entry), *pencenelle* in the area of Cupramontana, and *pincinelle* in Sassoferrato, but with different ingredients. In Tuscany, particularly in Versilia, *manifregoli* are a *polentina* of chestnut flour served with cold milk, and in the area bordering Umbria, they keep the shape of short, square *spaghetti.* In Umbria, *manfricoli* are actually *bringoli* (see entry), which are eaten especially in Orvieto.

154. MARICONDA

Pastina

INGREDIENTS: Wheat flour, parmigiano, eggs, and spices.

HOW MADE: The flour is sifted onto a wooden board and kneaded with parmigiano, eggs, and nutmeg. The dough is kneaded for a long time, then wrapped in a napkin, tied on the edges, and cooked in broth for a couple of hours, with the cooking time varying according to the size of the packet. The wrapped dough is allowed to cool, then the napkin is removed and the dough is cut into tiny dice, which will be served in broth.

ALSO KNOWN AS: No alternative names.

HOW SERVED: In meat broth.

WHERE FOUND: Emilia-Romagna.

REMARKS: *Mariconda* is a modification of the classic Mantuan *mariconda*, which is broth in which *gnocchetti* made of stale bread, parmigiano, and eggs are cooked. The Emilian *mariconda* resembles the preparation used in *zuppa reale*, a tasty dish served for feasts and holidays. At important meals, it was served first, to open the stomach for the subsequent succulent dishes.

The term, probably of Spanish derivation, indicates a mixture of cheese and eggs that could be sliced and fried, but that could also be used as stuffing for different preparations. It is in this sense we find it as *mariconda alla Ragonesa* in Messisbugo.[169]

155. MARUBINI

Pasta ripiena

INGREDIENTS: Wheat flour and eggs. For the filling, beef *stracotto,* roast veal, pork-bone marrow, formerly brains, parmigiano, and seasonings. Some versions call for *salame cremonese.*

HOW MADE: The flour is sifted onto a wooden board and kneaded long and vigorously with eggs until a firm, smooth dough forms. After resting, the dough is rolled out with a rolling pin into a thin sheet, and a toothed pasta cutter is used to cut out disks about 1½ inches (4 cm) in diameter. A generous mound of filling is placed in the center of half the disks. A second disk is placed on top, and the edges are carefully sealed. *Marubini* are usually cooked in broth.

ALSO KNOWN AS: *Maroon, maroubeen, marubiin,* and *marubieen.*

HOW SERVED: In broth, typically of various meats, but especially capon or hen, beef, and sometimes *salame da pentola.*

WHERE FOUND: Lombardy, typical of Cremona.

REMARKS: *Marubini* are a common feast-day dish, when a good *bollito* is traditionally served. The latter provides the broth in which the *ravioli* are cooked: a broth of various meats with the addition of a particular *salamella,* in Cremona known as the "three *brodi.*"

These very old *ravioli* also appear in Platina with an almost modern recipe.[170] The term could derive from the word *marù,* which means *castagna,* "chestnut," in the Cremonese dialect, perhaps in reference to the quantity of filling, which must be abundant, like the chestnut in its shell.

Local tradition gives this pasta an important role at a historic meal to which the captain of adventure Cabrino Fondulo, having become lord of Cremona, invited even the antipope John XXIII and the emperor Sigismond of Luxemburg. The year was 1414, and during the lavish banquet, these tasty *marubini* are said to have been served.[171] But returning to our own day, it is important to point out that, in 2000, the region of Lombardy added *marubini* to its list of traditional agrofood products to be safeguarded. In this list, the *marubino* appears not only in the traditional round form but also as a square and as a half-moon, which is how it is still made in the countryside.

156. MATASSE

Pasta lunga

INGREDIENTS: Durum-wheat flour and water, or durum-wheat flour and eggs.

HOW MADE: Factory-made dry *tagliatelle* (see entry), rolled up to form small *matasse,* or "skeins." They are sold in different widths and boiled in broth or abundant salted water.

ALSO KNOWN AS: *Nidi* (nests).

HOW SERVED: The thinnest are cooked in broth, the rest as *pastasciutta.*

WHERE FOUND: Widespread.

REMARKS: The name means literally "skeins." When making pasta at home was common, housewives often made noodles, both with eggs and with just flour and water to dry and store. In the south, after the pasta was cut and partially dried, the noodles were rolled into a *matassa* measured with an inverted *caffelatte* cup. They were then dried completely in the air and kept in the pantry.

Industry has exploited this type of packaging. By the beginning of the twentieth century, special machines were being used to wind up different shapes of pasta, such as *fidelini fini, spaghetti, vermicelli, fettuccine, capelli d'angelo,* and so on.

157. MENIETTI

Pastina

INGREDIENTS: Wheat flour and milk and oil, in equal parts.

HOW MADE: The flour is sifted into a large bowl. It is sprinkled first with oil and then with milk and at the same time is stirred with a fork until tiny lumps form. The mixture is sifted onto a wooden board to separate the lumps from the flour. The lumps are then laid out in a single layer to keep them from sticking together and are picked up a few at a time with the moistened palm of one hand. The tiny pieces of dough are rubbed between the palms into tiny rolls of pasta.

ALSO KNOWN AS: No alternative names.

HOW SERVED: Generally in vegetable soups (squash, leeks, potatoes, and the like).

WHERE FOUND: Liguria, especially typical of the Riviera di Ponente.

REMARKS: *Menietti* are similar to *cuscus* (see entry) except that they are rubbed between the hands to make tiny rolls instead of balls. The shape and rapidity of cooking must have been one of the compelling reasons why *cuscus,* under different names, spread through all Italian regions. But it was only its size that spread, because the preparation of authentic *cuscus* required a dexterity not all home cooks possessed. Instead, each figured out how to shape these small lumps of flour in her own way. Such was the case with the *menietti* of the Riviera di Ponente (western Liguria): unaware of the correct recipe for *cuscus,* the local people invented their own, using durum-wheat flour, and turned it into a delicate pasta for soup.

158. MENUZZE

Pastina

INGREDIENTS: Durum-wheat flour and water.

HOW MADE: Leftover cuttings of factory-made pasta, which are cooked in fish broth.

ALSO KNOWN AS: *Tretarielle.*

HOW SERVED: Generally in broth, especially fish.

WHERE FOUND: Molise.

REMARKS: When it was not yet obligatory to sell pasta wrapped in sealed packages, which was as late as the 1950s, it was sold in bulk, displayed in shops in large wooden boxes. The scraps that remained in the bottom of the container were sold at greatly reduced prices. The first pasta factories had the same problem, and they sold the leftovers of broken pasta, accumulated during processing, at lower prices. In Naples, where this pasta was common, the poor called it *munnezzaglia,* "trash."

159. MESCUETILLE

Pasta corta

INGREDIENTS: Durum-wheat flour, *semola,* and water. Other flours, such as whole wheat or *grano arso,* were also often used.

HOW MADE: The flours are sifted together onto a wooden board and kneaded long and vigorously with water. After resting, the dough is rolled out into a sheet, not too thin, and ¾-inch (2-cm) squares are cut from it. These are indented with a finger, and then boiled in plenty of salted water.

ALSO KNOWN AS: *Miscuitili.*

HOW SERVED: Usually with *vincotto.*[172]

WHERE FOUND: Puglia, in particular Altamura and Monteparano.

REMARKS: The use of whole-wheat and other dark flours was once very common in Puglia. In fact, in areas of extreme poverty, it was not uncommon even to use *grano arso.* These dark flours were ground from various cereals and legumes, such as barley and fava beans, and were often used with wheat flour for making bread as well as pasta.

The use of *vincotto* was reserved for ritual foods, and, in fact, *mescuetille* were prepared this way for the feast of Saint Joseph, March 19.

160. MIGNACULIS

Pastina

INGREDIENTS: Wheat flour, salt, and water.

HOW MADE: The flour is sifted with a little salt into a bowl. Enough water is added to make a batter, which is left to rest. The batter is dripped or poured from a spoon into simmering bean soup. It cooks quickly.

ALSO KNOWN AS: No alternative names.

HOW SERVED: In a typical bean soup.

WHERE FOUND: Friuli–Venezia Giulia, especially in the Carnia area.

REMARKS: The soup known as *fasui e mignaculis* is the pride of Friuli's gastronomy. It is dense with beans and potatoes, and thickened further with a flour-and-water batter. In the Carnia area, the irregular shapes of the cooked batter are called poetically *lis paveis,* or "butterflies." The soup is simple to make and only the final step is tricky: the irregular pasta that takes shape as the batter is added to the soup cooks almost immediately, but must form small lumps, not large masses.

161. MILLEFANTI

Pastina

INGREDIENTS: Durum-wheat flour, water, salt, and oil, or only durum-wheat flour and water.

HOW MADE: The technique varies according to place of production. In Abruzzo, the flour is sifted onto a wooden board and kneaded long and vigorously with water, a pinch of salt, and a little oil to produce a hard, firm dough. The dough is left to rest, then rolled into a thin sheet, and flat noodles about ⅝ inch (1.5 cm) wide are cut from it. Once the noodles are dried, they are broken into irregular lengths, or cut into uniform pieces ¾ or 1¾ inches (2 or 4.5 cm) long.

In Puglia, the pasta sheet is cut into very thin noodles, from which tiny pieces of pasta the size of a grain of rice are torn. In Sicily, they are tiny lumps of pasta.

Depending on the region, *millefanti* are cooked in broth or in abundant boiling salted water.

ALSO KNOWN AS: *Cettafanti, malefante, millafanti, millinfranti,* and *'mbilembande,* but also *tridde* or *triddhi.* In the Veneto, *menafanti, menai,* and *malafanti.* In Sicily, *melifanti* and *millefante.*

HOW SERVED: As *pastasciutta* or in broth, in general with a bean-based condiment. In northern Molise, bell peppers and tomato are added to the beans. In Puglia, they are always cooked in broth.

WHERE FOUND: Molise; Puglia, especially around Lecce, in Alessano; and Sicily.

REMARKS: The root word may derive from the Greek *milefatos*, which means "minced" or "ground." G. Alessio[173] constructs a long etymology of this term: from the Late Latin *bonifatus* to the Tuscan *manifatoli* to the *bonifatoli/tali* of Siena and Arezzo, the *melinfante* of Taranto, the *melifanti* or *milinfanti* of Sicily, and up to the Italian *millefanti*. The word has been greatly distorted by local dialects: we find this *pastina* in the south called *'mblband, bilbanti, melempant,* and many other almost-unpronounceable names (see *pasta grattata*).

The variations on the shape, over time and in the different production areas, are numerous: from small lumps of pasta to thin *tagliatelle,* hung to dry, then cooked in broth, to the *polentina* of the Veneto. A very old pasta type, *millefanti* even appeared in the first printed texts as a tiny shape suitable for broth.

In an early recipe book of the Kingdom of the Two Sicilies, we read: "Of such pasta, they make tiny pieces like grains of millet, or of wheat, and it is usual to make them by rubbing the pasta between the palms; they are cooked in plenty of good broth and garnished on top with parmigiano, or with *caciocavallo.*"

Artusi speaks of this *pastina* as a sort of *stracciatella* made of flour, eggs, and parmigiano, all inevitably flavored with nutmeg.

In Molise, *malefante* is combined with beans and pork rinds in a dish that can be considered a prototype of the poor peasant kitchen. Beans, the meat of the poor, and pork rind, one of the cheapest parts of the animal, supply the dish with needed protein and fats, creating an almost textbook balance of nutrients. Peasants knew nothing of this, but with the few things they had available, they learned to manage their diet wisely. Today, that same balance would be in line with the dictates of the Mediterranean cooking praised by nutritionists and dieticians.

In Puglia today, the dough is often enriched with cheese and parsley, and in Sicily, *millefanti* are made by mixing the flour with chopped parsley, salt, and pepper.

162. MINUICH

Pasta corta

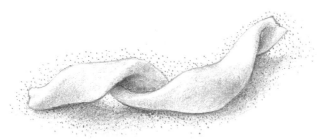

INGREDIENTS: Durum-wheat flour and water; in Puglia, *semolone*.

HOW MADE: The flour is sifted and kneaded long and vigorously with boiling water. The dough is covered and left to rest for at least a half hour. Walnut-sized pieces of dough are pinched off and rolled into sticks about 2 inches (5 cm) long. The sticks are laid on top of a square *ferretto*, pressed down, and rolled with hands on a wooden board. The small pasta coils are slid off the *ferretto* with a sharp rap of the hand and left to dry on a dish towel. They are boiled in plenty of salted water.

ALSO KNOWN AS: *Capunti, ferricieddi, fusilli,* and *minurich*. In Basilicata, in San Mauro Forte, Rotondella, and San Giorgio Lucano, they are called also *ferriciedd', frizzuli,* and *fusiedd'*; in Puglia, *ciambodre* and *mignuicchi*.

HOW SERVED: As *pastasciutta,* with various sauces, always including chili and the local pecorino.

WHERE FOUND: Puglia and Basilicata, especially around Matera.

REMARKS: Lucanian housewives are very skillful at making *minuich*: even three or four at a time on the same *ferretto*. Those who do not have a *ferretto* use knitting needles, the kind for socks or regular needles number 3.5 or 4, with the heads removed. In general, however, *minuich* or *capunti* are very small (see also *cavatelli* and *strascinati*).

The typical sauce, as usual for all Lucanian homemade pastas, is a *ragù* with *'ntruppicc,* small pieces of lamb or mutton and pork.

In Puglia, the Bari State Archive (Intendenza Prefetture) includes a registry of permits to make pasta in various towns (Bari, Terlizzi, Molfetta, Bitonto, Trani, Torritto, Triggiano, and others) during the years of the French occupation (1810–15). A look at it turns up numerous *maccheroni* factories "with device and warehouse," that is, with a sort of small factory-made production. Alongside these are found *maccheronari,* or retailers, which suggests the existence of a production sufficient to supply the commercial market.

In Basilicata, the existence of a commerce in home-style pasta is attested also by the *Statistica del Regno di Napoli,* 1811:[174] in the southern hinterland, only towns in Basilicata are listed as having, from the mid-1700s, a *maccaronaro* who makes and sells fresh pastas. He is also cited in the 1752 land register of Melfi;[175] after that year, there was a certain increase in the activity of pasta makers around Matera.

163. MISCHIGLIO

Strascinati

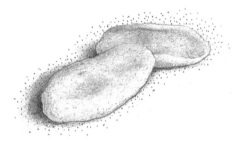

INGREDIENTS: Durum-wheat flour, barley flour, chickpea flour, fava-bean flour, and water.

HOW MADE: The flours are sifted together onto a wooden board and kneaded for a long time with water until a firm, smooth dough forms. The dough is left to rest, and then hazelnut-sized pieces of dough are pinched off and rolled with two fingers across the board to make smooth, open *strascinati* about 1¼ inches (3 cm) long and with a slightly raised edge. They are boiled in abundant salted water.

ALSO KNOWN AS: *Misckiglio* and *pasta a mischiglio.*

HOW SERVED: As *pastasciutta,* with a simple sauce of tomato, garlic, and oil to which *peperone crusco* (dried and fried bell peppers, specifically those of Senisi, in Basilicata) and *cacioricotta* are often added.

WHERE FOUND: Basilicata, in particular around the towns of Chiaromonte, Fardella, Teana, and Caldera; and in Calabria, in the area of the Pollino.

REMARKS: This pasta is already documented in the ancient county of Chiaromonte and in the marquisate of Caldera Falvella and Teana, which corresponds today to the area that includes the above-mentioned towns, by the late Renaissance. It was the pasta of the peasants who could not afford to buy much *semola,* which was quite expensive for their pockets. Instead, they added just a little to the dough, to have that modicum of gluten needed to keep it compact.

The area, at one time very depressed, made this pasta until the 1950s, when prosperity sent into oblivion anything that smacked of poverty and indigence.

But today, there is a new interest in everything that used to be locally produced. In fact, the search for old flavors has convinced one woman entrepreneur, Carmela D'Addiego, in Chiaromonte, to produce this antique pasta. It is enjoying considerable success even abroad for its delicate flavor and digestibility, which makes it almost a textbook Mediterranean-diet pasta. In fact, the water used for the dough springs from the rocks of the Caramola, which gives an added value to this excellent pasta.

The old people remember this pasta being served always with a light sauce of garlic, oil, bay leaf, tomato, and, if there was any, *cacioricotta* and the *peperoni cruschi* of the area. It must have been a very liquid sauce, because *mischiglio* was eaten with a spoon, like a soup.

164. NATALIN

Pasta corta

INGREDIENTS: Durum-wheat flour and water.

HOW MADE: Factory-made large, smooth tube, flattened, with the ends cut on the bias like *penne*. The tubes are cooked in broth.

ALSO KNOWN AS: In Genoa, *maccheroni*.

HOW SERVED: In broth, typically of tripe.

WHERE FOUND: Liguria.

REMARKS: This pasta in broth is typical for Christmas dinner and even for Christmas Eve, when many families make the broth from tripe. Pieces of sausage were often added to *natalin in to broddo* to symbolize wealth and prosperity. In eastern Liguria, along the Riviera del Levante, these *maccheroni* are dipped quickly in a batter of beaten egg, grated cheese, and marjoram, then dropped in broth. The batter fills the tube and sets in the hot broth, like a true filling.

165. 'NGRITOLI

Polenta

INGREDIENTS: Wheat flour and water.

HOW MADE: A sort of polenta made with wheat. The flour is poured, a little at a time, into boiling salted water and stirred with a wooden spoon to prevent lumps from forming. When cooked, the mixture is poured onto a wooden board and served.

ALSO KNOWN AS: No alternative names.

HOW SERVED: With garlic, oil, parsley, and mushrooms, but also with a sauce of crumbled sausage and pecorino.

WHERE FOUND: Lazio, province of Rieti (Castel di Tora).

REMARKS: The term probably derives from the fact that, even when mixed by an expert hand, the *polentina* almost inevitably forms small lumps. It was served very hot, sprinkled with the fragrant local pecorino.

This dish has almost disappeared from the Sabine tables, but at one time, it was not uncommon to hear housewives say, *"massera facemo 'i 'ngritoli"* (this evening we're having *'ngritoli*).[176]

166. OCCHI DI PASSERO

Pastina

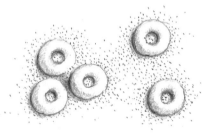

INGREDIENTS: Durum-wheat flour and water.

HOW MADE: Factory made of variable size, with a hole. They are cooked either in broth or in abundant boiling salted water.

ALSO KNOWN AS: *Occhi di elefante, occhi di giudeo, occhi di lupo rigati,* and *occhi di pernice* (eyes of elephant, Jew, wolf, and partridge, respectively).

HOW SERVED: In broth or as *pastasciutta,* depending on size.

WHERE FOUND: Widespread.

REMARKS: The name means literally "sparrow's eyes." The diameter of this round *pasta bucata* determines whether it is tiny *pastina* for broth, or a larger size for serving as *pastasciutta* or, more often, in legume soups.

A pasta shape inspired by the eye means it is generally small and round. But the size varies according to whose eyes the shape is named for. Thus, we have eyes of a wolf, partridge, sparrow, and on down to eyes of a flea and to pinpoints that can be considered eyes only under a microscope. There used to be eyes of a thief and eyes of a Jew, two shapes that today have disappeared from the catalogs. But the eyes can also be large, such as those of an elephant: in this case, the diameter is that of *cannelloni*.

167. OFFELLE

Pasta ripiena

INGREDIENTS: Wheat flour, potatoes, eggs, yeast. For the filling, meat, sausage, and spinach.

HOW MADE: The flour is kneaded with boiled, riced potatoes, eggs, and a little powdered yeast until a firm, smooth dough forms. After resting, the dough is rolled out with a rolling pin into a sheet, not too thin, and 2-inch (5-cm) squares are cut from it. A teaspoon of filling is placed on half the squares. A second square is placed on top and the edges carefully sealed. They are boiled in salted water, a few at a time.

ALSO KNOWN AS: No alternative names.

HOW SERVED: As *pastasciutta,* traditionally with melted butter and cheese *di malga.*

WHERE FOUND: Friuli–Venezia Giulia, especially Trieste.

REMARKS: The word *offa* used to mean the Roman spelt cake that was offered to the gods. Aeneas himself, when he came face to face with Cerberus at the gates to the underworld, managed to put the terrible dog to sleep by giving him an "*offa* made sleepy with honey and drugged meal."[177] The term had thus a precise meaning, a portion of food reserved for the gods. With time, the term evolved with the diminutives *offetta* and *offella,* and today the latter is the name of both a typical ring-shaped cake and a type of large *tortello* (see entry).

In general, *offelle* are sweets for Carnival, and as such are cited often in early cookbooks, as in Rossetti's valuable little book.[178]

Today, sweet *offelle* are found in many areas of central and northern Italy, such as Tuscany, Lombardy, and the Veneto. Friuli has developed this tasty and hearty *tortello* from the sweet version. But really sweet *tortelli,* especially for Carnival and sometimes also with meat *ragù,* are served in many regional cuisines as a *primo piatto.*

168. ORECCHIETTE

Pasta corta

INGREDIENTS: Durum-wheat flour, type 0 wheat flour, lukewarm water, and very often some whole-wheat flour and formerly some *grano arso*.

HOW MADE: The flours are sifted together and kneaded for a long time with lukewarm water. After the dough has rested, small pieces are pinched off and formed into cylinders as thick as a pencil. These are cut into lengths of about ⅝ inch (1.5 cm) or a bit more, according to the desired final size. Each piece is rolled across the board with a blunt knife point; around Bari, this is done with a *sferre*. Or the piece of dough is reversed on a fingertip to create the characteristic form of a small ear. The *orecchiette* are boiled in abundant salted water.

ALSO KNOWN AS: *Orecchini* in Rome, and *recchietelle* in Campania, Molise, and Basilicata. In Abruzzo and Basilicata, they are called *orecchie di prete* and *stacchiodde,* and in the area of Lagonegro in Basilicata, the wider ones are called *tapparelle*.

The different provinces of Puglia use different names. In Foggia, they are called *cicatelli* and *recchie de prevete;* in Bari, *chagghjubbi* or *fenescecchie, pestazzule, recchie, recchietedde, stagghiotte,* and *strascenate;* in Taranto, *chiancarelle* are the small ones and *pociacche* or *pochiacche* the larger ones; and in Lecce, they are called *stacchiodde*.

HOW SERVED: Generally as *pastasciutta,* with vegetables. In Puglia, this usually means the *broccolo (cime di rapa)* grown there, but also mushrooms (at Altamura) and different meat *ragù*. The dish is almost always completed with locally produced *ricotta marzolina* or *cacioricotta*.

WHERE FOUND: Central and southern Italy, in particular Puglia, especially around Bari.

REMARKS: The name means literally "little ears." The origin of *orecchiette* can possibly be traced back to the *crosets* of medieval Provence, which are about the same shape. Made in the south of France with the locally grown durum wheat, they could be dried and kept for a long time. This meant that, among other uses, they provided nutritious food for sailors on *galere.*[179] Some sources attribute their arrival in Puglia to the thirteenth-century domination of the Angevins, counts of Provence, who had dominions there.

The first mentions of this curious pasta appear in the mid-sixteenth century. The source is the Neapolitan Giambattista del Tufo, who describes them as "hollowed *strascinate* and *maccheroni* of Bari," evidence that they were already firmly established in Puglia.

The broad diffusion of *orecchiette* in Abruzzo and southern Molise is linked to the fact that, for centuries, these two regions constituted the northernmost territory of the Kingdom of Naples first, and that of the Two Sicilies later. This was especially true of Molise, which still has many border dishes. In 1891, twenty-one towns in the valley of the Fortore and in the coastal strip from Sant'Elia to Rotello and from Campomarino to Guglionesi[180] still belonged to the district of the Capitanata in Puglia, a fact that certainly also influenced the gastronomic practices of these later Molisan municipalities. Finally, there is the contribution of the agricultural laborers who migrated to the territory, especially toward the Tavoliere. The greatest numbers arrived during harvesttime, and their consequent presence in the local fairs and markets, precious places of exchange of culture and traditions, was important in the spread of all kinds of customs, not just gastronomic.

Today, this pasta is among the most typical of the south, and is common also in factory-made versions, both fresh and dry. The old wrinkled surface, well suited to gathering any type of condiment, is reproduced exactly.

In the past, the best sauce for *orecchiette* was a particular *ragù* of *castrato,* concentrated after very long cooking with lard and *odori.* Today, this pasta is the pride of the gastronomy of Puglia, and of Bari in particular, where it is served with turnip greens. But every town has its variations of both the pasta and the sauce: in Conversano, for example, *orecchiette* are made with whole-wheat flour and are served with anchovies.

This type of pasta has traditionally been made with durum-wheat flour, though often it is also made with whole-wheat flour or some *grano arso.* Indeed, the variations are numerous. Among the main ones are *pociacche,* wide, slightly flattened *orecchiette,* and *pestazzule,* which are even flatter *pociacche* and are also called *pizzarelle* in Foggia. It takes great skill to make them, since the dough is dragged under the *sferre,* while the pasta is held with a finger to keep it from rolling up. Large *orecchiette* are also called *stacchiodde,* typical of Foggia and today common throughout the region; around Lecce and Brindisi, they are open like a tile. So are *chjancaredde,* common around Taranto and Massafra. In contrast, *chagghjubbi* are closed in the form of a thimble, and *cuecce* are shaped like a shell.

In Basilicata, *orecchiette* have always been called *recchietelle* and are still a ritual dish: No religious or home feast was conceivable without a piping-hot dish of *recchietelle* at the center of the table. It had to be accompanied by a rich meat *ragù* that had simmered for hours in a large earthenware pot, perhaps set in the fireplace. In modern, aseptic kitchens, the tomato comes from a bottle, put up at home during the summer, or else *conserva*.

See also *cavatelli*.

169. PACCHERI

Pasta corta

INGREDIENTS: Durum-wheat flour and water.

HOW MADE: Factory-made short, wide tubes. They are boiled in abundant salted water.

ALSO KNOWN AS: *Maniche di frate, maniche rigate, rigatoni, rigatoncini, bombardoni,* and *tufoli rigati*. In the Marche and Umbria, *moccolotti*.

HOW SERVED: Traditionally as *pastasciutta*, with local sauces.

WHERE FOUND: Southern Italy; typical of Campania.

REMARKS: The origin of the word must be sought in the onomatopoeic Neapolitan *paccarià*, which means "to slap." The original large fresh pasta, put quickly in the mouth, supposedly slapped the face. The suffix *ero*, used to express disparagement in all the Italian dialects, here refers to a type of pasta considered poor and vulgar.

In Umbria, *moccolotti* are used to make the famous *sbombata*, a *pasticcio* that is made by lining a baking dish with a pasta sheet, filling it with *moccolotti* generously sauced with giblets and sprinkled with local pecorino, and then sealing and baking it.

170. PACCOZZE

Pasta corta

INGREDIENTS: Durum-wheat flour, eggs, and salt.

HOW MADE: The flour is sifted onto a wooden board and kneaded with eggs and a pinch of salt. The dough, worked long and energetically, is left to rest, then rolled out with a rolling pin into a thin sheet, and rhombuses the size of the palm of a hand (called a *pacca*, from which derives the term *paccozze*) are cut. The pasta is cooked in milk.

ALSO KNOWN AS: No alternative names.

HOW SERVED: As *pastasciutta*, with meat *ragù*, preferably of lamb, with a dusting of local pecorino.

WHERE FOUND: Molise; a specialty of Castelbottaccio.

REMARKS: This is the dish made for the feast of the Ascension,[181] a day on which, by age-old tradition, no one should work. A Molisan proverb says: *Pe l'Ascenza, 'nze chiante né se schiante, 'nze mette 'u file a l'aghe, né 'u pettene a la cape* ("For Ascension Day, no singing, no dancing, no sewing, no combing"—prescriptions that make decidedly more sense in the rhyme of the original). The only work allowed was milking the animals. However, the milk could be used only for the preparation of traditional dishes or as a gift to friends and relatives.

At the beginning of the twentieth century, in the small towns of the province of Isernia, a large bucket filled to the brim with milk was brought to the town piazza on Ascension Day, and everyone was invited to ladle some out. This ritual was believed to bring good luck to the cows and sheep returning from the transhumance in Puglia.

In Puglia, a similar pasta called *pizzelle* is made, but without eggs.

171. PAGLIA E FIENO

Pasta lunga

INGREDIENTS: For the white pasta, durum-wheat flour, eggs, and water; for the green pasta, durum-wheat flour, eggs, water, and spinach.

HOW MADE: Relatively thin factory-made *tagliolini* (see entry for *tagliatelle, tagliolini*), with each package containing half white pasta and half green pasta. They are boiled in abundant salted water.

ALSO KNOWN AS: No alternative names.

HOW SERVED: Generally as *pastasciutta*, with a hearty local *ragù* and a grating of cheese, usually parmigiano.

WHERE FOUND: Widespread.

REMARKS: The name means literally "straw and hay." This is a relatively recent pasta, given that it does not appear in Rovetta's manual,[182] which lists the factory-made pasta shapes found in Italy. Thin *tagliolini* appear already dried and formed into a nest, but not colored.

172. PANNICELLI

Pasta ripiena

INGREDIENTS: Wheat flour and eggs. For the filling, ricotta, spinach or chard, local cheese, and spices.

HOW MADE: The flour is sifted onto a wooden board and kneaded for a long time with eggs until a firm, smooth dough forms. The dough is left to rest, then rolled out with a rolling pin into a thin sheet, and 3-by-6-inch (7.5-by-15-cm) rectangles are cut from it. A spoonful of filling is placed in the center of each rectangle, and the sheet is folded in half, forming a large, square *raviolo*. The edge is sealed carefully to ensure the filling does not seep out during cooking. *Pannicelli* are boiled in salted water.

ALSO KNOWN AS: No alternative names.

HOW SERVED: As *pastasciutta,* usually covered with tomato sauce and gratinéed in the oven.

WHERE FOUND: Tuscany, in the Val di Chiana, in Arezzo Province.

REMARKS: The name means literally "swaddling clothes," which alludes to the size of this large *raviolo.* Around Arezzo, it used to be served with butter, parmigiano, and cinnamon.

173. PANSOTTI

Pasta ripiena

INGREDIENTS: Wheat flour, water, and white wine. For the filling, *preboggion,*[183] ricotta, and parmigiano.

HOW MADE: The flour is sifted onto a wooden board and kneaded for a long time with water and wine. The dough is left to rest, then rolled out into a sheet with a rolling pin, and 2-inch (5-cm) squares or disks are cut from it. A teaspoon of filling is placed in the center of a piece, and it is folded into a triangle or half-moon, or it is covered with a second piece to make a square. The *pansotti* are boiled in salted water.

ALSO KNOWN AS: *Pansooti.* In Genoa, they used to be called *gè in preixun* (chard in prison).

HOW SERVED: As *pastasciutta,* usually with a sauce of walnuts and pine nuts.

WHERE FOUND: Liguria.

REMARKS: *Pansotti,* in dialect *pansooti* (*panciuti,* "potbellied"), seem to have a date of birth, published by the Genoese newspaper *Il Secolo XIX* in an article on May 18, 1961, announcing the presentation of this curious meatless *raviolo* at a gastronomic festival in Nervi. In reality, the origin should be sought in Sant'Apollinare, on the hills behind Sori, where this meatless *raviolo* was traditionally made for the feast of Saint Joseph, March 19, which always falls during Lent. Probably the presenter of the *raviolo* at the Nervi festival simply dusted off an old recipe. Today, *pansotti* are a fixture of the Ligurian gastronomy. The walnut sauce was much in fashion on *trofie* and *gnocchetti* in the 1800s.

174. PAPPARDELLE
Pasta lunga

INGREDIENTS: For homemade, formerly wheat flour and water, or wheat flour, *cruschello,* and water; today, commonly made with eggs instead of water. For factory made, durum-wheat flour and water.

HOW MADE: The flour is sifted and kneaded with eggs and water long and vigorously until a firm, smooth dough forms. The dough is covered and left to rest for at least a half hour, then rolled out with a rolling pin into a sheet, not too thin. This sheet is cut into strips or squares whose size varies from region to region. Factory-made *pappardelle* sometimes have curled borders. The pasta is boiled in plenty of salted water.

ALSO KNOWN AS: *Paparele* in the Veneto, and *paspadelle* in the Marche.

HOW SERVED: As *pastasciutta,* preferably with hearty meat *ragù,* also based on game, as in Tuscany, the region where they are most commonly found. In some regions, they are often used in *pasticci* and *timballi.*

WHERE FOUND: Northern and central Italy, especially Emilia-Romagna, the Marche, Umbria, Tuscany, and Abruzzo, though today found throughout Italy.

REMARKS: *Pappardelle* is actually a Tuscan dialect term that derives from *pappare,* "to eat," and in the region they are extensively used, especially with hearty sauces, sometimes containing game. The term is also now used extensively elsewhere in Italy for wide noodles of differing thicknesses and widths.

It is an old term, included in the often-cited *Libro della Mensa*[184] as a preparation cooked in broth and with game. *Pappardelle* were—and are—traditionally served with a hearty *ragù* of game, both feathered and furred. Alessandro Tassoni, of Modena, whose mock epic *La secchia rapita* was published in 1622, recounts:

> . . . 'l miser Baccarin di San Secondo,
> che delle pappardelle era inventore, . . .[185]

[. . . the miser Baccarin of San Secondo, who was inventor of *pappardelle*, . . .]

In Romagna, they are served with a substantial *ragù* of pigeon, and in the Tosco-Emilian Apennines, with a hearty onion *ragù*. The Marche favor a sauce of quails *in porchetta*,[186] though in the Montefeltro area, a sauce of hare with chocolate is typical. In Lazio, boar is used; in Tuscany, hare; and in Umbria, either hare or pigeon. In Umbria, in fact, people have been raising pigeons for centuries. In the rural economy, pigeons used to be the women's job, just as small animals were, but every member of the family had his or her own pair of pigeons to raise and then sell or eat.

In the Veneto, the rather narrow *paparele* are made; in Verona, they were served with a duck sauce on the feast of Saint Zeno, patron saint of the city.

175. PAPPICCI

Pasta lunga

INGREDIENTS: Durum-wheat flour, salt, lukewarm water, and sometimes corn flour.

HOW MADE: The flour is sifted with a pinch of salt and kneaded with lukewarm water for a long time until a firm, smooth dough forms. It is then left to rest, wrapped in a dish towel. The dough is rolled out with a rolling pin into a sheet, not too thin, and sturdy noodles about 8 inches (20 cm) long are cut. Or small irregular triangles or rectangles of about ¾ inch (2 cm) are cut. The pasta is cooked in soup.

ALSO KNOWN AS: *Pappardelle* and *tajarille*.

HOW SERVED: They are served generally as a thick soup, made with a sauce of *lardo*, tomatoes, and local pecorino. Often they are accompanied with legumes.

WHERE FOUND: Abruzzo, where they are a specialty of the Teramo area.

REMARKS: *Pappicci* are a poor pasta even in their final elaboration. The term derives from *pappa*, a children's word that used to mean "bread, mush, soup." The word was probably originally used for a soup made with this type of pasta, and only later became the name for the pasta itself. In the past, *pappicci* in a meat broth was a food for new mothers to help the production of milk.

176. PARMATIELLI

Strascinati

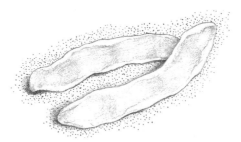

INGREDIENTS: Durum-wheat flour and water.

HOW MADE: The flour is sifted and kneaded long and vigorously with water, then the dough is left to rest. Hazelnut-sized pieces of the dough are rolled out with three fingers on the palm of the hand to form long, thin, pointed *cavatelli* (see entry). They are boiled in plenty of salted water.

ALSO KNOWN AS: *Parmatieddi, palmatielli.*

HOW SERVED: As *pastasciutta*, generally with a *ragù* of pork, *ricotta secca*, and chili.

WHERE FOUND: Campania, in the area of Teggiano and Padula.

REMARKS: The method for making the pasta, which used to involve the palm of the hand (*palma* in Italian, and probably the source of the pasta's name), today uses the *quadro*, the name for the wooden board used for making pasta in the area around Teggiano. It was the pasta made at home for Palm Sunday, and thus had the shape of a palm leaf. Some local scholars believe the pasta's name comes from the fact that *parmatielli* were made for this feast day. Moreover, they were served with meat *ragù*, a rare and special sauce served only on feast days.

177. PASSATELLI

Pasta corta

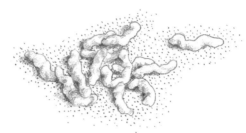

INGREDIENTS: Parmigiano, dry bread crumbs, eggs, beef marrow, spices (especially nutmeg and pepper), and sometimes also flour, vegetables, meat, or *salumi*.

HOW MADE: The parmigiano is blended carefully with dry bread crumbs, eggs, nutmeg, and melted bone marrow. The dough must be firm, but if it is too hard, it can be softened with a drop of broth or white wine. The dough is placed on a wooden board. With a special utensil made up a perforated convex disk and two opposing handles, the dough is pressed, with a slightly circular movement. Little cylinders of different lengths are extruded through the holes. These are laid on a dish towel until all the dough has been used up. The *passatelli* are then poured all at once into simmering broth and cooked briefly. They used to be dropped directly in boiling broth as they emerged from the utensil, but this led to uneven cooking.

ALSO KNOWN AS: *Lumachelle* (snails).

HOW SERVED: In broth, but today also as *pastasciutta,* and even with clams.

WHERE FOUND: Emilia-Romagna, the Marche, and Umbria.

REMARKS: Strictly speaking, *passatelli* do not belong in a catalog of pastas. But this tasty preparation deserves to be an exception. In both its home regions and

elsewhere in Italy, it is considered a sort of pasta for broth. In effect, Artusi makes *passatelli* with *semolino*, parmigiano, milk, and eggs, transforming them into a sort of pasta for all practical purposes. There are numerous variants, with the most famous *passatelli* made in Emilia and Romagna, home of *parmigiano-reggiano*. Today, people can afford to use fewer dry bread crumbs and more parmigiano in the mix.

Nowadays, meat is sometimes added to the mix, usually white meat, such as poultry, or else *salumi*, such as finely minced mortadella. The cooking broth is usually made with capon.

In the Marche, *passatelli* are common, especially in Montefeltro, around Pesaro. In Urbino, spinach and sometimes also meat are added, especially fillet; the dough is scented with lemon, a classic addition of the *cucina marchigiana*. The type of cheese, chosen from among the many excellent local products, can also vary.

Cougnet's *L'arte culinaria in Italia*[187] says *lumachelle* (see entry) are *passatelli marchigiani* made with meat.

Closer to the original recipe, the Umbrian *passatelli* are flavored only with lemon rind, which is added to the boiling broth. Today, around Gubbio, they are also eaten as *pastasciutta,* with butter and truffles.

178. PASTA GRATTATA

Pastina

INGREDIENTS: Wheat flour and eggs; formerly only wheat flour and water. In the south, durum-wheat flour and water. In Puglia, *triddi* often also contain pecorino and parsley. In poor kitchens, dry bread crumbs were included as well.

HOW MADE: The flour is sifted onto a wooden board and kneaded long and energetically with eggs. The dough, which must be very hard, is left to rest. The pasta is made by grating the dough on a large-holed grater, or crumbling it with the fingers, to make irregularly shaped minute *pastina*. This is put to dry on a dish towel. In Lombardy, the hard dough is sliced, dried, and then minced, with the final product the size of grains of rice. The *pastina* is cooked in broth.

ALSO KNOWN AS: In Friuli, *pasta grattada* and *mignaculis*. The Carinthians, an ethnic minority of northern Friuli, make a *pasta grattata* called *Griebenes Gerstl*. In the Veneto, it is known as *pasta gratada* or *gratadè* and *pestariei*. In Lombardy, it is called *pasta rasa*, but also *gratein* in the Po Valley. Around Mantova, they are *tridarini*; in Emilia, *grattini*; in Tuscany, *grandinina*; and in Umbria, *pasta grattata* and *mollichelle*. In Lazio, in the province of Rieti, particularly at Borbona, *'ntrisi*, and at Anticoli Corrado, *'nfranti*. In Abruzzo and Molise, it is *granitte*. In Basilicata, *mblband* Italianized into *bilbanti (trucioli)*, especially at Potenza; and at Genzano di

Lucania, *melempant* are large crumbs of pasta. In Puglia, in the Salento, they are *triddi;* and in Sicily, especially around Siracusa and Modica, *pasta rattedda.* Finally, *farfel* is *pasta grattata* in *cucina ebraica.*

HOW SERVED: Generally in meat broth; in Basilicata, also used in a bean soup.

WHERE FOUND: Present in almost all regions under different names.

REMARKS: The name means literally "grated pasta." Here is yet another type of pasta whose shape imitates the old *cuscus* (see entry), a type that must have encountered great favor to judge from its diffusion throughout Italy, albeit with different cooking methods (the Maghrebian and then the Sicilian and Sardinian were too complicated) and with different names.

In Friuli–Venezia Giulia, in particular in the province of Trieste, but also in other areas, this type of soup started important luncheons, such as those celebrating weddings, confirmations, or first communions. It was believed that it opened the stomach for the rich and hearty courses to come. In Trentino, in the eighteenth century, the *grataroi* or *formentoni* (graters) were already of antique tradition; they were used to make a tasty cake as well. In Basilicata, in the Agri valley, *pasta grattata* called *bilbanti,* that is, *trucioli* (wood shavings), is still served at weddings in a soup called *zuppa di patatelle,* made of hen broth.

This tiny pasta is common in Tuscany, too. There it is called *grandinina* and is found in the Val di Chiana and Casentino, where it is cooked in goose broth. In Umbria, *pasta grattata,* also called *mollichelle,* was cooked for new mothers in goose broth or in a broth made with a pork bone.

Finally, in an 1860 collection of recipes of Modena,[188] *gratini* are a mixture of grated bread, eggs, and cheese, just like the recipe given by Maestro Martino[189] for a soup called *zanzarelli,* made by grating a dough whose ingredients recall Emilian *passatelli* (see entry).

179. PASTA REALE

Gnocchi/gnocchetti

INGREDIENTS: Wheat flour, butter, and eggs; often also parmigiano.

HOW MADE: The flour is sifted and poured all at once into a saucepan containing lightly salted hot water and butter. The batter is stirred rapidly and then put back on the fire until it sizzles and comes away from the sides of the pan. The pan is removed from the fire, the eggs are added, one at a time, and then the dough is put into a pastry bag and little balls of it are squeezed into a greased baking dish. The balls of *pasta reale* are baked and then added to broth for serving. The dough can also be rolled into a sort of thick sheet that is baked whole and then diced. The Piedmontese technique differs slightly.

ALSO KNOWN AS: No alternative names.

HOW SERVED: In broth.

WHERE FOUND: Northern Italy, in particular Lombardy and Piedmont, but also Emilia-Romagna and the Marche.

REMARKS: The name means literally "royal paste." For serving, this pasta is first baked and then dropped into boiling broth, even at the table for the pleasure of the guests. The adjective *reale*, "royal," tells us how refined and delicious this dish was, by now totally supplanted by the factory-made product found in any food shop.

In the nineteenth-century recipe book of the Prinetti Adamoli family of Varese, macaroni—as *pasta reale* was called—appears rarely and is also described as soft bread dipped in cheese and gratinéed.[190]

180. PASTA STRAPPATA

Pasta corta

INGREDIENTS: Wheat flour and water; in the south, durum-wheat flour and water. In Friuli, sometimes the dough is enriched with parmigiano or other grated cheese and eggs; in Tuscany, it is colored with spinach.

HOW MADE: The flour is sifted onto a wooden board and kneaded long and vigorously with water. The dough is left to rest, then rolled out into a sheet, not too thin, and folded into quarters. Then, with the pasta resting on the edge of a pot of boiling salted water, small irregular pieces are torn from the sheet and dropped directly into the water. The process must be completed quickly so the pasta will cook as evenly as possible.

However, the method varies from place to place. Sometimes, lozenges or squares are cut rather than torn from the sheets, as in Trieste for *pasta strazada*. In Sicily and other regions, hazelnut-sized pieces are torn from the dough.

ALSO KNOWN AS: In Friuli–Venezia Giulia, *pasta strazada*, but also *Schinkenfleckerln;* and in Tuscany, *maccheroni alla garfagnanina* and *strapponi*, in particular the Mugello. In the Marche, *pezzole* or *cannacce;* and in Abruzzo, *stracce* or *carte da gioco*, but also *stracciatella*, and at Rocca di Cambio, *scinciata*. In Lazio, *cenciose, lacne stracciate, strappose,* and *pasta straccia*. In Sicily, in the Nebrodi, it is known as *pasta tappi tappi*, and in Siracusa, *frasquatuli*. In Sardinia, around Oristano, it is called *limbas 'e cane*.

HOW SERVED: As *pastasciutta*, with hearty meat *ragù*, especially of pork, and local pecorino. In Friuli, it is traditionally served with *sugo d'arrosto*, or *in bianco*, with béchamel with prosciutto. In Abruzzo, at Rocca di Cambio, *scinciata* is served with ricotta.

WHERE FOUND: Central and southern Italy, but also Friuli–Venezia Giulia (province of Trieste).

REMARKS: The name means literally "torn pasta." The method—rolling the pasta and then tearing or cutting it—is very old and has also been used for sweets. In antiquity, according to Chrysippus,[191] the *catillus ornatus* was a sort of *frappa*: dough rolled into a thin sheet, cut or torn into small pieces, and then deep-fried in oil.

Pasta strappata and its cooking method are identical to many regional preparations. One example is a particular type of pasta (see *volarelle*) in Abruzzo, which is added part fried and part boiled to a ritual soup.

The *stracciatelle* (literally "little rags") made in the area of Scanno are served with turnip greens and are cooked in the same water used for boiling the vegetable. This practice was introduced to Abruzzo by local shepherds who spent long months in Puglia for the transhumance, and with time it became a typical Abruzzese dish.

In the Marche, in particular in the Esino and Misa valleys, the simple flour-and-water dough for *pezzole* is called *sfoglia matta* (crazy). At Sassoferrato, *cannacce* merit a look: boiled squares of sheet pasta are filled with sautéed minced lamb innards and then rolled tight and served with a hearty sauce and the inevitable pecorino.

In Sicily, the *pizzulatieddi* mentioned by Pitré, and listed in the *Vocabolario siciliano-italiano*, are a small *pasta pizzicata* (pinched) usually served in broth. At Pachino, south of Siracusa, the flour-and-water dough used to make *frasquatuli* first breaks up into small pieces *(si muddìa)*, and then fragments further *(si spizzulia)* into tiny irregular chunks that are cooked in soup, often with broccoli and rice.

181. PASTINE MINUTE

Pastina

INGREDIENTS: Durum-wheat flour and eggs or sometimes water.

HOW MADE: Tiny factory-made pasta of various shapes. Gluten-free *pastine* are also available. The *pastine* are cooked in broth.

ALSO KNOWN AS: With holes, *anellini, occhialini, pepe bucato, ruotine,* and *tubetto minuto*. Seed shaped, *semi d'avena* (oat seeds), *di cicoria* (chicory), *di grano* (wheat), *di mele* (apples), *di melone* (melon), *d'orzo* (barley), and *di riso* (rice). Other shapes include *cuori* (hearts), *fiocchetti* (little bows), *funghetti* (little mushrooms), *stelle* (stars), and flower shapes such as *astri* (asters), *fiori di sambuco* (elderflowers), and *margheritine* (little daisies).

HOW SERVED: Usually in broth.

WHERE FOUND: Widespread.

REMARKS: Literally "tiny pastas," these small pastas, traditionally cooked in broth or milk, are of very old tradition. Maestro Martino speaks of *triti* and *formentini*, made from a thickish pasta sheet that is cut minutely. *Formentini*, from *frumento*, "wheat," in fact, must have been the size of a wheat kernel, thus the name.

Today, the term *pastina* covers an infinite variety of shapes: some rare, others disappearing, still others today unfindable. But most are still on the market. Many *pastine* that could be swallowed without chewing must have been studied by the industry for weaning babies. Some forms, like the *alfabeto* (see entry), today unfindable, were a way of introducing children to their ABCs. Many of these *pastine* are small versions of larger shapes, such as *assabesi* (see entry), *mafalde* (see entry), *tripolini,* and others.

182. PATELLETTE

Pasta corta

INGREDIENTS: Durum-wheat flour, corn flour, water, and salt.

HOW MADE: The flours are sifted together onto a wooden board and kneaded long and vigorously with water and a pinch of salt. The dough is left to rest, then rolled out into a thick sheet, and small triangles are cut from it. The *patellette* are boiled in salted water.

ALSO KNOWN AS: No alternative names.

HOW SERVED: As *pastasciutta*, with a *soffritto* of onions and pancetta.

WHERE FOUND: Abruzzo, in particular the province of Teramo.

REMARKS: According to tradition, this tasty pasta of Teramo is served with a rather liquid condiment and eaten with a spoon. Many poor pastas are prepared this way: serving them slightly watery was one way for the poor to fill their stomachs with a bit more volume.

183. PATERNOSTER

Pastina

INGREDIENTS: Flour and water.

HOW MADE: The flour is sifted and kneaded long and vigorously with lukewarm water. The dough is left to rest, then small pieces are pinched off and rolled on a wooden board into cylinders about the size of a pencil, which are cut into pieces about ¾ inch (2 cm) long. The pieces are then rolled over a special comb or on the tines of a fork and left to dry. They are boiled in plenty of salted water.

ALSO KNOWN AS: No alternative names.

HOW SERVED: In the area of Leonessa, where they are traditional, they are served with a ricotta-based sauce.

WHERE FOUND: Northern Lazio (Leonessa) and in Abruzzo.

REMARKS: The name means literally "Our Father." Every household in Leonessa used to have the comb for *paternoster,* which was made of wicker and was similar to the *pettine* used for weaving. The laborious preparation was cadenced by the recitation of prayers, Pater Noster (Our Father) and Ave Maria (Hail Mary), which was also how the cooking time was measured. In a catalog of factory-made pastas produced in America, the maker, probably of Italian origin, calls one shape *padrenosso.*

184. PENCARELLI

Pasta lunga

INGREDIENTS: Wheat flour and eggs; formerly only flour and water.

HOW MADE: The flour is sifted and kneaded long and vigorously with eggs. The dough is then covered and left to rest, after which small pieces are pinched off and elongated on a wooden board with hands, forming long, thick *spaghetti. Pencarelli* are boiled in plenty of salted water.

ALSO KNOWN AS: Formerly *pincarelle.* In the Marche, *pincinelle.*

HOW SERVED: As *pastasciutta,* with traditional local sauces.

WHERE FOUND: Lazio, province of Rieti, especially Leonessa and Antrodoco, and in the Marche.

REMARKS: In the past, *pincarelle* were also made in convents, which then sold them. The refined egg-rich ones made in Leonessa by the Poor Clares of the convents of Santa Lucia and San Giovanni Evangelista were famous. Along with sweets, they were sent as Christmas gifts to the town notables or the parish priest.

In Leonessa, *pencarelli* were made in homes on Fat Thursday (Thursday of Shrovetide) and Shrove Tuesday for a local festival at the end of Carnival. The condiment is something like carbonara; Small pieces of pancetta are sautéed in a large iron skillet together with crumbled sausage. The eggs were beaten separately in a bowl. When the pasta was cooked, it was drained against the pot lid; the pasta would keep warm and moist enough in the pot. To make the sauce, the skillet was not removed from the stove. First the pasta was poured over the fried pancetta and sausage and mixed well. Then it was the eggs' turn. They had to be perfectly incorporated, stirred constantly so as not to scramble. Finally, grated pecorino and a good handful of ground black pepper were added.

The *pincinelle* of the Marche are typical of the area of Sassoferrato.

In the province of L'Aquila in Abruzzo, in the area of Campo Felice, *piringhilli,* a type of pasta similar in shape to *pencarelli,* are made, but they are colored green with spinach.

185. PENCHI

Pasta lunga

INGREDIENTS: Flour, water, and salt; today, also eggs and a little wine.

HOW MADE: The flour is sifted with a pinch of salt onto a wooden board and kneaded long and vigorously with water until a firm, smooth dough forms. The dough is left to rest, then rolled out into a sheet about 1/16 inch (2 mm) thick, and strips as wide as the sheet is thick are cut from it. They are boiled in plenty of salted water.

ALSO KNOWN AS: *Strascinati di Monteleone.*

HOW SERVED: As *pastasciutta,* with traditional local ingredients, especially pancetta and pecorino.

WHERE FOUND: Umbria, typical of Monteleone di Orvieto and Monteleone di Spoleto.

REMARKS: The fifteenth and sixteenth centuries in Italy were dark days for the countryside and for the kitchens of the poor. They were turbulent years of skirmishes and wars among the more or less powerful lordlings, and of the comings and goings of armies on the plowed and cultivated fields. It was the last hurrah of the captains of adventure, brave *condottieri* who fought for whoever paid the most.

In this great cauldron of men and means, famous names bob up, from the Baglioni to the Orsini and the Farnese. Camillo Vitelli, with his brothers Paolo and Vitellozzo, belonged to that army of men who operated in the checkerboard of central Italy. We are at the end of the 1400s, and the armies that marched up and down the country with little or no pay made scorched earth of the fields, grain reserves, herds—of all that was edible in the countryside and in peasants' houses. It is not difficult to imagine the state of mind of the people in small towns as they awaited the arrival of this horde of locusts, whether friend or enemy. Some towns rebelled, but picks and shovels offered them little protection against the well-equipped soldiery, armed, among other things, with the new and terrible firearms.

In 1494, the brothers Vitelli passed into the service of the king of France, Charles VIII, who was preparing to descend into Italy. In 1496, the brothers participated in the sacking of Monteleone di Orvieto, which, unable to supply them with provisions, was destroyed. Tradition has it that two years previously, passing through the similarly named Monteleone di Spoleto, they asked for food and shelter at the castle of Vetranola, and were given pasta, badly made and badly sauced, that was called *penchi*. For punishment, the men of the town were dragged *(strascinati)* by the hair to the place of execution, evidently the source of another name for this pasta, *strascinati di Monteleone*.

Often stories of war are intertwined with those of food. In general, food prepared under duress or refused to the soldiery is what crops up in the local legends. *Canederli trentini,* for example, are large *gnocchi* of bread, the legend goes, similar to cannonballs, which were made by a female innkeeper awakened in the night by German mercenaries asking for food. A similar story is told about *penchi,* today a delicacy for tourists in Umbria.

Today, small producers of fresh pasta sell *penchi* in the shape of thick *tonnarelli*.

186. PENNE

Pasta corta

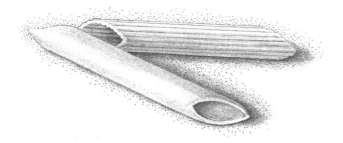

INGREDIENTS: Durum-wheat flour and water.

HOW MADE: Factory-made tubular pasta characterized by its oblique cut. It exists in both smooth and ridged versions, in different sizes, and is boiled in abundant salted water.

ALSO KNOWN AS: Depending on size, *mostaccioli, mostaccioli rigati, penne a candela, penne di Natale* (Christmas; also called *natalini*), *penne di ziti, penne di ziti rigati, penne di zitoni, penne rigate, pennoni, ziti tagliati, ziti tagliati rigati,* and *zitoni tagliati.*

For the smallest size, *penne di mezzane, pennette, pennette di mezzane rigate, pennette rigate, pennettine, pennettine rigate, pennine, pennine rigate, pennuzze,* and *pennuzze rigate.* For the largest size, *pennoni* and *zitoni,* both cut on the bias and cut straight, and both smooth and ridged.

In Sicily, *penne* are also called *maltagliati,* and when they are very short, *attupateddi.* See also *ziti, zite.*

HOW SERVED: Depending on size, as *pastasciutta* or in broth.

WHERE FOUND: Widespread.

REMARKS: The name means literally "quills." In 1865, Giovanni Battista Capurro, a pasta maker of San Martino d'Albaro (Genoa), asked for and obtained a monopoly on the manufacture of a diagonal cutting machine. The machine made it possible to cut the fresh pasta tubes on the bias, in various sizes between 1¼ and 2 inches (3 and 5 cm), without flattening the ends. We read: "Until today, it was impossible to make the diagonal cut except by hand with scissors, a method that, in addition to being too slow and costly, had the disadvantage of producing irregular cuts and of flattening the pastas."[192]

Originally, *penne* were a very different pasta because they were colored with pure saffron, which gave them a distinctive flavor, while many other pastas were tinted with a tasteless yellow coloring agent. As soon as *penne* became widespread, they were adopted in the rural areas as well as the cities: in the Ligurian Apennines, during the summer haying season, the *padrone* procured a basket of *penne* because pasta had to be served to the workers for at least one of the four meals provided in the fields—*culasiun* (for *colazione,* "breakfast"), *dinà* (lunch), *merenda* (snack), and *sena* (for *cena,* "dinner"). Today, *penne* are one of the most widely consumed pasta shapes in Italy.

The shape clearly refers to the old metal *pennino,* or "pen," that had to be dipped in ink, in use until after World War II, when ballpoints arrived from America. That pointed tubular form, which the pasta has diligently copied, served to collect a certain quantity of ink, making it possible to write a few words before dipping the pen again in the inkwell. And like the pen, this pasta shape adapts well to collecting the sauce, whether meat, fish, or vegetable based.

In the south, a very long *penna,* similar to *candele* (see entry), also exists, and it is used especially in pasta *timballi* for the Christmas festivities. In Genoa, the Christmas *maccheroni* are long *penne lisce,* which must not be broken up before cooking. In Sicily, *penne* are called *maltagliati* and are traditionally served with a special rich sauce called *aggrassatu,* made with meat, onions, and spices.

187. PESTAZZULE

Strascinati

INGREDIENTS: Durum-wheat flour, type 0 wheat flour, and water.

HOW MADE: The same technique used for making *orecchiette* (see entry) is used for this shape, but the dough is formed into disks about 1½ inches (4 cm) in diameter, like wide *orecchiette* but with the edge not rolled. They are boiled in plenty of salted water.

ALSO KNOWN AS: Around Foggia, *pizzarelle.*

HOW SERVED: As *pastasciutta,* with sauces typical of the region.

WHERE FOUND: Puglia.

REMARKS: Like *orecchiette,* this type of pasta requires great skill to make: small pieces of dough are rolled out with a *sferre,* but the pasta is held down with a finger so the edge does not roll up.

188. PEZZETELLI

Strascinati

INGREDIENTS: Durum-wheat flour, whole-wheat flour, and water, and often other flours or *grano arso*.

HOW MADE: The flours are sifted onto a wooden board and kneaded long and vigorously with water. The dough is left to rest, then formed into cylinders about ¾ inch (2 cm) in diameter. The cylinders are cut into small pieces of equal size, and each piece is indented with a quick rap of a *sferre* and an index finger. They are boiled in plenty of salted water.

ALSO KNOWN AS: *Pizzarieddhi* and *pizzidieddi*.

HOW SERVED: As *pastasciutta,* in general with a *ragù* of mixed meats.

WHERE FOUND: Puglia, especially around Lecce, in the towns of Casarano, Meledugno, and Muro Leccese.

REMARKS: Like many pastas in areas of extreme poverty in Puglia, *pezzetelli* could be made with such poor ingredients as *grano arso*.

189. PICAGGE

Pasta lunga

INGREDIENTS: Flour, eggs, oil, wine, and salt. For the green version, marjoram, borage, or chard is added.

HOW MADE: The flour is sifted and kneaded with eggs, oil, wine, salt, and sometimes tiny leaves of marjoram or finely minced borage. The dough is worked long and vigorously until firm and smooth, then covered and left to rest. It is rolled out with a rolling pin into a thin sheet, which is cut into flat noodles about ⅝ inch (1.5 cm) wide. They are boiled in plenty of salted water.

ALSO KNOWN AS: *Picaje* and *piccagge*.

HOW SERVED: As *pastasciutta*, with the traditional sauce of anchovies, tomato, and basil, but pesto is also classic. They go well with various other sauces, too.

WHERE FOUND: Liguria, in particular the province of Savona.

REMARKS: In the Savona dialect, the name means the ribbons that dressmakers once used as a finishing touch. In Genoese dialect, however, it means napkin, and indicates the shape and size of the pasta. *Picagge* can be white or green, with the addition of marjoram, borage, or even chard.

And here we need to talk about pesto, often considered the best condiment for *picagge*. In Liguria, pesto enjoys a long tradition: First, the ingredients: The basil must come from Pra and have small leaves and a distinctive scent. It is traditionally fertilized with horse manure and harvested seventeen or eighteen days after sowing in summer and thirty to thirty-five days after sowing in winter. The locals have a saying: *Se il basilico è foresto, di sicuro non è pesto* (If the basil comes from anywhere else, it is surely not pesto). The pine nuts must be Tuscan, the *pecorino sardo* and parmigiano must both be medium aged, and the oil must be the precious, delicately fruity olive oil of Liguria. Only if these ingredients are used, say the Genoese, is it true pesto.

For making the pesto, the basil leaves must number thirty and no more, and they must be cleaned with a damp cloth, not washed. They are not pounded, but instead rubbed against the wall of a mortar with garlic while coarse salt is gradually added (the salt helps the sauce maintain its bright green color). The ingredients are worked in the mortar until they become a beautiful green puree. Then it is time to add the cheese: but one or two? At one time, only pecorino was used, the milder one from Sardinia, with which Liguria has always had trade relations. And even if parmigiano is used today, it is still the flavor of the *pecorino sardo* that characterizes the true Genoese pesto. At this point, a stream of olive oil is added until the sauce is creamy. There are two schools of thought about pine nuts: with and without. But if they are added, they should be toasted very lightly in the oven and go into the mortar after the cheese.

190. PICCHIETTINI
Pasta corta

INGREDIENTS: Flour, eggs, and water.

HOW MADE: The flour is sifted onto a wooden board and kneaded with eggs and water. The dough is left to rest, then rolled out with a rolling pin into a sheet, not too thin, which is wrapped around the rolling pin. With a sharp knife, the dough is cut lengthwise along the pin into wide strips. These strips are folded lengthwise and cut again into matchsticks. They are boiled in plenty of salted water.

ALSO KNOWN AS: *Brudusi.*

HOW SERVED: As *pastasciutta,* with hearty *ragù* of lamb or mutton, almost always with truffles.

WHERE FOUND: Umbria, especially Valnerina, but also around Terni.

REMARKS: This pasta is typical of the Valnerina, in particular Ferentillo. In the province of Terni, the *brudusi* are customarily served in soup: the pasta is cooked in water, then a ladle or two of the pasta cooking water is added directly to individual bowls and mixed with the sauce.

The precious wheat flour for making the pasta used to be kept in a special *madia,* called a *mattera.* The different sieves, the flour, the board, and a rolling pin, called a *rasagnolo,* were kept in the lower part of the *mattera,* protected by a lid.

191. PICI
Pasta lunga

INGREDIENTS: Wheat flour, water, oil, and salt. In some areas, a small amount of *semolino* is added, which helps give the pasta a rougher surface. Today, eggs are sometimes added.

HOW MADE: The flour is sifted with the salt and kneaded with water (or eggs) and oil, and with the *semolino,* if used. The dough must be kneaded for a long time to make it homogeneous and firm. It is left to rest, then rolled out into a thickish sheet, and lozenges are cut from it. The lozenges are rolled with hands on a wooden board until they are thick, long *spaghettoni* of irregular size. They are boiled in plenty of salted water. There is also a factory-made version.

ALSO KNOWN AS: In Tuscany, they are called *pinci* in Montepulciano, and *lunghetti, ciriole, strangozzi,* and *stringozzi* in Montalcino. In Umbria and Lazio, they are called *umbrici* (see *umbricelli*).

HOW SERVED: As *pastasciutta*. Around Siena, the typical condiment is *rigatino* (pancetta) and crumbled bread, though a sauce of duck (called *nana*) or of garlic and tomato *(pici con l'aglione)* is also common. In Montalcino, *lunghetti* are served with a sauce of sausage and tomato, sometimes with mushrooms added.

WHERE FOUND: Tuscany, in Siena and the Val di Chiana; in Umbria and northern Lazio, with different names.

REMARKS: This is a very old pasta shape from southern Tuscany, which local historians try to trace to the Etruscans. Today, *pici* are a tasty and rich dish, and many popular *sagre* are dedicated to this pasta. It is characterized by its rough surface and irregular shape.

Around Siena, where *pici* are common in the triangle formed by Cetona, Chiusi, and Montepulciano, they were known as a poor folks' dish because they were the daily food of the peasants, who ate them with a simple garlic sauce or with crumbs of fried bread. Only those who could afford more prepared them with duck (*nana*), with a *ragù* of offal, or with a sauce of fish eggs (from *luccio*, "pike"), a dish that is still served around Lake Trasimeno. In the countryside south of Siena, in towns such as Trequanda, *lunghetti* are of variable size and irregular shape. In the area of Monte Amiata, *pici* are made with a coarse stone-ground flour.

192. PI.FASACC

Pasta ripiena

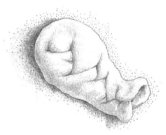

INGREDIENTS: Wheat flour, water, oil, salt, and very few eggs. For the filling, local cheeses, dried bread crumbs, *odori,* and spices.

HOW MADE: The flour is sifted and kneaded with water, oil, salt, and eggs for a long time until a firm, smooth dough forms. The dough is left to rest, then cut into disks with an inverted water glass. A teaspoon of filling is placed in the center of each disk, and the *raviolo* is closed into a long bundle. On one side, the sheet is opened like the round face of a newborn infant, for which it is named. The *ravioli* are boiled, a few at a time, in plenty of salted water until they float.

ALSO KNOWN AS: *Pipihahas* and *ravioli col manubrio.*

HOW SERVED: As *pastasciutta*, usually with foaming butter and sage.

WHERE FOUND: Lombardy, in particular in the Val Camonica, at Piazze d'Artogne.

REMARKS: The dialect name of these large and curious *ravioli*, which means "swaddled newborns," derives from their resemblance to swaddled infants who look as though they are in a bag. They require great skill to make.

They are typical of the area of Artogne, and in particular of Piazze d'Artogne, where they are also called *ravioli col manubrio* (with handle bars). Today, they have almost disappeared from the local everyday kitchen, but Artogne has an important annual *sagra* dedicated to this old and precious preparation, which in summer is found at almost all the festivals in the towns of the valley.

193. PIGNÈ

Pastina

INGREDIENTS: Durum-wheat flour, salt, water, and often whole-wheat flour, or other flours when these were in short supply, including *grano arso*.

HOW MADE: The flour is sifted onto a wooden board and kneaded with a pinch of salt and water until a firm, smooth dough forms. After the dough rests, a small piece is pinched off and is rolled into a thin cylinder. Tiny pieces are pinched off and rolled between thumb and index finger until they resemble pine nuts. They are cooked in broth.

ALSO KNOWN AS: In Taranto, *pasta scagghjola* (tiny scales).

HOW SERVED: In broth.

WHERE FOUND: Puglia.

REMARKS: The use of alternative grains to make pasta and bread used to be quite common, especially in periods of poor harvests or famine: in addition to barley and rye, legumes, such as fava beans, were milled. Sometimes even *grano arso* was used. Today, this unusual pasta has become popular in fashionable restaurants, and *grano arso* is marketed as a niche product.

194. PILLUS

Unusual shape

INGREDIENTS: Finely ground durum-wheat flour and eggs. For the filling, meat stew in tomato sauce and grated *pecorino sardo*.

HOW MADE: The flour is kneaded with eggs long and vigorously to make a firm and uniform dough. The dough is left to rest for a long time, then rolled out with a rolling pin into a sheet, and disks 7 to 8 inches (18 to 20 cm) in diameter are cut from it. The disks, called *pillus,* are dropped into boiling water, then drained, layered in a pan with the filling, and baked.

ALSO KNOWN AS: *Lisanzedas.*

HOW SERVED: Baked, like a classic *lasagna.*

WHERE FOUND: Sardinia.

REMARKS: The practice of making mutton broth is ancient and typical of all the highly pastoral regions. Indeed, it was widespread in ancient Greece, and mutton broth is still made today in Greece for Easter. The pairing of mutton broth and pecorino cheese is a classic combination of the cooking of Sardinia: when well made, the broth is delicate and marries particularly well with the flavorful pecorino of the island.

Around Cagliari, *pillus* made with saffron, known as *lisanzedas,* are favored.

195. PINGIARELLE

Pasta corta

INGREDIENTS: Wheat flour, yeast, lukewarm water, and sometimes eggs.

HOW MADE: The flour is sifted onto a wooden board and a well is made in the center. The yeast is crumbled into the well and mixed with a few tablespoons of lukewarm water and a little flour to make a thick batter. This is left to rest, covered, until the yeast foams. It is mixed and kneaded with the rest of the flour and lukewarm water until a soft, smooth dough forms. It is covered with a dish towel and left to rise until it has doubled in volume. The dough is then rolled into a rather thick sheet and cut into narrow, flat noodles about 4 inches (10 cm) long. The noodles are left to rise on a floured cloth, then boiled in plenty of salted water, like a normal pasta.

ALSO KNOWN AS: *Budillitti* and *penciarelle.* In the Marche, in the village of Campodonico, near Fabriano, they are called *manfricoli* (or *monfricoli*) or *surci;* and at Sassoferrato, they are *pencianelle.* At Colonna, in Lazio, they are known as *pincinelle.*

HOW SERVED: As *pastasciutta,* usually with meat *ragù,* especially lamb, but also with simple sauces of tomatoes and herbs or, as in the Marche, with a *soffritto* of pancetta and garlic. The dish is always finished with a grating of local pecorino.

WHERE FOUND: The Marche and Lazio.

REMARKS: Common especially around Macerata, *pingiarelle* used to consist of small pieces of pasta no larger than a chickpea, made with natural yeast, boiled, and served with melted *lardo*. The housewife would set aside a piece of raised dough when she was making bread, or she would use leftover bits of raised dough (which illustrates yet again the close cultural and material link between bread and pasta, twin pillars everywhere of the peasant diet).

Today, the name *pingiarelle* can be applied to pasta of various shapes, including flat noodles. In the area of Sassoferrato, in the Marche, they are thick, short *spaghetti*. In Cupramontana, *pencenelle* are large squares, or they are flat noodles made from a dough of polenta and flour and served with *baccalà* (salt cod) or a sauce of tomato and pork rinds.

196. PINGUNI

Pasta lunga

INGREDIENTS: Wheat flour, corn flour, water, and salt.

HOW MADE: The two flours are sifted onto a wooden board with a pinch of salt and kneaded with water to make a dough that is not too hard and that is not left to rest. Walnut-sized pieces are pinched off and rolled with hands on the board into *spaghetti* about 10 inches (25 cm) long. They are boiled in plenty of salted water.

ALSO KNOWN AS: No alternative names.

HOW SERVED: As *pastasciutta,* usually with a simple condiment of garlic, oil, tomato, chili, and the inevitable local pecorino.

WHERE FOUND: Lazio, province of Rieti.

REMARKS: Until the economic boom of the 1960s, the practice of mixing different flours for making bread and, to a lesser extent, pasta was common everywhere on the peninsula where the diet was defined by survival. These flours were milled from such grains as barley, millet, emmer, rye, and oats; from legumes such as fava beans and chickpeas; and often also from acorns and chestnuts. The advent of corn, which was both pest resistant and easy to grow, was a big step forward. For decades, it was the only sustenance in vast rural areas of northern Italy, where the diet of exclusively polenta was responsible for the tragedy of pellagra.

In central and southern Italy, corn did not push out other crops, as it did in the north. But it did insinuate itself into the kitchen in a significant way: sweets, breads, and pasta began to include corn among their ingredients, though it never completely replaced wheat. These *pinguni* could not have been rolled into *spaghetti* if they had not also contained the gluten of at least a little wheat flour.

197. PISAREI

Pasta corta

INGREDIENTS: Very fine dry bread crumbs, wheat flour, and warm water.

HOW MADE: The dry bread crumbs are sifted well to make almost a flour. They are sprinkled lightly with warm water to soften them, then kneaded with sifted flour and water until a firm, smooth dough forms. The dough is left to rest, then small pieces are pinched off and rolled with an open hand on a wooden board to form pencil-thick *spaghetti*. These are cut into pieces about ⅜ inch (1 cm) long. The pressure of a finger gives them a sort of shell shape. They are cooked in soup.

ALSO KNOWN AS: *Cazzetti d'angelo* (angels' weenies).

HOW SERVED: In Piacenza, they are combined with beans in the traditional soup *pisarei e fasò*.

WHERE FOUND: Emilia-Romagna, in a typical dish of Piacenza.

REMARKS: The name means literally "baby penises." Pasta names that allude to genital organs—in this case those of children—are not rare.[193]

Pisarei paired with beans is a common dish in peasant households. It used to be made with *pistà 'd grass*, that is, *lardo* minced with garlic and parsley, which provided not only fat but also flavor. Today, the dish is in demand in the typical restaurants of the Piacenza area, where it provides a taste of a rustic, popular food in the otherwise rich local gastronomy. By pairing the pasta with *fasò*, one author suggests, the peasants of Piacenza's countryside combined grains and legumes to provide protein for the table where meat was too costly, in anticipation of macrobiotic cooking.[194]

There used to be a curious custom around Piacenza. When a young man presented his prospective fiancée to his family, his mother checked the girl's right thumb: if she found small imperfections or, better yet, a callus, it meant the girl was an experienced maker of *pisarei* and was thus a suitable bride for her son.

198. PIZZARELLE

Pasta lunga

INGREDIENTS: Wheat flour, corn flour, and formerly lukewarm water only and today also eggs.

HOW MADE: The flours are sifted together and kneaded for a long time with lukewarm water and then with eggs until a smooth, firm dough forms, which is left to rest. It is rolled out into a sheet, not too thin, and cut into strips about 4 inches

(10 cm) wide. The strips are cut into narrow, flat noodles that are allowed to dry before they are boiled in plenty of salted water.

ALSO KNOWN AS: No alternative names.

HOW SERVED: As *pastasciutta,* generally with traditional local sauces, such as a sauce of snails, *castrato, baccalà* (salt cod), and so on.

WHERE FOUND: Lazio, around Subiaco, in particular Cerreto Laziale.

REMARKS: *Pizzarelle* were once the food for feast days, served with a sauce enriched with *baccalà.* When there was no money or anything to trade for the *baccalà,* the people gathered snails after a day of rain. These tasty gastropods, indicators of a time of limitless poverty, were plentiful in marshy areas and along streams. They were a good source of protein and, most important, did not cost money. Nowadays, the sauce with snails, flavored with mint, is made only at certain country festivals. At the September *sagra* in the town of Cerreto Laziale, not far from Rome, the *pizzarelle* are served with a simple sauce of tomato and chili.

199. PIZZICOTTI

Pastina

INGREDIENTS: Wheat flour, lukewarm water, and salt; also natural yeast if making a raised dough.

HOW MADE: The flour is sifted onto a wooden board and kneaded with lukewarm water and a pinch of salt until a firm, smooth dough forms. It is then wrapped in a dish towel and left to rest. Pieces of dough are pinched off and tossed directly into boiling salted water. The same method is used for *pizzicotti* made from yeast-leavened dough.

ALSO KNOWN AS: *Pizziconi.*

HOW SERVED: As *pastasciutta,* with local sauces and grated pecorino. The traditional sauce is garlic, oil, and tomato.

WHERE FOUND: Lazio, province of Rieti (*pizzicotti* made from raised dough are a specialty of Contigliano and Cittaducale) and of Viterbo (Bolsena, Gradoli, and Marta).

REMARKS: The name means literally "pinches." A richer type of dough, containing eggs, used to be made in the province of Rieti for the feast of Saint Anatolia. Today, it is almost an everyday pasta and is easy to find in local trattorias. The skill lies in pinching the dough just hard enough to obtain uniform pieces that will cook evenly.

200. PIZZOCCHERI

Pasta lunga

INGREDIENTS: Buckwheat flour, type 00 wheat flour, and water. Today, milk and eggs are sometimes added.

HOW MADE: The flours are sifted together and kneaded long and vigorously with water or milk and sometimes egg. When the dough is firm and smooth, it is covered and left to rest. It is then rolled out into a sheet ⅛ inch (3 mm) thick, and the sheet is cut into flat noodles about ⅜ inch (1 cm) wide and 3 inches (7.5 cm) long. The noodles are boiled in plenty of salted water.

ALSO KNOWN AS: *Fugascion,* in the form of a wide noodle, and *pizzocher de Tei.*

HOW SERVED: Typically cooked with potatoes and Savoy cabbage and sauced with melted butter and local cheese, especially *casera* and *bitto.*

WHERE FOUND: Lombardy, in the Valtellina. They are a specialty of the towns of Teglio and Tirano. *Fugascion* is typical of Castione Andevenno.

REMARKS: Today, *pizzoccheri* are the symbol of the simple gastronomy of the Valtellina to the point that, in 2001, the Accademia del Pizzocchero di Teglio was founded to safeguard the genuineness of the product, and especially to protect it from imitations that would obscure its nature and historical value. At Teglio, a *sagra* celebrating the *pizzocchero* is held on the last weekend of July.

The etymological hypothesis traces the word *pizzocchero* to the superimposition of two terms: The first is *pita,* "bread" in Arabic, from which the word *pizza* also derives. The second is *bizochus,* from the *bizzochi,* who were adherents of a sect of monks condemned by Pope Boniface VIII. Because of the presence of the suffix *ero,* which signals disparagement, the word *pizzocchero* alone refers to a poor food. But it could also refer to the color of the habit of the *bizzochi* monks, who wore gray (*bigi* in Italian, and *bizi* in northern dialect), the same dark color as the pasta.

Because of its easy adaptability to poor terrains and its short growing season, the buckwheat *(Fagopyrum)* traditionally used for making *pizzoccheri* has acquired a certain importance in mountainous areas. In the Valtellina, it is grown for polentas, but also for the production of the famous *pizzoccheri; sciatt; chisioi,* which are disk shaped; and *taiadin mugni,* which contain beer and grappa.

Today, much of the native buckwheat of the Valtellina has been supplanted by more profitable foreign varieties, but regulations defining cultivation have recently been enacted to ensure the conservation of this unique food product. Different species of the *Fagopyrum* genus are used for green manure (cover crops) and for honey.

The cultivation of buckwheat in the alpine valleys from Lombardy to Trentino was already widespread toward the end of the fourteenth century, especially in Carnia and the Valtellina. According to one tradition, the plant owes its Italian name, *grano saraceno* (also known as *formentino, fraina,* and *fagopiro*), to its seed color, which is "dark as a Saracen." Another, more likely theory attributes the name to the arrival of the seeds with the Saracen invasions of the tenth century, during the struggles between Hugo of Provence and Berengario di Ivrea for the crown of Italy. *Grano saraceno* is sometimes also called *grano pagano,* or "heathen wheat." In fact, in German, buckwheat is called *Heidenkorn,* or "heathen wheat," though the name itself does not imply Mediterranean origin.

Geographically isolated from the rest of Lombardy, the Valtellina, in the center of territorial disputes involving the Visconti and Sforza families,[195] France, and Spain, has sought over the centuries to isolate itself among its own terrible mountains, and thus has kept its food habits and way of life intact. That meant corn did not penetrate, as it did in other parts of northern Italy, but buckwheat, together with rye, millet, and Italian millet, spread, and all appear as important crops in the Jacini inquest.[196]

201. PTRESENELLE

Pastina

INGREDIENTS: Durum-wheat flour, eggs, parsley, and water.

HOW MADE: The flour is sifted onto a wooden board and kneaded with eggs, water, and finely chopped parsley, which gives the dough a uniform green color. The dough is left to rest, then rolled out with a rolling pin into a thin sheet. This is cut into flat noodles about ⅜ inch (1 cm) wide, and then cut again into tiny rhombuses. They are cooked in broth.

ALSO KNOWN AS: No alternative names.

HOW SERVED: Generally in hen broth.

WHERE FOUND: Molise.

REMARKS: In Molise, recipes calling for flour never spoke of hectograms or kilograms, but rather specified *jemmelle.* The *jemmella* was the amount of flour that could be held by two cupped hands.

This pasta takes its name from parsley, called *ptresine* in Molisan dialect, which imparts a lovely bright green to both pasta and broth.

202. PURULZONI

Pasta ripiena

INGREDIENTS: Durum-wheat flour, salt, and lukewarm water. For the filling, fresh *pecorino sardo* and sugar.

HOW MADE: Durum-wheat flour is sifted onto a wooden board and kneaded long and hard with a pinch of salt and lukewarm water. When the dough is smooth and firm, it is left to rest. It is then rolled out with a rolling pin into two thin sheets. On one sheet, teaspoonfuls of filling are placed at intervals of 1¼ inches (3 cm). The second sheet is laid over the first sheet, and the pasta is pressed around the mounds of filling to seal it well. Square or half-moon *ravioli* are cut out with a pasta cutter and boiled in plenty of salted water.

ALSO KNOWN AS: No alternative names.

HOW SERVED: As *pastasciutta,* traditionally with a simple sauce of tomato and basil.

WHERE FOUND: Sardinia, typical of the Gallura.

REMARKS: A fresh, sweet sheep's milk cheese, the pride of the Gallura pastures, is used in the filling of these tasty *ravioli.*

203. QUADRUCCI

Pastina

INGREDIENTS: For homemade, wheat flour, eggs, and sometimes also nutmeg. In the Marche, a mixture of wheat flour and corn flour is used. In central and southern Italy, only flour and water are used. In Lazio (upper Aniene valley), emmer is often mixed with the wheat flour. For factory made, durum-wheat flour, water, and eggs.

HOW MADE: The flour is sifted, sometimes with a pinch of nutmeg, and kneaded with eggs until the dough is firm and smooth. The dough is left to rest, then rolled out into a very thin sheet, from which ¼-inch (6-mm) squares are cut. The size can vary according to the areas of production, as can the use of nutmeg.

Quadrucci are made differently in the Marche: the ball of dough is cut into thick slices and then into small dice. The *pastina* is cooked in broth.

ALSO KNOWN AS: *Quadrellini, quadretti,* and *quadrotti.* In Emilia, *quaternei;* in the Marche, *quadrelli pelosi* and *patacchelle;* in Umbria, *squadruccetti;* and in Lazio *ciciarchiola* and *cicerchiole,* but also *tajurini.* In factory-made production, *lucciole.*

HOW SERVED: Typically in broth-based soups, especially factory-made *quadrucci.* Around Urbino, they are also used in a traditional soup with fava beans. In the upper Aniene valley, they are added to a soup made with local beans (especially *fagiolina di Arsoli, cioncone di Riofreddo,* and others).

WHERE FOUND: Widespread.

REMARKS: The name means literally "little squares." This classic pasta fashioned from scraps was usually made, like *maltagliati* (see entry), from the odd bits of the pasta sheet that remained after the *fettuccine* were cut for the feast day.

In the Marche, especially in the town of Staffolo, *quadrucci pelosi* (hairy) were called *u pastu di puritti* and constituted one of the seven meals consumed during harvest: 6 A.M. *u' boccò,* coffee and sweets; 8 A.M. *a colaziò,* frittata and stewed rabbit; 10 A.M. *a colaziò, ciambellone,* water, and wine; noon *u pranzu, quadrucci pelosi* in goose broth, *pastasciutta,* roast goose; 2 P.M. *u svejari,* vermouth or Marsala; 6 P.M. *a merennuccia,* bread with oil, salt, and pepper and a sweet in wine; 9 P.M. *a cena, lonza,* salad, bread. Terminology and number of courses vary from area to area; although there are usually seven, there can be as many as ten or more, as in the area of Ascoli Piceno.[197]

In Umbria, *squadruccetti* were served as the opener at the luncheon for communions, confirmations, and weddings, but were also given, cooked in goose or hen broth, to the workmen who had taken part in the husking of the corn.

Quadrucci and peas in fish broth is a typical dish of Gubbio, where it is made for the vigil of the Festa dei Ceri (Festival of the Candles).[198] The town of Gubbio once extended as far as Pergola, that is, some eighteen miles (thirty kilometers) from the sea, and the fish arrived by the ancient via Flaminia, directly from the Adriatic.

The Latian term *cicerchiola* indicates the dimensions of the little square, which must be the size of a *cicerchia* to fit well with the regional recipes. This legume had practically disappeared until a few years ago, but is now making a comeback, especially in restaurants that try to revive traditional local recipes. For example, in the upper Aniene valley, *cicerchiole* are cooked with a particular type of locally grown bean, the *cioncone* or *fagiolina.* In Rome, *quadrucci* or *cicerchiole* are essential for the famous *minestra di quadrucci e piselli,* made with peas.

204. RAMICCIA

Various shapes

INGREDIENTS: Wheat flour, but also other flours, such as emmer, water, and a few eggs.

HOW MADE: The flour is sifted onto a wooden board and kneaded long and vigorously with water and some eggs until the dough is very hard. The dough is left to rest, then rolled out into a very thin sheet from which fine threads are cut. They are boiled in salted water.

ALSO KNOWN AS: No alternative names.

HOW SERVED: As *pastasciutta,* with the characteristic condiment based on liver sausage and pork spareribs.

WHERE FOUND: Lazio, around Subiaco; they are a specialty of Roviano and Percile, but are also found in the Monti Lepini area, where they are one of the traditional dishes of the town of Norma.

REMARKS: This pasta was typical of Carnival time, when it was present on every peasant table on Shrove Tuesday and Fat Thursday. It seems to have been designed to use up the last sausages left in the pantry before the sacrifice of the new hog. In fact, the sauce often includes both liver and meat sausages.[199] In Norma, in Latina Province, the pasta is served with a meat sauce in which the meat is finely diced, not ground.

Much care is required to cook this delicate pasta in the *cutturella,* the old copper pot that hung above the fire in the fireplace. When the water boiled, the *ramiccia* was dropped in and, given its lightness, rose immediately to the surface. It was drained quickly, poured onto a wooden board, and slathered with a sauce of sausages and tomato. The pasta is so thin it practically melts in the mouth.

205. RASCATIELLI

Strascinati

INGREDIENTS: Durum-wheat flour, water, and often also potatoes or fava-bean flour.

HOW MADE: The flour is sifted onto a wooden board and kneaded with water and often with a small amount of boiled, riced potato or another kind of flour. The dough is kneaded long and vigorously, then left to rest. A small piece of dough is pinched off and rolled out in a stick as thick as a pencil, then cut into ⅜-inch (1-cm) lengths. These are dragged with the fingertip to make small *cavatelli,* which are cooked in abundant boiling salted water.

ALSO KNOWN AS: *Cavateddri* and *rascatieddi;* in Puglia, *rasckatieddi, cavatini,* and *rachetielli.*

HOW SERVED: As *pastasciutta,* with meat sauces, especially lamb. In Basilicata, a simple tomato sauce with the local *cacioricotta.*

WHERE FOUND: Puglia, Basilicata, and Calabria.

REMARKS: In Calabria, as is often the case in the south, meat *ragù* was always served for the Sunday lunch on the wealthier tables. Nicola Misasi, in his *In provincia, l'ambiente calabrese al tempo dei Borboni,*[200] tells us how each day had its food: Monday vegetable soup, Sunday *ragù.* Rarely were the poorer classes able to have a meat *ragù,* even on feast days. As Misasi tells it, among the poorest of the poor, "the struggle for existence there is harsh and without scruples . . . at 18 years they are already old, at 30 already decrepit. . . ."

206. RAVIOLE

Pasta ripiena

INGREDIENTS: Formerly wheat flour, a few eggs, and water; today, only flour and eggs. The filling used to be made of finely diced leftover cheeses, bound with eggs, but today it is made of a selection of local cheeses.

HOW MADE: The flour is sifted onto a wooden board and kneaded long and vigorously with water and a few eggs. The dough is left to rest, then rolled out into a thin sheet, and 4-inch (10-cm) squares are cut from it. A spoonful of filling is placed at the center of each square, the square is folded in half, and the edges are carefully sealed. The *raviola* is first fried, then simmered in milk until the milk boils completely away.

ALSO KNOWN AS: No alternative names.

HOW SERVED: Fried and then finished in milk.

WHERE FOUND: Piedmont, in particular the valleys around Biella.

REMARKS: This type of stuffed pasta has the same name as a preparation made by the Walser community in the valleys of northern Piedmont, a clear sign that recipes, and especially their names, traveled with trade (see *raviole alagnesi*). The fillings, however, were left to the imagination of the women and the ingredients that could easily be found nearby. *Raviore* (see entry) are made in the territory where the flocks pass on their way from the Maritime Alps to the coast for the winter, and with the shepherds came their foods.

207. RAVIOLE ALAGNESI

Pasta ripiena

INGREDIENTS: Corn flour, a little wheat flour, stale bread, water, and butter. For the filling, salami, sausage, and local cheeses.

HOW MADE: The wheat and corn flours are kneaded with the bread, which has been soaked in water and squeezed out, and a small piece of butter. When the dough is quite firm, walnut-sized balls are formed, which are shaped and stuffed. The exact shape of the pasta—oval, round, flattened, and so on—differs with the filling. The *raviole* are cooked in broth or milk.

ALSO KNOWN AS: No alternative names.

HOW SERVED: Boiled in meat broth or in milk and served with melted butter.

WHERE FOUND: Piedmont, in the valleys of Anzasca, the upper Formazza, and the Valsesia (specialty of Alagna Valsesia).

REMARKS: The Walser ethnic minority, which settled in the valleys of northern Piedmont, are descendants of the ancient Alemanni, who came from the German regions of the Rhine and Main and from the upper Rhône valley. The settlement dates back to the twelfth and thirteenth centuries, when the climatic conditions convinced the Walser shepherds, who in summer brought their flocks to pasture in the Piedmontese valleys, to accept promises of privileges from lords of the territory and some rich monasteries in exchange for farming the new lands of the valleys of the Lys, Anzasca, Formazza, and Sesia. Although separated from their homeland by mountain chains, the Walser did not lose contact with their confreres in the other Piedmontese valleys and kept alive their language, Titsch, and their gastronomic traditions. Their cuisine was rich in game, fresh cheeses, and potatoes, ingredients still found today in the traditional recipes of these valleys. Among these dishes is *raviole alagnesi,* which was once made on feast days and is now sought out by tourists in the restaurants of Gressoney, Macugnaga, and Alagna.

208. RAVIOLI, RAVIOLINI

Pasta ripiena

INGREDIENTS: Wheat flour and eggs, and sometimes water and salt.

HOW MADE: In the modern version, the flour is sifted, sometimes with a pinch of salt, and kneaded long and vigorously with eggs and sometimes a little water. When the dough is firm and smooth, it is covered and left to rest. It is then rolled out with a wooden rolling pin into a thin sheet and cut into small disks, squares, or rectangles. A teaspoon of filling is placed in the center of each piece. The shape of the *raviolo* varies from place to place—half-moons, rectangles, triangles—but the edges must always be carefully sealed to prevent the filling from escaping during cooking. They are boiled, a few at a time, in plenty of salted water.

ALSO KNOWN AS: See individual *ravioli* entries. Formerly *raffiolo, rafiolo, ravaiolo, raviuolo,* and *ravviolo.*

HOW SERVED: Generally as *pastasciutta,* with local sauces.

WHERE FOUND: Widespread.

REMARKS: Stuffed pasta first appears in Italian gastronomy in the 1500s, especially in the north, in Lombardy at the courts of Milan and Mantova, and then travels thanks to the great cooks of the day. Messisbugo, Scappi, Romoli, and Stefani, to mention only a few, transcribed the recipes of the court, and over time certain preparations became popular and trickled down to the humbler classes, who served them on feast days. Thus, stuffed pastas passed from the Italian court to the Italian regional kitchen. It is also important to stress that, although stuffed pasta was more common in the north, by the 1800s it had become a feast-day dish in the south as well, where the filling was usually vegetables and local cheeses.

But the first written sources that name a preparation similar to the *raviolo* date as far back as 1100. What follows here is a bibliographic excursus from the Middle Ages to the period between the two world wars. It is not a history of the *raviolo,* but rather a series of reference points in time and geography. We can do no more than this because we are talking about early food prepared by illiterate people, which by definition lacks documentary sources. In fact, the numerous texts from the 1300s and later that cite or explain this type of pasta are the work of educated people, who are an insignificant percentage of all the users. It is risky indeed to state that this or that filling, this or that ingredient applies to the broader preparation of any *raviolo* just because it is cited in a text. It is more reasonable to assume that the housewife typically used the type of meat or of cheese and greens she had on hand.

The *Liber de coquina* and the *Tractatus de modo preparandi et condiendi omnia cibaria* contain in the appendix the *Liber de ferculis* of Giambonino da Cremona,

who collected some eighty Arabic recipes of gastronomic and nutritional interest, drawn from a monumental gastronomic work in Arabic by a physician who
lived in Baghdad and died in 1100.[201] It contains what may be the first description
of the *raviolo*, which Giambonino calls *sambusaj*, the term for a triangular piece
of pasta (hence the Arabic name, itself probably of Persian origin) filled with
ground meat.

In the more than two centuries of Arab domination in Sicily, many of the
dishes of the Muslim kitchen were adopted by the indigenous peoples and became their own, first during the Norman period and then even more so during
the reign of Frederick II, at whose court the Arabic recipes probably began to be
translated. His son Manfred, for his part, initiated the translation into Latin by
Ibn Butlan of an important text on Arabic cooking and nutrition called *Tacuinum
sanitatis* (Notebook of health), which experienced enormous success in the West.
And it was none other than Ibn Butlan who suggested as the translation for the
Arabic *sanbusaj* the Latin *raviolus* or *calizon panis*.

Do we owe the introduction of the *raviolo* into Italy to the diffusion of this
work? We cannot know. But what is certain is that the Arab cooks in Sicily had
been making it for at least two hundred years before Ibn Butlan. The occurrence
of the word *raviolo* in the early and often coeval Genoese documents attests the
vitality of the exchanges between that people of navigators and Sicily, center of
an extended network of commerce and trading.

The etymology of the word *raviolo* is uncertain, but is documented in medieval Latin. We find one of the first citations in Salimbene da Parma, who names
the *"raviolus sine crusta de pasta,"*[202] noting it already as a delicacy. That the term
appears in a Latin text does not mean that it belonged to the vocabulary taught at
the grammar schools; more simply, the author must have borrowed from the vulgate the only term he felt was suitable to describe the *raviolo,* but which did not
have an equivalent in classical Latin. This is likely evidence that by the end of the
1200s the term *raviolo* belonged to the language spoken in the northern area. In
fact, in a document from Cremona dated 1243, a similar *raviolo* is mentioned as a
specialty of the area (see *marubini*). Important, too, is the vernacular testimony in
the 1344 *Libro della mensa.*[203] Moreover, at the beginning of the fourteenth century,
a miscellaneous collection of recipes appeared at the Angevin court of Naples.
Considered one of the first attestations of the existence of a southern cuisine, it
contains a citation of the *raviolo.*

In the sixteenth century, there is terminological uncertainty on the making of
the *raviolo* in printed texts. In general, it is described as a sort of *gnocco,* prepared
with cheese and flavorings and then fried, rather than wrapped in a sheet of
pasta. In some texts, a similar preparation is called *raviolo gnudo,* which is still found
today in the Tuscan kitchen. Numerous writers mention the *raviolo.* Giovio[204]
records: "... replied Aragonia, distinguishing between *ravioli* with wrapping

and without wrapping."[205] Ortensio Lando offers another example: "Libista, a Lombard peasant woman from Cernuschio, was the inventor of *ravioli* wrapped in pasta and *spogliati,* called by the Lombards *mal fatti.*"[206] And Domenico Romoli instructs: ". . . take that pasta that you will have made for the eggs stuffed only with capon meat; add a little flour, take the frying pan with good lard and boil it on the fire and right away put the frying pan on the coals; flour the back of the cheese grater, take a bullet of the mixture, and rub it over the holes and you will make a little packet with the balls and let them go gradually into the pan."[207]

In Giambullari's *Vocabolario fiorentino* (1551), *rauiuolo* is a "food in small pieces made of cheese, eggs, greens, and the like," while *tortello* is defined as "food of the same material as the *torta,* but in smaller pieces."

The next century opened the door to the definitions. Specifically, the vocabularies of the Accademia della Crusca[208] began to define the terms. In the first edition (1612), we read under *raviuolo,* "food in small pieces made of cheese, eggs, greens, and the like," while under *tortello,* we find "from *torta,* but rounder and wrapped in pasta." The later editions of the *Vocabolario della Crusca* keep this definition.

In 1691, Politi's *Dittionario toscano* describes *rauiuolo* as "delicate food in small pieces, made of cheese, eggs, greens, and spices," and *tortello* as "a sort of *rauiuolo* with a wrapping of pasta," surely borrowing the description from the *Vocabolari della Crusca.* The eighteenth-century vocabularies keep these definitions.

But the terminological uncertainties are not over. The *Libretto di cucina,* manuscript of Gio Batta Magi (1842–85), a cook of Arezzo, describes the Tuscan preparation of the *raviolo gnudo* under the term *ravioli.* Fanfani's *Vocabolario dell'uso Toscano* (1863), staying with the old dictionaries of the Accademia della Crusca, defines *raviuoli* as "food in small pieces, made of minced greens with ricotta, cheese, eggs, flour, and other," or the modern *ravioli* of ricotta, but without the pasta wrapping. Different interpretations on the type of wrapping also exist. The *Enciclopedia* edited by Guarnaschelli Gotti gives an interesting etymology for *ravioli*—from the medieval *rabiola,* in turn from the Latin *rapa* (turnip), to indicate the old filling made from ricotta wrapped in turnip leaves or that the leaves were used in the filling. And this is not an isolated interpretation.

Thus, the idea that the *raviolo* was gradually wrapped in greens or pasta to become what is essentially the modern preparation cannot be denied.

In his *Manuale del cuoco e del pasticcere,*[209] Vincenzo Agnoletti creates new confusion by describing the *raviolo alla romana* as the modern *raviolo* of ricotta and spinach, wrapped in pasta and cut in a half-moon, and the Piedmontese *agnolotto* as a *gnocco* cooked and served in broth. He does not mention the *tortello,* but speaks of *tortellini* and *cappelletti* as small *ravioli* with varied fillings. A few years later, the first edition of the *Cucina teorico-pratica,* by Ippolito Cavalcanti, duke of

Buonvicino,[210] gives almost the same definition of *raviolo:* a tiny disk (as big as a Neapolitan *tari* or a Tuscan *paolo,* both old coins), filled with meat and ricotta.

On the other hand, *Il cuoco sapiente,* published in 1881, describes the *raviolo* as a *gnocco* of chard, ricotta, and parmigiano cooked in broth. In other words, it is the *raviolo gnudo* of Tuscany. According to Artusi, the *raviolo* is actually a croquette of cheese, chard, eggs, and spices, floured and cooked like a modern *gnocchetto,* again as was customary in Tuscany. In his *ravioli romagnoli,* the type of vegetable is different, and those made in Genoa contain meat.

Caterina Prato's *Manuale di cucina* (1906)[211] describes the *raviolo* in its present-day form, and accompanies the description with a drawing that shows the *raviolino* as a half-moon with toothed edge, with the wheeled pasta cutter next to it.

In 1932, *Il vero re dei cucinieri*[212] speaks of the *raviolo alla milanese* as a *gnocco* of meat boiled in broth. In *Altre ricette di Petronilla,*[213] the Christmas *ravioli* is recalled: "remember the superlative soup, the Christmas classic; the one that requires an ultra-delicious filling . . . called *ravioli,* or *tortellini,* or *agnolotti* or *cappelletti.*"

Thus, in the decades between the two world wars, the word *raviolo* came to be applied to a variety of different preparations. This is confirmed by the numerous vocabularies of the Italian language published since World War II.

The former variants distinguished *ravioli* and *tortelli* in meatless and meat versions. In the meatless version, the fillings used mainly cheeses and greens, and the pastas themselves were called by various terms in the old recipe books: *tortelli da quadragesima* (for Lent), *ravioli bianchi in die senza charne* (white ravioli on meatless days), and *ravioli herbozij* (with herbs) or *de zuche* (squash), according to the predominant ingredient in the filling. Among the meat versions are *tortelli di polastro alla bolognese* (poultry), or the more common *de carne del porco,* because pork ruled in the world of antique meat-filled pastas.

The modern regional variants change not only the filling—meat, fish, fresh cheeses, and various flavorings—but also the ingredients used in the dough, such as olive oil, particularly in the south, and especially the shape, which can be square, rectangular, round, or half-moon and with straight or pinked edges.

See also *tortelli.*

209. RAVIOLI ALLA GENOVESE

Pasta ripiena

INGREDIENTS: Wheat flour, eggs, and water. For the filling, sow's udder, brains, *filoni,*[214] veal, vegetables, and spices.

HOW MADE: The flour is sifted onto a wooden board and kneaded long and vigorously with eggs and a little water until a firm, smooth dough forms, which is left to rest. The dough is then rolled out with a rolling pin into a thin sheet, and little balls, spaced 1 to 1½ inches (2.5 to 4 cm) apart, are placed on half of it. The other half is folded over and pressed firmly with fingers around the filling. The *ravioli* are cut into rectangles with a wheel-type pasta cutter, and then put to dry on a floured dish towel. The *ravioli* are boiled, a few at a time, in abundant salted water.

ALSO KNOWN AS: No alternative names.

HOW SERVED: As *pastasciutta,* with the Ligurian meat sauce known as *il tocco di carne* (a touch of meat).

WHERE FOUND: Liguria.

REMARKS: The *raviolo alla genovese* is traditionally served with *il tocco di carne,* a meat-and-mushroom sauce, much reduced and long cooked with wine, *odori,* and tomato. At one time, these *ravioli* were the Ligurian food for feasts and gourmands—yes, with the *tocco*—but only after being religiously cooked in capon broth.

Today, this dish is commonly found in the region's restaurants, though the meat fillings often vary from the traditional recipe. Mushrooms, an important ingredient for the preparation of the *tocco,* are almost omnipresent in Ligurian recipes, their presence guaranteed by the wealth of the wooded valleys that climb gently from the sea toward the Apuan Alps. Mushrooms are also used in the filling of Ligurian *ravioli* in the 1880 *Cucina di strettissimo magro,* the manual published by Father Gaspare Dellepiane that includes fish-based *ravioli,* one filled with caviar and another with oysters.

Near Ventimiglia, one type of Ligurian *raviolo* was filled with squash, and another, older type was filled with greens, ricotta, raisins, and pine nuts and fried.

210. RAVIOLI ALLA NAPOLETANA

Pasta ripiena

INGREDIENTS: Wheat flour, eggs, and water. For the filling, fresh cheeses (usually mozzarella and ricotta), prosciutto, and spices.

HOW MADE: The flour is sifted onto a wooden board and kneaded long and energetically with eggs and a little lukewarm water until a firm, smooth dough forms. The dough is wrapped in a dish towel, left to rest, and then rolled out with a rolling pin into a thin sheet. Little balls of filling are placed, well spaced, on half of the sheet, and the other half is folded over to cover the filling. The pasta is pressed with fingers around the filling, to keep it from coming out during cooking. A wheel-type pasta cutter is used to cut out half-moon *ravioli,* which are boiled, a few at a time, in plenty of salted water.

ALSO KNOWN AS: No alternative names.

HOW SERVED: As *pastasciutta,* generally with the famous *ragù alla napoletana.*

WHERE FOUND: Campania.

REMARKS: Ippolito Cavalcanti[215] cites these *ravioli* only once, while there are numerous *gattò*[216] *di fedelini* and *lasagne, timballi di maccheroni* and *timpani di tagliolini,* because the baroque opulence of the tables of the Kingdom of Naples favored *pasticci* of pasta and *sartù,*[217] work of the French *monsù,*[218] who adapted the refined and heavy French dishes to Mediterranean taste.

But what penetrated the racket of the seething, starving backstreets in this muffled world of foods? For the poor, there were the *maccheronai,* who sold long, steaming *maccheroni* with cheese that were popped into the mouth with a practiced movement of the hands, and the *pizzaioli,* where food could be bought on credit.[219]

It was the middle bourgeoisie of lawyers, doctors, and notaries, but also merchants and large-scale artisans, who could afford *ravioli* on their tables for feast days. At the time, they were meat-filled *ravioli* because it was meat that separated the classes, even if one of the numerous cheeses produced in the kingdom provided most of the flavor in the filling.

Today, now that *ravioli alla napoletana* are on everybody's tables on feast days, the filling has lightened up and the numerous variations even include fish. There are also *ravioli* called *panzarotti,* which are filled with Neapolitan salami and ricotta, fried, and served piping hot.

211. RAVIOLI ALLE CIME DI RAPA

Pasta ripiena

INGREDIENTS: Wheat flour, salt, eggs, and water. For the filling, turnip greens sautéed with garlic and local oil.

HOW MADE: The flour is sifted onto a wooden board with a pinch of salt and kneaded for a long time with eggs and a goodly amount of water. The dough is left to rest, then rolled out into a very thin sheet, and disks about 4 inches (10 cm) in diameter are cut from it. Each one is topped with a teaspoon of filling and folded into a half-moon, and its edges are carefully sealed. They are boiled, a few at a time, in plenty of salted water.

ALSO KNOWN AS: No alternative names.

HOW SERVED: As *pastasciutta,* traditionally with pork *ciccioli* (cracklings) and chili.

WHERE FOUND: Puglia.

REMARKS: The stuffing for these typical Puglian *ravioli* uses the famous turnip greens, *cime di rapa,* pride of the horticulture of the Tavoliere.[220] Although they are a dish for feast days, they are of secondary importance in the universe of Puglian pastas, where shapes that were rolled, indented, and formed on the *ferretto* predominate. They appear here because, like all stuffed pastas of the various regions, their filling reflects the typical products of the territory.

212. RAVIOLI AMARI

Pasta ripiena

INGREDIENTS: Durum-wheat flour, salt, and formerly a few eggs but more usually water. For the filling, ricotta and marjoram or sometimes mint.

HOW MADE: The flour is sifted onto a wooden board and kneaded for a long time with salt and eggs or water until a firm, smooth dough forms. After resting, the dough is rolled out with a rolling pin into a thin sheet. The sheet is cut into 3-inch (7.5-cm) squares, and a spoonful of filling is placed in the center of each square. The *raviolo* is then folded into a triangle and boiled in plenty of salted water.

ALSO KNOWN AS: *Raviola.*

HOW SERVED: As *pastasciutta,* usually with pork *ragù.*

WHERE FOUND: Sicily.

REMARKS: The adjective *amari* (bitter) serves only to distinguish these *ravioli* from the sweet ones, which are much more common in the island's rich pastry repertory. Around Messina, they are flavored with mint, and in Ragusa, with marjoram.

213. RAVIOLI DELLA PUSTERIA

Pasta ripiena

INGREDIENTS: Rye flour, wheat flour, eggs, oil, and water. For the filling, spinach, ricotta, and potatoes, but also poppy seeds, nettles, or sauerkraut.

HOW MADE: The flours are sifted onto a wooden board and kneaded long and vigorously with a few eggs, a drop of oil, and some lukewarm water to form a dough, which is then left to rest. The dough is rolled out with a rolling pin into a thin sheet, and a mold or inverted glass is used to cut out disks about 2 inches (5 cm) in diameter. A teaspoon of filling is placed in the center of each disk, which is then folded into a half-moon and the edges carefully sealed. The half-moons are boiled in plenty of salted water.

ALSO KNOWN AS: *Schlutzer.*

HOW SERVED: As *pastasciutta,* with melted butter and grated cheese.

WHERE FOUND: In the Val Pusteria, in Trentino–Alto Adige.

REMARKS: In the mountain areas, where the climate does not permit the wealth of vegetables found in the south, the filling is made with seasonal products: sauerkraut in winter, nettles and poppy seeds in spring, but also ricotta, spinach, and potatoes in the warmer months.

214. RAVIOLI DI CARNE

Pasta ripiena

INGREDIENTS: Wheat flour, eggs, and water. For the filling, meats, prosciutto, spinach, ricotta or cheese, and sometimes Marsala.

HOW MADE: The flour is sifted and kneaded long and vigorously with eggs and water to form a dough, which is then covered and left to rest. The dough is rolled into a wide, thin sheet, and small balls of filling, spaced 1 to 1½ inches (2.5 to 4 cm) apart, are placed on half of it. The other half of the sheet is folded over the filling, and the pasta is pressed around the filling. The *ravioli* are cut apart with a wheel-type pasta cutter, with the shape—half-moon, triangle, rectangle—varying from place to place. They are boiled in plenty of salted water, a few at a time.

ALSO KNOWN AS: In Lazio, *cappelletti*, and in the Marche, *li griù*.

HOW SERVED: Traditionally in capon broth, or else as *pastasciutta*, usually with meat *ragù* and parmigiano.

WHERE FOUND: Widespread.

REMARKS: Here, the old *raviolo sine crusta*, of which Salimbene da Parma speaks in his *Cronica*,[221] is definitively wrapped in a thin sheet of pasta. As prosperity increased, the fillings became richer, with meats and other costly ingredients.

Every regional cuisine now has its typical meat-filled *ravioli, tortelli,* or *agnolotti.* The specific filling is what distinguishes one kind from another, both in the choice of meat and in how it is prepared, using cooked meats (and more rarely raw) together with local ricotta or other cheeses. (The most important meat *ravioli* have their own entries.) Until a few decades ago, for example, *cappelletti* were obligatory for Christmas in Rome. They were made on December 23, before the trip, around midnight, to the *cottio,* the famous fish market, which overflowed for the occasion with all Neptune's most fabulous bounty. The *cappelletti* stayed there on a wooden board, lined up, counted, and covered with a clean dish towel, waiting to bless the table on December 25.

A similar rite once took place in many regions of Italy, but today technology has deprived homes of the modest pleasure repeated each year by rich and poor alike—a pleasure guaranteed because nobody would willingly do without a Christmas bowl of *cappelletti, anolini, tortellini,* or *ravioli.* Nowadays, we can buy the *ravioli,* aseptic and dry, at the corner store or the supermarket, and they have become an easy, quick-cooking dish—maybe with a little butter—for the everyday table.

215. RAVIOLI DI PESCE

Pasta ripiena

INGREDIENTS: Wheat flour and eggs. For the filling, usually cod, dogfish, or *pesce azzurro;* ricotta; lemon rind; and other local ingredients.

HOW MADE: The flour is sifted onto a wooden board and kneaded long and vigorously with eggs until a smooth, firm dough forms. The dough is left to rest, then rolled out into a thin sheet. Teaspoons of filling are placed 1¼ to 1½ inches (3 to 4 cm) apart on half of the sheet. The other half of the sheet is folded over and pressed around the filling. The *ravioli,* square or round according to local custom, are cut apart with a wheel-type pasta cutter. They are boiled, a few at a time, in plenty of salted water.

ALSO KNOWN AS: No alternative names.

HOW SERVED: As *pastasciutta,* often with a fish-based sauce, especially sole, flavored with the local wines.

WHERE FOUND: Veneto, Liguria, the Marche, and Campania, in particular the island of Ischia.

REMARKS: The filling for this type of *raviolo* exploits the great abundance and quality of Mediterranean *pesce azzurro.* The fragrance imparted by the grated rind of untreated lemons is omnipresent in the cooking of the Marche and is also found in the filling of Campanian *ravioli,* for which the famous lemons of the Amalfi coast are used.

The smaller Ligurian *raviolini,* always served in fish broth, are flavored with nutmeg instead of lemon. *La cuciniera genovese*[222] recommends filling them with *pesce cappone,*[223] hake, *bianchetti,* or *rossetti* (both of the latter tiny fish), depending on the season, and calls for adding mushrooms, very important in Ligurian cooking, to the fish sauce.

216. RAVIOLI DI RICOTTA

Pasta ripiena

INGREDIENTS: Wheat flour and eggs. For the filling, ricotta, parsley or spinach, and pecorino, or, more simply, ricotta and pecorino, but also other local cheeses.

HOW MADE: The flour is sifted onto a wooden board and kneaded long and vigorously with eggs until the dough is firm and smooth. The dough is left to rest, then rolled out with a rolling pin into a thin sheet, from which long strips about 4 inches (10 cm) wide are cut. On half of each strip, little piles of filling are lined up, then the strip is folded over and the pasta is pressed around the filling. The *ravioli* are cut into half-moons about 2 inches (5 cm) in diameter with a wheel-type pasta cutter or an inverted glass. However, the filling method and the shape can vary from area to area. The *ravioli* are boiled, a few at a time, in abundant salted water.

ALSO KNOWN AS: In Campania, especially in the Cilento, *coronetta;* in Puglia, in the Salento, *scarfiuni;* in Sicily, *cassatedde.*

HOW SERVED: Generally as *pastasciutta*, with traditional local sauces. In Sicily, *cassatedde* are served in broth, including fish broth.

WHERE FOUND: Central and southern Italy, in particular Abruzzo; the Marche; Campania, where they are found in the Vallo di Diano; Puglia, especially in the province of Brindisi; Basilicata; and Sicily.

REMARKS: Ricotta-filled *ravioli* are found almost everywhere, but what distinguishes them is what else is added to the filling in the way of seasonings or other local cheeses. The *ravioli di ricotta* made in Abruzzo include a type of pecorino known as *pecorino di Pizzoli.* In general, parsley is added to the ricotta, and sometimes also spinach. But various spring herbs and other greens are found, too, including nettles, used especially in the area of Fermignano (Pesaro Urbino).

In Campania, the ricotta-filled *raviolo* is also called *coronetta,* for its toothed half-moon form. In the Cilento, the *coronetta* is said to be in honor of Princess Costanza, daughter of Federico of Montefeltro, duke of Urbino, who married a Sanseverino lord of Diano. To celebrate the event, a *sagra delle coronette* is held each year.

The Sicilian *cassatedde,* with their tasty filling of local ricotta, allude to the extremely sweet *cassate* and *cassatine* of the island's pastry repertory.

Ravioli with ricotta filling are classic on the Hanukkah table.

217. RAVIOLI DI SAN LEO

Pasta ripiena

INGREDIENTS: Wheat flour, eggs, and water. For the filling, mixed wild greens bound with ricotta and parmigiano and flavored with lemon rind and spices.

HOW MADE: The flour is sifted onto a wooden board and kneaded with eggs and a little lukewarm water. The dough must be worked long and vigorously, and then is left to rest. It is rolled out into a thin sheet, from which disks about 2 inches (5 cm) in diameter are cut. A teaspoon of filling is placed in the center of each disk, the disk is folded into a half-moon, and the edges are carefully sealed. The *ravioli* are boiled, a few at a time, in plenty of salted water.

ALSO KNOWN AS: No alternative names.

HOW SERVED: As *pastasciutta,* with a hearty meat *ragù* and a grating of local cheese.

WHERE FOUND: In the Marche, where they are a specialty of San Leo.

REMARKS: In the small town of San Leo, famous for the Rocca, a fortress in which the sinister Count of Cagliostro was imprisoned, these tasty *ravioli* flavored with lemon are made. They recall the days when wild greens were used in soup, for a one-dish peasant meal.

No precise recipe specifies which and how many kinds of greens must go into the filling, because it depends on what is found in the fields. This means that these *ravioli* always have a different aromatic component. Meat *ragù* is the ideal complement.

218. RAVIOLI DI SEIRASS E MAIALE

Pasta ripiena

INGREDIENTS: Wheat flour, egg yolks, and often spinach. For the filling, Piedmontese ricotta *(seirass)* and stewed pork.

HOW MADE: The flour is sifted onto a wooden board and kneaded long and vigorously with egg yolks and often also finely minced boiled spinach to color the dough green. When the dough is firm and smooth, it is left to rest, then rolled out with a rolling pin into a thin sheet, and little balls of filling are placed, well spaced, on half of it. The sheet is folded over and pressed around the filling. A special pasta cutter or inverted glass is used to cut out half-moons about 2 inches (5 cm) wide. The *ravioli* are boiled, a few at a time, in abundant boiling salted water.

ALSO KNOWN AS: No alternative names.

HOW SERVED: These ravioli are generally served as *pastasciutta, in bianco* with foaming butter *di malga,* sage, and parmigiano.

WHERE FOUND: Piedmont.

REMARKS: *Seirass* is the name given in Piedmont to the fragrant mountain ricotta, which imparts an unmistakable flavor. It is made by heating the whey of cow's, sheep's, and goat's milk, singly or together.

The *seirass* (or *saras*) *del fen* comes from the pastures around Pinerolo, in particular the Chisone, Pellice, and Germanasca valleys. This traditional product is made by adding milk to the whey and aging the forms for twenty-five to thirty days, then wrapping them in alpine hay, which becomes the characteristic covering of the cheese.

The addition of stewed pork to the filling enriches the dish, whose ideal condiment is the region's excellent mountain butter.

219. RAVIOLI DOLCI DI RICOTTA

Pasta ripiena

INGREDIENTS: Wheat flour and eggs. For the filling, sheep's milk ricotta, sugar, lemon, and cinnamon.

HOW MADE: The flour is sifted onto a wooden board and kneaded with eggs until a firm, smooth dough forms. The dough is left to rest, then rolled out with a rolling pin into a thin sheet, from which disks about 4 inches (10 cm) in diameter are cut. A teaspoon of filling is placed in the center of each disk, and the *raviolo* is closed into a half-moon and the edges carefully sealed. The half-moons are boiled, a few at a time, in plenty of salted water.

ALSO KNOWN AS: In Basilicata, *ravioli materani* and *u cazini*.

HOW SERVED: As *pastasciutta,* traditionally with melted butter and parmigiano.

WHERE FOUND: Abruzzo, typical of Teramo, and Basilicata, especially in the area of Matera.

REMARKS: Sweet *ravioli,* typical for feast days and especially Carnival, actually belong to the sweets repertory of almost every Italian region, with local variants, including the cooking method. In Abruzzo, despite their sweet taste, they are served as a *primo piatto* at important luncheons, recalling ancient traditions from elsewhere as well.

In Basilicata, especially in the province of Matera, the *raviolo* is typically served with a lamb *ragù* and is also called *u cazini,* "the *calzone.*"

220. RAVIORE

Pasta ripiena

INGREDIENTS: Wheat flour and water. For the filling, wild herbs and greens, such as costmary, lemon verbena, wild spinach (called *engrari*), mint, and nettles.

HOW MADE: The flour is sifted onto a wooden board and kneaded long and vigorously with water until a smooth, firm dough forms. The dough is left to rest, then rolled out into a sheet, which is cut into rectangles of about 3⅛ by 2½ inches (about 8 by 6 cm). Some filling is placed on each rectangle, the pasta is rolled closed, and the ends are twisted like a candy wrapper. The *raviore* are boiled in salted water.

ALSO KNOWN AS: No alternative names.

HOW SERVED: As *pastasciutta,* traditionally with the cooking water, butter, and local pecorino, but also with chopped walnuts and cream.

WHERE FOUND: Liguria, in particular Montegrosso Pian Latte and Cosio d'Arroscia.

REMARKS: In Liguria, a thin thread in the Maritime Alps links the transhumance routes, along which foodways traveled with the flocks for centuries, with the Occitan valleys of the province of Cuneo. The local cuisine exploits not only the monochromatic foods of *cucina bianca* but also the area's wild herbs, like those that go into the filling for *raviore.* Together with the traditional sauce of walnuts and cream, these *raviore* attest the poverty that once afflicted this land in winter: there was nothing else to use. But today, this unusual pasta is the pride of the valley's gastronomy.

221. REGINETTE TOSCANE

Pasta lunga

INGREDIENTS: Durum-wheat flour and water.

HOW MADE: Factory-made flat noodle with one or both edges ruffled. They are boiled in abundant salted water.

ALSO KNOWN AS: Depending on width, *fettuccelle ricche, frese, lasagne doppio festone, lasagnette, mafaldine, mezze lasagne, nastri, nastrini, reginelle, sciabò, sciablò, signorine, tagliatelle nervate,* and *tripolini.*

HOW SERVED: As *pastasciutta,* typically with a sauce of hare or rabbit.

WHERE FOUND: Throughout Italy, but particularly in Tuscany.

REMARKS: The name means literally "Tuscan queenlets." This pasta is particularly common in Tuscany, especially in the Val di Chiana. The ruffled edge(s) have the practical purpose of collecting the sauce, but are also reminiscent of the crown worn by queens and princesses in the popular imagination.

222. RICCIOLINI

Pasta corta

INGREDIENTS: Durum-wheat flour or type 00 wheat flour, salt, and a few eggs.

HOW MADE: The flour is sifted with a pinch of salt onto a wooden board and kneaded long and vigorously with only a few eggs, so the dough will be quite hard. After the dough has rested, small pieces are pinched off and worked with oiled hands into narrow strips 1¼ or 1½ inches (3 or 4 cm) long. These are curled to resemble a corkscrew. The *ricciolini* are cooked in broth.

ALSO KNOWN AS: No alternative names.

HOW SERVED: In broth.

WHERE FOUND: Emilia-Romagna, in particular Ferrara.

REMARKS: The name means literally "little curls." *Ricciolini* are typical of the *cucina ebraica* of Ferrara, where they are customarily made for Yom Kippur.

223. RIGATONI

Pasta corta

INGREDIENTS: Durum-wheat flour and water.

HOW MADE: Factory-made thick, tubular pasta with ridges. They are boiled in plenty of salted water.

ALSO KNOWN AS: *Bombardoni, cannaroni, cannerozzi rigati, maniche, rigatoni romani, rigatoncini, trivelli,* and *tufoloni rigati.* In Calabria, *scaffittuni.*

HOW SERVED: As *pastasciutta,* with hearty local sauces.

WHERE FOUND: Southern Italy.

REMARKS: The name comes from *rigato,* or "ridged." Adding striations to the dies, which are what give ridges to certain pastas, must have been one of the first problems faced by the nascent pasta industry. With ridging, pasta made a great advance in quality because ridged pasta collected the sauce and grated cheese better than smooth pasta. In fact, ridged forms, from thin *sedani* to thick *rigatoni,* are the best sellers.

Rigatoni, in particular, are perennial favorites in southern Italy, especially in Sicily, where they are the great protagonists of such preparations as the *taganu* of Aragona Caldaro, near Agrigento, typically served for Holy Saturday. In dialect, the *taganu* is an earthenware pan with flared sides that was once used for a succulent *pasticcio.* To prevent the *pasticcio* from losing its shape when it was unmolded, the *taganu* was broken, leaving the *pasticcio,* in the shape of a panettone, standing in all its majesty on the serving dish.[224]

Maccheroni were also prepared in earthenware pots in Basilicata, and some housewives still prepare them that way: the large *cannerozzi* were layered and served with sauce and cheese. In the past, they assembled the pots of pasta in the morning and sent them into the countryside for the harvesters to eat still warm.

In Roviano, in Lazio, near Subiaco, the popular imagination has given *rigatoni* the name *scorzasellari,* "celery peelers," because the ridging makes them look like ribs of celery. In Abruzzo, *rigatoni* used to be called *gnocconi,* and *ciofelloni* when they were larger. They were the pastas for Sundays.

224. ROTOLO RIPIENO

Pasta ripiena

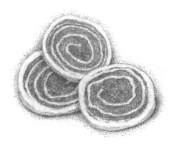

INGREDIENTS: Wheat flour, eggs, and water, but sometimes only flour and water. For the filling, various ingredients usually, but not always, bound with ricotta.

HOW MADE: The flour is sifted onto a wooden board and kneaded long and vigorously with eggs and water. The dough is left to rest, then rolled out with a rolling pin into a more or less rectangular sheet, on which the filling is spread evenly. The sheet is then rolled up, wrapped in gauze, and simmered in salted water.

The gauze is carefully removed, and the *rotolo* is sliced. The slices are arranged in an ovenproof dish; covered with béchamel, *ragù*, or simple tomato sauce, depending on local custom; and gratinéed.

ALSO KNOWN AS: *Rotolo imbottito* (stuffed roll). In Trentino–Alto Adige, *strudel;* in the Marche, *pasta al sacco.*

HOW SERVED: As *pastasciutta,* usually gratinéed with traditional local ingredients.

WHERE FOUND: Widespread.

REMARKS: Literally "stuffed roll," *rotolo ripieno* is a relatively modern preparation, probably originally a variant of the sweet strudel of Trentino. It is popular today throughout Italy for its practicality and ease of execution. The filling depends on local products, and can be meat, fish, cheese, or a mixture. In Lombardy, but also in other regions, the *rotolo* is usually filled with ricotta and spinach, then sliced, covered with sauce, and browned in the oven.

Gubbio boasts a tasty variant of the *rotolo.* To make it, a sheet of pasta is spread with a layer of *broccoletti* and one of *zite* (see entry) mixed with a sauce of goose giblets. The sheet is folded over to seal in the contents, covered with more sauce, and cooked in a wood-burning oven.

225. RUFIOI DELLA VALLE DEI MOCHENI

Pasta ripiena

INGREDIENTS: Wheat flour, eggs, water, and salt. For the filling, Savoy cabbage, leek, cinnamon, and *grana trentino* cheese.

HOW MADE: The flour is sifted onto a wooden board and kneaded long and hard with eggs, water, and a pinch of salt until a firm, smooth dough forms. The dough is left to rest, then rolled out into a sheet, not too thin. Teaspoons of filling are placed 1¼ to 1½ inches (3 to 4 cm) apart on half of the sheet. The sheet is folded over and pressed around the filling. A wheel-type pasta cutter is used to cut out large, square *tortelloni,* which are boiled in salted water.

ALSO KNOWN AS: No alternative names.

HOW SERVED: As *pastasciutta,* generally with foaming butter and *grana trentino.*

WHERE FOUND: Trentino–Alto Adige, in the Valle dei Mocheni.

REMARKS: *Rufioi* are a specialty of the hills that stand above the town of Pergine Valsugana, along the Valle dei Mocheni. They used to be served for lunch on feast days, and the housewives would make large quantities of them to offer visiting friends and relatives. *Kropfen, ravioli* filled with sauerkraut and rice, were also typical of the valley.

The Mocheni are an ethnic German minority who, fleeing the wars for succession among the principalities, took refuge in Italy, in this mining area of the Trentino, in the fourteenth and fifteenth centuries. Until the 1700s, they constituted the largest workforce in the mines, but after the shafts were closed, they became itinerant vendors of artisanal products and later traveled through the mountain villages carrying a permit from Maria Teresa, empress of Austria, to which Trentino belonged in the nineteenth century. Today, the Mocheni practice small-scale commerce and livestock raising, and maintain their customs, language, and food culture.

226. RUOTE

Pasta corta

INGREDIENTS: Durum-wheat flour and water.

HOW MADE: Factory made in a spoked wheel shape. They are boiled in abundant salted water.

ALSO KNOWN AS: For the smallest sizes, *rotelle* and *rotelline,* but also *rotine.*

HOW SERVED: Generally as *pastasciutta,* but the smallest size is cooked in broth.

WHERE FOUND: Widespread.

REMARKS: Many machine-inspired pasta shapes of various sizes arrived with the industrial age, and particularly the automobile, in the early twentieth century. Thus, we have not only *ruote* (wheels), but also *radiatori* (radiators) and *lancette* (a *pastina* shaped like pen nibs). And there are others: *Frese, fresine,* and *sfresatine* (variations on a kind of cutter) are in the *tagliatelle* (see entry) family, but are wider and longer and have a slightly ruffled edge. *Trivelli* are short, ridged tubes, just as the first *trivelle* (industrial drills) must have been. *Gomiti* (elbows) are curved tubes of various sizes, and *eliche* ("helixes," but also "propellers") are shaped like propellers and include two variants, *eliche grandi* and *elicoidali.* Very similar are *spole* and *spolette* ("spools" or "bobbins"). In the 1950s, a decade when people had Martians on the mind, there were even disk-shaped *dischi volanti* (flying saucers).

227. SAGNE

Pasta lunga

INGREDIENTS: Wheat flour, water, and sometimes eggs. In some towns, *sagne* are made with the local *farro* flour.

HOW MADE: The flour is sifted onto a wooden board and kneaded long and vigorously with water and sometimes also eggs, then the dough is left to rest. It is rolled out into a thick sheet, and flat noodles of variable width and length, depending on the area of production, are cut from it. They are boiled in abundant salted water.

ALSO KNOWN AS: *Sagnarelle, sagnette,* and *sagnettine.* In Friuli–Venezia Giulia (Carnia), *lis agnis* or *las agnas;* in northern Lazio, *sagnotte, sagnozzi,* and also *sagne 'mpezze;* and in Molise, *lajanelle, malefante, sagne di casa,* and *sagnetelle.*

HOW SERVED: Generally as *pastasciutta,* with various meat *ragù,* but also with vegetable sauces. In Abruzzo, a typical soup of *sagne* with *cicerchie* is made, but the noodles are also served as *pastasciutta* with wild asparagus.

WHERE FOUND: In general, central Italy, and in particular, the Marche, Abruzzo, Molise, and northern Lazio (Tivoli-Subiaco), but also Friuli (Carnia).

REMARKS: Antonio de Magistris da Introdaqua, in the *Biografia del Beato Bernardino da Fontavignone* (1794), recounts how the *beato* prescribed *sagne* as a medication:

> . . . Lucantonio of Fonte Avignone suffering many complicated infirmities . . . since the physicians gave a very bad estimate of his being cured . . . eating the *sagne* made by his wife (medicament left to the whole town by the Servant of God) immediately began to improve and in a few days was perfectly free and healthy. . . .

The term *sagne* is used in different localities and usually indicates fresh pasta of different shapes. For example, in Lazio, around Subiaco, the term *sagne 'mpezze* is used for a sort of rhombus-shaped *maltagliato.* In Riofreddo, in the upper Aniene valley, *sagnozze* are thick *spaghetti* about 2¾ inches (7 cm) long, which are served both in broth with beans and as *pastasciutta.*

Today, *sagne* are almost always made with eggs. In northern Lazio and Abruzzo, flour milled from emmer, which is the pride of the local agriculture of the hills and which has never been subject to rationing, even during wartime, is used. In the past, these *sagne* were often sold to buy salt, the only item for which the grocery stores would not give credit.

The homemade pasta was dark and had an unappealing appearance. This was because the nighttime dew turned the sheaves black, which meant they had to be washed, with consequent loss of volume. To avoid this job, many housewives made *sagne* with the dark grain, and then, so the darker color of the pasta would be less obvious, they closed the shutters when they served it.

In some towns in Abruzzo, in season, the women known as *sagnarelle* make *pastasciutta* with the wild asparagus that grows spontaneously in the *macchia mediterranea* (maquis). These are the same asparagus that the poet Martial liked so much,[225] and the ones that the poet Juvenal's slave woman, leaving her wool work, went to look for in the mountains so that she could make them for his friend Persicus.[226]

The small Abruzzese town of Fontavignone, founded on the Altipiano delle Rocche by the populations fleeing the Valle dell'Aterno, which had been invaded by outsiders, lacked communication links, which isolated it for centuries. It was thus able to remain a faithful guardian of culinary traditions forgotten elsewhere, such as polenta and these *tagliolini,* which are still today cooked in milk. They are common in Molise as well, where *sagne brodose* (watery) are served cooked in broth and as *pastasciutta in bianco,* with the local cheeses and chili. Also in Molise, an appetizing *pasticcio* of wide *tagliatelle* with *scamorza* and *ragù,* called *sagna 'mbuttita* in dialect, is made for Carnival. In the Molise town of Trivento, housewives make *sagne 'nche le curredure,* broad, flat noodles that they cut with a toothed cutter called a *curredure,* which gives the pasta a slightly wavy shape. This noodle is so well liked in these parts that almost all of the pasta factories in Molise—and they are numerous—have reproduced it as a broad, curly *fettuccia.*

228. SAGNE CHJNE

Pasta ripiena

INGREDIENTS: Durum-wheat flour, salt, and water. For the filling, tiny meatballs, artichokes, mushrooms, herbs, *caciocavallo,* pecorino, and hard-boiled eggs.

HOW MADE: The flour is sifted onto a wooden board and kneaded long and vigorously with a pinch of salt and lukewarm water until a hard, smooth dough forms. The dough is left to rest, then rolled out with a rolling pin into a thin sheet, and 4-inch (10-cm) squares are cut from it. The squares are dropped into boiling salted water, drained, and laid out on a dish towel to dry. The squares are layered in an oiled pan with the typical *ragù, caciocavallo,* and hard-boiled eggs, and baked.

ALSO KNOWN AS: *Lasagna ripiena.*

HOW SERVED: Layered with *ragù, caciocavallo,* and hard-boiled eggs and baked like *lasagna.*

WHERE FOUND: Calabria.

REMARKS: The word *chjne* (also spelled *chine* or *kine*) means *ripiene,* "filled" or "stuffed." In Calabria, but also in some areas bordering it, such as in Basilicata, the concept of stuffed pasta is not limited to the small pasta-wrapped packages of the rest of Italy. Stuffed pasta here can mean only a vegetable *lasagna* with tiny meatballs no larger than those used to fill *tortellini* (see entry) or *anolini* (see entry). In Calabria, the *timballo,* which came from the aristocratic kitchens of the Kingdom of the Two Sicilies and reached the tables of the people only at the end of the 1700s, replaced the commonly understood concept of the stuffed pastas.[227] *Ravioli* and *tortelli* are recent introductions to the region, their arrival dating from after World War II.

Sagne chjne are traditionally served on feast days.

229. SAGNE INCANNULATE

Pasta lunga

INGREDIENTS: Durum-wheat flour and water.

HOW MADE: The flour is sifted onto a wooden board and kneaded long and vigorously with water until a solid, smooth dough forms. It is left to rest, then rolled out with a rolling pin *(minnaturu)* into a thin sheet, from which strips about ⅝ inch (1.5 cm) wide are cut. The end of a strip is held still on the wooden board with one hand, while the strip is rolled against the board with the palm of the other hand *(incannulata)* three times. Alternatively, the strip is wound around a wooden stick about ⅜ inch (1 cm) in diameter, then slid off. The *sagne* are boiled in plenty of salted water.

ALSO KNOWN AS: *Sagne, lagane incannulate,* and *sagne torte.*

HOW SERVED: As *pastasciutta,* with traditional local sauces, usually a *ragù* of mixed meats.

WHERE FOUND: Puglia.

REMARKS: Shaping this pasta requires great dexterity, and it used to be made by girls in convent-orphanages *(conservatori)*. The 1811 *Statistica del Regno di Napoli*[228] records that the pastas made in the two such institutions in Foggia, delle Orfane and della Maddalena, were famous. The convents sold their products in neighboring Molise. Making pasta was practically the only labor these institutions could practice to support their good works.

Today, the shape is extensively used by industry but with different names, usually *fusilli.*

230. SBROFADEJ

Pasta corta

INGREDIENTS: Wheat flour, eggs, *grana padano,* and spices; on Lake Garda, corn flour is added.

HOW MADE: The flour is sifted onto a wooden board and kneaded with eggs, a little grated *grana padano,* and a pinch of nutmeg. The dough is kneaded quickly and must be soft and well blended. It is left to rest, then placed in a potato ricer and riced directly into boiling broth. The final product is short, thick *vermicelli*— the diameter of the ricer's holes—that are cooked in broth. The composition and shape are different for the Val Camonica.

ALSO KNOWN AS: *Brofandei.* In the Val Camonica, *brofadei.*

HOW SERVED: In meat broth.

WHERE FOUND: Lombardy, in Brescia and around Lake Garda.

REMARKS: The name *sbrofadej* derives from the Lombard dialect word *sbroffà,* which means "spill food on oneself" or "splash oneself," which can happen when eating this short, thick pasta shape in broth.

In the Val Camonica, ball-shaped *brofadei* are made from a mixture of corn and wheat flours. They are poured into boiling water and stirred rapidly.

231. SCARFIUNI

Pasta ripiena

INGREDIENTS: Durum-wheat flour, water, some eggs, and salt. For the filling, ricotta and pecorino.

HOW MADE: The flour is sifted onto a wooden board and kneaded long and vigorously with water, eggs, and a pinch of salt. The dough is left to rest, then rolled out into a thin sheet, and an inverted water glass is used to cut out small disks. A spoonful of filling is placed in the center of each disk, the disk is folded into a half-moon, and the edges are sealed carefully. The half-moons are boiled in plenty of salted water.

ALSO KNOWN AS: *Ravioloni.*

HOW SERVED: As *pastasciutta,* generally with a hearty meat *ragù* and grated pecorino.

WHERE FOUND: Puglia, especially around Brindisi.

REMARKS: The decoration of the border of this large *raviolo* is left to the skill of the housewife. For example, the edge can be flattened with two fingers held close together to make tiny, shallow folds. But each housewife seals her *scarfiune* the way she likes.

232. SCARPINOCC

Pasta ripiena

INGREDIENTS: Flour, milk, eggs, and butter. For the filling, cheese, dry bread crumbs, garlic, and spices.

HOW MADE: The flour is sifted onto a wooden board and kneaded with milk, eggs, and room-temperature butter, then covered and left to rest. The dough is rolled out with a rolling pin into a sheet, and disks 2½ to 3¼ inches (6 to 8 cm) in diameter are cut from it. A spoonful of filling is placed in the center of each disk, the disk is folded into a half-moon, and the edges are carefully sealed. The filled half-moon is pressed with a finger to resemble a rustic shoe. The half-moons are dropped into abundant boiling salted water.

ALSO KNOWN AS: *Betoi.*

HOW SERVED: As *pastasciutta,* with butter and local cheese.

WHERE FOUND: Lombardy, in Parre in the upper Val Seriana.

REMARKS: The name comes from the word *scarpa,* or "shoe." In the upper Val Seriana, as in many valleys of the Orobian Alps, sheep rearing has constituted the principal form of subsistence for centuries. This explains the extensive use of dairy products (butter and cheeses) in the preparation of these *tortelli,* which manage to be tasty, even in their simplicity and poverty of ingredients.

Both the shape and the ingredients are indigenous. The *scarpinocc* are flattened in the middle to look vaguely like the traditional footwear worn by the inhabitants of the town of Parre until a few decades ago. Because of their shape, *scarpinocc* are also called *orecchie* (ears).

Today, *scarpinocc* are also marketed by small local pasta factories, but they must bear a specific mark that guarantees their conformity to the standards established by a specific commission.

233. SCHIAFFETTONI

Pasta ripiena

INGREDIENTS: Durum-wheat flour and eggs, but also flour and water and sometimes a little oil. For factory made, durum-wheat flour and water. For the filling, meats and local *insaccati*.

HOW MADE: The flour is sifted onto a wooden board and kneaded long and vigorously with eggs or water and sometimes a little oil. The dough is left to rest, then rolled out with a rolling pin into a thin sheet, and 4-inch (10-cm) squares are cut from it. A spoonful of filling is placed in the center of each square, the pasta is rolled into a tube, and the edges are tightly sealed. Today, large *rigatoni* or *canneroni* are the factory-made equivalent. They are boiled in plenty of salted water.

ALSO KNOWN AS: In Campania, in Naples, *schiaffuni;* in Molise, *schiaffune;* in Puglia, *sckaffune;* and in Basilicata and Calabria, *scaffettune.*

HOW SERVED: Generally as *pastasciutta*, with meat *ragù,* always with chili.

WHERE FOUND: Campania, especially in the province of Avellino; Molise; Puglia; Basilicata, typical of Sant'Arcangelo and Brindisi Montagna; and Calabria.

REMARKS: The name means literally "slaps." In the town of Brindisi Montagna in Basilicata, *schiaffettoni* used to be made from the trimmings left over after *ravioli* were cut with an inverted glass from a sheet. The irregular rhombuses that remained were filled and served with the *ravioli.*

Today in Calabria, *schiaffettoni* are identified with large commercial *rigatoni* that are both stuffed and used empty in *timballi.* The filling consists of meats, hard-boiled eggs, and pork *insaccati.* They are closed at the ends, boiled, and served with sauce and cheese.

234. SCHNALZERNUDELN

Pasta lunga

INGREDIENTS: Rye flour, ricotta, water, sometimes eggs, and salt.

HOW MADE: Rye flour is kneaded for a long time with ricotta, water, sometimes an egg, and a pinch of salt until a very hard dough forms. Then pieces of dough are fed into a *torchio*, from which extremely thin *spaghetti* emerge.

The particularity of this pasta lies in the fact that it is not boiled. Instead, it is browned in a goodly amount of foaming butter, stirred, and broken up with a fork while cooking.

ALSO KNOWN AS: No alternative names.

HOW SERVED: As *pastasciutta*, with butter and cheese.

WHERE FOUND: Alto Adige, typical of the Val di Senales.

REMARKS: This old preparation of the Val di Senales is an index of the poverty of the area's cuisine. It can be a *primo piatto*, served simply with the cooking butter and a little local cheese, but it can also accompany game, or it can be paired with a jam of red bilberries and served as a dessert.

Although the preparation of the compact, firm dough is simple, great strength is required to force it through the *torchio*. For this reason, the *torchio*, very similar to the Venetian *bigolaro*, is clamped to a wooden stand.

235. SCHULTZKRAPFEN

Pasta ripiena

INGREDIENTS: Rye flour, wheat flour, eggs, oil, and water. For the filling, spinach, ricotta, and potatoes, but also poppy seeds, chives, nettles, or sauerkraut.

HOW MADE: The flours are sifted onto a wooden board and kneaded long and vigorously with eggs, a little oil, and lukewarm water. The dough is left to rest, then rolled out into a thin sheet, and disks about 2 inches (5 cm) in diameter are cut with a mold or an inverted glass. A teaspoon of filling is placed in the middle of each disk, the disk is folded into a half-moon, and the edges are carefully sealed. They are boiled in plenty of salted water.

ALSO KNOWN AS: *Ravioli atesini, ravioli della Pusteria,* and *roffioi* or *rofioi.*

HOW SERVED: As *pastasciutta*, with melted butter and local cheese, especially the so-called gray cheese, *Graukäse.*

WHERE FOUND: Alto Adige, especially the Val Pusteria.

REMARKS: The picturesque villages set into mountainsides and valleys in the Dolomites have maintained culinary ties to Austria. In the mountains, where the climate prohibits the wealth of vegetables found in the south, *ravioli* are filled with what is available in each season: sauerkraut in winter, nettles and poppy seeds in spring, but also ricotta, spinach, and potatoes in the warm-weather months. And these very special *ravioli,* symbol of the cooking of the Val Pusteria, owe their fame to the particular ricotta used for the filling.

In the peasant homes, *ravioli* were not necessarily considered food for feast days. Traditionally, a different food was made for each day of the week, and *Schultzkrapfen* were for Saturday. They have been made for centuries in the Val Pusteria. Their ancestors, the *calisons* of Trentino, were sweets fashioned from almond paste covered with host and made in a wide variety of shapes, including hearts for lovers' gifts. The so-called *pasticcetti,* tasty *ravioli* baked in the oven and served in broth, were also made in the Val Pusteria.

236. SCHUNCHENFLETZ

Pasta corta

INGREDIENTS: Wheat flour and eggs.

HOW MADE: The flour is sifted onto a wooden board and kneaded with eggs until a firm, smooth dough forms. The dough is left to rest, then rolled out with a rolling pin into a sheet, not too thin. A wheel-type pasta cutter is used to cut squares of unspecified size. They are boiled in abundant water.

ALSO KNOWN AS: No alternative names.

HOW SERVED: As *pastasciutta,* sauced and gratinéed.

WHERE FOUND: Trentino–Alto Adige.

REMARKS: These small squares of pasta are layered in a pan with bits of prosciutto and abundant butter and cheese and browned in the oven.

Schunchenfletz are documented in the home recipe book of the Montel household. Inside the front cover is written: "This copy of the cookbook of the Montel house was transcribed by Pio Mancini, tax collector of the German cemetery, on behalf of Teodolindo Montel, who has custody of the original; he gave the copy to his sister Maria Gerloni de Montel. The original certainly dates to before 1820."[229] The transcriber copied the book in Rome on April 9, 1871.

237. SCIALATIELLI
Pasta lunga

INGREDIENTS: Durum-wheat flour and water. For factory made, durum-wheat flour and water and today sometimes cheese.

HOW MADE: The flour is sifted onto a wooden board and kneaded long and vigorously with water until a firm, smooth dough forms, which is then left to rest. Next, two customary procedures are possible: For one, the dough is rolled out into a sheet, thick noodles are cut from it, the noodles are rolled around a *ferretto*, and then they are rolled back and forth on the wooden board into long *bucatini*. For the other, small pieces of dough are pinched off and rolled directly on the *ferretto* to the length and the thickness desired. There are also factory-made versions of various shapes: a flat noodle about ⅛ inch (2 mm) thick and about 6 inches (15 cm) long, and spiral *spaghetti*. *Scialatielli* are boiled in abundant salted water.

ALSO KNOWN AS: In Campania and Basilicata, *sciliatelli;* in Calabria, *ricci di donna, salatielli, scilatelli, scivateddi,* and *strangugliapreviti.*

HOW SERVED: Generally as *pastasciutta,* with traditional local sauces, including *ragù* of brains (of lamb, not too young) in Calabria, but more commonly pork *ragù.*

WHERE FOUND: Campania, a specialty of Minori, on the Amalfi coast; Basilicata; and Calabria, especially Cosenza.

REMARKS: The origin of the word lies in the Neapolitan dialect verb *sciglià*, for Italian *scompigliare,* "to dishevel," referring to hair: these *sciliatelli* must be thin and *scompigliati,* or "disheveled," which is how they look, steaming in their dish.

In Basilicata, *sciliatelli* are thick *fettuccine,* not longer than 4 to 5 inches (10 to 12 cm), made with a particular die and produced today by small local pasta factories. They are suitable for fish sauces.

In certain areas of Calabria, the name *scialatielli* is used for a thick *spaghetti* about 4¾ inches (12 cm) long. In some areas, *strangugliapreviti,* which means *strozzapreti* (see entry for *strangolapreti, strozzapreti*), are simple *gnocchetti* rolled on a wooden board with one or two fingers; in others, they are *fusilli* made from *fettuccine* rolled on a *ferretto,* called *roncu.*

238. SCORZE DI MANDORLE

Pasta corta

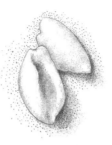

INGREDIENTS: Durum-wheat flour, water, and salt.

HOW MADE: The flour is sifted with salt onto a wooden board and kneaded long and vigorously with water until a smooth, firm dough forms, which is left to rest. With the rounded tip of a knife, pea-sized pieces of dough are drawn downward on the wooden board in such a way that they form little curls that resemble almond shells. They are boiled in abundant salted water.

ALSO KNOWN AS: *Skorzel d'amell.*

HOW SERVED: As *pastasciutta,* with local sauces.

WHERE FOUND: Basilicata, especially around Matera, where they are typical of the small town of Pomarico.

REMARKS: The name means literally "almond shells." The variety of homemade-pasta shapes in Basilicata is great. The work is always done on a wooden board known as an *'mpastapan,* a curious dialect term that derives from the Italian *impasta pane,* or "knead bread."

Often the *cavatello* shape takes slightly different forms, smaller or larger, more closed or more open, the edges flat or upturned, and so on. The different shapes also have their typical condiments, ranging from lamb *ragù* to the more common sauce of garlic, oil, tomato, and chili, with a final dusting of one of the excellent pecorino cheeses produced in the region.

239. SCORZE DI NOCELLA

Pasta corta

INGREDIENTS: Durum-wheat flour, sometimes also whole-wheat flour or *grano arso,* and water.

HOW MADE: The flour is sifted and kneaded long and vigorously with water until a smooth, firm dough forms. After the dough has rested, small pieces are pinched off and rolled into little balls. Each ball is poked in the middle with a finger, to yield a pasta that looks like half of a hazelnut shell. They are boiled in plenty of salted water.

ALSO KNOWN AS: *Abissini, cappettine,* and, around Molfetta, *scagghjuzze.*

HOW SERVED: Generally with legumes or ricotta, or in broth.

WHERE FOUND: Puglia, in particular the area of Taranto.

REMARKS: The name means literally "hazelnut shells." The use of flours other than wheat flour was common in Puglia, especially in depressed areas or during periods of famine when grasses or legumes might be ground. Sometimes *grano arso* was also used. Doughs made from these flours were hard work to knead, which explains the easy-to-make shapes such as this one.

240. SCUCUZZU

Pastina

INGREDIENTS: Durum-wheat flour, eggs, water, and salt; formerly only flour and water.

HOW MADE: The flour is sifted with a pinch of salt and then kneaded with eggs and water until a dough forms, which is left to rest. Tiny pieces are pinched off and rubbed between the hands into little balls no bigger than grains of rice. The pasta is dried for twenty-four hours before it is cooked in broth.

ALSO KNOWN AS: No alternative names.

HOW SERVED: In vegetable soup or in broth.

WHERE FOUND: Liguria.

REMARKS: This tiny pasta, made in imitation of couscous (see *cuscus*), was the product of the intense commercial exchanges between Genoa and North Africa. Ligurian cooks, however, were unfamiliar with the difficult original preparation. The word itself is probably taken from the term *cuscus*.

The characteristic tiny pasta, which, under different names, has kept its popularity over the years throughout Italy, must be thoroughly dried before cooking. If it is not perfectly dry, it will disintegrate in the soup and turn a clear broth into a sort of *polentina*.

241. SEDANI

Pasta corta

INGREDIENTS: Durum-wheat flour and water.

HOW MADE: Factory-made short tubes, usually ridged and slightly curved. They are boiled in abundant salted water.

ALSO KNOWN AS: Depending on size, *cornetti* (horns), *diavoletti* (imps), *diavolini*, *fagiolini* (green beans), *folletti* (elves), *sedanetti* (little celeries), *stivalettini* (tiny boots), *stortini* (little crooked), and *tubetti lunghi* (long tubes). For the small shapes, *cannolicchi*, *fagioloni* (beans), *gnocchetti di ziti*, *gramignoni*, *sciviottini*, *svuotini* (empties), *sedani rigati* (ridged celeries), and *maccheroncini*.

HOW SERVED: Generally as *pastasciutta*, with traditional local sauces.

WHERE FOUND: Widespread.

REMARKS: The name means literally "celeries." *Sedani* are short, ridged pastas, similar to *rigatoni* (see entry). The alternative names refer to both vegetables and the world of fairy tales, with imps and elves, and certainly come from old homemade pastas.

242. SEMI D'AVENA

Pastina

INGREDIENTS: Durum-wheat flour and water.

HOW MADE: Factory-made tiny shape cooked in broth.

ALSO KNOWN AS: *Lenti, lentine* (lenses), *midolline, semi di peperone* (pepper seeds), *perline* (beads), *punte d'ago* (needle points), *semi di cicoria, semi di grano, semi di mele, semi di melone, semi d'orzo, semi di popone, semi di riso, telline,* and *tempestine.*

HOW SERVED: Generally in broth.

WHERE FOUND: Widespread.

REMARKS: The peasant's strongbox of long ago, if it had existed, would have contained his most precious possessions, the seeds on which his work and his family's sustenance depended. The better the seeds he selected, the better the harvest. The name of this pasta, literally "oat seeds," reflects that history.

Many other tiny *pastina* shapes also allude to seeds of fruits, grains, and legumes: *semi di cicoria* (chicory seeds), *semi di grano* (wheat), *semi di mele* (apples), *semi di melone* (melon), *semi d'orzo* (barley), *semi di peperone* (bell pepper), *semi di popone* (melon), and *semi di riso* (rice). Other shapes can be added to this group for their size and use, such as *punte d'ago, lentine, midolline, tempestine,* and so on.

Comparing the catalogs of the pasta makers of yesterday with those of today, we see that the shapes vary little, and remain tiny: less imagination, certainly, but the products are more marketable.

243. SEMOLA BATTUTA

Pastina

INGREDIENTS: Durum-wheat *semolone,* eggs, cheese, and parsley.

HOW MADE: The flour is sifted into a bowl and kneaded with grated cheese, eggs, and chopped parsley until a hard, smooth dough forms. Chickpea-sized pieces are pinched off and rolled into tiny balls between the hands. They are cooked in broth.

ALSO KNOWN AS: No alternative names.

HOW SERVED: In vegetable or meat broth, formerly turkey.

WHERE FOUND: Puglia, typical of the province of Foggia.

REMARKS: The name means literally "beaten flour." This soup used to be obligatory for Easter. Durum-wheat flour, used for almost all the pastas made in Puglia, was classified, according to quality, as *cappelle, grefone,* or *saragolla.* The latter, which was considered by far the best, was used to make *semola battuta.*

Today, the same dough but slightly softer is also forced through a potato ricer to make a special pasta called *stracciatella.*

244. SHTRIDHËLAT

Pasta lunga

INGREDIENTS: Durum-wheat flour, type 00 wheat flour, and water.

HOW MADE: The flours are sifted together and kneaded for a long time with water. The dough is left to rest, then divided into small loaves. The loaves are pierced in the center with a special utensil (in Arbëreshë, *kesistra*) or with hands, and work proceeds much as for *manate* (see entry). They are boiled in abundant salted water.

ALSO KNOWN AS: *Maccaruni a centinara, maccaruni a cento,* and *maccheroni a fezze.* In Lazio, in the Sabine country of the province of Rieti, the pasta is known as *jacculi;* and in Abruzzo, around Teramo, as *pasta alla molenara.* In the area of Vaglio Basilicata, a similar pasta is called *manare* or *manatelle;* and in Calabria, in the provinces of Cosenza and Catanzaro, it is *salatielli, sciliatelli,* and *scivateddi,* but the technique is different.

HOW SERVED: Traditionally in soup with beans, but also *pastasciutta,* with typical local sauces.

WHERE FOUND: In the Albanian communities of Lazio, Abruzzo, Molise, Basilicata, and Calabria.

REMARKS: This pasta is typical of the Arberia, the Italo-Albanian communities in Italy. The Albanians crossed the Ionian Sea between 1470 and 1540 to flee the Turkish invasion and settled in the south of Italy, thanks both to the welcome by the local population (not without some episodes of exploitation) and to the marriage of Irene Castriota Scanderbeg, granddaughter of Giorgio Castriota Scanderbeg, leader of the Albanian troops against the Turks, to the feudal lord Pietro Antonio Sanseverino. Other migrations followed, spurred by different historical events over the centuries, until our own day.

The 1991 census counted just over 90,000 Italian citizens of Albanian ethnicity. Of these, about 7,000 lived in Basilicata and almost 41,000 in Calabria. Other significant clusters live in Molise and in Sicily, where the Arbëreshë settlement is found around the town of Piana degli Albanesi. Within the Pollino National Park, which spans Calabria and Basilicata, ethnic Albanians are present in nine towns: Frascineto (Frasnita), Eianina (Purcilo), Civita (Çiftí), San Paolo Albanese (Shën Pali), San Costantino Albanese (Shën Kostadini), Acquaformosa (Firmoza), Lungro (Ungra), Plataci (Pllatani), and San Basile (Shën Vasili). They are resident in big cities like Rome, Milan, and Turin as well—without counting the 250,000 new Albanian immigrants into Italy.[230]

In most of these communities, language, customs, and festivities have remained firmly rooted. The religious feasts were considered particularly important until the 1940s and 1950s. In the different *gjitonie* (Albanian communities), during the week before the feast of the Nativity of the Virgin (September 8), a large copper vase in which the faithful poured offerings of oil was displayed on the windowsill. At dusk the oil was lit, and the members of the *gjitonia*, seated in a circle, sang ritual Albanian and Calabrian songs to the Virgin. In the Albanian community of Lungro, the tradition of the torches, prepared with *verbasco* (mullein), a type of herb that was picked and dried during the year, called for lighting torches on Christmas Eve to illuminate the way to Midnight Mass. This ritual continued until the 1930s.[231]

Many of the gastronomic customs still alive in the Albanian communities, such as *taralli* and *cullura*,[232] have passed into traditional Italian cuisine. Even *shtridhëlat* are now part of the gastronomic heritage of many towns in central and southern Italy, including where there were no ethnic Albanian settlements. The pasta takes on different names but has maintained the typical preparation technique.

The writer Carmine Abate recalls a meal from his childhood:

> Bravo the cook of Arberia. I think that none of us knew then that the Arberia meant the Italo-Albanian communities in the south of Italy as a whole; personally I was convinced that it was the bizarre name of the cook's mother. . . . For our good fortune, the cook clapped his hands to admit five women who brought in platters of steaming *shtridhëlat* . . . they were truly good. I ate two plates of them.[233]

This type of pasta is curiously common also in areas where there have never been any Albanian communities, as in the Sabine country of Lazio, or at Fabrica di Roma, where a similar pasta is called *mesatoli*. The same pasta at Carbognano (Viterbo) is known as *gavinelle*.

245. SLICOFI

Pasta ripiena

INGREDIENTS: Flour, oil, and water. For the filling, potatoes, dry bread crumbs, cheese, fragrant herbs, and sometimes cooked ham.

HOW MADE: The flour is sifted onto a wooden board and kneaded with a little oil and water until a smooth, firm dough forms. After resting, the dough is rolled out with a rolling pin into a thin sheet, and 2¾-inch (7-cm) squares are cut from it. A spoonful of filling is placed on each square, and the square is closed in a rectangle.

The edges are carefully sealed so the filling does not come out when the pasta is boiled in salted water.

ALSO KNOWN AS: *Gnocchi di Idria, gnocchi di pasta ripieni di patate, slikrofi,* and *zlikofi.* In one variant, the filling is bread, soaked in cream, and prosciutto.

HOW SERVED: Generally as *pastasciutta,* sauced with dry bread crumbs sautéed in butter.

WHERE FOUND: Friuli–Venezia Giulia, province of Trieste, in particular San Daniele, in the Carso.

REMARKS: These particular *ravioli,* whose filling in springtime is redolent of chives, are typical of the hilly area that rises toward the Carso and the part of Istria that is no longer Italian. The Croatian restaurants near the present-day border often make them as a local specialty.

246. SORCETTI

Pastina

INGREDIENTS: Flour, potatoes, spinach, and eggs. Sometimes corn flour is mixed with the wheat flour.

HOW MADE: The potatoes are boiled and riced while still warm. The spinach is boiled separately, then squeezed and finely chopped. Cold potatoes and spinach are kneaded with sifted flour and eggs. It is not necessary to leave the dough to rest. Small pieces of dough are pinched off and rolled between the hands to make little logs about ⅜ inch (1 cm) in diameter. These are cut on the bias into lengths of about ¾ inch (2 cm), which are boiled briefly in salted water and drained as soon as they float.

ALSO KNOWN AS: In the Marche, they are called *sorcetti pelosi* (hairy mice), when the dough contains some polenta, but also *suricitti.*

HOW SERVED: As *pastasciutta,* usually with a sauce of *castrato,* with a final dusting of local pecorino.

WHERE FOUND: Abruzzo, but also the Marche.

REMARKS: The name means literally "little mice." Popular gastronomy is full of references to animals considered filthy (rats, mice, worms, snails, and so on) to indicate extremely poor foods of little value, like *sorcetti*.

Around Macerata, *sorcetti* or *suricitti* are fried *gnocchi* made of polenta and wheat flour.

247. SPAGHETTI

Pasta lunga

INGREDIENTS: Durum-wheat flour and water.

HOW MADE: Long, string-shaped durum-wheat pasta, originally rolled by hand and, later, extruded through a die. Today, it is long-format factory-made pasta. The types and names vary according to the diameter of the pasta and the region of production. They are boiled in plenty of salted water.

ALSO KNOWN AS: *Fide;* in Sicily, *fidillini.* For the thinnest, *capelli d'angelo* (angel hair), *capellini* (hair), *capelvenere* (Venus's hair), *fedelini, fidelini,* and *sopracapellini,* but also *mezzi vermicelli, spaghettini,* and *vermicellini.* For the thickest, *filatelli, spaghettoni, vermicelloni,* and *vermicelloni giganti.*

HOW SERVED: The thin shapes in broth; the thicker ones as *pastasciutta,* with traditional local sauces.

WHERE FOUND: Widespread.

REMARKS: The root of the word *spaghetti* is simple: it means a small string, exactly as the first, handmade, vaguely irregular *spaghetti* must have been. The name for this pasta is a household word on every continent and a synonym for "made in Italy." The writer Giuseppe Prezzolini said that "*spaghetti* have the same right or more to belong to Italian civilization that Dante has." Without doubt, behind the surface meaning of a string-shaped pasta made from durum-wheat flour, there is a deeper meaning that contains the philosophy of a civilization—a meaning difficult to grasp if examined only superficially.

Pasta has indeed become a true civilization in Italy: it has the place of honor on the menu, and because of the variability of the condiments that can be combined with it to make a substantial and balanced one-dish meal, it is now, at the dawn of the third millennium, the most popular food on Italian tables for all walks of life.

Spaghetti—and here Prezzolini is right—travel the world in the company of pizza, with the label "Italy" written in large letters: good taste and quality of life in a single word.

Foreigners must think the debates on *spaghetti* very strange indeed—on the degree of doneness, on the thickness of the strand, on the best sauce—because for anyone who considers *spaghetti* just food, any type of pasta goes well with any sauce. But for those for whom this pasta is a way of life, there exist various schools of thought. In the north, the preference is to cook *spaghetti* longer; in the south, they are eaten *al dente* and, for many pasta fanatics, they are cooked barely beyond raw. While most call it *spaghetti,* others say *vermicelli,* and still others *fidelini.* The sauce, or the herbs, used to tell us what region we were in. And it is not uncommon to hear in the same region, or often in the same family, discussions about whether garlic, oil, and chili go better with no. 12 or no. 8 *spaghetti.*[234]

If this stringlike pasta appears in cookbooks later than, say, *lasagna,* it does not mean that it was not firmly established in Italy by the twelfth century. A more in-depth study on such archival documents as notarial acts, inventories, tax registries, and the like, all of which often contain precious information, would say for sure.

If we want to establish a chronology, we can say with certainty that during the twelfth, thirteenth, and fourteenth centuries dry pasta had already been traveling around the Mediterranean for some time, leaving the ports of Sicily and Sardinia on vessels flying the flags of the maritime republics of Genoa and Pisa. There were also other poles of production, such as the enclave of Amalfi, though it was still the early days and the scale was relatively small.

The entry on *fidelini* outlines the history of pasta in Liguria. Here we will concentrate on other areas, starting with Sicily, true cradle of dry pasta, attested with the Muslim conquest. According to *The Book of Roger,* authored by the Arab geographer al-Idrisi in 1154 and pinnacle of geographic knowledge of the day:

> In Sicily there is a town called Trabia, an enchanted place endowed with perennial waters and mills. In this town they make a food of flour in the form of strings in quantities such as to supply in addition to the towns of Calabria, those of the Muslim and Christian territories.[235]

The "strings" were known as *itryya,* and they were dried and sold in the Mediterranean also under the Arabic term *fidaws,* which later became the Castilian *fideos,* hence the Italian *fidelini.*

Similar exports also left from Sardinia. The researcher Laura Galoppini, who has studied old customs documents of Cagliari, maintains that, at the end of the fourteenth century, the trade in dry pasta was well launched on the island. The fact that a type of stringlike pasta was cited in even older texts, such as the Talmud, is marginal to our work, because the long, slow metamorphosis that made pasta, of all shapes, into a cultural patrimony that has no equal in the world began when it encountered the culture and traditions of life of the Italic peoples.

The Kingdom of Naples was one of the great production centers of dry pastas. In the 1200s, different producers of *maccheroni* were already documented, even if the large and important production of the Bay of Naples and Amalfi did not get under way until some centuries later.

By the sixteenth century, pasta was widely consumed among the middle classes, so much that, in 1579, the Arte dei Vermicellari broke off from the corporation of the bakers to assume managerial autonomy, especially in the supply of grains. A statute dated October 16, 1699, and kept in the Naples State Archive, establishes the trade guild's official headquarters (with chapel) in the church of the Carmine Maggiore. Pasta at the time was under the watchful eye of the government, which controlled the quality, prices, and distribution. This was when the Neapolitans changed from being *mangiafoglie* (leaf eaters) to *mangiamaccheroni* (macaroni eaters). It was also when Naples and the other provinces of the kingdom, including the towns along the Bay of Naples from Torre Annunziata to Gragnano, were pulsing with large and small pasta-making shops, each of which had a *gramola a stanga* (a type of kneading machine) and often also a *torchio,* a requirement for admittance to the Arte dei Vermicellari. The pasta was hung to dry on long sticks, a system that took advantage of the area's unique air, which ensured that these coastal pasta makers would have good fortune and stay at the top of their profession over the centuries. Mechanization came two centuries later, toward the middle of the 1800s, with the introduction of machines that made production both faster and cheaper. However, raw materials of excellent quality, such as the famous *grano saragolla,* were the primary reason the kingdom's pasta makers enjoyed great success.

From the sixteenth century on, the so-called *maccheroni* of Naples and pasta of Genoa were considered the best pastas in Europe.

In Puglia, documents in the Bari State Archive reveal that the pasta makers of Molfetta had won, by the end of the 1400s, a reduction on the tax on pasta sold in northern Italy. In the Cagliari State Archive, various contracts from the 1400s show the exportation of barrels of pasta destined for the Aragonian court. John II seems to have been particularly fond of it; Queen Sybil, fourth wife of Peter IV, counted it among her favorite dishes; and Martin I even wanted it, accompanied with the cheese of Majorca, among the dishes served at his coronation banquet.[236]

The great demand for pasta in Rome is evident from the numerous edicts regulating its distribution and price that date from the end of the fourteenth century.[237] In 1602, the powerful Confraternita dei Vermicellari was founded. Its importance can be inferred from the contract it received to decorate a portion of the street down which the papal cavalcade traveled en route to the Lateran Palace to take possession of the basilica of St. John.[238]

In the first years of the 1800s, in Puglia, in many towns around Bari, there were already numerous manufacturers of *maccheroni* "with *ingegno* and warehouse," that is, with a small factory-made production of their own. Retail *maccheronari* existed as well, which presupposes a substantial supply to send to market.[239]

With the twentieth century, *spaghetti* became the common food of all the Italians, even those living overseas, and Italian immigrants in the United States became the largest importers of the precious Sicilian and Neapolitan pastas.

Although the overseas market was firmly in the hands of the Italian pasta makers, some small local operations had begun to make some headway by the mid-1800s: In 1865, the baker Goodman moved from Manhattan to Philadelphia and opened a small *macaroni* and *spaghetti* factory. In 1867, the young American pasta maker Frederick Mueller opened a factory in Jersey City. But it was not until 1914 that the Italian American Vincent La Rosa laid the foundation in Brooklyn for a pasta empire that would offer serious competition to the Italian imports.[240]

When did the word *spaghetti* supplant the earlier *vermicelli,* which was still used in Italian homes, especially in the north, up to World War II? Probably at the turn of the twentieth century. Prezzolini[241] stresses that the term *spaghetti* is not found in the seventeenth-century edition of the *Dizionario della Crusca,* or in other northern dictionaries published in the nineteenth century, though it does appear in Carena's *Vocabolario domestico* published in Naples in 1859. Again according to Prezzolini, the term makes a hesitant first appearance in a short poem by Viviani (1824).

In the sonnet *La politica,* dated 1915, Trilussa, the Roman dialect poet, represents the lively discussions that arose in a family among the father, a Vatican employee and Christian Democrat, and his three sons, a socialist revolutionary, a monarchist, and a republican:

> . . . *ma appena mamma*
> *ce dice che so' cotti li spaghetti*
> *semo tutti d'accordo ner programma.*

[. . . as soon as Mamma tells us the *spaghetti* are done, we are all of one mind.]

Would a political agreement on *vermicelli* be possible?

248. SPÄTZLI

Gnocchi / gnocchetti

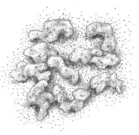

INGREDIENTS: Wheat flour, but also buckwheat flour, water, eggs, and sometimes milk.

HOW MADE: It is made with a specific utensil, which looks like a flat grater on which a little carriage with holes is mounted. A soft dough of flour, water, eggs, and sometimes milk is put into the carriage and passes through the holes into boiling broth or salted water.

ALSO KNOWN AS: In the Valtellina, *menedici;* a smaller variety in the Val Camonica is called *spezzali.*

HOW SERVED: As *pastasciutta* or in broth, according to local customs.

WHERE FOUND: Trentino–Alto Adige, in particular in the Tyrol, but also Lombardy, in particular in the Valtellina, in the area between Sondalo and Bormio.

REMARKS: *Spätzli* are *gnocchetti* with links to the gastronomic culture of southern Germany, and are also made in Switzerland and France. They are common in the Tyrol, where they are often an accompaniment to game dishes, and in the Valtellina, they are served in soup. One variant calls for adding spinach to the dough to color it green.

For centuries, *bisi* (peas) *di pasta* were found in the home recipe collections in Trento. They were made by dropping batter from a sieve directly into foaming butter, then sprinkling the pasta with grated cheese and serving it in broth.

Maneghi de zuc, a related preparation, were made by using a syringe to inject the batter directly into the butter for frying. *Straboi* were similar but sweet.

249. SPINATSPÄTZLE

Gnocchi/gnocchetti

INGREDIENTS: Wheat flour, eggs, spinach, and sometimes milk.

HOW MADE: The flour is sifted onto a wooden board and kneaded with eggs and with spinach that has been boiled, squeezed dry, and finely chopped. A small amount of milk is added if needed. Small *gnocchetti* are formed from the dough and boiled in plenty of salted water.

ALSO KNOWN AS: *Gnocchetti di spinaci.*

HOW SERVED: As *pastasciutta,* with traditional local sauces.

WHERE FOUND: Trentino–Alto Adige, in particular in the Tyrol.

REMARKS: Wild spinach and other wild greens were very likely used originally instead of spinach.

250. STELLE

Pastina

INGREDIENTS: Durum-wheat flour and water.

HOW MADE: Factory-made tiny stars. They are cooked in broth.

ALSO KNOWN AS: *Astri* (stars), *fiori di sambuco* (elder flowers), and *stellette, stellettine,* and *stelloni* for the largest, though they are still small enough to be considered *pastina.*

HOW SERVED: In broth.

WHERE FOUND: Widespread.

REMARKS: The name means literally "stars." The term is old: it was used in the sixteenth century, in Messisbugo,[242] for a sweet star-shaped pasta that was clearly fresh rather than dry.

The factory-made *stellina* is described in Carena's *Vocabolario domestico* as *pastina* for broth.

251. STRACCI

Pasta corta

INGREDIENTS: Wheat flour, often whole wheat but also fine bran, eggs, and water.

HOW MADE: The flour is sifted onto a wooden board and kneaded with eggs and water for a long time, then wrapped in a dish towel and left to rest. The dough is rolled out with a rolling pin into a sheet, from which *lasagne* of varying sizes are cut. These are often torn into irregular pieces, according to the customs of where the pasta is made, but may also be neatly cut. The dough is sometimes colored green with spinach. The *stracci* are boiled in plenty of salted water.

ALSO KNOWN AS: In Lazio, Abruzzo, and Molise, *stracce,* but also *sagne stracce.*

HOW SERVED: As *pastasciutta,* with traditional local sauces.

WHERE FOUND: Liguria, but also Tuscany (Garfagnana in particular), Lazio, the Marche, Abruzzo, and Molise.

REMARKS: The name means literally "rags." Typical of the towns of the Monti Simbruini, such as Camerata, in Lazio, *sagne stracce* are generally served with a sauce of onion, tomato, a great deal of chili, often also pork, and, of course, grated local pecorino.

This type of pasta, like other so-called poor pastas, was reserved for feast days and anniversaries. In northern Ciociaria, on the border with Abruzzo, *stracci* often contained borage, wild spinach, or even cardoon leaves. In the Marche, the pasta squares were topped with lamb *corata* (innards), folded like a handkerchief, and baked.

Stracci were usually homemade, but in almost every town the *maccaronaro* sold them as well. He was also often the miller in whose establishment women made pasta to sell.

The batter used for *stracce* in Abruzzo resembles that for *crespelle* (see entry).

252. STRACCI DI ANTRODOCO
Unusual shape

INGREDIENTS: Wheat flour, eggs, salt, water, and sometimes milk. For the filling, generally meat and *scamorza*.

HOW MADE: A batter is made, rather than a dough. Eggs are beaten in a bowl. Then, while the batter is being stirred constantly to keep lumps from forming, flour and a pinch of salt are allowed to fall through a sieve into the eggs. At the end, a little water or cold milk is added in a stream to make a semiliquid batter, which is covered and left to rest.

Small crepes, about 6¾ inches (17 cm) in diameter, are cooked in oil and then filled.

ALSO KNOWN AS: No alternative names.

HOW SERVED: Baked, covered with rich meat *ragù*.

WHERE FOUND: Lazio, a specialty of Antrodoco, in the province of Rieti; and Abruzzo, in the village of Sella di Corno.

REMARKS: The *crespella* (see entry) entered Italian gastronomic culture only in modern times. Nevertheless, we find it in L'Aquila, capital of Abruzzo, and curiously also in Antrodoco, in Lazio, where the tradition may have been brought from the city of Rieti. Today, stuffed *stracci* can be tasted at one of Lazio's oldest gastronomic *sagre*, which has been held at Antrodoco, in the province of Rieti, on the first Sunday of August since the period after World War II. Making *stracci* is a long and complicated job and employs many of the able local housewives. Normally, ten thousand to fifteen thousand portions of *stracci* are fried, containing some five thousand eggs. And to think that the old recipe called for just "one egg, an eggshell of water, and an eggshell of flour"!

253. STRANGOLAPRETI, STROZZAPRETI
Various shapes

INGREDIENTS: Water and various types of flours, but also bread or potatoes, sometimes with fine bran flour or with vegetables to color the dough.

HOW MADE: The ingredients are kneaded with water, and various shapes of pasta are formed, depending on the area. They are boiled in abundant salted water. In some areas they are made with raised bread dough.

ALSO KNOWN AS: In Friuli, in Carnia, *gnocchi di prete;* in the Marche, around Genga, *frigulelli, piccicasanti,* or *strozzafrati;* in Lazio, *cecamariti;* in Abruzzo, *maccheroni alla molinara;* in Naples, *strangulaprievete;* in Calabria, *strangugliaprjeviti;* and in Sicily, *affogaparrini.*

HOW SERVED: As *pastasciutta,* usually with typical local sauces and grated local cheese.

WHERE FOUND: Central and southern Italy, but also common in some areas of the north, such as Carnia, in Friuli, where they are a specialty of Raveo and Ovaro.

REMARKS: The name means literally "priest stranglers." According to Cesare Marchi, in his *Quando siamo a tavola,* "To see them in the dish, they look like those mossy stones that stick up around the edges of a pond; greenish, velvety, irregular, and on the menu they bear a name that, in Catholic Trentino, sounds blasphemous, *strangolapreti.*" [243]

The name was, however, already in use many centuries ago. In a manuscript in the Biblioteca Nazionale of Naples titled *Apparecchi differenti da mangiare et rimedii* and dated by the anonymous author (probably a prelate),[244] we find the term *strangolaprietij* (as well as *strangola prevjtj*) and a description of the composition of the dough: *caciocavallo,* ricotta, eggs, and almonds. And if the dough is too hard, he suggests adding some rose water. As for the best way to cook the pasta, he suggests chicken broth. Unfortunately, the author does not talk about the shape, possibly because he takes for granted that his readers know what he is talking about, which would be a sort of small *gnocco.*

Strozzapreti also appear in a manuscript from near Perugia, datable to the end of the 1500s and brought to light by Casagrande.[245]

Vincenzo Tanara, in his *Economia del cittadino in villa,*[246] writes, "Others grate a loaf of bread, and they give it body, like a mediocre pasta, . . . a little flour and water, and make it into bite-sized pieces; they press the pieces with a finger on the back of a grater and call them *strozzapreti, macaroni,* and we call them *gnocchi.*" Further on, he says that they can also be made with millet bread, cooked in milk, and served with parmigiano and a great deal of butter, and heated up for the evening meal.

Why *strozzapreti?* At the origin lies the popular belief in the gluttony of priests confirmed by the tale of Gian Battista Alvino, who, in the middle of the eighteenth century, wrote:

> There has almost never lived a priest so passionate for the hunt as the parasites are gluttonous for game, which they get at the hunt: It was one day that this priest, after wandering back and forth through valleys and woods, finding himself by chance short of supplies for his mouth, and went back home so hungry that not a nice fat chicken would he have devoured, but even a great *polenta* poor and dry. The serving woman had made him this dish of *gnocchi* with greens, which he set about eating with such voracity that it stuck in his throat. He would have suffocated if the compassionate servant, seeing no other remedy, had not struck him with her fist repeatedly harder and harder between neck and back until he spat out the great mouthful.

The Roman dialect poet Gioacchino Belli considered them less dangerous, however. After tasting a dish of *strozzapreti "cor sughillo"* (with a poor sauce), he wonders in his poem *La scampagnata* (November 16, 1834):

Ma a proposito qui de strozzapreti:
io nun posso capì pe' che raggione
s'abbia da de' che strozzeno li preti:
Quanno ogni prete è un tipo de cristiano
da inghiottisse magari in un boccone
er sor Pavolo Biondi sano sano.

[But à propos of *strozzapreti*, I can't understand why they say they choke the priests: when every priest is the kind of man able to swallow Mister Paolo Biondi whole in a single bite.]

In Patriarchi's *Vocabolario veneziano e padovano* (1821),[247] *strozzapreti* are defined as "*raviuoli*, a food made of greens with eggs, cheese, and other." And later, F. Alvino, in his 1845 *Viaggio da Napoli a Castellammare*, explains that "macaroni made by hand are called priest-stranglers [*strangolapreti*] by monks, and by priests they are dubbed monk stranglers [*strangolamonaci*]." And, again, D'Ambra's *Vocabolario napolitano-toscano* (1873)[248] defines them as a "kind of homemade pasta called *maccheroni di casa*, which are indented with three fingers and rolled on the board." Finally, according to the 1931 Touring Club Italiano gastronomic guide,[249] *gnocchi strangolapreti* are made with flour and water, or with the addition of a few potatoes.

Once prevalent in southern Italy, where they were made with different kinds of dough—various flours, potatoes, bread, and other ingredients—*strozzapreti* have now spread throughout the country. But the variety of the types makes single classification impossible: in fact, every region, and every town—but especially where the clergy had a more marked temporal or social power—has its form of *strozzapreti*.

For example, in the Marche, at Matelica, they are small, irregular pasta squares made from whole-wheat flour; at Fabriano, corn flour is added and the squares are large; and at Genga, raised bread dough is kneaded to make sticks as thick as a finger and these are cut into *gnocchetti*. All they have in common is a poor condiment, a *sugo finto* of tomato and *odori*. Leonardo Bruni, in *Ricette raccontate: Marche*,[250] tells of a custom around Macerata in which flour-and-water pastes were used to attach holy cards to the kitchen wall or the calendar of Saint Anthony, whence the name *piccicasanti*, or "saint stickers."

Sometimes the *strozzaprete* changes shape over time within a single area. For example, today in Naples it is a *gnocco* of potatoes, but only two centuries ago, in the text of Cavalcanti,[251] it was made with flour and *semolino*.

In Trezzo, in Lombardy, *strozzapreti* are *gnocchi* of greens and *odori* that are baked for Carnival. In Istria, they are tasty spinach *ravioli*, which used to be served to the priest visiting for Easter or for the feast of the Madonna Piccola (September 8) and Madonna Grande (August 15).

They take different forms in other regions, too, but are always made by hand, with only flour and water. Besides *gnocchetti*, they can be a sort of *cavatelli*, or they can be thick *spaghetti* or noodles more or less long and more or less wide.

254. STRASCINATI

Strascinati

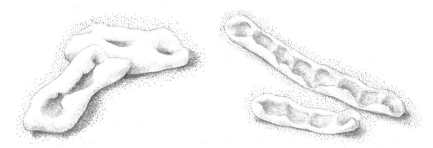

INGREDIENTS: Durum-wheat flour, but also alternative flours such as whole wheat, *semolone*, barley, *grano arso*, or others, and water.

HOW MADE: The flour or flours are sifted onto a wooden board and kneaded long and vigorously with water until a firm, smooth dough forms, which is left to rest. Pieces are then pinched off and rolled with the hands into cylinders of variable diameter. These are cut into short lengths of variable size, and the pieces are drawn across a wooden board or other typical utensil, with the fingers or with a *sferre*. The shapes will depend on the particular gesture with which the dough pieces are rolled. They are boiled in abundant salted water.

ALSO KNOWN AS: In Campania, *cortecce*. In Puglia, *capunti* and *capuntini*, *cavati*, *cuppetiedde*, *mignuicchi*, *minchialeddi*, *minchjaleddi*, and *pezzetelli*, or *pizzidieddi*, and in Lecce, *rasckatieddi* and *stagghiotte*. In Basilicata, *cantaroggni*, *capunti*, and *minuich*.

HOW SERVED: Generally in legume or vegetable soups, but also as *pastasciutta*, with traditional local sauces.

WHERE FOUND: Campania, Puglia, Basilicata, and Calabria.

REMARKS: It is practically impossible to make sense of the Babel of *strascinati* in the regions of southern Italy. The dough, usually of durum wheat, can also contain *semolone* or other alternative flours such as whole wheat or, in Puglia, *grano arso*. Another variable is the weight of the dough that is shaped, which will define the size of the pasta.

Strascinati can be rolled with one finger to make simple *cavatelli;* with two fingers to make *cecatelli* (see entry) and the like; or with three, four, or eight fingers. Each method produces a longer or shorter pasta with a different name, sometimes in conflict with a similar name in another area.

Strascinati can also be differentiated by their opening: some are wide open, others are open but with the edges slightly raised, and still others have edges sharply raised. In this case, the names invoke objects from nature, such as *foglie di oliva,* or "olive leaves"; *faianelle,* which resemble carob pods; or *palmatielli,* which resemble palm leaves.

Here follow the most common names, divided by the four regions involved. It should be kept in mind that the same type of pasta can acquire different names in bordering areas, or even within the same region, only because, let us say, size varies or the dough or sauce is a bit different.

Campania: In the Vallo di Diano, the *palmatiello* (see entry for *parmatielli*) is rolled with two fingers on the palm of the hand. In the Cilento, *cortecce* are rolled with four fingers.

Puglia: In this region, *strascinati* are rolled with a *sferre. Orecchiette* (see entry) and similar pastas also belong to the *strascinati* family, because their manufacture begins with the same kind of rolling with the finger(s), or *trascinamento.* For example, *cuppetiedde,* which are similar in shape to *orecchiette,* recall a little bowl, or *coppetta,* whence the name. In Alezio, Castro, Lecce, Gallipoli, and Parabita, *minchialeddi* are long, narrow *cavatelli.* On the Salento peninsula, similar long, narrow *cavatelli* are prepared differently, with wheat flour and barley.

Basilicata: *Cantarogni lucani* are rolled with three fingers; the closed ones are slightly larger, made with the tips of four fingers; and those rolled with two fingers, also called *capunti,* are literally "rolled with the point." There is also a particular type of *cantarogni,* sometimes made with eggs, and with a completely different shape (see *gnocchetti di Tricarico*).

Calabria: Calabrian *strascinati* repeat the shapes and sauces of Lucania, across the border. They were often made with flours other than wheat, since the rural population there was among the poorest in Italy. The isolation of the peoples of Calabria between the coast and the mountains, which was caused by the Saracen invasions only at the first, gave rise to a strange series of costs and benefits that can be summed up: "Thanks to their backwardness the Calabrians regained their peace and health but condemned themselves to poverty and emargination."[252]

255. STRASCINATI UMBRI

Strascinati

INGREDIENTS: Durum-wheat flour and water.

HOW MADE: The flour is sifted and kneaded long and vigorously with water. When the dough is smooth and firm, it is left to rest, then rolled out with a rolling pin into a sheet, not too thin, from which wide, flat noodles are cut. These are boiled in plenty of salted water and drained very *al dente,* then finished by being sautéed in a frying pan where the sauce is sizzling.

ALSO KNOWN AS: No alternative names.

HOW SERVED: As *pastasciutta,* with smoked *guanciale,* sausage, and eggs.

WHERE FOUND: Umbria.

REMARKS: Pasta dressed with *guanciale* and eggs, which kept well, constituted the typical meal of the *carbonari,* "charcoal makers," who stayed away from home for long periods making charcoal in the *carbonaie,* traces of which can still be seen in the woods of Umbria.

The expression *alla carbonara* then entered the Latian kitchen to indicate a typical pasta preparation, but also for an equally famous lamb dish.

256. STREPPA E CACCIALÀ

Pasta corta

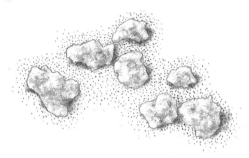

INGREDIENTS: Wheat flour, salt, water, and a little oil.

HOW MADE: The flour is sifted and kneaded for a long time with a pinch of salt, a little oil, and lukewarm water, then the dough is left to rest. Later, small pieces of dough are pinched off, flattened with fingers, and tossed into boiling soup.

ALSO KNOWN AS: *Maccheroni strappati.*

HOW SERVED: In a typical vegetable soup.

WHERE FOUND: Liguria, in the Maritime Alps, in particular upper Valle Arroscia.

REMARKS: The name means literally "tear and throw there," Italian *strappa e caccia là*. This flavorful soup, which is made when the Savoy cabbage is white and firm, after the first winter frosts, belongs to the typical *cucina bianca*. The pasta is cooked in the water in which leaves of Savoy cabbage, turnips, and potatoes are boiling.

True monument of culinary archaeology, this pasta, which today is a feather in the cap of the restaurants of Liguria's alpine valleys, has many relatives in the *cucina povera* (the cuisine of poverty) of other Italian regions, where it is always served with condiments typical of the place.

257. STRETTINE

Pasta lunga

INGREDIENTS: Wheat flour, nettles, and eggs.

HOW MADE: The flour is sifted onto a wooden board and kneaded long and vigorously with eggs and with nettles that have been boiled, squeezed dry, and finely chopped. When the dough is firm and smooth, it is wrapped in a dish towel and left to rest. It is rolled out with a rolling pin into a sheet, not too thin, and cut into narrow, flat noodles. They are boiled in plenty of salted water.

ALSO KNOWN AS: No alternative names.

HOW SERVED: As *pastasciutta,* generally with *ragù* of white meats and, of course, parmigiano.

WHERE FOUND: Emilia-Romagna.

REMARKS: The name means literally "little narrows." Spinach is often used to make this dough, but nettles are also popular, especially in spring, when they are nice and green. The sprouts and tenderest leaves are picked and boiled, like spinach, in very little water. The leaves are squeezed dry, then chopped as finely as possible to give the pasta a uniform color.

258. STRINGOZZI

Pasta lunga

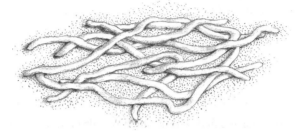

INGREDIENTS: *Farro* flour, type 00 wheat flour, eggs, and water, but also often only wheat flour, salt, and water.

HOW MADE: The flours are sifted together and kneaded with eggs and water for a long time until a smooth, solid dough forms, which is then wrapped in a dish towel and left to rest. Next, the dough is rolled out on a wooden board into a sheet ⅛ inch (2 mm) thick and cut into strips about ⅛ inch (2 mm) wide and 8 inches (20 cm) long. The exact size can vary from place to place, but the surface must be rough (from the wooden board), to hold the sauce. They are boiled in plenty of salted water.

ALSO KNOWN AS: *Ciriole, strangozzi, umbricelli,* and *strigliozzi* (the latter at Castel di Tora, in Lazio). They are often also called *strozzapreti* (see entry for *strangolupreti, strozzapreti*). In Emilia-Romagna, *stringotti.*

HOW SERVED: With various sauces, with herbs, truffles, or *funghi porcini.* In Lazio, meat sauces prevail, especially lamb, with the local pecorino.

WHERE FOUND: Umbria, especially Foligno and Spoleto; in Emilia-Romagna; and in northern Lazio.

REMARKS: Some people believe the name derives from the word *stringa,* literally "string" or "shoelace," from the elongated shape that recalls the thick shoelaces of long ago.

   Like other so-called poor pastas, this pasta was reserved for feast days and other holidays. In Emilia-Romagna, *stringotti* were always served on Christmas Eve, with olive oil, walnuts, and pepper, and often accompanied the traditional *brod ad cuciarul* (for Italian *brodo al cucchiaio,* or "spoon broth"), a broth of dried chestnuts enriched with a small piece of salt cod.

   This pasta was usually homemade, but in almost all the towns the *maccaronaro*—who was often the miller—also made and sold it. The monastery of Santa Croce of Montefalco, in Umbria, was famous for its *strangozzini,* with a sauce of tomato and herbs.

Today, *stringozzi* are used extensively on Umbrian tables, and the sauces exploit the local products. Factory-made *strangozzi* are sometimes made with gluten-free flour, and local small-scale pasta makers produce fresh *strangozzi* under climate-controlled conditions.

259. STRONCATELLI

Pasta lunga

INGREDIENTS: Durum-wheat flour or type 00 wheat flour, salt, and some eggs.

HOW MADE: The flour is sifted with a pinch of salt onto a wooden board and kneaded long and vigorously with some eggs (not a great many) to make a very hard dough, which is then left to rest. Small pieces are pinched off and worked with oiled hands into long, thin *spaghetti,* which are cooked in broth.

ALSO KNOWN AS: No alternative names.

HOW SERVED: Cooked in broth.

WHERE FOUND: The Marche, in Ancona area.

REMARKS: Although the Italian territory was once divided into many small states, it is interesting to note how certain techniques for making pasta and certain pasta shapes, especially the ritual ones, spread rapidly throughout the Boot. The recipe for *stroncatelli* comes from the *cucina ebraica* of Ancona, and it was used for the feasts of the Jewish New Year. A variant calls for adding tiny meatballs to the soup.

The practice of oiling the hands for shaping pastas that have to be manipulated for a long time is not limited to Ancona, but is instead quite widespread. It is typical of certain pastas of the Albanian communities (see *shtridhëlat*) and has a precise function: it allows for working with the dough for an extended time without it sticking to the hands, which can cause a long *spaghetto* to break.

260. STRUNCATURA

Pasta lunga

INGREDIENTS: Various flours, sometimes including carob flour or rye flour; bran; and water. For factory made, durum-wheat flour and bran.

HOW MADE: The flours and bran are sifted onto a wooden board and kneaded long and vigorously with water. When the dough is firm and smooth, it is left to rest, then rolled out into a rather thick sheet, which is cut into *fettuccelle,* or flat noodles as wide as factory-made *trenette* (see entry). They are boiled in abundant salted water. The factory-made version are shaped like *linguine.*

ALSO KNOWN AS: No alternative names.

HOW SERVED: As *pastasciutta,* with anchovies, garlic, and chili.

WHERE FOUND: Calabria, the plain of Gioia Tauro, as far as Vibo Valentia.

REMARKS: The name means literally "sawdust." No pasta better represents the unimaginable poverty of the poorest families in rural Calabria that lasted almost until the 1950s. It was made at home from the sweepings of flour and bran from the mill floors. Different kinds of grain were mixed indiscriminately, but rye—with risk of ergot poisoning—was almost always included, as well as everything one can imagine would be found on a floor of beaten earth. Not surprisingly, the pasta had a sharp, acrid taste and a low price. To temper the acidity, it was served with very piquant sauces or with anchovies and garlic.

The term comes from *struncaturi,* the long saw that threw sawdust onto the ground, and in the collective imagination, this rough pasta resembles the sawdust swept up from the floor.

Today, factory-made *struncatura* has become a niche product. The dark color and the chewiness of the cooked pasta are the result of using high-quality durum wheat and bran in the manufacture.

261. SUCAMELE

Pasta lunga

INGREDIENTS: Durum-wheat flour, and often also whole-wheat flour, yeast, and water.

HOW MADE: The flour is sifted and kneaded with the yeast and with water as needed. The dough is rolled out into a thin sheet, narrow strips are cut from it, and the strips are rubbed between the hands to form strings. The pasta is left to dry in the sun, then boiled in abundant salted water. In one variation, the pasta strings are wound around a straw, as for *fusilli* (see entry).

ALSO KNOWN AS: *Maccheroni filati;*[253] in Sicily, *sussameli.*

HOW SERVED: As *pastasciutta,* typically with honey and cinnamon.

WHERE FOUND: Puglia, typical of Lecce, and Sicily.

REMARKS: This is a very old dish—a ritual dish—still widely found in the countryside around Lecce. The pairing of a sweet condiment with pasta is of Arab-Sicilian origin.

The Sicilian *sussameli,* today a normal *pasta bucata* served with pork *ragù,* owe their name to the old sweet preparation used on children's pasta on feast days. In the Valle del Belice, *sussameli* were very thin *tagliolini,* which were deep-fried and served with chopped pistachios and candied fruit for the feast of Saint Benedict.

262. SUDDHI

Pasta lunga

INGREDIENTS: Barley flour, salt, and water.

HOW MADE: The flour is sifted with a pinch of salt onto a wooden board and kneaded long and vigorously with water. The dough is left to rest, then rolled out into a sheet, not too thin, from which flat noodles of variable width are cut. They are boiled in abundant salted water.

ALSO KNOWN AS: No alternative names.

HOW SERVED: As *pastasciutta,* with traditional local sauces, usually based on pork.

WHERE FOUND: Sicily, typical of Canicattini Bagni.

REMARKS: This rare pasta was made in the province of Siracusa, in particular at Canicattini Bagni. In fact, the precious flour of a particular type of durum wheat grown in eastern Sicily was used to make the pasta. The use of other flours, such as the barley flour indicated here, was likely associated with famines, plagues, or other extraordinary events. In Sicily, unlike in poorer regions, homemade pasta was usually made with eggs and wheat flour, and the use of alternative flours, such as barley or legume, was almost unknown.

263. SUGELI

Gnocchi/gnocchetti

INGREDIENTS: Wheat flour, salt, oil, and water.

HOW MADE: The flour is sifted onto a wooden board and kneaded for a long time with a pinch of salt, a little oil, and lukewarm water, and the dough is left to rest. The dough is then formed into rolls about ⅝ inch (1.5 cm) in diameter, which are cut crosswise into small pieces. Unlike *cavatelli* (see entry), these little pieces are flattened against the board with a rotary movement of the finger, then over-turned, as for *orecchiette* (see entry), to make the classic form of a small hat. They are boiled in plenty of salted water.

ALSO KNOWN AS: *Corpu de diu* (body of God).

HOW SERVED: As *pastasciutta,* traditionally with fermented cheese.

WHERE FOUND: Liguria (Maritime Alps) and in Piedmont, Cuneo in particular.

REMARKS: *Sugeli* are the flagship pasta of the Maritime Alps, common in the whole area of Monte Saccarello, in the alpine *malghe* of Mendatica, at Triora, and in the Valle Argentina. In these mountains, *sugeli* are served with a fermented, sour ricotta called *brusso*, already mentioned at the end of the 1800s in the Inchiesta Jacini,[254] where it was shown to be typical of Triora.

For centuries, this part of the Ligurian mountains, dotted with the towns of Cosio d'Arroscia, Mendatica, Montegrosso Pian Latte, Pornassio, and Triora, and the adjacent Occitan valleys of the province of Cuneo exchanged customs and gastronomic practices. Here, also, developed the traditional cuisine known as *cucina bianca*. In Cuneo, *sugeli* are sauced with local cheeses.

For a curious variant, see *streppa e caccialà*.

264. TACCONI
Pasta corta

INGREDIENTS: Corn flour, type 00 wheat flour, and water. In Molise, durum-wheat flour. In Campania, also whole-wheat flour. Leftover polenta was often used.

HOW MADE: A polenta is made with corn flour, chilled, and kneaded with wheat flour and water to make a homogeneous and rather firm dough. The dough is left to rest, then rolled out with a rolling pin into a sheet, not too thin, from which strips about ¾ inch (2 cm) wide are cut. These are cut again into squares or rhombuses, *tacconi* in Italian.

Factory-made *tacconi* are 1½-inch (4-cm) squares, made with flour and water. They are boiled in plenty of salted water.

ALSO KNOWN AS: *Quadrucci* if small; otherwise, *tacconelle, taccozze de muline,* and *taccozzelle*. In some towns near Chieti (Abruzzo), they are called *sagnarelle degli antichi* and *volarelle;* in the Marche, *taccù* and *cannarù;* in Sicily, *taccuna* and *taccuna de mulinu*.

HOW SERVED: As *pastasciutta*, with typical local sauces, but always with a dusting of local pecorino. The small ones are also cooked in broth. In Abruzzo, along the coast, there is a typical soup of *tacconelle* with chickpeas and *pannocchie* (mantis shrimp), and in Molise, *taccozzelle alla molenara* are served with tomato.

WHERE FOUND: The Marche, Umbria, Abruzzo, Molise, Campania, and Sicily.

REMARKS: Etymologically, the term comes from the word *tacca*, which used to mean "patch" or "rag." The root goes back to the Germanic *tak*, Italian *tacca*, originally a chip of wood.

Some local scholars give a different explanation: The area of Ascoli Piceno in the Marche has a long tradition of manufacturing footwear, and in the past shoe-makers traveled the region to sell their wares at low prices. These sturdy shoes, widely used for slogging around the countryside, had characteristic large heels, or *tacchi*. Thus, the pasta squares were named for their resemblance to the *tacchi* of those clodhoppers.

In Abruzzo, *sagnarelle degli antichi* were *ammassate*, meaning they were kneaded with fine bran, a little oil, salt, and warm water.

In Molise, the women who worked directly in the mills used to make *sagne a tacconi*, also called *taccozze de muline* (of the mills), for sale. To make the dough, they used the water of the same stream, in many cases the Verrino, that provided power to the mills, and the buyers boiled the pasta in water from the same source.

Taccozze were rhomboid, larger or smaller depending on the condiment, and were often mixed with legumes to make a tasty and substantial one-dish meal. The *taccozze* or *taccozzelle*, goes an old Molisan adage, must be the size of a child's hand and be cooked together with the tomato in a large terra-cotta pan.

In Sicily, *taccuna de mulinu* are served with garlic, oil, chili, *ricotta salata*, and eggplant. There the word is believed to derive from the Spanish *taccù*.

265. TACUI
Pasta corta

INGREDIENTS: Chestnut flour, wheat flour, salt, and water.

HOW MADE: The flours are sifted together onto a wooden board and kneaded long and vigorously with a pinch of salt and lukewarm water until a firm, smooth dough forms. The dough is left to rest, then rolled out into a sheet, not too thin, from which lozenges are cut. They are boiled in abundant salted water.

ALSO KNOWN AS: No alternative names.

HOW SERVED: As *pastasciutta*, usually with a sort of pesto of walnuts, basil, and marjoram.

WHERE FOUND: Liguria, typical of the upper Nervia valley.

REMARKS: In the past, this pasta was made with two-thirds chestnut flour and one-third wheat flour; the latter was too expensive for the meager finances of the peasants, while chestnuts abounded in the extensive groves scattered throughout the mountains that surround Liguria.

266. TAGLIATELLE, TAGLIOLINI
Pasta lunga

INGREDIENTS: Wheat flour and eggs, but formerly also flour and water or whole-wheat flour and water. The same ingredients are used for the factory-made versions.

HOW MADE: The flour is sifted and kneaded long and vigorously with eggs. The classic dough uses 100 grams (3½ ounces) of flour per medium egg. The dough must be smooth and firm; it is left to rest, covered, and then rolled into a thin sheet. The sheet is cut into flat noodles that vary in width from place to place. The wider noodles are called *tagliatelle,* the thinner *tagliolini.* Green noodles, a classic of Emilia and today found everywhere in Italy, come from the addition of cooked spinach to the dough.

Factory-made *tagliatelle* and *tagliolini* are made of flour and eggs or flour and water. Both types are also sold in nests.

Tagliatelle are boiled in plenty of salted water. *Tagliolini,* especially the factory-made versions, are extremely thin and usually cooked in broth.

ALSO KNOWN AS: In Trentino–Alto Adige, *tagliatelle smalzade;* in Veneto, around Cortina d'Ampezzo, *lesagnetes;* and in Lombardy, *bardele.* In Tuscany, in the Valdarno, they are called *maccheroni;* in Lazio, they are *fettuccine,* though at Colonna, the term *pincinelle* is used for certain locally made flour-and-water *fettuccine.*

For the *tagliolini, tagliatini, taglierini, tagliarini,* and *tagliolini pelosi,* but also *tajulì* and *taglioli pelosi.* In Emilia-Romagna, *bassotti,* and in the Marche, the dialect term is *tajulin sa'l sgagg.* In Lazio, around Subiaco, they are called *tajurini* or even *sciaquabaffi* (mustache rinsers) when served in broth; and in the Sabina, *curioli.* In Abruzzo and Molise, they are *tajarille,* and in Puglia, around Taranto, *tagghjarine* and *tagghjaridde.* In Sicily, they are *tagghiarini;* and in Sardinia, in Gallura in particular, *taddarini.*

For factory-made *tagliatelle, nastri* (tapes), *fettucce romane, fettuccelle, fresine,* and *tagliarelli.* For factory-made *tagliolini, capelvenere.* Some are packaged in nests.

HOW SERVED: As *pastasciutta,* with the typical regional sauces, or in broth, depending on whether they are *tagliatelle* or *tagliolini.*

WHERE FOUND: Widespread.

REMARKS: The name derives from the verb *tagliare,* "to cut." *Tagliatelle* used to be reserved for feast days, but are extremely common today, served any day of the week.

Bologna boasts that it is the birthplace of *tagliatelle,* citing the legend of Zafirano (or Zaffirino), court cook of Giovanni II Bentivoglio, who supposedly invented them in 1501 to serve to Lucrezia Borgia. She was passing through the city on her way to Ferrara, to join her new husband, Alfonso I d'Este, and the cook, the story goes, was inspired by the beautiful blond hair of the bride, magnificently painted by Pintoricchio in the Borgia apartment in the Vatican.

But only legend holds Bologna the birthplace of *tagliatelle.* It is much more likely that a pasta already being made elsewhere in Italy achieved perfection in Bologna, where the use of eggs—whole or just yolks—and a finer flour made it possible to roll the sheet to a proverbial thinness—so thin that when the sheet is held up to a window, the silhouette of the Colle della Guardia,[255] with the Basilica di San Luca, is visible through it. With the passage of the centuries, *tagliatelle* have become embedded in the DNA of true Bolognesi.

The early definition of the meter as $\frac{1}{10,000,000}$ of the length of the earth's meridian through Paris from the pole to the equator (or one-fourth of the earth's circumference), a length measurable against a platinum-iridium bar, was well-known to the students of the period between the two world wars. Clearly, that definition was in the minds of the members of the Bologna delegation of the Accademia Italiana della Cucina on April 16, 1972, when, led by Renato Zangheri, mayor of Bologna, they registered the dimensions of the authentic *tagliatella bolognese* with the city notary, Aldo Vico. Cooked and served, it must measure exactly 8 mm (about ⅓ inch) wide, corresponding to $\frac{1}{12,270}$ of the height of the Torre degli Asinelli. "Any other size," the act says, "would make it lose its inimitable character." To ensure that the cooked *tagliatella* meets this standard, the act permits a fluctuation of about ¼ inch (6.5 to 7 mm) for the freshly cut noodle, depending on how stiff the pasta sheet is. A golden *tagliatella* of regulation size is available for comparison at the offices of the local Chamber of Commerce, much like the old official meter in the National Archives in Paris.

We cannot talk about Bolognese *tagliatelle* without also mentioning the inseparable *ragù* of mixed meats, a true gastronomic monument of the food culture of Bologna that acquires its reddish brown color over four or more hours of sputtering on the fire.

An irreplaceable product in the popular gastronomic imagination, *tagliatelle* also used to be fried and sweetened with sugar and anise, as in Romagna, or added to a sweet cake known as *rizulòena*, as in Emilia. In Bologna, extremely thin *taglioline da suora* (nun) contained a tiny bit of parmigiano.

And in the countryside? The beginning of autumn was the time to set aside a supply of eggs for the winter, when the hens stopped laying. They were stored in *lole* (terra-cotta jars) and buried in a solution of water and lime. This way the precious *tagliatelle* could be made at any time of year. They were served with a rustic sauce of sausages, sometimes also with peas, if they were in season, and with a small amount of *conserva*. Less refined than in the cities, certainly, but nonetheless tasty, and embellished, in any case, by the ever-present *forma*, as parmigiano was familiarly called in Emilia and Romagna.

For the numerous ways in which the gastronomic literature speaks of this type of pasta, see *maccherone*. Many authors mention the thinness of *tagliolini romaneschi*. To cite just one, Antonio Latini dubs them *tagliolini di monica* (nun), to emphasize the convent practice of making the noodles thin.[256] The adjective *romanesco* does not indicate that *tagliatelle* are native to the Eternal City; rather, it documents how widespread they were in Rome in that period. In fact, in the sixteenth century, convents in Rome made thin *tagliolini* for new mothers in important families (see *capelli d'angelo* for an account). But the spread of *tagliolini* as a food for new mothers was not limited to Rome. In Molise and in Puglia, for example, it was believed that eating egg *tagliolini* improved the quality of the milk of a woman who had just delivered. Thus, the gift from her relatives was a wooden *spasa*[257] full to the brim with *tagliolini* and two pigeons to make the broth. This was a valuable gift, because it was not easy to make pasta as thin as *capelli d'angelo*, or "angel's hair." The housewife had to have cold hands to keep the dough from drying out during the kneading.

The quality of the flour was important, and old texts often specify that it must be good, white *fior di farina* (best quality). Soft-wheat flour was used extensively because valuable durum wheat, considered far superior, was preferred for factory-made dry pastas or for homemade pastas that were dried. This was true especially in the south, although by the beginning of the eighteenth century, there were already edicts regulating durum wheat in the north.

What we know today as *tagliatelle* were first defined in 1859:[258]

> With flour moistened with very little water, not cold, sometimes with eggs, the pasta is made on a board or the inside of the *madia* cover. The dough is kneaded for a long time, then floured, rolled into a large, thin sheet with a rolling pin, the sheet is rolled up, flattened down, and cut with a knife crosswise into thin strips.

Tagliatelle, taglierini, or *tagliolini* and other pastas of similar shape are assigned to a given region both by the ingredients that go into the dough and by the sauce that accompanies them. Let us look at how they appear from north to south, and to what local traditions and customs they belong. Obviously, the list cannot be exhaustive.

In Alto Adige, particularly in the Val Pusteria, and in Friuli–Venezia Giulia, or in Istria, fresh pork blood is added to the flour-and-egg dough. This hearty one-dish meal was served with a side dish of kohlrabi (see *Blutnudeln*).

The old *tagliatini trentini* were extremely thin and made with *pasta frolla*, or short pastry. They were used to make a *torta di foiete,* or *feuilleté, pasta frolla* disks fragrant with spices layered alternately with *tagliolini* and baked.

In Lombardy, *bardele coi morai* (see entry) are *tagliatelle* that contain borage, and Piedmont, especially the Langhe, is famous for the rich *tajarin* (see entry), made with flour and egg yolks and sometimes a small amount of white wine. They are served with a sort of *finanziera* and, in season, a grating of the area's famous white truffles. One variation, *tajarin di meliga,* called for adding a small amount of corn flour to the dough.

In Liguria, *tagliolini verdi* get their green from borage; and the *gialli,* "yellow," from saffron. A particular type of *tagliatelle* called *cappellasci* is traditionally served with *sugo alla genovese,* that is, the so-called *tocco di carne* (see *ravioli alla genovese*), or with a mushroom sauce.

In the Apennines of Piacenza, *tagliatelle* are paired with a walnut sauce that recalls the neighboring Ligurian cuisine, and a specialty of some towns of the Apennines around Parma is *tagliatelle* made with chestnut flour. *Bassotti,* a specialty of Civitella di Romagna, are submerged in broth and baked, garnished with a rich cream of eggs and cheese and flavored with cinnamon.

In the Marche, *tajulin sa'l sgagg,* literally *col chiasso,* or "with noise," are so called because of the sizzling sound the *soffritto* of *lardo* or pancetta makes when added to the water in which the pasta is cooking. In the rural areas, *tagliatelle* were made with whole-wheat flour and served with *sugo finto* and *sardella* (salted sardines). The convent of Santa Caterina at Ripatransone made them for the feast of the Madonna della Pace, December 15, to commemorate a miracle. Evidence collected by Sebastiana Papa in that convent describes in detail the ritual of making the *tagliolini:* A small, extremely thin pasta sheet was left to dry just until it could be rolled up into two small rolls, started from opposite sides of the sheet and rolled to meet in the center. One roll was placed on top of the other and flattened slightly, and only two sisters were able to cut the pasta as thin "as a cotton thread."

Still in the Marche, girls used to give *tagliolini pelosi* (see entry) to their fiancés to prove they were able to cut them thin. The adjective *peloso* (hairy) gives the sense of the roughness imparted to the pasta by rolling it out on a wooden board.

The Molisan custom of cooking *tagliolini* in milk can be traced to the habits that developed during long periods of fasting and of abstinence from meat, which extended well beyond the forty days of Lent for a total of some one hundred fifty days a year.

In Umbria, *tagliolini* must have a generous grating of the local black truffle. In Perugia, extremely thin *tagliolini* are used in a soup called *"blò blò,"* named for the noise they make as they simmer slowly in the pot.

In Tuscany, around Siena, *tagliatelle* are used in the so-called *timballo della mietitura* (harvest). In the Valdarno, they are called *maccheroni* and an old saying differentiates the thicknesses: *maccheroni,* rolled thin and cut thick; *tagliolini,* rolled thick and cut thin. "Cut thick" meant that the *tagliatelle* were at least 1½ inches (4 cm) wide, and these are still served with a sauce of rabbit (see *pappardelle*).

Tagliolini, with different names, are a pillar of the Lazio kitchen. They are cut so thin one wonders how they can survive the cooking, brief though it is. How they are served varies and is strictly local. On Lake Bolsena, freshwater fish is favored, such as the soup made with tench (*tinca* in Italian, a white freshwater fish) and *tagliolini.* In the Sabine hills of the province of Rome, not so far away, the most popular sauce is made with lamb, and in some towns around Viterbo, delicious cakes are made with *tagliolini.* At Roviano, in the upper Aniene valley, *tajurini* are cooked in a soup made with a special locally grown bean, the *fagiolo cioncone.* Also Latian are *maccaruna o fieno,* made of just flour and egg yolks and cut as thin as a blade of hay, or *fieno.*

The cuisine of Naples, in contrast with that of Lazio, has remained showy and baroque, as it was when the city was a royal capital. Thin *tagliolini* are used to make *ordura,* a large croquette filled with everything under the sun and fried.

In Puglia, *taglioline* are made only with durum wheat and water, and are often the flagship dish of certain religious holidays. Among them is the feast of Our Lady of the Star, held on the second Sunday in October, at Palagiano, in the province of Taranto. It is one of many rustic feasts whose origin lies in ancient pagan propitiatory rites belonging to the agrarian world. Today, these festivals, which were still going strong in the 1950s, have almost disappeared, and it is thus interesting to attend this survivor, held in a country church on the edge of the area called Lama di Lenne. After the procession, in the square in front of the church, an enormous quantity of *tagghjarine* is first blessed in memory of the ancient custom of providing food to the peasants returning from work in the fields and then distributed to the faithful.

In Basilicata, *tapparelle* is the name given to the typical *tagliatelle* around Matera and Pisticci. In the Vulture area, special *tagliolini,* cooked in milk and flavored with cinnamon, are made for the feast of the Ascension. Formerly, it was prohibited to curdle the milk on this holy day. As a result, it became customary (and still is) for the shepherds to give away the milk in which the *tagliolini* were boiled. The milk was also believed to bring good fortune in the form of a generous forage harvest.

In Sicily, at Modica, egg *tagliatelle* about ¾ inch (2 cm) wide are called *lasugne* (see entry).

267. TAGLIOLINI PELOSI

Pasta lunga

INGREDIENTS: Wheat flour, but also durum wheat, some eggs, salt, and water.

HOW MADE: The flour is sifted with a pinch of salt onto a wooden board and kneaded long and vigorously with the eggs and with water as needed. When the dough is firm and smooth, it is left to rest, then rolled out with a rolling pin into a thin sheet, which is cut into flat noodles, *tagliatelle* or *tagliolini,* of variable width. They are boiled in salted water or broth.

ALSO KNOWN AS: No alternative names.

HOW SERVED: *Tagliatelle* as *pastasciutta, tagliolini* in broth, also with legumes.

WHERE FOUND: The Marche and Umbria.

REMARKS: *Peloso,* or "hairy," indicates the wrinkly surface the pasta gets from being rolled out on a wooden board. This roughness is important because it helps the pasta better collect the sauce.

Tagliatelle, tagliolini, bread, and other pastas made at home had their ritual. For example, if someone entered the house while the pasta was being made, he or she had to say *"San Martino l'accresca"* (May Saint Martin make it), to help ward off the *malocchio* (evil eye).

Tagliolini pelosi in a soup of chickpeas and chestnuts used to be customary in Orvieto for Christmas Eve. There was also a sweet variant of *tagliatelle pelose,* with chopped walnuts, sugar, and cinnamon. At Christmas lunch, *tagliolini* were cooked in hen broth, and a sauce of chicken giblets was served for the evening meal. It was not until economic conditions improved in the first decades of the 1900s that a main course of lamb followed the *tagliatelle* on both the Christmas and Easter menu.

Today, this pasta, now a luxury dish, is normally served at weddings, usually with a sauce made with giblets.

Tagliolini pelosi were also on the menu for the harvest meals, which were as follows: the *beverino,* or snack, at 7 A.M., which consisted of pork jowl and belly cooked with vinegar, oil, and sage, washed down with wine; at 10 A.M., beans with olive oil, with prosciutto and cheese; at 1 P.M., soup, boiled meat, and salad; and at 5 P.M., *pastasciutta,* meat, and salad.

There were separate tables for the threshing lunch, with the machine operators at one and the workmen at the other. The former were served the *tagliatelle pelose,* and the latter were given a generic *pastasciutta.* For the dinner, after the *scartocciatura,*[259] *tagliatelle* with tomato sauce were served, or else *spaghetti* with a sauce of sardines.

268. TAJARIN

Pasta lunga

INGREDIENTS: Wheat flour, eggs (today, on occasion only a great many yolks), salt, and sometimes a little oil or white wine. Formerly, a little butter was used instead of oil. For *tajarin di meliga,* wheat flour, corn flour, and eggs (variable number).

HOW MADE: The flour is sifted with a pinch of salt onto a wooden board and kneaded for a long time with whole eggs, or with only the yolks, and often also with a little olive oil or white wine. When the dough is firm and smooth, it is covered and allowed to rest. It is then rolled out into a thin sheet, and equally thin *tagliolini* are cut from it. They are boiled in salted water.

ALSO KNOWN AS: *Tajarin d'la nona;* at Ceresole, they are called *ceresolini.*

HOW SERVED: As *pastasciutta,* with local sauces, the most famous of which is *comodino,* a sumptuous *ragù* of organ meats. At Alba, they are graced with the famous white truffle.

WHERE FOUND: Piedmont, in the Langhe; Monferrato, especially Asti; and Alessandria.

REMARKS: The name is Piedmontese dialect for *tagliarini*. Pride of the rich and flavorful *cucina piemontese, tajarin* are regarded today with the respect due a true culinary monument.

Massimo Alberini, in his *Piemontesi a tavola,* tells us how much Victor Emanuel II liked them. The monarch used to protect his uniform with a large napkin knotted behind his neck. The *"bela* Rosin," promoted to Contessa di Mirafiori, and later the king's morganatic wife, used to make them for her august consort with her own hands.

The standard formula of one egg per 100 grams (3½ ounces) of flour is regarded with disdain by Piedmontese gastronomes: whole eggs or even just the yolks are added with abandon, twenty yolks and more per kilo of flour.

In one variant of *tajarin,* the dough contains a small amount of corn flour *(meliga),* and so they are called *tajarin di meliga.*

Some local scholars consider *tajarin* the only example of fresh pasta of certain Piedmontese origin, probably around Alba. And in fact, today each cook and every farm in the Langhe still has its recipe. The same is true for the *ragù,* made strictly with chicken and rabbit innards and cooked for a long time on the corner of the stove until it is brownish. It is a sort of *finanziera* that at one time was called *comodino.*

A recipe book published in Turin at the beginning of the nineteenth century[260] gives *tajarin* a tasty sauce of oil and anchovies, or of butter and mushrooms, which shows how versatile this superb pasta is. Even if today the condiments are more varied—and it is not difficult to find *tajarin* served with a *sugo di arrosto* or other meat sauce—in Alba, the famous local truffles are still the finishing touch. The same fresh pasta, made by artisanal pasta makers, is also sold.

In the past, peasants considered *tajarin,* and the equally famous *agnolotti,* the meal for feasts, and making them and their sauce was a ritual no housewife would miss. Poultry and rabbits were raised at home, the latter fed vegetables discarded by the numerous gardeners who grew the prized produce in the area, and the offal of animals fed on these same vegetables must have given the *ragù* a flavor impossible to duplicate today.

269. TESTAROLI

Unusual shape

INGREDIENTS: Durum-wheat flour, salt, and water. In some areas, formerly emmer or chestnut flour.

HOW MADE: The flour is sifted with a pinch of salt into a bowl, and then enough water is added to make a light batter, which is left to rest for a long time. To make the *testaroli,* a special utensil called a *testo* is used: A ladleful of batter is poured into the lower part of the *testo,* called the *testo sottano,* which is quite hot (and was once greased with a piece of pork rind). The upper part of the *testo,* the *testo soprano,* radiates heat that cooks the batter into a thin crepe. The *testaroli* are subsequently cut into large lozenges, tossed into salted water that has been brought to a boil and turned off, and left for two or three minutes. They are then drained and sauced. Traditionally, the *testo* is put into a wood-fired oven or directly on the hearth.

ALSO KNOWN AS: *Testaroi;* in Liguria, *testaieu.*

HOW SERVED: The usual sauce is *pesto alla genovese.*

WHERE FOUND: Tuscany, the Lunigiana, especially around Pontremoli. They are also common in the Garfagnana and surrounding areas, and in Liguria, especially in the Graveglia valley.

REMARKS: The name comes from the traditional *testo* of glazed terra-cotta, a sort of shallow cake pan. Over time, these were replaced with *testi* made of cast iron of the same size and shape.

The *testarolo* has early origins. The Bible gives Elijah a surprise (I Kings 19:6): "And he looked, and, behold, there was a cake baked on the coals. . . ." The Roman historian Varro[261] calls *testuacium* a sort of *focaccia* baked on brick (*testuacium quod in testu caldo coquebatur*).

The peoples of Lunigiana, and certainly they are not alone, have been eating these *focacce* since the Middle Ages. The *testaroli* used to be made at home in the same rooms, *gradili,* used for the drying of chestnuts. In the *gradili,* the fire was lit on the floor and the *testo* was heated on the embers. After it was used to cook the *testaroli*, it was used to cook bread, meat, and vegetables, imparting an inimitable flavor to the food.

Corrado Barberis has shown[262] how, in the High Middle Ages, the diet was much better in the Longobard area than in the Byzantine.

> Politically, the two jaws of the vise which from Romagna and the Ligurian Apennines sought to choke the Longobard corridor that ran from Emilia to the duchies of Spoleto and Benevento were Byzantine. Gastronomically, they are still represented by the two most elementary flours known to the Italian white art: the *piadina romagnola* and the *testaroli* of the Lunigiana, in both cases flour mixed with water, and all that is needed to cook them is a red-hot brick.[263]

Today, *testaroli* are a monument of gastronomic archaeology, sought out by gourmets and tourists in the Lunigiana, who can buy them vacuum-packed to take home.

A peasants' dish, homemade *testaroli* can be served simply with cheese and local olive oil, today enriched with *salumi*. The particular *testarolo* of Pontremoli is noticeably thicker and larger, about 16 to 20 inches (40 to 50 cm) in diameter, and is cut into squares. *Panigacci* are a smaller variation, though at Aulla, this name is used incorrectly for small *focacce* of raised dough.

Finally, there is *lu coccu illa zidda,* an unleavened *focaccia* of Sardinia cooked on a brick under the ashes.

270. TIRACHE TREVIGIANE

Pasta lunga

INGREDIENTS: Wheat flour and water.

HOW MADE: The flour is sifted onto a wooden board and kneaded with water until a firm, smooth dough forms. The dough is left to rest, then rolled out into a rather thick sheet, which is cut into wide, flat noodles. They are boiled in water or in soup.

ALSO KNOWN AS: No alternative names.

HOW SERVED: As *pastasciutta,* with traditional local sauces, or broken into pieces and used in the typical *pasta e fagioli.*

WHERE FOUND: Veneto, in particular Padova and Treviso.

REMARKS: *Tirache* is dialect for "suspenders" (or braces), which these long, thick *tagliatelle* resemble; *trevigiano* is the adjective for Treviso. Most often these noodles are broken up and used as the pasta in the dense *pasta e fagioli* that is commonly served around Padova and Treviso.

271. TOPPE

Pasta lunga

INGREDIENTS: Durum-wheat flour, type 00 wheat flour, and eggs.

HOW MADE: The flours are sifted together and kneaded for a long time with eggs until a firm, smooth dough forms, which is then left to rest. The dough is rolled out into a sheet, not too thin, and flat noodles 1½ to 2 inches (4 to 5 cm) wide and about 6 inches (15 cm) long are cut from it. They are boiled in abundant salted water.

ALSO KNOWN AS: No alternative names.

HOW SERVED: As *pastasciutta*, with simple condiment of Tuscan olive oil, pepper, and local pecorino, but also with various tomato sauces.

WHERE FOUND: Tuscany, especially the Casentino.

REMARKS: The name means literally "patches." The pasta is probably thought to resemble the cloth patches that the poor, unable to afford new clothes, used to repair their old ones.

272. TORCELLI

Pasta lunga

INGREDIENTS: Wheat flour and eggs.

HOW MADE: The flour is sifted onto a wooden board and kneaded long and vigorously with eggs. When the dough is firm and smooth, it is covered and left to rest. Hazelnut-sized pieces of dough are then pinched off and rolled between well-oiled hands into extremely thin *spaghetti*.

ALSO KNOWN AS: In the Marche, *stroncatelli*.

HOW SERVED: In general, cooked in broth, or as *pastasciutta*, with a meat *ragù*.

WHERE FOUND: Typical of *cucina ebraica*.

REMARKS: *Torcelli* were always served at the closing dinner of Yom Kippur, along with stewed yellow squash and the ritual *ciambelle di Kippur*,[264] which were covered and placed in the center of the table. That night it was believed an angel would come and quench his thirst and bless the house.[265]

The *stroncatelli* of Ancona are cooked in broth, to which celery and tomato are added.[266]

273. TORDEI

Pasta ripiena

INGREDIENTS: Wheat flour, salt, eggs, and water. For the filling, minced mortadella, chicken giblets, and herbs.

HOW MADE: The flour is sifted with a pinch of salt and kneaded long and vigorously with eggs and sometimes a little water until a smooth, firm dough forms. The dough is left to rest, then rolled out into a sheet, not too thin, and small disks of variable size are cut from it. A spoonful of filling is placed on each disk; the disk is folded in half to form a half-moon, and the edges are sealed with the tines of a fork. The *tordei* are cooked in plenty of lightly boiling salted water.

ALSO KNOWN AS: No alternative names.

HOW SERVED: As *pastasciutta,* with traditional local sauces.

WHERE FOUND: Tuscany, in particular the Lunigiana.

REMARKS: The Valle del Magra has a long tradition of *tortelli*. They are similar in shape to the *tordelli* (see entry) of Versilia, but are larger and the filling is very different.

274. TORDELLI

Pasta ripiena

INGREDIENTS: Wheat flour, some eggs, salt, and water. For the filling, veal, brains, sausage, chard, and grated cheese. For the meatless filling, bread soaked in milk or ricotta. In Liguria, the filling is a mixture of ricotta and grated cheese.

HOW MADE: The flour is sifted onto a wooden board and kneaded long and vigorously with some eggs, a pinch of salt, and water. When the dough is firm and smooth, it is left to rest, then rolled out into a sheet, and an inverted glass is used to cut out disks about 2 inches (5 cm) in diameter. A spoonful of filling is placed in the center of each disk, the disk is folded in half to form a half-moon, and the edges are sealed with the tines of a fork. The *tordelli* are boiled lightly in salted water.

ALSO KNOWN AS: No alternative names.

HOW SERVED: As *pastasciutta,* with hearty meat *ragù.*

WHERE FOUND: Tuscany, in particular the areas of Lucca, the Garfagnana, and Upper Versilia, but also the Lunigiana, on the Ligurian border.

REMARKS: Let no one call these *tortelli* by mistake, or they risk the scorn of the aficionados of this tasty dish. *Tordelli* used to be filled with ricotta and bread for fast (that is, meatless) days, but the leniency of church rules today finds them often given a hearty and complex meat filling.

When it comes to which herbs are used in the filling, every town, practically every family, has its own recipe. At Camaiore, for example, the filling is flavored with wild thyme leaves. In the meatless filling, the treatment of the bread can vary slightly. In some towns it is moistened with milk, and in others with water.

275. TORTELLI

Pasta ripiena

INGREDIENTS: Wheat flour and eggs. Various fillings, depending on place and feast days.

HOW MADE: The flour is sifted onto a wooden board and kneaded long and vigorously with eggs. When the dough is smooth and firm, it is wrapped in a dish towel and left to rest. It is then rolled out with a rolling pin into a thin sheet and cut into small disks or squares of variable size. A teaspoon of filling is placed at the center of a disk or square, and the *tortello* is closed in one of three ways: a second square or disk is placed on top, the disk is folded into a half-moon, or the square is folded into a triangle. The edges are always carefully sealed. Size, type of closing, and shape of the *tortello* vary from area to area. They are boiled, a few at a time, in abundant salted water.

ALSO KNOWN AS: In Emilia-Romagna, *turtlò,* and around Piacenza, *turtej cu la cua* (see entry); in Tuscany, in the areas of Versilia and the Lunigiana, *tordelli.* Often also called *ravioli.*

The fillings vary according to the area of production. Those called "of the vigil" are generally filled with ricotta, and in some areas, spinach or parsley is used. Squash is customary in the province of Piacenza and in Ferrara, where they are called *cappellacci di zucca* (see entry), and in Mantova, where amaretti are added to the squash (see *tortelli di zucca*). But the filling of greens in Parma remains the most famous.

HOW SERVED: As *pastasciutta,* with traditional local sauces.

WHERE FOUND: Widespread.

REMARKS: The term *tortello,* used for some types of stuffed pasta, can be traced to the Latin root *turta,* which means a dish that is stuffed in one way or another. For centuries, the *turta* has been documented in recipe books as something similar to the *torta rustica* of modern times, a pie with two crusts, the dough customarily made with flour and butter or lard and the filling usually a sweet-and-sour mixture of vegetables and/or fruits. *Tortello* derives from the term *torta,* "cake" or "pie," and is a commonplace from remote times. In fact, we read in Pulci's *Il Morgante* (XVIII-116): "Credo nella torta e nel tortello: l'uno è la madre e l'altro il suo figliolo." (I believe in the *torta* and the *tortello:* the one is the mother, the other the child.)

From the Middle Ages on, the *torta,* also called a *pastello,* has signaled its filling by its shape, and we can see this in a wealth of images: not only still lifes, but also set tables on which the painter depicts in detail objects, ornaments, and dishes, realistically copying them from what he saw around him.

The origin of the *tortello* was probably as meatless food. Not only are *tortelli* found in the first recipe collections in the vernacular, but their goodness, and therefore their diffusion, is mentioned in writings from the fourteenth century on, when they became differentiated by shape and filling. In fact, the earliest *tortello* was made in various shapes that are unusual to us today:

> On *tortelli.* Of pasta you can make any instrument you want, that is, horseshoe, pins, letters, and any animal you like. And you can fill them, if you want, and cook them in a skillet with *lardo* and with oil and fish and color them as you wish.[267]

Thus, the early *tortelli* were in the shape of small, closed tartlets, similar to certain pastries made today.

Sweet *tortelli,* nowadays eaten especially on such religious occasions as the feast of Saint Joseph (the Italian Father's Day) and also Carnival, are baked or deep-fried.

For the different ways to close them, see Piedmontese *agnolotti col plin* (see *agnolotti*) and the entry for *turtej cu la cua,* made in and around Piacenza: especially in the towns of Besenzone, Castelvetro, Cortemaggiore, Fiorenzuola, Monticelli d'Ongina, and San Nazzaro, where the ends are twisted to resemble a candy wrapper—almost like a braid with two tails. For the preparation and variety of fillings, see *ravioli* entry.

It is worth citing an example from a document dated 1226 mentioned in the *Glossarium* of Du Cange[268] under *tortellus:* "he entered the tomb of Saint Ebrulf and, after having reverently lifted the tombstone, gathered like *tortelli* the dust of the holy flesh."

276. TORTELLI BASTARDI
Pasta ripiena

INGREDIENTS: Wheat flour, chestnut flour, eggs, milk, and salt. For the filling, ricotta and grated cheese.

HOW MADE: The flours are sifted together onto a wooden board and kneaded long and vigorously with eggs, milk, and a pinch of salt until a firm, smooth dough forms. The dough is left to rest, then rolled out with a rolling pin into a sheet, which is cut into wide strips. Well-spaced walnut-sized heaps of filling are placed on one-half of each strip, and the other half is folded over and the pasta is pressed around the filling with fingers to seal. The filled strip is cut into half-moons with an inverted glass or special cutter. The *tortelli* are boiled in abundant salted water.

ALSO KNOWN AS: No alternative names.

HOW SERVED: As *pastasciutta,* generally with local condiments.

WHERE FOUND: Liguria, toward the Tuscan border.

REMARKS: Similar to the Tuscan *tordelli* (see entry), these strictly meatless *tortelli* are unusual for the use of chestnut flour in the dough. Chestnut flour—an important resource of the economy of the woods—is used more in Liguria than in any other Italian region.

277. TORTELLI CREMASCHI
Pasta ripiena

INGREDIENTS: Wheat flour, eggs, and water. For the filling, amaretti, raisins, candied citron, *mustazzitt* (see below), mint, parmigiano, and spices.

HOW MADE: The flour is sifted onto a wooden board and kneaded long and vigorously with very few eggs and with water as needed, then the dough is left to rest. It is rolled out into a very thin sheet and cut into squares large enough to hold a spoonful of filling at the center. The filled squares are folded into a triangle and the edges sealed carefully. They are cooked, a few at a time, in abundant lightly boiling salted water.

ALSO KNOWN AS: No alternative names.

HOW SERVED: As *pastasciutta,* with melted butter.

WHERE FOUND: Lombardy, especially around Crema.

REMARKS: Every family living in the towns around Crema believes it is the custodian of the true, original recipe for this feast-day dish. The filling contains *mus-*

tazzitt, a hard, spicy *biscotto* that greatly resembles its medieval ancestors, known as *mustacei.* Clearly, little has changed over the centuries in the preparation of these *tortelli.*

278. TORTELLI DEL MELO

Pasta ripiena

INGREDIENTS: Wheat flour, eggs, and water. For the filling, chard, local cheese, ricotta, dry bread crumbs, and spices.

HOW MADE: The flour is sifted and kneaded with eggs and water for a long time until a smooth, firm dough forms. The dough is left to rest, then rolled out into a sheet, and 1½-inch (4-cm) squares are cut from it. A spoonful of filling is placed in the center of half of the squares. A second square is placed on top and the edges carefully sealed. The *tortelli* are boiled in plenty of salted water.

ALSO KNOWN AS: *Raviolo del Melo.*

HOW SERVED: As *pastasciutta,* traditionally with a mushroom sauce or a meat *ragù.*

WHERE FOUND: Tuscany, in the province of Pistoia, at Melo, a part of Cutigliano.

REMARKS: In the tranquil hamlet of Melo, on the right-hand slope of the Lima valley, in the upper Apennines of Pistoia, life must not have been easy when the only resources were water and the forest and, to some extent, sheep raising, which led to the production of local cheeses and excellent ricotta.

The identifying characteristic of these *tortelli* is the particular local ricotta used in the filling. It was a dish for special occasions, made for guests and always for the feast of the patron saint, San Nicolao, September 25. Today, the *tortelli* are a feature of *sagre* in mid-August, when the local tourism is higher.

279. TORTELLI DEL MONTEFELTRO

Pasta ripiena

INGREDIENTS: Wheat flour and eggs. For the filling, fresh cheese, ricotta, honey, and lemon rind.

HOW MADE: The flour is sifted onto a wooden board and kneaded long and vigorously with eggs. The dough is left to rest, then rolled out into a thin sheet, and small balls of filling, spaced about 1¼ inches apart, are arranged on half of the sheet. The other half of the sheet is folded over the filling and the pasta is pressed around the filling with fingers to seal. A pasta cutter or an inverted glass is used to cut out round *ravioli* about 2¾ inches (7 cm) in diameter. They are boiled in plenty of salted water.

ALSO KNOWN AS: No alternative names.

HOW SERVED: Generally as *pastasciutta* served *in bianco,* with butter, parmigiano, sage, and *mentuccia.*[269]

WHERE FOUND: The Marche.

REMARKS: Like almost everything else in the *cucina marchigiana,* these *tortelli* are flavored with grated lemon rind, and it is this fragrance that still today makes the dish unmistakable.

Flavoring foods with lemon is an old practice that may have been spread in the 1500s by the court of the Montefeltro, a beacon of culture, including gastronomic. The classic books, such as Scappi's weighty *Opera,* often call for lemon, which must have been fashionable on the noble and curial tables from the Middle Ages on.

280. TORTELLI DEL MUGELLO

Pasta ripiena

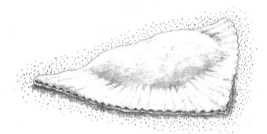

INGREDIENTS: Wheat flour and eggs. For the filling, chestnuts, grated cheese, spices, and olive oil.

HOW MADE: The flour is sifted onto a wooden board and kneaded long and vigorously with eggs. After the dough is allowed to rest, it is rolled out with a rolling pin into a thin sheet, which is cut into 1½-inch (4-cm) squares. A teaspoon of filling is placed in the center of each square, the square is folded into a triangle, and the edges are carefully sealed with the tines of a fork. The *tortelli* are boiled in plenty of salted water.

ALSO KNOWN AS: No alternative names.

HOW SERVED: Traditionally as *pastasciutta,* served with butter and the local cheese.

WHERE FOUND: Tuscany, in particular the Mugello.

REMARKS: The traditional cooking of Tuscany has always been one of the most attentive to the products of the territory. Over the centuries, the people of the

Mugello have preserved a profound attachment to the land and what it produces, as evidenced by these *ravioli,* which exploit the chestnuts of the woods that extend toward the Apennines and characterize the cooking of the towns of Dicomano, San Godenzo, Firenzuola, and Marradi.

281. TORTELLI DI PATATE

Pasta ripiena

INGREDIENTS: Wheat flour, eggs, and salt. For the filling, potatoes, local cheese, and spices.

HOW MADE: The flour is sifted with a pinch of salt onto a wooden board and kneaded with eggs long and vigorously until a smooth, firm dough forms. The dough is covered and left to rest, then rolled out into a thin sheet, which is cut into wide strips. Teaspoons of filling are placed about 1¼ inches (3 cm) apart on a strip. A second strip is placed on top, and the sheet is pressed carefully with fingers around the filling. Large, square *ravioli* are then cut apart with a wheel-type pasta cutter. They are boiled, a few at a time, in salted water.

A limited factory-made production of this *tortello* also exists.

ALSO KNOWN AS: No alternative names.

HOW SERVED: As *pastasciutta,* traditionally with a hearty meat *ragù.*

WHERE FOUND: Tuscany, in the province of Prato and in the Mugello.

REMARKS: This *tortello* has been made in Tuscany by the same method for at least two centuries. It is associated with the local cultivation of potatoes, which have a particularly delicate flavor. In the Mugello, in spring, when the extraction of the precious tubers begins, numerous *sagre* are held in honor of these equally precious *tortelli.* At Borgo San Lorenzo, for example, they are the ritual dish for the feast of the local patron saint, Saint Lawrence, August 11. In the Valle del Sieve, they are served with a sauce of *nana,* as the Tuscans call duck.

282. TORTELLI DI ZUCCA

Pasta ripiena

INGREDIENTS: Wheat flour and eggs. For the filling, *zucca mantovana* (Mantuan squash), amaretti, *mostarda di Cremona,* parmigiano, and nutmeg.

HOW MADE: The flour is sifted onto a wooden board and kneaded forcefully with eggs for a long time until a firm, smooth dough forms, which is left to rest. It is rolled out with a rolling pin into a sheet, and 4-inch (10-cm) squares or disks are cut from it. These are topped with a walnut-sized bit of filling and closed into a rectangle or half-moon, and the edges are carefully sealed. They are boiled, a few at a time, in plenty of salted water.

ALSO KNOWN AS: *Tortei;* at Viadana, near Mantova, *blisgon,* literally "slippery."

HOW SERVED: As *pastasciutta,* generally with abundant butter and parmigiano.

WHERE FOUND: Lombardy, in particular Mantova, but also Cremona and Brescia.

REMARKS: *Tortelli di zucca* were served in Mantova typically for Christmas Eve. This large *tortello* is shaped like a Napoleonic hat, part of the costume of the Mantuan wine bearers. The vernacular poet Ettore Berni describes it thus:

> . . . *dag la form d'on capèl;*
> *e s'at vol po' fart' onor,*
> *d'on capèl da "portador";*
> *e s'at vol chi diventa fin*
> *fai pu gros d' on agnolin.*[270]

[. . . give it the shape of a hat of a "bearer" and if you want it to be more valuable, give it the form of *agnolino.*]

But the *tortello di zucca* is also exemplary of a good use of local products: The squash that has been produced for centuries in the Po Valley has a very high sugar content, a quality it owes not only to the terrain, but also to the light fog that protects it from the burning summer sun, maintaining that degree of humidity it needs to grow and ripen. In fact, in times of scarcity of sugar, it was also used as a sweetener.

283. TORTELLI MAREMMANI

Pasta ripiena

INGREDIENTS: Wheat flour and eggs. For the filling, spinach or nettles, local cheese, ricotta, and spices.

HOW MADE: The flour is sifted onto a wooden board and kneaded for a long time with eggs, then the dough is left to rest. It is rolled out with a rolling pin into a thin sheet, which is cut into strips about 5 inches (12 cm) wide. Well-spaced hazelnut-sized piles of filling are placed on half of each strip. The other half is folded over and the pasta is pressed closed around the filling with fingers. A wheel-type pasta cutter is used to cut the strip crosswise at intervals of about 2½ inches (6 cm) to make square *ravioli,* which are dried and then boiled, a few at a time, in salted water.

ALSO KNOWN AS: No alternative names.

HOW SERVED: As *pastasciutta,* with hearty meat *ragù.*

WHERE FOUND: Tuscany, at Maremma grossetana (the strip of Grosseto Province near the coast).

REMARKS: This *tortello* is common not only along the Maremma grossetana, but also in the hills and other areas surrounding Monte Amiata. In recent years, the consumption of this *tortello,* with its poor filling, has slowly declined as improved economic conditions, even for the country women, have favored the richer *tortello,* with a meat filling.

284. TORTELLI ROMAGNOLI

Pasta ripiena

INGREDIENTS: Wheat flour and eggs. For the filling, field greens, ricotta, and nutmeg. One variant uses potatoes and ricotta.

HOW MADE: The flour is kneaded energetically for a long time with eggs until the dough is firm and smooth. The dough is left to rest, then rolled out into a thin sheet and cut into 2-inch (5-cm) squares. Each square is filled and folded into a triangle, and the edges are carefully sealed. The *tortelli* are boiled, a few at a time, in plenty of salted water.

ALSO KNOWN AS: *Cappelletti romagnoli.*

HOW SERVED: As *pastasciutta,* with various sauces; sometimes with *strigoli.*[271]

WHERE FOUND: Emilia-Romagna.

REMARKS: In Romagna as well as in Emilia, homemade pasta, the noble kind made with wheat flour and eggs, is a well-established tradition. This is work for strong arms, since the dough, known here as *spassèll,* must be kneaded with both skill and force; then the sheet, under the *staciadur* (rolling pin), must be rolled to a rare and difficult thinness. For these precious *tortelli,* it must be almost transparent.

Strigoli, also called *stridoli* in dialect, are found in many parts of Italy, but are abundant in the pine forests around Ravenna. They are a common, simple *contorno* in the *cucina romagnola,* and they give the pasta filling a characteristic flavor.

A particular *tortello* called *tortello di erbette* has a filling of chard and ricotta; it is made throughout the region.

285. TORTELLI SGUAZZAROTTI

Pasta ripiena

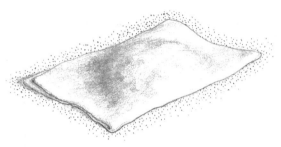

INGREDIENTS: Wheat flour, eggs, and water. For the filling, *borlotti* (cranberry-type) beans and *salsa saorina*.

HOW MADE: The flour is sifted onto a wooden board and kneaded for a long time with some eggs and with water until a firm, smooth dough forms. The dough is left to rest, then rolled out into a thin sheet, and 4-inch (10-cm) squares are cut from it. A spoonful of filling is placed in the center of each square, the square is folded into a rectangle, and the edges of the large *ravioli* are carefully sealed so the filling will not escape during cooking. The *tortelli* are boiled in salted water.

ALSO KNOWN AS: *Turtei sguassarot.*

HOW SERVED: As *pastasciutta,* served warm or cold, with *salsa saorina.*

WHERE FOUND: Lombardy, Mantova in particular.

REMARKS: A true hallmark of gastronomic archaeology, this *tortello* seems to have come off the dusty pages of a Renaissance recipe book of the Gonzaga court.

Salsa saorina is an indispensable ingredient. It is mixed with bean puree for the filling, and is also the sauce in which the *tortelli* must *sguazzare,* "flounder" or "swim," hence the name. It is an old sauce made with *vincotto,* sugar, walnuts, apples, squash, and orange rind. The fragrance comes from cinnamon and cloves, though these last two ingredients are eliminated from the sauce when it is served with *ravioli.*

286. TORTELLINI

Pasta ripiena

INGREDIENTS: Type 0 wheat flour and eggs. For the filling, mortadella, prosciutto, meat (veal, chicken, or pork), parmigiano, beef marrow, and spices. Small variants on the filling exist.

HOW MADE: The flour is sifted onto a wooden board and kneaded long and vigorously with eggs. The dough is left to rest, then rolled out with a rolling pin into a very thin sheet, and ¾-inch (2-cm) squares are cut from it. Each square is topped with a hazelnut-sized bit of filling and folded into a triangle, and the edges are carefully sealed. Then the edge is folded, the *tortellino* is wound around a fingertip, and the points are pressed together. The *tortellini* are boiled in broth.

ALSO KNOWN AS: *Presuner* (for *prigionieri*, "prisoners," at Carpi).

HOW SERVED: In broth.

WHERE FOUND: Emilia-Romagna, Bologna and Modena in particular.

REMARKS: The pride of Emilian gastronomy, *tortellini* stand with *lasagne* and *tagliatelle* in the famous triad that defines Bolognese cooking in the eyes of the world—even if Bologna and Modena dispute the origin of the recipe.

The controversy over the true and original recipe has been disputed ad infinitum for decades by gourmets, scholars, and philologists and by the citizens of Bologna, where every family makes its *tortellini* with small variations and considers its own to be the only true and authentic recipe. To put an end to the controversy, on December 7, 1974, the Accademia Italiana della Cucina, Bologna section, and the Confraternita del Tortellino registered with notarial act and deposited with the Bologna Chamber of Commerce the ingredients and quantities of the "true and authentic" *tortellino*. Here, then, is the definitive recipe to fill about one thousand *tortellini*: 300 grams *lombo* (loin) of pork, browned in butter; 300 grams *prosciutto crudo;* 300 grams true Bolognese *mortadella;* 450 grams *parmigiano-reggiano;* 3 hen's eggs; and 1 nutmeg (whose weight it would be more correct to state in grams).

It was a long road that began with Bartolomeo Scappi, secret cook of the inappetent Pius V. In chapter 178 of the second book of his *Opera*, published in

Venice in 1570, we find a recipe "to make *tortelletti* with pork belly, and other material, called *annolini* in the vernacular." A long description of the filling follows: boiled fresh *pancetta,* udder of heifer well cooked, lean meat of young pig half roasted on the spit or boiled, abundant parmigiano and other cheeses, sugar, cinnamon, pepper, cloves, nutmeg, raisins, grilled *enula* roots, fresh eggs, and saffron. At this point Scappi prescribes: "Take a sheet of pasta and make *anolini* small as beans or chickpeas and join their points so they have the shape of little hats."[272]

Here, then, are all the elements of confusion that keep the debate amusing and make synonyms of *tortellini* (or *tortelletti*), *anolini* (variously spelled), and *cappelletti*. In truth, the synonymy invests the *cappelletti* of Reggio, but also those of Romagna, whose filling is strictly meatless.

What they have in common is the outside: the Emilian pasta sheet must be thin and fragrant. All the housewives who today have gray hair have in their DNA the extraordinary ability to make this pasta, different from that of all the other Italian regions, even if the ingredients are the same. And it is not only a question of thickness. If two properly made pasta sheets were placed side by side, every housewife born under the Two Towers[273] would be able to pick out which one was Bolognese. Thus, the *tortellino* must be as small as possible. In this, Reggio Emilia claims supremacy. Hence the mention of the chickpea or bean already found in Scappi.

A certain freedom in preparing the filling would affect the name. According to Gabriele Ronzoni,[274] the *anolino* would owe its name not to its ring shape, as is commonly believed, but to containing *enula* in the filling, according to Scappi: Costanzo Felici, in a letter to the great naturalist Ulisse Aldrovandi (1572), even proposed calling them *enulini*.

When did *tortelletti* become *tortellini?* Almost certainly at the origin of this terminological mutation is the Bolognese Vincenzo Tanara,[275] who, writing in the mid-seventeenth century, uses *tortelletti* as a synonym for *anolini*. Earlier in the same century, Alessandro Tassoni of Modena, whose mock epic *La secchia rapita* was published in 1622, still spoke of *tortelletti:*

Tutte nostre saran senza sospetti
queste ricche campagne e queste armenti;
le salsicce i capponi e i tortelletti
da casa ci verran cotti e bollenti.

[These rich lands and foods will be all ours; the sausages, capons, and *tortellini* will come from home, cooked and boiling.]

Was it was only a need for rhyme that made Tassoni keep the designation *tortelletti* for what were already being called *tortellini?* It cannot be ruled out, even though it would have been easy to find rhymes ending in *ini*. Therefore, in the rivalry between Bologna and Modena as birthplace of the *tortellino,* Tanara's testimony is certainly to Bologna's advantage—it still being understood that the word is one thing, the substance, which is to say the filling, quite another. We also know that in Modena the *tortelletto* quickly took the name *tortellino.* A stimulating essay by Gabriele Ronzoni[276] recalls the youthful verses in which Ludovico Antonio Muratori,[277] writing between 1688 and 1690, not even half a century after Tanara, gave vent to the literally macaronic fame of the two friends Marforio and Pasquino:

> *Tortellinorum nobis mangianda minestra est*
> *Quia panzam scaldant.*

[We should eat a soup of *tortellini* because it warms our belly.]

Until a few decades ago, *tortellini* were always served in broth, but today they may be treated as *pastasciutta* or put in a *pasticcio,* such as the sumptuous one made with pigeon in Reggio Emilia.

In the second half of the 1800s, *tortellini* were already a myth in honor of which unlikely compromises were invented, like the one that attributed their paternity to Castelfranco, a small city halfway between Bologna and Modena. An industry also grew up. Corrado Barberis[278] documents how in Bologna, the Dall'Osso factory was employing forty workers by around 1880. And with industry blossomed the legend that derives the product from the navel of Aphrodite. Having the goddess as a guest in his hotel and having had the chance to contemplate her undressed,

> *l'oste che era guercio e bolognese*
> *Imitando di Venere il bellico*
> *L'arte di fare il tortellino apprese.*[279]

[the landlord, who was cross-eyed and Bolognese, imitating the umbilicus of Venus, learned the art of making the *tortellino.*]

See also entries for *tortelli* and *ravioli.*

287. TORTELLO SULLA LASTRA

Pasta ripiena

INGREDIENTS: Wheat flour and the water used to cook the squash for the filling. For the filling, squash, potatoes, flavorful cheese such as *cacio raviggiolo* or pecorino, *lardo,* and seasonings.

HOW MADE: The flour is sifted onto a wooden board and kneaded with the squash water until a firm, smooth dough forms. The dough is left to rest, then rolled out into a thickish sheet. Large rectangles, about 2 by 4 inches (5 by 10 cm), or 4-inch (5-cm) squares are cut from the sheet. A spoonful of filling is placed on each cutout, the pasta is folded in half, and the edges are carefully sealed. The *tortello* is cooked on both sides on a sandstone griddle.

ALSO KNOWN AS: No alternative names.

HOW SERVED: Plain, from the grill.

WHERE FOUND: In the mountainous border area between Romagna and Tuscany.

REMARKS: The name means literally "*tortello* on the slab," the slab being a griddle. We have found no written sources for this particular *tortello*, considered a true delicacy of the towns on the Apennine crest that separates Tuscany from Romagna, though tradition suggests that it has been there for quite some time.

The particular preparation on the slab recalls the method common in Romagna for making the local flat bread called *piadina*. It is certainly also what our ancestors used when they left the caves and started to grow grains and grind flour. The *piadina* is not traditional in this part of Romagna, but this *tortello* can be considered its distant relative, in both how it is made and how it is cooked.

Tortello sulla lastra used to be made only when the squash was ripe, from the end of summer through late autumn, but today it is made year-round.

288. TORTIGLIONI

Pasta corta

INGREDIENTS: Durum-wheat flour and water.

HOW MADE: Ridged factory-made tubes with twisted shape. *Tortiglioni* are boiled in abundant salted water.

ALSO KNOWN AS: Depending on size, *eliche, fusilli, fusilli a spirale, fusilloni, spirali* (all types of spirals), *gemelli* (twins), and *riccioli* (curls).

HOW SERVED: Generally as *pastasciutta*, with typical local sauces.

WHERE FOUND: Throughout Italy, but especially southern Italy, Campania in particular.

REMARKS: The name refers to the shape and derives from the Vulgar Latin *tortillare,* which in turn is derived from the Classical Latin *torquere,* or "twist" (as in English "torsion"). *Tortillare* evolved into the Vulgar Italian *tortigliare;* thus, the noun *tortiglione* is literally a thing twisted in a spiral.

The same term must at one time have been used for a particular fresh pasta, similar to *fusilli,* since it is attested in the *Libro della mensa.*[280]

Industrial pasta makers have exercised their imagination with variations on the twist theme by coiling both thick *spaghettoni* and *fettuccelle* into a spiral.

289. TRENETTE, TRENETTE AVVANTAGGIATE

Pasta lunga

INGREDIENTS: Durum-wheat flour and water. For *trenette avvantaggiate,* durum-wheat flour, whole-wheat flour, and water.

HOW MADE: Narrow factory-made ribbons. *Trenette* are boiled in plenty of salted water.

ALSO KNOWN AS: *Linguine* and *bavette.*

HOW SERVED: As *pastasciutta,* with the typical sauces of Liguria. *Trenette* are usually boiled together with potatoes and green beans and served with *pesto alla genovese.*

WHERE FOUND: Liguria, Genoa in particular.

REMARKS: Today, it is a gourmet treat, but both yesterday and today "advantaged" pasta—which is what *avvantaggiata* means literally, that is, containing some whole-wheat flour—costs less than the normal white pasta made entirely with white flour: this was actually the advantage for the consumer, who could rarely afford to buy wheat pasta. *Pasta avvantaggiata* could also contain 20 percent chestnut flour, which accentuated its dark color and further lowered the price.

The province of La Spezia used to have *trenette a stuffo,* which were served with a bean *ragù:* a balanced, nourishing one-dish meal in line with the dictates of the Mediterranean diet. It is so called because the pasta is *stufata* (stewed) in its sauce of beans. But the sauce par excellence for *trenette* is *pesto alla genovese* (see *picagge*).

290. TRIA

Pastina

INGREDIENTS: Durum-wheat flour and eggs, but formerly water.

HOW MADE: The flour is sifted and kneaded for a long time with eggs or water. The dough is covered and left to rest, then rolled into a thin sheet, which is cut into various shapes and sizes, depending on the area of production. They are usually flat noodles, more or less wide and thick, and are cooked in soup.

ALSO KNOWN AS: In Puglia, *tridde* and *ruvitti*.

HOW SERVED: Usually in chickpea soup, but also in other combinations of vegetables, meats, fish, and legumes.

WHERE FOUND: Puglia and Sicily.

REMARKS: A very old pasta, *tria* appears already in a description by the Arab geographer al-Idrisi (see *spaghetti*). According to some historians, this document must be read correctly, in the sense that the title of "granary" assigned to Sicily for the production of durum wheat does not indicate broad consumption of the grain on the part of the population, though it does identify it as an object of profitable commerce. Moreover, the Sicilian lands were particularly well suited to grain production, but success was also due to the habitual stubbornness of the medieval peasant in plowing and tilling the soil.

Tria is the ancient generic name of pasta, which was noted in the fourteenth century by Mastro Barnaba di Reggio, in a manuscript in the Biblioteca Laurenziana of Florence,[281] under *Capitulum de tri:*

> Tri vulgariter habet different vocabula: a quibusdam enim dicitur tria, ut a Contanis, a quibusdam vermicelli ut a Thuscis, a quibusdam oreti ut a Bononiensibus, a quibusdam minytelli ut a Ven(etis) et quibusdam formentini ut a Reg(iensibus) et a quibusdam pancardelle ut a Man(tuanis).

> [*Tria* are popularly called by different names: for some it is *tria,* as in Contani; for some *vermicelli,* as for the Tuscans; others call them *oreti,* such as the Bolognesi; some *minytelli,* as the Venetians; some *formentini,* as in Reggio; and some *pancardelle,* as in Mantova.]

Itryya was sold also under the Arabic name *fidaws,* which became the Castilian *fideos.* String-shaped dry pastas, abundantly cited in Arab-Andalusian culinary treatises, find space very late in the Italian culinary treatises. However, they are often cited in archival documents of various kinds, such as notarial acts, inventories, tax rolls, and the like, which attest how *spaghetti* dried in the sun were found throughout the Mediterranean basin as early as the twelfth century. They were also exported from Sardinia as Galoppini has noted with regard to the traffic of dry pastas. The same thesis is sustained by Rosenberger in his study of Arabic cooking texts.[282]

Today, the old word *tria* lingers in many parts of southern Italy, especially Sicily, where a pasta called *tria* is still common. In Puglia, *ciceri e tria* is the dialect name of one of the region's most popular *primi piatti,* which contains some boiled noodles and some fried. In many towns in the province of Lecce, on March 18, the day before the feast of Saint Joseph, which is the Italian Father's

Day, *ciceri e tria* used to be offered to three poor people, symbolizing Saint Joseph, the baby Jesus, and the Virgin Mary.

291. TROCCOLI

Pasta corta

INGREDIENTS: Durum-wheat flour, but also type 00 wheat flour, water, and sometimes also egg whites.

HOW MADE: The flour is sifted and kneaded with water, and sometimes also with egg whites, for a long time until a firm, smooth dough forms, which is then left to rest. Pieces are pinched off and rolled into cylinders 5 to 6 inches (13 to 15 cm) long, which are then flattened with the palm of the hand. A special grooved rolling pin, called *u 'ntrucele,* made of brass or wood is rolled over these irregular strips to cut thick *tonnarelli.*

In Abruzzo, the technique changes slightly: the piece of dough is rolled out with a smooth rolling pin into a strip about ⅜ inch (1 cm) thick; the strip is then pressed hard with the grooved rolling pin to cut the noodles.

The *troccoli* are boiled in abundant salted water.

ALSO KNOWN AS: *Torchioli.* In Abruzzo, *maccheroni al rintrocilo, rentrocelo,* and *ritrocilo;* and in Basilicata, *truoccoli.*

HOW SERVED: As *pastasciutta,* with typical local *ragù* and, invariably, grated local pecorino.

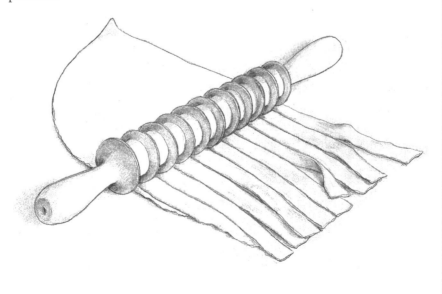

WHERE FOUND: Lazio (the Sabine country of the province of Rieti); Abruzzo, province of Chieti; Puglia, province of Foggia; and Basilicata.

REMARKS: The curious utensil for making this pasta, *u 'ntrucele,* is quite old in Italy. In the sixteenth century, Scappi calls it *ferro da maccaroni.* In his day, it was made of iron, heavier, yes, but it could be sharpened to make more regular shapes. Today's wooden utensil is not as sharp but is also cheaper. Hard-woods were gradually replaced by softer, neutral woods, such as the beech used today.

In Puglia, the grooved rolling pin for making *troccoli* is called *torcolo* or *troccolo,* from the Latin *torculum,* from which the pasta takes its name.

A typical Pugliese sauce for this type of pasta is *ragù del macellaio,* so called because the butcher *(macellaio)* himself used to select the variety of meats needed, probably from leftovers, and always including lamb and pork.

292. TROFIE

Pasta corta

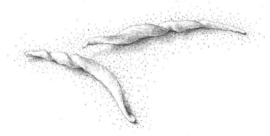

INGREDIENTS: Wheat flour enriched with bran; potatoes, bread, or chestnut flour; and water. For factory made, durum-wheat flour and water.

HOW MADE: The sifted flour or flours, or potatoes or bread, are kneaded for a long time with water. If potatoes are used, they are boiled and riced, and if stale bread is used, it is soaked in water and squeezed well. Then the dough is left to rest, to give the gluten time to develop and make the dough elastic. Bean-sized pieces are pinched off and rubbed between the hands into a sort of spindle shape, tapered at the ends. *Trofie* are boiled in plenty of salted water. Factory-made *trofie* are small spirals tapered at both ends.

ALSO KNOWN AS: *Rechelline, trofiette, troffie,* and *troffiette.*

HOW SERVED: As *pastasciutta,* with *pesto alla genovese* made with Ligurian basil, garlic, pecorino, *prescinsoea,*[283] pine nuts, salt, and olive oil of the Ligurian Riviera. In Recco, fava beans are added to the pesto. It is traditional to boil *trofie* with green beans and potatoes. Nowadays, instead of pesto, the sauce may be of mushrooms, *ragù*, fish, or other ingredients.

WHERE FOUND: Liguria in general, in particular the area of Camogli; but also some areas of Tuscany bordering Liguria.

REMARKS: The word is of Greek derivation, from τροφή, meaning "nourishment." It is one of the many shapes that descend from the medieval flour-and-water *gnocco*, typically made with poor flours and other local ingredients to enrich the dough. The addition of potato imparted softness to the finished *trofie*.

At the beginning of the 1800s, the potato spread rapidly in Liguria, on the terraced terrains planted to vines and olive trees. The town of Borgotaro grew thirteen varieties, and the cultivation of the tuber quickly extended to the hinterland of Recco and Chiavari.

In the depressed areas of the Ligurian-Emilian Apennines, from the middle of the 1800s almost up to World War II, chestnuts were a basic component of the peasant diet. Every poor home had a place to dry chestnuts, and much more space was dedicated to storing chestnut flour than wheat or corn flour. For six months of the year, the peasant family lived on chestnuts, and the flour was present in at least two daily meals. Dried chestnuts were also a precious commodity of exchange, and the shells were fed to the pigs.

This attachment to the chestnut was challenged at the beginning of the nineteenth century, with the arrival under Napoléon of new ideas on converting the land to agriculture. When the older peasants objected to the uprooting of the trees, the young would-be farmers of Castagnola and Cattaragna, in the mountains around Piacenza, went out at night and stripped trees of their bark to make them dry out.

An early condiment for *trofie*, now disappeared, was a melted fresh cow's milk cheese, typical of the Valbrevenna, whose flavor and aroma blended perfectly with that of chestnuts.

Today, chestnut *trofie* are a niche product always served with pesto.

293. TUBETTI

Pasta corta

INGREDIENTS: Durum-wheat flour and water.

HOW MADE: Factory-made tubes, usually small, both smooth and ridged. They are cooked in soups or with legumes.

ALSO KNOWN AS: *Tubettini, ditali, ditaletti* (thimbles), *gnocchetti di ziti, gnocchettini,* and *coralli* (corals). In Puglia and Sicily, *denti di vecchia* (old woman's teeth), *denti di cavallo* (horse's teeth), *ganghi di vecchia* (old woman's legs), and *magghietti.*

HOW SERVED: The small shapes in broth or in legume soups.

WHERE FOUND: Widespread.

REMARKS: The name means literally "little tubes." In Puglia, where the *pasta d'ingegno* was widespread by the beginning of the 1800s, these irregularly shaped, small, curved tubes could be produced with the *torchio* or with the appropriate die.

The spread of the small local pasta makers at the beginning of the 1800s was extensive, especially around Bari. A sampling of patent registries for a number of towns (including Bari, Molfetta, Bitonto, Trani, Terlizzi, Torritto, and Triggiano)[284] shows the presence of manufacturers of *maccheroni* "with *ingegno* and warehouse," that is, local producers who had a small or large trade extending beyond the surrounding towns.

In Calabria, *ditali* are traditionally served with *ca trimma,* a sauce made from beaten eggs, pecorino, and parsley.

In Sicily, the *maccheronai* made *denti di vecchia,* and many other shapes, throughout the 1800s: this pasta, which is ridged, appears in both Perez's *Vocabolario siciliano-italiano* and Pitré's catalog made some twenty years later.[285]

294. TUFOLI

Pasta corta

INGREDIENTS: Durum-wheat flour and water.

HOW MADE: Factory-made tubes of varying diameter, both smooth and ridged. They are boiled in abundant salted water or in broth.

ALSO KNOWN AS: *Cannaroni, cannaruncielli,* and *cannerozzi.* For small sizes, *cannelli, cannolicchi, diavoletti, diavolini, spolette, stortini, svuotini,* and *tubetti.* For larger sizes, *cannelloni da ripieno* (to be filled), *canneroni, cannerozzi, fascette* and *mezze fascette, fischioni, fischiotti, maniche, schiaffettoni, schiaffoni,* and *sigarette.*

An old terminology from eastern Sicily included, among similar shapes, *napoleoni* and *zitelle,* which are slightly curved, and *cavour* and *damigelle* (damsels), which are straight.

HOW SERVED: The large shapes as *pastasciutta,* and the smaller ones in broth or soups.

WHERE FOUND: Widespread.

REMARKS: The vast terminology of pasta—and all the alternative names for *tufoli* are a good example—varies depending on where the pasta is made. The Neapolitan term *cannerone* refers to the animal gullet, which the pasta resembles in the popular imagination.

The old handmade *tufoli* were formed by rolling a small piece of dough across a small board on which a design—or simply lines or points—was incised.

295. TURLE

Pasta ripiena

INGREDIENTS: Wheat flour and water and sometimes eggs. For the filling, potatoes and mint.

HOW MADE: The flour is sifted onto a wooden board and kneaded long and vigorously with water and sometimes a few eggs. The dough is left to rest, then rolled out with a rolling pin into a thin sheet, and disks or rectangles of variable size are cut from it. The disks are filled and folded into half-moons; the rectangles are filled and folded into squares. The *turle* are boiled in abundant salted water.

ALSO KNOWN AS: No alternative names.

HOW SERVED: As *pastasciutta,* with cream and walnuts, or with butter, garlic or leek, and hazelnuts.

WHERE FOUND: Liguria, in the Maritime Alps, in particular the upper Valle Arroscia.

REMARKS: The transhumance paths that link the Maritime Alps of Liguria with the Occitan valleys of the province of Cuneo, in Piedmont, carried culinary traditions back and forth along with the flocks. This is the land of the *cucina bianca,* to which belongs the old condiment of walnuts or hazelnuts and dairy cream. In winter, there was nothing else to put on these particular *ravioli,* which today are the pride of the local gastronomy.

296. TURTEI DELLA VALLE TANARO

Pasta ripiena

INGREDIENTS: Flour, cream from mountain pastures, and salt. For the filling, potatoes and tips of nettles or other wild greens.

HOW MADE: The flour is sifted onto a wooden board with a pinch of salt and kneaded with cream (today also with olive oil) for a long time until a firm, smooth dough forms. The dough is left to rest, then rolled out into a thin sheet. Tablespoons of filling are placed on half of the sheet at generous intervals. The sheet is folded over and pressed closed around the filling. A wheel-type pasta cutter is used to separate large *ravioloni.* They are deep-fried or cooked on a griddle.

ALSO KNOWN AS: No alternative names.

HOW SERVED: Deep-fried or cooked on a griddle.

WHERE FOUND: Piedmont, a specialty of the upper Valle Tanaro.

REMARKS: These curious *ravioli* used to be cooked on the griddle of a wood-burning stove, or they were deep-fried and sprinkled with sugar as a tasty snack for children.

297. TURTEJ CU LA CUA

Pasta ripiena

INGREDIENTS: Wheat flour and eggs. For the filling, ricotta and greens, or even ricotta and mascarpone.

HOW MADE: The flour is sifted onto a wooden board and kneaded long and energetically with eggs. The dough must be firm and silky. It is left to rest, then rolled out into a very thin sheet, and rhombuses or rectangles about 1½ by 2½ inches (4 by 6 cm) are cut from it. A spoonful of filling is placed lengthwise on each piece, and the pasta is closed with a series of folds to make a braid on the surface and a sort of tail at the end. The *tortelli* are dropped into abundant lightly boiling salted water.

ALSO KNOWN AS: *Tortelli piacentini.*

HOW SERVED: As *pastasciutta,* with melted butter and parmigiano, or with meat *ragù.*

WHERE FOUND: Emilia-Romagna, typical of Piacenza.

REMARKS: *Cu la cua* is dialect for *con la coda,* or "with the tail." *Turtej cu la cua* used to be obligatory for the evening of the feast of Saint John the Baptist, June 24. After the green walnuts were picked and the *nocino* (walnut liqueur) was prepared and put to age, it was time for a dinner of these traditional *tortelli. Tortelli alla parmigiana,* which are made in Parma today and served on feast days, are very similar.

298. TURTRES LADINE

Pasta ripiena

INGREDIENTS: Rye flour, wheat flour, eggs, water, butter, and salt. For the filling, sauerkraut, onion, juniper berries, and cumin.

HOW MADE: The flours are sifted together onto a wooden board and kneaded with eggs, lukewarm water, a little melted butter, and salt. After the dough rests, it is rolled out into a very thin sheet, and disks 4 to 5 inches (10 to 12 cm) in diameter are cut from it. A spoonful of filling is placed in the center of a disk, a second disk is placed on top, and the edges are carefully sealed. The *turtres* are fried in plenty of very hot oil.

ALSO KNOWN AS: *Turtres de craut.*

HOW SERVED: As *pastasciutta*, fried in very hot oil.

WHERE FOUND: All the valleys straddling the regions of Trentino–Alto Adige and Veneto, in particular Val Gardena, Val Badia, Val di Fassa, around Cortina d'Ampezzo, and Comelico.

REMARKS: The Ladins, an ethnic group in the Trentino–Alto Adige region, trace their origin to an exact date, the year 15 B.C. in the reign of the emperor Augustus, when the Romans conquered the Alps and founded Rhaetia.

The Rhaetians, Reti in Italian, were made up of various small ethnic groups drawn from the Celts, Ligurians, and Illyrians. It is from exactly this potpourri of different ethnicities that the Ladins proudly claim they descend. They live in villages at high altitudes and cultivate impassable lands, where they grow buckwheat, rye, potatoes, beans, and poppies for their precious seeds. They have kept their language and traditions, including gastronomic, and in fact many recipes found in the Dolomites are of Ladin origin, such as the *casonsei ampezzani* (see *casonsei*).

299. UMBRICELLI

Pasta lunga

INGREDIENTS: Wheat flour, or part durum-wheat and part soft-wheat flour, eggs, and water.

HOW MADE: The flour is sifted and kneaded with eggs and water for a long time and left to rest. The dough is sliced, the slices are rolled with the hands into thick *spaghetti,* and then further rolled with the hands on a wooden board until they are thinner. They are boiled in plenty of salted water. A thickish factory-made type also exists.

ALSO KNOWN AS: *Pici* (see entry), *strangozzi, umbrichielle, umbrichielli,* and *umbrici.* In Narni, they are called *manfricoli;* in Sangemini, *picchiarelli;* and in Terni, *ciriole.*

HOW SERVED: Generally as *pastasciutta,* with a *sugo finto* or meat sauce typical of the various localities, and often with local black truffles.

WHERE FOUND: Umbria, especially in the towns of Castiglione del Lago, Città della Pieve, Città di Castello, Orvieto, Panicale, Perugia, Tavernelle, and Todi.

REMARKS: This pasta, which is widespread under different names in many regions of central and southern Italy, probably refers to the thick and precious *lombrichi,* or "earthworms," that peasants have always relied on to fertilize and enrich the soil. The fact that *umbricelli* are typical of Umbria has led some local scholars to think that the name may also derive from their place of origin.

In Orvieto, they are called *cavatelli,* a synonym of *pici,* and the housewives warn against letting them dry out too much. In general, they should be consumed the same day they are *appiciati,* or "kneaded" in the local dialect.

300. VERMICELLI

Pasta lunga

INGREDIENTS: Durum-wheat flour and water.

HOW MADE: *Spaghetti*-shaped factory-made pasta of durum wheat produced in different thicknesses. They are boiled in plenty of salted water.

ALSO KNOWN AS: *Spaghetti* (see entry). According to thickness and length, *capelli d'angelo, capellini, mezzi spaghetti, spaghettini, vermicellini,* and *vermicelloni.*

HOW SERVED: As *pastasciutta,* with traditional local sauces or broken into broth.

WHERE FOUND: Southern Italy.

REMARKS: The name, which means literally "little worms," is the old name for *spaghetti* and is still widely used in parts of the south.

Spaghetti and *vermicelli* were once served with *pesce fuggito* (fish that has fled), whose fishy fragrance was provided by seaweed and porous stones taken from the sea floor and boiled with other ingredients. Then *spaghetti* or *vermicelli* were cooked in the tasty broth.

The use of *pesce fuggito* was common to many coastal areas of southern Italy, including the Pontina area of southern Lazio, where the simple soup was the origin of the now-popular *acqua pazza* (crazy water). Sada gives an eighteenth-century recipe that was still in use along the Italian coasts until the 1960s.[286]

301. VINCISGRASSI

Pasta ripiena

INGREDIENTS: Durum-wheat flour, type 00 wheat flour, butter, and Marsala.

HOW MADE: The flours are sifted together and kneaded with Marsala and butter (melted, then chilled) until a firm, smooth dough forms. The dough is left to rest, then rolled out with a rolling pin into a thin sheet, from which strips of pasta about 4 inches (10 cm) wide are cut. These are parboiled in salted water, laid out to dry on a dish towel, and then layered with sauce and baked.

ALSO KNOWN AS: No alternative names.

HOW SERVED: In a *timballo* with *ragù* of chicken and mushrooms.

WHERE FOUND: The Marche, around Macerata.

REMARKS: A curious story accompanies these baroque *lasagne,* with their sumptuous sauce of giblets, which are the object of a literary debate among scholars of local history.

Some attribute their invention to the cook of the Austrian general Windisch-Graetz, who in 1799, during the Napoleonic wars, was stationed with his troops at Ancona. This theory makes the term *vincisgrassi* a macaronic elaboration of the unpronounceable name of the general.

But in 1781, well before the general arrived in Ancona, Antonio Nebbia, in his *Cuoco maceratese,* speaks of a *"salza per il princisgras,"* a cream sauce enriched with truffles and prosciutto, evidence that the dish was already known in Italy.

A century later, the anonymous *Cuoco perfetto marchigiano* gives two recipes: *visgras,* layered like *lasagne,* and *gattò alla misgrasse,* an elaborate baked dish enriched with the sauce of the *vincisgrassi.* We can thus reasonably establish that this rich and important baked pasta is a traditional dish of the Marche, especially of the province of Macerata. And, even if today it is sometimes made with tomato and a not-very-Italian béchamel, it is considered a symbol of the regional gastronomy. At one time, according to the upper bourgeois model of life to which Nebbia's text refers, truffles were indispensable, and they had to be the white truffles of Acqualagna,[287] which were in no way inferior to their Piedmontese cousin. Today, especially around Pesaro and Urbino, mushrooms and peas often replace the truffle in *vincisgrassi.*

302. VIPERE CIECHE

Pasta lunga

INGREDIENTS: Wheat flour, water, and sometimes eggs.

HOW MADE: The flour is sifted onto a wooden board and kneaded long and vigorously with water and sometimes with a few eggs. When the dough is firm and smooth, it is covered and left to rest. Small pieces of dough are then pinched off and rolled on the wooden board to elongate them into the long, rough *spaghetti*. These are coiled, like sleeping vipers, and then dropped into abundant boiling salted water.

ALSO KNOWN AS: No alternative names.

HOW SERVED: Generally as *pastasciutta,* with tomato, oil, garlic, and chili.

WHERE FOUND: Lazio, province of Rieti.

REMARKS: The name means literally "blind vipers." The shape of this tasty and very common pasta must have reminded some housewife of the vipers that sleep under rocks. And then, when it is drained in the bowl, awaiting the sauce, that mass of blind vipers, under the expert hand that stirs them, moves and twists just like the small reptiles in their lair.

And yet when laid out to dry, or in the dish, voluptuously covered in the lucid tomato sauce and sprinkled with pecorino, they scarcely look like a bowlful of snakes!

303. VOLARELLE

Pasta corta

INGREDIENTS: Durum-wheat flour and water.

HOW MADE: The flour is sifted and kneaded with cold water long and vigorously, then left to rest. It is rolled out into a thin sheet, and ⅝-inch (1.5-cm) squares or lozenges are cut from it. The *volarelle* are deep-fried in olive oil and served with soup in place of toasted bread.

ALSO KNOWN AS: In Puglia, *quadrucci;* and at San Ferdinando di Puglia, *fanze.*

HOW SERVED: Typical Abruzzese pasta, traditionally combined with cardoons in broth for Christmas Day. At Capestrano, *volarelle* are added to soup with the locally produced beans, and they are often associated with other legumes as well. In Puglia, they are cooked in broth.

WHERE FOUND: Abruzzo (L'Aquila), but also Molise and Puglia.

REMARKS: The Abruzzese term *volarelle* probably refers to their particular lightness (*volare* means "to fly"), and their size varies according to the soup they accompany. In L'Aquila on Christmas Day, a broth of *cardi* (cardoons) and *volarelle* is typically served. The dish is known in this beautiful city, built by the emperor Frederick II in the thirteenth century to defend his possessions from arrogant barons, as the "prince of gastronomic inventions."

The broth is enriched with tiny meatballs, smaller than a pea, which are the pride of the skillful Abruzzese housewives. The soup is made with giblets, meat, and *conserva,* but its main ingredient is the *cardo aquilano,* a gigantic, tender, and flavorful local variety of cardoon, a beautiful sight to see in the stalls in the magnificent piazza on market days.

Some of the *volarelle* are boiled in the same soup and some are added fried, a practice also followed in Puglia, where a part of the *taglioline* for *ciceri e tria* (see *tria*) are fried before they are added to the broth. The practice of frying the pasta and then of finishing the cooking by plunging it into a liquid is ancient; the Romans fried a particular type of pasta, *catillus ornatus,* which was rolled in a sheet and cut (see *pasta strappata*).

304. ZAVARDOUNI

Pasta corta

INGREDIENTS: Wheat flour, corn flour, salt, and water.

HOW MADE: The flours are sifted together and kneaded long and vigorously with a pinch of salt and some lukewarm water. The dough is left to rest, then rolled out into a sheet as thick as a *piadina,* which is cut into small squares or lozenges with a toothed wheel. They are boiled in salted water.

ALSO KNOWN AS: No alternative names.

HOW SERVED: As *pastasciutta,* with simple tomato sauce and sheep's milk cheese.

WHERE FOUND: Emilia-Romagna, a specialty of the peasants of Romagna.

REMARKS: The dialect word *zavardouna* means "slovenly woman." Presumably, it refers to the coarse flour used to make this pasta, which does not share the refined character of its sister pastas in the region.

305. ZEMBI D'ARZILLO
Pasta ripiena

INGREDIENTS: Wheat flour and water. For the filling, leftover fish, ricotta, borage, and herbs.

HOW MADE: The flour is sifted onto a wooden board and kneaded for a long time with water. When the dough is firm and smooth, it is left to rest, then rolled out into a thin sheet. Little balls of filling are placed at generous intervals on half of the sheet, and the other half is folded over. The pasta is pressed with fingers around the filling, and *ravioli* are cut apart with a wheel-type pasta cutter. They are boiled, a few at a time, in plenty of salted water.

ALSO KNOWN AS: *Zembi d'arziglio.*

HOW SERVED: As *pastasciutta,* usually with mushroom sauce.

WHERE FOUND: Liguria.

REMARKS: The etymology is hard to interpret. The Genoese dialect term *zembo* (*gobbo* in Italian), meaning "hump" or "hunchback," may allude to the bulbous shape of the filling. It probably derives from the Arabic *zembil,* meaning "basket made of braided palm leaves." And, in fact, the pasta is usually put to dry in baskets. Frisoni's Genoese-Italian dictionary [288] translates *arzillo* as "marine flavor of shoal fish," and *arzillo du ma* is Genoese dialect for the fragrance of just-caught shoal fish. Like all the coastal peoples, the Ligurians use the scented products of the sea as fillings and not just of pastas. "And what is this odor of mountain herbs that mixes so strangely with the limpet of the shoals and spans the coast between Lerici and Turbia?"[289] The fish filling was flavored with local herbs.

The nineteenth-century recipe book *La cucina di strettissimo magro*[290] lists the following ingredients for the filling *for zembi d'arzillo:* "boiled escarole, raw monkfish and hake, soft bread crumbs, oil, anchovies, pine nuts, and mushrooms."

306. ZENGARIELLE
Pasta lunga

INGREDIENTS: Dark grains, water, and often also emmer.

HOW MADE: *Spaghetti*-like dark-colored factory-made pasta produced by artisanal makers in Molise. They are boiled in abundant salted water.

ALSO KNOWN AS: No alternative names.

HOW SERVED: Generally as *pastasciutta.*

WHERE FOUND: Molise.

REMARKS: Molise has always been the granary of Naples. The spelt grown by the ancient Romans in the Larinum—the ancient name of the land occupied by present-day Molise—is solidly attested there also in the Middle Ages and after. Toward the end of the 1700s, wheat replaced the rustic and resistant spelt. Soft-wheat varieties took hold, especially in the areas surrounding the towns of Campobasso, Casacalenda, Montagnano, and San Giovanni, while durum wheat was grown around Isernia and the district of Larino.

The extreme poverty of Molise was the reason for these dark *spaghetti*, which used different grains that were rich in fiber and certainly healthful and, more important, had the advantage of a very low price. The name and color bring to mind the dark complexion of *zingarelle*, Gypsy women, but a seventeenth-century text[291] gives a recipe for *"zagarelle,"* meaning *fettucce*, which are light because they contain egg whites.

Zengarielle used to be served on Christmas Eve with a condiment of anchovies fried in oil. They have almost disappeared from the market, because their rustic flavor does not suit today's exigent palates.

307. ZITI, ZITE
Pasta lunga

INGREDIENTS: Durum-wheat flour and water.

HOW MADE: Factory-made long tube. *Ziti* are boiled in plenty of salted water.

ALSO KNOWN AS: *Busiata* (see entry) and *maccheroni di zita*. In Molise, they are called *a pasta d'à festa*, and in Puglia, *stivalette*.

HOW SERVED: As *pastasciutta*, with traditional local sauces.

WHERE FOUND: Originally Sicily; today throughout Italy.

REMARKS: The name means literally "grooms" or "brides." This is the pasta for feast days in different regions. Popular belief in Molise, for example, calls for making it on the Feast of the Epiphany (January 6) to ward off seeing the devil on your deathbed.

In Puglia, *zite* are used for *pasta seduta*, or "seated pasta": the pasta is covered with tomato sauce, fried meatballs, and abundant grated cheese, then poured into a bowl, where it must remain "seated" for some minutes, while the covered bowl is immersed in a boiling bain-marie. Also in Puglia, a *zita mezzana* is a specialty of Grumo Appula and is called *stivalette*, or "short boots."

In Sicily, *zite* used to be de rigueur at weddings: the succulent *maccarrune di zita*, served with stewed pork, were made in large quantity, because tradition called for bringing a gift of a hearty plate of pasta to all the neighbors, both rich and poor.

Today in Sicily, the term *zita* still means "bride," as do the children's words *cita* and *citta* in some parts of Tuscany. This neutral meaning, attested at least until the 1600s, has been lost in standard Italian, where the only form to survive is *zitella*, meaning "spinster."

Maccheroni di zita got its name from its role in wedding banquets; the name meant *maccheroni della sposa,* "of the bride."

308. ZIZZIRIDD'

Pasta corta

INGREDIENTS: Durum-wheat flour, water, and salt.

HOW MADE: The flour is sifted onto a wooden board and kneaded long and vigorously with water and salt, and the dough is left to rest. It is rolled out into a sheet about ⅜ inch (1 cm) thick, allowed to dry a bit, and then cut into flat noodles about ⅜ inch (1 cm) wide. The noodles are cut crosswise into ⅜-inch (1-cm) cubes. They are cooked in soup.

ALSO KNOWN AS: *Zziridd'.*

HOW SERVED: Typically in a bean soup.

WHERE FOUND: Basilicata, typical of Acerenza.

REMARKS: The name is dialect for the Italian *stuzzichini del gargarozzo,* or "gullet ticklers." The spread of legume- and vegetable-based soups was a sign of poverty, especially in Calabria. We learn from the Inchiesta Jacini, conducted in the 1880s across the entire new Kingdom of Italy, that Lucanian peasants seem to have eaten exclusively bread and vegetables, with an absolute absence of foods containing protein, a diet at the limit of survival. The Inquiry on Poverty conducted by the Italian Parliament in 1953 produced much the same results.

309. ZUGOLOTTI

Pasta lunga

INGREDIENTS: Wheat flour, water, and salt.

HOW MADE: The flour is sifted onto a wooden board with a pinch of salt and kneaded long and vigorously with water until a firm, smooth dough forms. After resting, the dough is rolled out into a very thick sheet, and stout noodles about ⅝ inch (1.5 cm) wide are cut from it. They are boiled in plenty of salted water.

ALSO KNOWN AS: *Fregoni, mazzancrocchi, stringotti,* and *zaccagnotti.*

HOW SERVED: As *pastasciutta,* with a *soffritto* of *lardo, odori,* and marjoram, and local pecorino.

WHERE FOUND: Umbria, typical of Gubbio.

REMARKS: These wide, thick Umbrian noodles, usually served with very simple sauces, are made for Christmas and New Year's, and also for October 31, the eve of All Saints' Day.

In the countryside around Gubbio, they are also served in a sweet version, flavored with lemon rind, walnuts, honey, and dry bread crumbs.

310. ZUMARI

Pasta lunga

INGREDIENTS: Durum-wheat flour and water.

HOW MADE: The flour is sifted onto a wooden board and kneaded for a long time with water until a firm, smooth dough forms. The dough is left to rest, then rolled out into a sheet, not too thin, from which flat noodles of unspecified size are cut. They are boiled in salted water.

ALSO KNOWN AS: No alternative names.

HOW SERVED: Traditionally in legume soups.

WHERE FOUND: Puglia, especially Corigliano d'Otranto, Martano, Serrano, and Sternatia.

REMARKS: This is a rustic *tagliatella* that used to be made with chickpea soup for the feast of Saint Joseph (March 19). Today, it has practically disappeared, but its presence was documented as late as the 1950s.[292]

GLOSSARY

Frequently Used Italian Words

ARBITRIO Old southern Italian and Sicilian word for *"torchio* [see below] for making pasta"; *d'arbitrio,* made with the *arbitrio.*

BIANCO, IN Said of a food served with a sauce or condiment that contains no tomato.

BUCATO, -A, -I, -E From the past participle of the word *bucare,* "to pierce a hole in," *bucatino* is both the name of a specific pasta (see *bucatini,* page 49) and a generic name for many kinds of long pasta pierced down the center. See *bucatini* for their origin and technique.

CACIOCAVALLO A *pasta filata* (plastic curd) cow's milk cheese with the characteristic shape of a large ball with a small appendage. The odd name (literally "horse cheese") is said to derive from the practice of tying two cheeses together and slinging them "astride" a horizontal bar.

CACIO RAVIGGIOLO Fresh cow's milk cheese from the Tosco-Romagnolo Apennines; mentioned in medieval texts but still produced today.

CACIORICOTTA A cheese, typical of Basilicata but found throughout southern Italy, made from sheep's milk and a small amount of goat's milk. It is aged for four months and packaged in conical baskets like those used for ricotta, hence the name. The flavor resembles that of sheep's milk ricotta, but the cheese is hard enough to grate over pasta.

CANNA, CANN- A reed and, by extension, a tube of any kind. The name turns up in various mutations with a large variety of suffixes throughout the vocabulary of pasta shapes.

CASTRATO A young male sheep that has been castrated.

CAVATELLI Both a specific kind of pasta (see *cavatelli,* page 71) and a generic term to describe a type of *gnocchetto* that has been rolled on a wooden board and indented or hollowed with the pressure of one or more fingers.

CICERCHIA, PL. CICERCHIE Chickling vetch, a traditional legume of central Italy. It looks something like a cross between a fava and a chickpea, but it has its own distinctive flavor.

CONSERVA The flesh of ripe tomatoes, sieved and dried in the sun until it has the consistency of a dense puree, or tomato paste. It is kept in glass jars protected by a film of oil and is used in winter in certain sauces.

CRUSCHELLO Type of fine bran containing some flour.

CUCINA BIANCA Literally, "white cuisine," a traditional cuisine in the mountains of Cuneo Province, in Piedmont, based on white or light-colored foods, such as flour and dairy products, and light-colored vegetables, such as potatoes, garlic, onions, turnips, and leeks.

CUCINA EBRAICA The cuisine of the Jews of Italy. Although respectful of Jewish dietary laws, it is a flavorful, distinctly Mediterranean—Italian—cuisine. In fact, many recipes today considered Italian are actually classics of *cucina ebraica,* such as *pollo con i peperoni, crostata di ricotta, carciofi alla romana,* and others. Because the Jews were restricted to ghettos for so long, they maintained their culinary traditions better than many other groups.

FARINA Literally, "flour," but by law in Italy the word *farina* is used only for soft-wheat flour. In this book, the English word *flour* is used in its common English sense, and thus translates the Italian words *farina, semolina,* and *sfarinato* (a flour made from substances other than wheat).

FERRETTO, PL. FERRETTI From *ferro,* "iron" or "tool," a utensil, something like a square knitting needle, used for making long, tubular pasta shapes, such as *bucatini* (see page 49). The first *ferretto* was a reed or stick, but as the name suggests, this developed into something made of metal, such as a wire or a purpose-made utensil.

FINANZIERA This is a garnish for poultry or veal dishes in the traditional Piedmontese kitchen. It is a sort of *ragù* made with coxcombs, sweetbreads, veal spinal cord, chicken livers, mushrooms, and truffles, all stewed in Marsala wine. It is also served alone as an antipasto. The name refers to the fact that the dish used to be only for the wealthy, such as those from the world of finance (*finanza*).

FOCACCIA, PL. FOCACCE From *focolare,* the Italian word for "hearth," *focaccia* is a generic word for flat bread, not a specific preparation.

GRANA Term for any of several hard, grainy cheeses suitable for grating. The most famous is *parmigiano-reggiano,* followed by *grana padano* and *pecorino romano.*

GRANO ARSO Literally, "burnt wheat." After the threshing of the grain, the gleaners went into the fields to gather the few grains that remained on the ground. The fields were then burned to fertilize the land. The grain that had escaped the expert eye of the gleaners was burnt along with the stubble and remained on the ground. The poorest peasants gathered this burnt grain and milled it, thus making a black, smoky-flavored flour, which they added to other flours when making their bread and pasta. For generations a symbol of the abject poverty the people of the south long endured, today pleasantly smoky pasta made with what now passes for *grano arso* is sold as a niche product.

INGEGNO The early *torchio* (see below) with dies, ancestor of the modern industrial pasta machines; the word is found mostly in Sicily.

INSACCATI Salamis and similar products preserved in a casing.

LARDO Cured pork fat in a solid piece that can be sliced. Lard, in the English-language sense of a spreadable product used for shortening, is *strutto* in Italian. In this book, *strutto* is translated, but *lardo* is left in Italian.

MADIA A sort of rustic wooden chest, traditionally kept in the kitchen to hold bread and flour and where dough was kneaded.

MALGA, PL. MALGHE In the alps of northwestern Italy, a wooden structure used by cowherds, where, among other things, they have always made cheeses and butter from unpasteurized milk. The phrase *di malga* means "made in the mountains."

MINESTRINA A broth-based soup in which *pastina* is cooked.

ODORI In Italian cooking, the word *odori* refers to a small group of fresh, aromatic ingredients used to flavor sauces and other preparations. The basic *odori* usually consist of an onion, a rib of celery, a carrot, sometimes a clove of garlic, and a few sprigs of parsley, but these can be varied or enriched with additional herbs, such as thyme, rosemary, marjoram, or others.

PAGLIA E FIENO Literally, "straw and hay." The term refers to a combination of white and green (the latter usually from the addition of spinach) pasta, independently of shape.

PAPPA, PL. PAPPE A mush or pottage. A *pappa* can be a baby food or a very thick soup, such as the Tuscan *pappa al pomodoro.*

PASTASCIUTTA The term *pastasciutta* or *pasta asciutta,* which means "dry pasta," is used for pasta served with a sauce or condiment. It is thus distinguished from pasta served in a broth or soup. This distinction should not be confused with that between fresh pasta *(pasta fresca)* and dry or factory-made pasta *(pasta secca).*

PASTICCIO, PL. PASTICCI A baked pasta.

PESCE AZZURRO Literally, "blue fish"; includes many of the stronger-tasting, darker-fleshed fish, such as tuna, mackerel, herring, swordfish, anchovies, and others.

PETTINE (DEL TESSITORE) Literally, "(weaver's) comb"; a utensil resembling a weaver's comb used for creating ridges in pasta. It consists of a series of parallel wires held firmly by a small frame of reeds. The artisans who made these utensils worked mostly in the lake areas around Ravenna, where reeds grew in abundance.

PRIMO PIATTO "First course"; the first course of an Italian meal, which may be pasta, rice, polenta, or soup.

PROVOLA Spherical buffalo's milk cheese that forms strings when melted (called *pasta filata*), typical of the Campania region, but also made elsewhere in southern Italy with cow's milk. It is usually consumed medium aged and is sometimes smoked *(affumicata).*

SAGRA, PL. SAGRE Popular festival, with adjacent fair or market, often held on the occasion of a religious holiday or saint's day.

SAPA Syrup made from grape must or wine that is used to give food a sweet-and-sour taste.

SAVOR, SAOR A sauce of white onions cooked in oil, white wine, and vinegar; typical of Venetian cooking.

SCALCO From the fourteenth century, this was the term for a carver. During the sixteenth century, he was placed in charge of the kitchen and table service.

SEMOLA Used synonymously with *semola di grano duro.*

SEMOLINO A hard-wheat flour ground slightly coarser than what is known as *semola di grano duro.* When cooked, as Cream of Wheat, it is sometimes called *farina* or semolina in English.

SEMOLONE A hard-wheat flour considerably coarser than what is known as *semola di grano duro.*

SFERRE A typical knife of Puglia used to make many types of pasta. It has no handle, so it can also be used horizontally to make long *strascinati* (see page 267).

SOFFRITTO The basis of many Italian sauces and other preparations, a *soffritto* is, unless otherwise stated, usually minced onion, celery, and carrot, and sometimes also garlic, sautéed with a fat (oil, lard, or butter).

SPAGHETTONE, PL. SPAGHETTONI Extra-thick or extra-long *spaghetti.*

STRACOTTO Long-cooked beef pot roast.

SUGO D'ARROSTO Pan juices from a roast used as pasta sauce.

SUGO FINTO Literally, "bogus sauce"; an almost-meatless yet hearty sauce for pasta.

TIMBALLO "Timbale"; traditionally a pie or varied ingredients molded and baked. Also, a generic term for a baked pasta dish with or without a crust.

TORCHIO Hand-cranked machine for extruding certain shapes of pasta, famously *bigoli* (see page 44). The name comes from *torcere,* "to twist."

Explanations of Other Terms Used

ARBËRESHË (ADJ.) The Albanian community of central and southern Italy and Sicily.

CHEESE Translates the Italian *formaggio,* meaning "cheese," even when the cheese is quite young. Ricotta, mozzarella, and similar products considered fresh cheeses in English are classified in Italian as *latticini,* "dairy products," rather than as *formaggi.*

CONDIMENT Translates the Italian *condimento,* which for pasta can mean anything from a handful of pork cracklings or grated cheese to an elaborate sauce.

DURUM-WHEAT FLOUR Translates the Italian *farina, semola di grano duro,* or *semolina.*

EMMER The Italian *farro* has numerous meanings, but in this book it means *Triticum dicoccum,* which is "emmer" in English.

FEAST DAY Translates the Italian *festa* or *giorno di festa,* and today also used simply to mean "Sundays and holidays." In the traditional rural society that underlies much of this book, the holy days, saints' feast days, and Sundays were the principal occasions for special meals, village festivals, and other celebrations.

HOST Translates the Italian *ostia* (not to be confused with the port of Rome), a thin flour-and-water wafer used in pastry making. It is the same substance used in Communion hosts, but has no inherent religious associations. Large hosts for use in the kitchen are today sold in pharmacies.

LAMB, MUTTON Italian has the convenient term *carne ovina,* which covers the meat of lamb and sheep of all ages. Most English-speaking countries have the equally convenient term "sheepmeat" or "sheep meat," its exact equivalent. Unfortunately, the

United States does not recognize the term, and so it is not available to this book. The American sheep industry uses "lamb" for animals under one year of age and "mutton" for animals one year or older, and so, to the extent such precision is possible, those are the terms used in this book. Where the Italian states *abbacchio* or *agnello,* the translation is "lamb." Where the Italian is *pecora,* the ewe is meant, and the translation is "mutton." When the *castrato,* a castrated older lamb, is called for, it is usually specified, though its meat could certainly be included under "mutton." The ram *(montone)* is not eaten in Italy.

LARD Translates the Italian *strutto;* the Italian *lardo,* cured fatback, is left in Italian.

LUNCH, LUNCHEON Translates the Italian *pranzo,* which should be understood as a main meal.

NOODLES Translates *fettuccine, tagliatelle, tagliolini,* and similar terms in Italian used generically to mean a long, flat strip of pasta cut from a rolled-out sheet.

PARMIGIANO Short for *parmigiano-reggiano,* hard cow's milk cheese from the designated zone in part of the Emilia-Romagna and Lombardy regions. Similar grainy, hard cheeses suitable for grating are generically known as *grana.*

PECORINO Generic term for any kind of sheep's milk cheese.

RITUAL FOOD Translates the Italian *cibo rituale;* food or foods made for particular feast days of pagan origin that later became Christian.

SHEET Translates the Italian *sfoglia,* the rolled-out sheet of pasta before it is cut into different shapes to become *tagliatelle, ravioli, fettuccine,* or any number of others.

SOFT BREAD CRUMBS Translates the Italian *mollica.*

SPICES The word *spices* in the ingredient lists in this book usually means nutmeg, cinnamon, or pepper, or a combination, but home cooks would use what they had. Chili is usually listed separately.

SQUASH Translates the Italian *zucca,* which is used for various varieties of yellow winter squash.

TYPE 0 AND TYPE 00 WHEAT FLOUR The Italian *farina tipo 0 (zero)* and *farina tipo 00 (doppio zero)* are soft-wheat flours; type 0 is slightly coarser and richer in gluten.

WHEAT FLOUR Translates the Italian *farina di grano,* which can mean either hard-wheat or soft-wheat flour. Often it is simply not known, or did not matter, what kind of flour was used for making traditional shapes. Whatever was on hand was used.

WOODEN BOARD Translates the Italian *spianatoia,* a large wooden board used for making pasta by hand. The wood imparts a desirable rough texture to the pasta surface.

NOTES

1. Manuscript II, XI, 15, Biblioteca Nazionale, Florence.

2. L. Pulci, *Il Morgante,* cat. XVII, ed. G. Fatini (Torino: UTET, 1948). Pulci was a Florentine poet (1432–84).

3. Clematis *(Clematis vitalba).*

4. The Valli Valdesi, or Waldensian Valleys, comprise the Pellice, Germanasca, and lower Chisone valleys, in the Piedmont region, near the French border.

5. For more on the *mostardele* and their *agnoli,* see G. and W. Eynard, *Supa barbetta La cucina delle Valli Valdesi* (Torino: UTET, 1996), 57.

6. O. Lando, *Commentario delle più notabili, et mostruose cose d'Italia* (1548; reprint, Bologna: Pendragon, 1994). Ortensio Landi, a nobleman of Piacenza, is better known by the singular form of his name, Ortensio Lando. During the Renaissance, it was customary to decline surnames (like Latin adjectives), that is, to change their endings according to number and gender, as is still done, for example, in Russian (e.g., Anna Karenina). According to this practice, families would collectively be known in the plural (as in English today, "the Browns"). With time the plural became the only form of the name and was used by all its members without variation.

7. The illustrious statesman Camillo Benso Conte di Cavour (1810–61) was architect of the Unification of Italy and minister in the reign of Carlo Alberto di Savoia.

8. *Il cuoco piemontese perfezionato a Parigi* (Torino: Carlo Giuseppe Ricca Stampatore, 1766).

9. *La cuciniera piemontese che insegna con facil metodo le migliori maniere di acconciare le vivande* (Torino: Fratelli Reycend e C., 1831. First published in 1798).

10. F. Chapusot, *La cucina sana, economica e dilicata* (Torino, 1851; reprint Sala Bolognese: Forni, 1990).

11. G. Vialardi, *Cucina borghese semplice ed economica* (Torino: Roux e Viarengo, 1901).

12. In R. Novelli, *Le Marche a tavola* (Ancona: Il lavoro editoriale, 1987).

13. Giacinto Carena, *Vocabolario domestico. Prontuario di vocaboli attenti a cose domestiche, e altre di uso comune* (Napoli: Marghieri e Boutteaux coeditori, 1859).

14. See R. Rovetta, *Industria del pastificio o dei maccheroni,* 1st ed. (Milano: Hoepli, 1951).

15. *Fondo casa e corte Farnese*, in the Parma State Archive.
16. Manuscript in Biblioteca Palatina, Parma.
17. B. Scappi, *Opera di M. Bartolomeo Scappi, cuoco secreto di papa Pio V* (Venezia: Tramezzino, 1570. Reprint Sala Bolognese: Forni 1981).
18. P. Artusi, *La scienza in cucina e l'arte di mangiar bene*, 16th ed. (Firenze, 1913), 76. Pellegrino Artusi (Forlimpopoli 1820–Florence 1911), writer and gastronome, is the author of perhaps the most famous cookbook still consulted today in Italian households. The first of numerous editions was printed in Florence in 1891.
19. Maria Luigia, duchess of Parma (Vienna 1791–Parma 1847), firstborn of the emperor François I de Bourbon and wife of Napoléon I. After Napoléon's fall, the Congress of Vienna, in 1815, assigned her the Duchy of Parma, where she lived until her death.
20. *Geography of Italy* 5.4.4.
21. L. Frati, "Libro di cucina del secolo XIV," in *Raccolta di rarità storiche e letterarie* (Livorno: L. Frati, 1899).
22. Also written *cagliata*, from *caglio*, "rennet"; a fresh, barely coagulated cheese. In Liguria, it is called *prescinsoea*.
23. Occitania, a cultural area identifiable today only with sociolinguistic criteria, comprises numerous valleys in the province of Cuneo and some valleys in the province of Turin, in particular the Pellice, the Chisone, and the upper Germanasca.
24. Pietro Fanfani, *Vocabolario dell'uso toscano* (Firenze: Barbera, 1863).
25. "The soup of the grain beating": a soup offered for the workers' lunch. The wheat was beaten on the threshing floor to separate the grain from the pericarpus that covered it.
26. Bleak (*Alburnus alburnus*), a freshwater fish of northern and central Italy.
27. M. Savonarola, *Libreto de tutte le cosse che se manzano* (Venezia: Bernardino Benalio Bergomêse, 1515).
28. *Tavola da tagliatelle*, "noodle board."
29. "Il vitto in Friuli attraverso la mensa degli educandati femminili—secoli XVII–XVIII," in *Archivi per la storia dell'alimentazione*, vol. 2, 1330 (Roma, 1995).
30. G. Perusini Antonini, *Mangiare e ber friulano* (Milano: Franco Angeli, 1984).
31. B. Platina, *Il piacere onesto e la buona salute*, ed. E. Faccioli (Torino: Einaudi, 1985), 160 and 163.
32. In *Atti del Convegno internazionale di studi su Maestro Martino da Como e la cultura gastronomica del Rinascimento* (Como, 1989), 2:37.
33. L. Bolens, *La cuisine andalouse, un art de vivre, XI–XIII siècle* (Paris: A. Michel, 1990).
34. Maestro Martino of Como, *The Art of Cooking: The First Modern Cookery Book*, ed. Luigi Ballerini, trans. Jeremy Parzen (Berkeley: University of California Press, 2005), 70.
35. E. Faccioli, *Arte della cucina dal XIV al XIX secolo* (Milano: Il Polifilo, 1966; reprint 1972).
36. Fried sweets filled with walnuts, honey, and spices, a specialty of *cucina ebraica*.
37. G. Ascoli-Vitali Norsa, *La cucina nella tradizione ebraica* (Padova: Adei Wizo, 1970).

38. A. Bertoluzza, *La cucina Trentina all'epoca degli Asburgo* (Trento: U.C.T., 1997) and *Cucina trentina del Settecento* (Trento: U.C.T., 1990).

39. F. Libera, *L'arte della cucina: ricette di cibi e dolci: manoscritto trentino di cucina e pasticceria del XVIII secolo*, ed. A. Mazzoni (Sala Bolognese: Forni, 1986).

40. In Alto Adige, *maso chiuso* was a local legal concept whereby an agricultural property was subject to primogeniture, that is, it was left to the eldest son in order to preserve the family's wealth and avoid fragmentation of the land holdings. The farm was completely self-sufficient. *Maso* is a dialect word for "farmhouse."

41. See G. Brunetti, *Cucina mantovana di principi e di popolo* (Mantova: Istituto Carlo Darco, 1963), 174.

42. V. Corrado, *Il cuoco galante. Opera meccanica dell'oritano Vincenzo Corrado* (Napoli: Stamperia Raimondiana, 1778).

43. Dialect for *il fagiolo si è messo la cravatta*, meaning "the bean is wearing a necktie."

44. O. Zanini De Vita, *The Food of Rome and Lazio: History, Folklore, and Recipes*, trans. M. B. Fant (Rome: Alphabyte, 1994), 29.

45. A soft cow's milk cheese with a pleasantly acidic taste, produced in Emilia-Romagna.

46. Extremely tender and soft cow's milk cheese with a sweet, delicate flavor, produced in Emilia-Romagna. It must be consumed within three days of production.

47. Cf. G. Maioli and G. Roversi, *Sua maestà il tortellino* (Bologna, 1993), 140.

48. The Regno d'Italia or Regno Italico (1805–15) was a pre-Unification state founded by Napoléon after his Italian campaigns. It comprised eastern central Italy and part of the north, and its capital was Milan.

49. G. Leopardi, *Tutte le opere* (Milano: F. Flora, 1949), 5:613.

50. Touring Club Italiano, *Guida gastronomica d'Italia* (Milano, 1931), 416.

51. *"Sunt ibi costerae freschi, tenerique botiri / in quibus ad nubes fumant caldaria centum / plena casoncellis, macaronibus atque fojadis"* (I, 45). See below, n. 90.

52. A. Latini, *Scalco alla moderna* (Napoli: Parrino e Mutii, 1692), 300.

53. L. Messedaglia, *Vita e costume della rinascenza in Merlin Cocai* (Padova: Antenore, 1973), 457.

54. A variety of broccoli rabe typical of the countryside around Naples.

55. Il Tavoliere delle Puglie is a vast plateau in the Puglia region where a special durum wheat is grown. The name derives from *tavola*, "table."

56. See T. De Mauro, *Parole straniere nella lingua italiana: dizionario moderno*, ed. M. Mancini (Milano: Garzanti linguistica, 2001).

57. *Agrocybe agerita.*

58. Ms. Lat. 9328, Bibliothèque Nationale, Paris, brought to light by Anna Martellotti, *Il Liber de ferculis di Giambonino da Cremona. La gastronomia araba in Occidente nella trattatistica dietetica* (Fasano: Schiena, 2001).

59. See also O. Redon, F. Sabban, and S. Serventi, *La gastronomie au Moyen Age* (Paris, 1993).

60. See G. Cosetti, *Vecchia e nuova cucina di Carnia* (Tavagnacco: Arti Grafiche Friulane, 1996).

61. The acts of the parliamentary commission investigating poverty in Italy.

62. *Liber de coquina ubi diuersitates ciborum docentur,* in M. Mulon, "Deux traités inédits d'art culinaire médiéval," *Bulletin philologique et historique* (Paris, 1968).

63. The classic copper pot for polenta.

64. Many more are cited in L. Monod, *Cucina fiorentina* (Firenze: Coppini tipografi, 1914).

65. T. Scully, "Du fait de cuisine par Maistre Chiquart, 1420," in *Vallesia, Bulletin annuel de la Bibliothèque et des Archives cantonales du Valais, des Musées de Valère et de la Majorie* (1985), 101.

66. *Scripto in Nerula, lo Ano 1524, Adi 3 de Agusto.*

67. Book II, ch. 153.

68. *Giudicati* were administrative districts into which Sardinia was divided in the Middle Ages.

69. The Doria were an ancient and powerful family of Genoese merchants, who became *signori,* or lords, of the city. They were at their height in the sixteenth century.

70. But they are known in English by the equally descriptive name bow ties. Of course, in Italian an actual bow tie, for the neck, is called a *farfalla.*—MBF

71. Rovetta, *Industria.*

72. Giovanna Micaglio Ben Amozegh, personal communication.

73. A game something like backgammon.

74. Latini, *Scalco,* 292–93.

75. *Il Cuoco perfetto marchigiano* (Loreto, 1891; reprint Ancona: E. Faccioli, 1982).

76. Giovanna Micaglio Ben Amozegh, personal communication.

77. The word is Latin for soldier. During the Middle Ages, it meant a high-ranking soldier, thus also financially well-off.

78. S. Serventi and F. Sabban, *La pasta, storia e cultura di un cibo universale* (Bari: Laterza, 2000), 95.

79. From the *Verbale della riunione dei censori genovesi del 13 febbraio 1654.*

80. Warships used also for transport of goods.

81. C. Bitossi, "L'alimentazione delle forze armate della Repubblica di Genova: sondaggi archivistici e problemi di ricerca," in *Archivi per la storia dell'alimentazione* (Roma, 1995), 2:800 ff.

82. See G. Folengo [Clara Ippolito], "Maccheroni: avventure linguistiche di una pasta," in *Cucina & Vini* (May 2004), 56.

83. I. Arieti, *Tuscia a tavola* (Viterbo: Quatrini Archimede, 1987), 91.

84. N. Misasi, *In provincia. L'ambiente calabrese al tempo dei Borboni* (Napoli: Chiurrazzi, 1896).

85. Sardinian novelist (1871–1936) who won the Nobel Prize in Literature in 1926.

86. Prehistoric Sardinia, from the conical stone structures called *nuraghi.*

87. Vincenzo Lancellotti, *Lo scalco prattico* (Roma, 1627), 2.

88. Dialect for the Italian *formaggio del pascolo,* a hard cheese produced in the upper Val Brembana, in the province of Bergamo. It has a delicate, slightly piquant flavor, and is best when made in summer.

89. A cheese similar in flavor to *formai del mut,* named for the town of Branzi, also in Val Brembana, where it is produced.

90. "Sunt ibi costerae freschi, tenerique botiri / in quibus ad nubes fumant caldaria centum / plena casoncellis, macaronibus, atque fojadis," I, 43. "Here the coasts are of soft, fresh butter, and one hundred cauldrons, full of *tortelli, gnocchi,* and *tagliatelle,* send their smoke to the clouds." The poet refers to the coasts of Lake Garda, birthplace of the Roman poet Catullus.

91. That is, a sort of liquid polenta that is eaten with a spoon.

92. See research by the Province of Terni published as *Le opere e i santi: tradizione alimentare e festività rituali in provincia di Terni,* ed. G. Baronti (Terni, n.d.).

93. L. Sada, *Spaghetti e compagni* (Bari: Edizioni del Centro Librario, 1982). This invaluable booklet was compiled for a Bari restaurant and only three hundred copies were printed. Luigi Sada (1920–95) was a historian, principally of the folklore and linguistics of Puglia; he also wrote numerous works on food.

94. *Atti governativi e amministrativi,* Cagliari State Archives, various vols.

95. *Inferno,* IX, 113–14.

96. The Istrian peninsula, which for many centuries belonged to the Republic of Venice, passed to then-Yugoslavia after World War II. It is now part of Croatia.

97. Dialect term for Italian *condimento,* a sauce made with *lardo,* onions, herbs, and tomatoes.

98. Giovanbattista and Giovanni Ratto, *Cuciniera Genovese ossia la vera maniera di cucinare alla genovese* (Genova: Fratelli Pagano, 1893).

99. Maestro Martino da Como, *Libro de arte coquinaria composto per lo egregio Maestro Martino coquo olim del reverendissimo monsignor Camerlengo et Atraiarcha de Aquileia,* mid-fifteenth century.

100. Napoleonic inquest on consumption and traditions in the Kingdom of Italy. With the Italian campaign (1805–15), Napoléon I founded the Kingdom of Italy (Regno Italico) and named himself king of Italy. The purpose of this inquest was to evaluate the real economic and agrarian conditions of the new kingdom.

101. Not raisins. Bunches of grapes were hung and preserved without drying out completely.

102. A. Boni, *Il Talismano della felicità* (Roma: La Preziosa, 1925).

103. Bertoluzza, *La cucina trentina all'epoca degli Asburgo.*

104. A. Nebbia, *Il cuoco maceratese* (Macerata: Luigi Chiapini and Antimonio Cortesi, 1781), 196–97.

105. See V. Mora, "Fonti per la storia dell'alimentazione nella Sezione di Archivio di Stato di Verbania," in *Archivi per la storia dell'alimentazione* (Roma, 1995), 1:180 ff.

106. O. Guerrini, *A tavola nel Medioevo* (Bologna, 1877), 80.

107. *Pastume* is chicken feed, a mix of corn flour, bran, and other ingredients. Here it is used figuratively to indicate a tasteless food.

108. The *cavarola* is a wooden board, usually incised with small designs that are transferred to the *gnocchi* as they are rolled over the board.

109. Tommaso Lucchetti, "Cucina e banchetto nelle Marche centrali del Seicento: analisi dei testi e fonti iconografiche," *laurea* thesis (University of Viterbo, 1999).

110. *Il cuoco sapiente, ossia l'arte di piacere ai gusti degl'italiani* (Firenze: Enrico Moro, 1881).

111. G. Vialardi, *Cucina borghese semplice ed economica*.

112. *Biblioteca di gastronomia* (Milano: La cucina italiana, 1932).

113. Petronilla is the pseudonym of the Mantuan journalist Amalia Moretti, who wrote a popular column in *Corriere della Sera* during World War II. Her recipes were subsequently collected in very successful books. A. Moretti Foggia Della Rovere, *Altre ricette di Petronilla* (Milano: Sonzogno, 1937).

114. Salimbene de Adam, *Cronica* (Bari: Laterza, 1966), 2:797. Salimbene de Adam, known as Salimbene da Parma (1221–87), was a chronicler and author of one of the most important historical sources of the thirteenth century, written in Vulgar Latin.

115. *Libro di cucina del secolo XIV* (Livorno: R. Giusti, 1899).

116. Pastas made with a *torchio* called the *arbitrio*.

117. See T. M. Vinydes i Vidal, *La vida quotidiana a Barcelona vers 1400* (Barcelona, 1985), 170 ff.

118. "Istituti e alimenti dagli statuti dell'area friulano-giuliana," in *Archivi per la storia dell'alimentazione* (Roma, 1995), 1:608 ff.

119. Today, the word *biade* is used only for animal fodder, but in official documents as late as the nineteenth century it is used generically for grains (wheat, emmer, barley, millet, rye). However, it was not used for wheat in the Friulana-Giuliana area, the coastal part of the region.

120. From the Salento peninsula, the heel of the Boot, part of the Puglia region.

121. ". . . *inde domum me ad porri et ciceris refero laganique catinum,*" *Satires* 1.4.115.

122. Appendix Vergiliana.

123. *Tracta* is the past participle of the Latin verb *trahere*, to draw or pull, which corresponds to the Italian *tirare*, which means not only "to draw or pull" but also "to roll out" (the pasta).

124. See Caelius Apicius, *De re coquinaria*; also J. André, *L'alimentation et la cuisine à Rome* (Paris: Librairie C. Kilncksieck, 1961); A. Dosi and F. Schnell, *A tavola con i romani antichi* (Roma: Quasar, 1984).

125. Large terra-cotta pots.

126. In Mulon, *Deux traités*.

127. A. Bertoluzza, *De coquina. Cucina di vescovi principi, cucina di popolo nel Principato di Trento* (Trento, 1988).

128. Joachim (Gioacchino) Murat was a brother-in-law of Napoléon and king of Naples from 1808 to 1815. N. D'Arbitrio and L. Zivello, *Carolina Murat. La Regina francese del Regno delle Due Sicilie* (Napoli: Bavarese, 2002).

129. The lunch of the *consolo* (from the verb *consolare*, "to console") is still offered to bereaved families and friends. It is usually brought to their home.

130. A high plateau in northern Calabria.

131. The *oncia* (pl. *once*) was an old unit of measure that varied from state to state. It was approximately equal to just under an ounce (28 grams).

132. S. Salomone Marino, *Costumi e usanze dei contadini di Sicilia* (Palermo: Sandron, 1897).

133. Matilde di Canossa (1046–1115), great supporter of the papal policy. During the 1077 duel between the Church and the Holy Roman Empire, the now-famous episode occurred in which the emperor Henry IV asked pardon of Pope Gregory VII, who had

taken refuge with Matilde in the impregnable castle of Canossa. Henry, dressed humbly as a peasant and barefoot, was made to wait three days in the snow before being admitted to the papal presence.

134. A type of *focaccia* made of a simple flour-and-water batter and usually cooked between heated terra-cotta plates, then either used directly as a crepe or cut up for *testaroli* (see entry).

135. An area of northern Lazio corresponding to the modern province of Viterbo.

136. The *Albo nazionale dei prodotti agroalimentari tradizionali* is a ministerial document listing all the typical Italian products recognized by law.

137. Seat of the Montefeltro during the Renaissance.

138. See *lagane* entry.

139. Giuseppe Pitré (1841–1916) was an illustrious Sicilian ethnologist and pioneer of the study of folklore.

140. G. Pitré, *Usi, costumi, credenze e pregiudizi del popolo siciliano* (Palermo: Pedone-Lauriel, 1889).

141. G. Perez, *Vocabolario siciliano-italiano* (Palermo, 1870).

142. A part of the *torchio*.

143. Sugar-coated almonds still traditionally distributed to guests at weddings, christenings, and the like.

144. F. Stancati, *Il mio paese: tradizioni popolari nella famiglia nella vita nell'arte* (Nicastro: Arti Grafiche Nicotera, 1949).

145. See P. Cartechini, "Disposizioni di carattere annonario negli Statuti comunali della Marca d'Ancona," in *Archivi per la storia dell'alimentazione* (Rome, 1995), 1:409 ff.

146. T. Lucchetti, "Caleidoscopio alimentare storiografico. La pasta come chiave di volta di molte letture storico-culturali," master's thesis (University of Bologna, 2003).

147. Hazard Analysis and Critical Control Points.

148. Carena, *Vocabolario domestico*.

149. *Archivio di Stato di Napoli, Ministero interni, primo inventario, statistiche.*

150. *Dizionario Garzanti della lingua italiana* (Milano: Aldo Garzanti, 1965).

151. G. Prezzolini, *Maccheroni & C.* (Milano: Rusconi, 1998), 142.

152. *Nuovo Vocabolario, ossia raccolta di vocaboli italiani e latini* (Parma, 1759).

153. Giovanni Boccaccio (1313–75), great poet and prose author, best known for the *Decameron*.

154. "Enjoyment," from *bene*, "well," and *godere*, "to enjoy."

155. ". . . una contrada che si chiamava Bengodi, nella quale si legano le vigne con le salsicce . . . ed eravi una montagna tutta di formaggio parmigiano grattugiato, sopra la quale stavan genti che niuna altra cosa facevan che far maccheroni e ravioli e cuocerli in brodo di capponi e poi li gettavan quindi giù, e chi più ne pigliava più se n'aveva." *Decameron*, day VIII, novella 3.

156. Teofilo Folengo (1491–1544), satiric poet who wrote in macaronic Latin. His most famous work is the *Baldus*.

157. Giordano Bruno (1568–1600), the great philosopher burned at the stake in Rome.

158. Costanzo Felici, *Lettera sulle insalate* (Urbino, 1577).

159. T. Garzoni, *Piazza universale di tutte le professioni del mondo* (Venezia, 1599), 297.

160. C. di Messisbugo, *Banchetti compositioni di vivande, et apparecchio generale* (Ferrara: De Buglhat e Hucher, 1549).

161. B. Platina, *Il piacere onesto e la buona salute,* ed. E. Faccioli (Torino: Einaudi, 1985), 160 and 163.

162. In *Atti del Convegno internazionale di studi su Maestro Martino da Como e la cultura gastronomica del Rinascimento* (Como, 1989), 2:37.

163. Piglia de la farina bellissima et impastala con bianco dovo . . . acqua comuna . . . fa' questa pasta ben dura, da poi fanne pastoncelli longhi un palmo sottili quanto una paglia. Et togli un filo di ferro longo un palmo o più sottile quanto uno spago, ponilo sopra 'l ditto pastoncello e dagli una volta con tutte doi le mani sopra una tavola, da poi caccia fora il ferro, ristira il maccherone pertusato in mezo.

164. Emilio Sereni (1907–77), journalist and writer, author of many important works on the agrarian world.

165. See E. Sereni, "I napoletani da mangiafoglia a mangiamaccheroni," in *Terra nuova e buoi rossi* (Torino: Einaudi, 1981).

166. See *tria* entry.

167. Lando, *Commentario,* 9.

168. Vol. 3 (Rome: Accademia Nazionale dei Lincei, 1988). When Joachim Murat (see n. 128) was named king of Naples, he ordered a collection of data on the real economic and social conditions of his new kingdom.

169. Messisbugo, *Banchetti,* 11.

170. B. Platina, "De honesta voluptate et valetudine," manuscript, Library of Congress, Washington, ed. E. Faccioli (Torino: Einaudi, 1985).

171. See C. Bertinelli Spotti and A. Saronni, *I marubini di Cremona* (Cremona, 2003). Unfermented grape must aged in large jars for a month; the resulting syrup was often used to sweeten foods or in sweet-and-sour preparations.

172. Unfermented grape must aged in large jars for a month. The resulting syrup was often used to sweeten foods or in sweet-and-sour preparations.

173. "Storia linguistica di un antico cibo attuale: i maccheroni," in *Atti dell'Accademia Pontaniana,* 1960, 8:261–80.

174. Vol. 3, Accademia Nazionale dei Lincei (Roma, 1988).

175. ASN. Ministero Interno, primo inventario.

176. See G. Truini Palomba, *La cucina sabina* (Padova, 1991).

177. *Aeneid* 6.420–21.

178. G. B. Rossetti, *Dello scalco* (Ferrara, 1584).

179. See n. 80.

180. See A. M. Lombardi and R. Mastropaolo, *La cucina molisana* (Campobasso: Cultura & Sport, 1995).

181. Always a Thursday, forty days after Easter. It commemorates Jesus's ascension into heaven.

182. Rovetta, *Industria.*

183. A bunch of wild herbs and greens that varies with the season. In general it comprises *verza primaticcia* (cabbage), borage, lovage, chard, wild radicchio, chervil, *cicerbita* (a wild plant of the genus *Sonchus*), and *talegua*, also known as *dente di leone*. It comes with a curious etymological anecdote: it was used as a medication that seems to have cured Goffredo di Buglione, the great *condottiero* of the First Crusade, when he was gravely ill; hence, *"pro Buglionis, pro Buggion."*

184. G. Frosini, *Il cibo e i signori: La mensa dei Priori di Firenze nel quinto decennio del sec. XIV* (Firenze: Accademia della Crusca, 1993).

185. *La secchia rapita,* canto IV, 30, 15.

186. *In porchetta* is an herb-based flavoring usually used for roast piglets (hence the name); it calls for garlic, herbs, and especially a great deal of wild fennel. It is widely used for other types of meat as well.

187. A. Cougnet, *L'arte culinaria in Italia* (Milano: Bocca, 1910).

188. F. Cavazzoni, *Libro di cucina* (Modena, 1870).

189. *Libro de arte coquinaria.*

190. A. Bazzi, "Il ricettario di Lucia Prinetti Adamoli," in *Archivi per la storia dell'alimentazione* (Roma, 1995), 2:1266 ff.

191. Chrysippus of Tyana in Athenaeus, *Deipnosophistai* 647 E.

192. Archivio centrale dello Stato, *Privativa industriale 11 marzo 1865,* vol. 6, n. 52, completivo 21 giugno 1865, vol. 6, n. 165.

193. For reasons beyond the scope of this book to ponder—but one thinks of the apotropaic phalli found at Pompeii and other archaeological sites—references to sex organs in Italian language and life cannot be judged by Anglo-Saxon standards. Although certainly to be kept under control in polite company, references that in English would, at the very least, shock may in Italian (when not used in anger) be quite harmless and even jovial or affectionate.—MBF

194. C. Artocchini, *400 ricette di cucina piacentina* (Piacenza: Stabilimento Tipografico Piacentino, 1985).

195. The Visconti were a noble Italian family that ruled the Duchy of Milan from the twelfth to the fifteenth century. They were succeeded by the Sforza, who governed Milan until the sixteenth century.

196. *Atti della giunta per l'inchiesta agraria sulle condizioni di vita della classe agricola* (1882).

197. G. Crocioni, *La gente marchigiana nelle sue tradizioni* (Milano: Corticelli, 1951), 59 ff.

198. Very old festival still held at Gubbio every year on May 15. It includes a procession to the Basilica di Sant'Ubaldo on Monte Igino in which giant candles, or *ceri,* formerly of wax but today of richly decorated wood, are carried.

199. G. Senzanonna and O. Zanini De Vita, *Tradizioni vive, il folklore e la tavola nella provincia di Roma* (Roma: Cucina & Vini, 2003), 142.

200. Misasi, *In provincia.*

201. Martellotti, *Liber de ferculis.*

202. *Cronica,* 2:797.

203. See Frosini, *Il cibo.*

204. Paolo Giovio (1483–1552), or Paulus Jovius, was a humanist and historian whose work contains much about daily life.

205. *Epistularium* (Roma, 1956).

206. In *Commentario*, 126.

207. D. Romoli, *Lo scalco. Della qualità dei cibi e reggimento della Sanità* (Venezia: Tramezzino, 1560).

208. A Florentine academy, founded in the sixteenth century and still vital, whose purpose is to protect the Italian language and philology. It has published important Italian dictionaries and continues to do so.

209. V. Agnoletti, *Manuale del cuoco e del pasticcere* (Pesaro: Nobili, 1834).

210. I. Cavalcanti, duca di Buonvicino, *Cucina teorico-pratica* (Napoli, 1846; reprint Milano: Bietti, 1904).

211. C. Prato, *Manuale di cucina* (Verona and Padova: Fratelli Drucker, 1906).

212. G. Belloni, *Il vero re dei cucinieri* (Milano: Madella, 1932).

213. Moretti Foggia della Rovere, *Altre ricette di Petronilla*, 76.

214. More commonly called *schienali*, pieces of the spinal cord of a calf.

215. Cavalcanti, *Cucina teorico-pratica*.

216. From the French *gâteau*, "cake."

217. A timbale, from the French *surtout*, literally "above all."

218. From the French *monsieur*, title given in Naples to the great cooks of the private houses.

219. See also F. de Bourcard, *Usi e costumi di Napoli e contorni* (Milano: Longanesi, 1955).

220. Extensive plateau in Puglia, one of Italy's most important agricultural areas.

221. 2:797.

222. G. B. Ratto and G. Ratto, *La cuciniera genovese ossia la vera maniera di cucinare alla genovese* (Genova: Fratelli Pagano, 1893).

223. Gurnard, a member of the Triglidae family.

224. Cf. G. Coria, *Profumi di Sicilia. Il libro della cucina siciliana* (Palermo: Vito Cavalletto, 1981), 198.

225. Martial, *Epigrams* 13.21.

226. ". . . et montani asparagi, posito quos legit villica fuso." Juvenal, *Satires* 4.65–70.

227. V. Olivieri, "Un'ipotesi di diffusione del modello pasta ripiena nel meridione d'Italia," master's thesis (University of Bologna, 2003).

228. Vol. 3, Accademia Nazionale dei Lincei (Roma, 1988).

229. Cf. Bertoluzza, *La cucina trentina all'epoca degli Asburgo*.

230. Caritas Italiana e Fondazione Migrantes. *Dossier statistico Immigrazione* (Roma, 2004).

231. See also G. B. Rennis, *La tradizione bizantina della comunità italo-albanese* (Cosenza: Progetto, 2000, 1993).

232. An Easter cake decorated with whole eggs.

233. Carmine Abate, "Il cuoco d'Arberia" in *Mangiare Meridiano, le culture alimentari di Calabria e Basilicata*, ed. V. Teti (Cosenza: Carical, 1996), 243.

234. The secret numbers on pasta packages indicate the size and thickness of the contents.

235. Quoted in M. Amari and C. Schiapparelli, eds., *L'Italia descritta nel "libro di re Ruggero" compilato da Edrisi* (Roma: Salvucci, 1883).

236. Vinydes i Vidal, *La vida quotidiana,* 170 ff.

237. *Regesti di bandi editti notificazioni e provvedimenti diversi relativi alla città di Roma ed allo Stato pontificio,* 1:7 (Roma, 1920).

238. G. Moroni, *Dizionario di erudizione storico-ecclesiastica* (Venezia: Tipografia Emiliana, 1842), 84:233.

239. *Intendenza prefetture,* 1810–15, Bari State Archive.

240. J. Trager, *The Food Chronology: A Food Lover's Compendium of Events and Anecdotes, from Prehistory to the Present* (New York: Henry Holt, 1995).

241. Prezzolini, *Maccheroni,* 137.

242. Messisbugo, *Banchetti.*

243. C. Marchi, *Quando siamo a tavola* (Milano: Rizzoli, 1990), 44.

244. Scripto in Nerula, lo Ano 1524, Adi 3 de Agusto.

245. *Gola e preghiera nella clausura dell'ultimo '500* (Foligno, 1989), 214.

246. V. Tanara, *L'economia del cittadino in villa del signor Vincenzo Tanara, divisa in sette libri, coll'aggiunta delle qualità del Cacciatore del medesimo Autore* (Bologna: Eredi dal Dozza, 1658), 34.

247. G. Patriarchi, *Vocabolario veneziano e padovano co' termini e modi corrispondenti toscani* (Padova, 1821).

248. R. D'Ambra, *Vocabolario napolitano-toscano di arti e mestieri* ([Napoli], 1873).

249. Touring Club Italiano. *Guida gastronomica d'Italia* (Milano, 1931).

250. L. Bruni, *Ricette raccontate: Marche* (n.p., 1999).

251. Cavalcanti, *Cucina.*

252. A. Placanica, *Storia della Calabria* (Catanzaro: Meridiana libri, 1993), 104.

253. Alberto Consiglio, *La storia dei maccheroni* (Roma: Canesi, 1959), 79.

254. *Atti della giunta per l'inchiesta sulle condizioni di vita della classe agricola* (Roma: Forzani, 1882).

255. The Colle della Guardia, on which the sanctuary stands, is located outside the city and is visible from every house.

256. Latini, *Scalco.*

257. A sort of large tray with raised borders.

258. Carena, *Vocabolario domestico.*

259. Corn husking. The husks were dried and used to stuff mattresses.

260. *La cuoca di buon gusto* (Torino, 1801).

261. *De lingua latina* 5.22.

262. Corrado Barberis, *Le campagne italiane da Roma antica al Settecento* (Bari: Laterza, 1997), 130.

263. The two flours are *grano tenero,* soft wheat, and *grano duro,* durum wheat. The flat bread *piadina,* typical of Romagna, on the Adriatic, is made of the former; *testaroli,* from the opposite coast, are made of durum wheat.

264. Ring-shaped cookies made of flour, oil, sugar, lemon rind, vanilla, and cinnamon.

265. J. Bassani-Liscia, *La storia passa dalla cucina* (Pisa: E.T.S., 2000), 27.

266. Ascoli-Vitali Norsa, *La cucina nella tradizione ebraica.*

267. Anonimo Toscano LXVI 1–51.

268. G. Du Cange, *Glossarium mediae et infimae latinitatis conditum a Carolo du Fresne domino Du Cange auctum a monachis ordinis S. Benedicti* (Paris, 1937).

269. In the Marche, *mentuccia* is *Calamintha nepeta,* of the Laminaceae family. See *Atlante dei prodotti tipici. Le erbe* (Roma: Agra Eri Rai, 2005), s.v.

270. Ettore Berni, *Brevi e facili poesiole per gli alunni delle scuole elementari e degli asili, con una raccolta di indovinelli* (Torino: G. B. Paravia, 1900).

271. Wild spinachlike greens, *Silene cucubalus.*

272. Book II, ch. 178, p. 71.

273. Le Due Torri, or Two Towers, in the center of Bologna, are often used as an epithet for the city itself.

274. G. Ronzoni, *Le origini del tortellino e la tradizione modenese* (Modena: Aedes muratoriana, 1992).

275. Tanara, *L'economia del cittadino,* 551.

276. Ronzoni, *Le origini del tortellino.*

277. L. A. Muratori, *Carmina* (Modena, 1956), 116.

278. Corrado Barberis, *Le campagne italiane dall'Ottocento ad oggi* (Bari: Laterza, 1997), 170.

279. G. Ceri, "La nascita del tortellino," in Maioli and Roversi, *Sua maestà il tortellino.*

280. Frosini, *Il cibo e i signori.*

281. Mastro Barnaba di Reggio. *De naturis et proprietatibus alimentorum.* Manuscript. 1338. Firenze: Biblioteca Laurenziana. Gaddi Reliqui 209, c.44.

282. B. Rosenberger, "Les pâtes dans le monde Musulman," in *Médiévales* (Saint-Denis: Presses universitaires de Vincennes, 1989), 16–17:77–89.

283. See n. 22.

284. *Intendenza Prefetture,* 1810–15. Bari State Archive.

285. Pitré, *Usi, costumi.*

286. L. Sada, *La cucina della terra di Bari* (Padova: Muzzio, 1991), 55.

287. A small town in the province of Pesaro Urbino, in the Marche, best known for its truffles. An annual truffle fair is held there.

288. G. Frisoni, *Dizionario moderno genovese-italiano e italiano-genovese arricchito di una raccolta di mille proverbi liguri e seguito da un rimario dialettale* (Genova, 1910; reprint Sala Bolognese: Forni, 1969).

289. Paolo Monelli, *Il ghiottone errante* (Milano: Treves, 1985), 97.

290. G. Dellepiane, *La cucina di strettissimo magro senza carne, uova e latticini* (Genova, 1880. Reprint Milano: Jaca Book/Alce Nero, 1990). The author was father superior of the Padri Minimi of Genoa.

291. Latini, *Scalco,* 292–93.

292. G. Rohlfs, ed., *Vocabolario dei dialetti salentini (terra d'Otranto)* (München: Bayerische Akademie der Wissenschaften, 1959).

BIBLIOGRAPHY

Accademia Nazionale dei Lincei. *Statistica del Regno di Napoli.* Vol. III. Roma, 1988.

Agnoletti, V. *Manuale del cuoco e del pasticcere.* Pesaro: Nobili, 1834.

Alberini, M. *4000 anni a tavola.* Milano: Fabbri, 1972.

———. *Piemontesi a tavola.* Milano: Longanesi e C., 1967.

———. *Storia del pranzo all'italiana.* Milano: Rizzoli, 1966.

Aleandri, G. *La difesa di Adone.* Venezia, 1630.

Alessio, G. "Storia linguistica di un antico cibo attuale: i maccheroni." In *Atti dell'Accademia Pontaniana.* Vol. III. 1960.

Alvino, F. *Viaggio da Napoli a Castellammare.* Napoli: Stamperia dell'Iride, 1845.

Amari, M., and C. Schiapparelli, eds. *L'Italia descritta nel "libro di re Ruggero" compilato da Edrisi.* Roma: Salvucci, 1883.

André, J. *L'alimentation et la cuisine à Rome.* Paris: Librairie C. Kilncksieck, 1961.

Aricti, I. *Tuscia a tavola.* Viterbo: Quatrini Archimede, 1987.

Artocchini, C. *400 ricette di cucina piacentina.* Piacenza: Stabilimento Tipografico Piacentino, 1985.

Artusi, P. *La scienza in cucina e l'arte di mangiar bene, Manuale pratico per le famiglie.* Firenze, 1891, and numerous subsequent editions.

Ascoli-Vitali Norsa, G. *La cucina nella tradizione ebraica.* Padova: Adei Wizo, 1970.

Atti della Commissione parlamentare di inchiesta sulla miseria e sui mezzi per combatterla. Milano: Istituto Editoriale Italiano, 1953.

Atti della giunta per l'inchiesta agraria sulle condizioni di vita della classe agricola. Roma: Forzani, 1882.

Babbi Cappelletti, L. *Civiltà della tavola contadina in Romagna.* Milano: Idealibri, 1993.

Baltzer, E. *Cucina vegetariana.* 1910.

Barberis, C. *Le campagne italiane da Roma antica al Settecento.* Bari: Laterza, 1997.

———. *Le campagne italiane dall'Ottocento ad oggi.* Bari: Laterza, 1999.

Baronti, G., ed. *Le opere e i santi: tradizione alimentare e festività rituali in provincia di Terni.* Terni: Provincia di Terni, n.d.

Bassani-Liscia, J. *La storia passa dalla cucina.* Pisa: E.T.S., 2000.

Bauer, C. A., and A. L. Bauer. *La cucina trentina.* Trento: Reverdito, 1988.

Bazzi, A. "Il ricettario di Lucia Prinetti Adiamoli." In *Archivi per la storia dell'alimentazione.* Vol. II. Roma, 1995.

Belloni, G. *Il vero Re dei cucinieri.* Milano: Madella, 1933.

Berni, E. *Brevi e facili poesiole per gli alunni delle scuole elementari e degli asili, con una raccolta di indovinelli.* Torino: G. B. Paravia, 1900.

Berti, A. *La cucina dei Gonzaga.* Milano: Franco Angeli, 1971.

Bertinelli Spotti, C., and A. Saronni. *I Marubini di Cremona.* Cremona, 2003.

Bertoluzza, A. *De coquina. Cucina di vescovi principi, cucina di popolo nel Principato di Trento.* Trento, 1988.

———. *La cucina trentina all'epoca degli Asburgo.* Trento: U.C.T., 1997.

———. *La cucina trentina del Settecento.* Trento: U.C.T., 1990.

Biblioteca di gastronomia. Milano: La cucina italiana, 1932.

Bitossi, C. "L'alimentazione delle forze armate della Repubblica di Genova: sondaggi archivistici e problemi di ricerca." In *Archivi per la storia dell'alimentazione.* Vol. II. Roma, 1995.

Boccaccio, G. *Il decamerone di M. Boccaccio nuovamente corretto et con diligentia stampato.* Firenze: Filippo Giunta, 1527.

Boccalatte Bagnasco, N., and R. Bagnasco. *La tavola ligure ovvero le ricette tradizionali per la cucina d'oggi.* Milano: Artes, 1991.

Bolens, L. *La cuisine andalouse, un art de vivre, XI–XIII siècle.* Paris: A. Michel, 1990.

Boni, A. *Il Talismano della felicità.* Roma: La Preziosa, 1925.

Boucard, F. de. *Usi e costumi di Napoli e contorni.* Milano: Longanesi, 1955.

Brunetti, G. *Cucina mantovana di principi e di popolo.* Mantova: Istituto Carlo Darco, 1963.

Bruni, L. *Ricette raccontate: Marche.* N.p., 1999.

Calussi, G. *Sapori di Dalmazia.* Trieste: MGS Press, 1997.

Camera dei Deputati. *Atti della Commissione parlamentare di inchiesta sulla miseria in Italia.* Roma, 1953.

Carena, G. *Vocabolario domestico. Prontuario di vocaboli attenti a cose domestiche, e altre di uso comune.* Napoli: Marghieri e Boutteaux coeditori, 1859.

Cargnelutti, L. "Il vitto in Friuli attraverso la mensa degli educandati femminili, secoli XVII–XVIII." In *Archivi per la storia dell'alimentazione.* Vol. II. Roma, 1995.

Caritas Italiana e Fondazione Migrantes. *Dossier statistico Immigrazione.* Roma, 2004.

Cartechini, P. "Disposizioni di carattere annonario negli Statuti comunali della Marca d'Ancona." In *Archivi per la storia dell'alimentazione.* Vol. I. Roma, 1995.

Casagrande, G. *Gola e preghiera nella clausura dell'ultimo '500.* Foligno: Edizioni dell'Arquata, 1989.

Cavalcanti, I., duca di Buonvicino. *Cucina teorico-pratica.* Napoli, 1846. Reprint Milano: Bietti, 1904.

Cavazzoni, F. *Libro di cucina.* Modena, 1870.

Cecchini, P. *La corte squisita del Duca Federico, mense imbandite nel più bel palazzo del Rinascimento italiano.* Bologna: Calderini, 1995.

Chapusot, F. *La cucina sana, economica e dilicata.* Torino, 1851. Reprint Sala Bolognese: Forni, 1990.

Chirico, F. *Mitico Aspromonte. Tradizioni popolari nel Reggino.* Reggio Calabria: Laruffa, 1998.

Cirillo, S. *Belle tipiche e famose, 240 formati di pasta italiana.* Perugia: ali&no editrice, 2002.

Codacci, L. *Civiltà della tavola contadina in Toscana.* Firenze: Sansoni, 1981.

Coltro, D. *La cucina tradizionale veneta. Ricette, sapori, aromi noti o dimenticati di una cucina varia e multiforme, dal mangiare rustico dei contadini e delle genti alpine alle specialità marinare dell'alta costa adriatica.* Roma: Newton Compton, 1983.

Consiglio, A. *La storia dei maccheroni.* Roma: Canesi, 1959.

Corda, E. *Terra barbaricina: documenti, vicende, folclore del circondario di Nuoro tra '800 e '900.* Milano: Rusconi, 1993.

Coria, G. *Profumi di Sicilia. Il libro della cucina siciliana.* Palermo: Vito Cavallotto, 1981.

Corrado, V. *Il cuoco galante. Opera meccanica dell'oritano Vincenzo Corrado.* Napoli: Stamperia Raimondiana, 1778.

Cosetti, G. *Vecchia e nuova cucina di Carnia.* Tavagnacco: Arti Grafiche Friulane, 1996.

Costanzo Felici da Piobbico. *Lettera sulle insalate.* Urbino, 1577.

Cougnet, A. *L'arte culinaria in Italia.* Milano: Bocca, 1910.

Crocioni, G. *La gente marchigiana nelle sue tradizioni.* Milano: Corticelli, 1951.

Le cucine della memoria, Testimonianze bibliografiche e iconografiche dei cibi tradizionali italiani nelle Biblioteche Pubbliche Statali. Roma: De Luca, 1995.

La cuciniera piemontese che insegna con facil metodo le migliori maniere di acconciare le vivande. Torino: Fratelli Reycend e C., 1831.

La cuoca di buongusto. Torino, 1801.

Il cuoco perfetto marchigiano. Loreto, 1891. Reprint Ancona: E. Faccioli, 1982.

Il cuoco piemontese perfezionato a Parigi. Torino: Carlo Giuseppe Ricca Stampatore, 1766.

Il cuoco sapiente, ossia l'arte di piacere ai gusti degl'italiani. Firenze: Enrico Moro, 1881.

D'Ambra, R. *Vocabolario napolitano-toscano di arti e mestieri.* [Napoli], 1873.

D'Arbitrio, N., and L. Zivello. *Carolina Murat. La Regina francese del Regno delle Due Sicilie.* Napoli: Bavarese, 2003.

Dellepiane, G. *La cucina di strettissimo magro senza carne, uova e latticini.* Genova, 1880. Reprint Milano: Jaca Book/Alce Nero, 1990.

Dosi, A., and F. Schnell. *A tavola con i romani antichi.* Roma: Quasar, 1984.

Du Cange, C. *Glossarium mediae et infimae latinitatis conditum a Carolo du Fresne domino Du Cange auctum a monachis ordinis S. Benedicti.* Paris, 1937.

Durante, C. *Il tesoro della sanità nel quale s'insegna il modo di conservar la Sanità e prolungar la vita.* Roma: Jacomo Tornieri & Jacomo Biricchia, 1586.

Eustacchi Nardi, A. M. *Contributo allo studio delle tradizioni popolari marchigiane.* Firenze: Olschki, 1958.

Fabrizi, A. *La pastasciutta, ricette e considerazioni in versi.* Milano: Mondadori, 1970.

Faccioli, E. *Arte della cucina dal XIV al XIX secolo.* Milano: Il Polifilo, 1966. Reprint 1972.

Fanfani, P. *Nuovo dizionario della lingua italiana scritta e parlata.* 1863. Reprint Napoli: Morano, 1897.

————. *Vocabolario dell'uso toscano.* Firenze: Barbera, 1863.

Fant, M. B., and H. M. Isaacs. *Dictionary of Italian Cuisine.* Hopewell, N.J.: Ecco Press, 1998.

Fast, M. *La cucina istriana.* Padova: Muzzio, 1990.

————. *Mangiare triestino. Storia e ricette.* Padova: Muzzio, 1993.

Ferrero da Valdieri, A. *La gnoccheide.* 1774.

Firpo, L. *Gastronomia del Rinascimento.* Torino: UTET, 1974.

Folengo, G. [Clara Ippolito]. "Maccheroni, avventure linguistiche di una pasta." *Cucina & Vini,* maggio 2004.

Folengo, T. *Baldus.* Edited by M. Chiesa. Torino: Unione tipografico-editrice torinese (UTET), 1997.

Forni, M. *La realtà e l'immaginario nelle valli ladine dolomitiche: quotidianità della vita, tradizioni e credenze popolari fra passato e presente.* San Martino in Badia: Istitut Cultural Ladin de Ru, 1997.

Francesconi, J. C. *La cucina napoletana.* Roma: Newton Compton, 1992.

Frati, L. "Libro di cucina del secolo XIV." In *Raccolta di rarità storiche e letterarie.* Livorno: L. Frati, 1899.

Freda, S. *Roma a tavola.* Milano: Longanesi, 1973.

Frisoni, G. *Dizionario moderno genovese-italiano e italiano-genovese arricchito di una raccolta di mille proverbi liguri e seguito da un rimario dialettale.* Genova, 1910. Reprint Sala Bolognese: Forni, 1969.

Frosini, G. *Il cibo e i signori: La mensa dei Priori di Firenze nel quinto decennio del sec. XIV.* Firenze: Accademia della Crusca, 1993.

Fumi, L. *Usi e costumi lucchesi.* Palermo: Edikronos, 1981.

Fusco, R. *Pagine di storia viste dalla parte degli sconfitti, ovvero La pasta, evoluzione di una lotta.* Massalubrense: Edizioni Lubrensi, 1989.

Garzoni, T. *Piazza universale di tutte le professioni del mondo.* Venezia: Roberto Merotti, 1599.

Gelsi, S. *Zucca e tortelli. Archeologia, mito, storia.* Mantova: Tre Lune, 1998.

Giambullari, P. F. *De la lingua che si parla & scriue in Firenze.* Firenze, [1551?].

Gianni, G., ed. *Quando la cucina si chiamava "casa." Sapori perduti e ritrovati dagli alunni delle scuole elementari e medie della provincia di Arezzo.* Arezzo: Accademia Italiana della cucina, 1991.

Giaquinto, A. *Cucina di famiglia e pasticceria.* Roma: Stabilimento Tipografico, 1903.

————. *I quattro volumi riuniti della cucina di famiglia.* Roma: Stabilimento Tipografico, 1907.

Giochi, F. M. *Costume, tradizione, ambiente nella campagna marchigiana nei sec. 17–19.* Loreto, 1978.

Goldoni, C. *Le baruffe chiozzotte.* Milano: Sonzogno, 1886.

Gosetti della Salda, A. *Le ricette regionali italiane.* Milano: Solares, 1967.

Guarnaschelli Gotti, M., ed. *Grande enciclopedia illustrata della gastronomia.* Milano: Reader's Digest, 1990.

Guerrini, O. *A tavola nel Medioevo.* Bologna, 1887.

Inchiesta napoleonica sui consumi e le tradizioni nel Regno italico (1805–15).

INSOR [Istituto Nazionale di Sociologia Rurale]. *Atlante dei prodotti tipici. I salumi.* Roma: Agra Eri Rai, 2002.

Iona, M. L. "Istituti e alimenti dagli Statuti dell'area friulano-giuliana." In *Archivi per la storia dell'alimentazione*. Roma, 1995.

Jannattoni, L. *La cucina romana e del Lazio*. Roma: Newton Compton, 1998.

Lancellotti, V. *Lo scalco prattico*. Roma: Francesco Corbelletti, 1627.

Lando, O. *Commentario delle più notabili, et mostruose cose d'Italia*. 1548. Reprint Bologna: Pendragon, 1994.

Latini, A. *Scalco alla moderna*. Napoli: Parrino e Mutii, 1692.

Leopardi, G. *Tutte le opere*. Milano: F. Flora, 1949.

Libera, F. *L'arte della cucina: ricette di cibi e dolci: manoscritto trentino di cucina e pasticceria del XVIII secolo*. Edited by A. Mazzoni. Sala Bolognese: Forni, 1986.

Limentani Pavoncello, D. *Dal 1880 ad oggi la cucina ebraica della mia famiglia*. Roma: Carucci, 1982.

Lirici, L. *Manuale del capo pastaio. Controlli di fabbricazione. Analisi–legislazione–pastificazione ieri e oggi*. Pinerolo: Chiriotti, 1983.

Lombardi, A. M., and R. Mastropaolo. *La cucina molisana*. Campobasso: Cultura & Sport, 1995.

Lombroso, C. *In Calabria, 1862–1897: studi*. Catania, 1898.

Lorini, T. *Mugello in cucina, Storie, prodotti, tradizioni, ricette*. Borgo San Lorenzo (Firenze): Stabilimento tipografico Toccafondi, 1985.

Lucchetti, T. "Caleidoscopio alimentare storiografico. La pasta come chiave di volta di molte letture storico-culturali." Master's thesis, University of Bologna, 2003.

"Maestro Martino da Como Libro de arte coquinaria." In *Atti del Convegno internazionale di studi su Maestro Martino da Como e la cultura gastronomica del Rinascimento*. Vols. I and II. Milano: Terziaria, 1989.

Maffioli, G. *La cucina padovana*. Padova: Muzzio, 1984.

———. *Storia piacevole della gastronomia*. Milano: Bietti, 1976.

Magi, G. B. *Libretto di cucina di Gio Batta Magi aretino, 1842 1885*. Arezzo: De Filippis, 1989.

Magistris da Introdaqua, A. de. *Biografia del Beato Bernardino da Fontavignone*. 1794.

Maioli, G., and G. Roversi. *Civiltà della tavola a Bologna*. Bologna: Aniballi-Ges, 1981.

———. *Sua maestà il tortellino*. Bologna: Enzo Editrice, 1993.

Marchi, C. *Quando siamo a tavola*. Milano: Rizzoli, 1990.

Martellotti, A. *Il Liber de ferculis di Giambonino da Cremona. La gastronomia araba in Occidente nella trattatistica dietetica*. Fasano: Schiena, 2001.

Mastro Barnaba di Reggio. *De naturis et proprietatibus alimentorum*. Manuscript. 1338. Firenze: Biblioteca Laurenziana.

Mazzara Morresi, N. *La cucina marchigiana tra storia e folclore*. Ancona: Aniballi, 1978.

Medagliani, E., and F. Gosetti. *Pastario ovvero atlante delle paste alimenari italiane*. Milano: Bibliotheca culinaria, 1997.

Messedaglia, L. *Vita e costume della rinascenza in Merlin Cocai*. Padova: Antenore, 1973.

Messisbugo, C. di. *Banchetti. Compositioni di vivande, et apparecchio generale*. Ferrara: De Buglhat e Hucher, 1549.

Ministero dei Beni Culturali e Ambientali. *Archivi per la storia dell'alimentazione. Atti del Convegno, Potenza–Matera, 5–8 settembre 1988*. Roma, 1995.

Misasi, N. *In provincia. L'ambiente calabrese al tempo dei Borboni.* Napoli: Chiurazzi, 1896.

Monelli, P. *Il ghiottone errante.* Milano: Treves, 1985.

Monod, L. *Cucina fiorentina.* Firenze: Coppini tipografi, 1914.

Monte, M. da. *A tavola in Casentino.* Stia: Fruska, 1995.

Mora, V. "Fonti per la storia dell'alimentazione nella Sezione di Archivio di Stato di Verbania." In *Archivi per la storia dell'alimentazione.* Vol. I. Roma, 1995.

Morelli, A. *In principio era la sfoglia. Storia della pasta.* Pinerolo: Chiriotti, 1991.

Moretti Foggia Della Rovere, A. *Altre ricette di Petronilla.* Milano: Sonzogno, 1937.

Moroni, G. *Dizionario di erudizione storico-ecclesiastica.* Vol. 84. Venezia: Tipografia Emiliana, 1842.

Mulon, M. "Deux traités inédits d'art culinaire médiéval." In *Bulletin philologique et historique.* Paris, 1968.

Muratori, L. A. *Carmina.* Modena, 1956.

Nascia, C. *Li quatro Banchetti Destinati per le Quatro Stagioni dell'Anno.* Vol. I and II. Manuscript. 1683. Reprint San Giovanni in Persiceto: Li Causi, 1982.

Nebbia, A. *Il cuoco maceratese.* Macerata: Luigi Chiapini and Antimonio Cortesi, 1781.

Novelli, R. *Le Marche a tavola.* Ancona, 1987.

Nuovo Vocabolario, ossia raccolta di vocaboli italiani e latini. Parma, 1759.

Olivieri, V. "Un'ipotesi di diffusione del modello pasta ripiena nel meridione d'Italia." Master's thesis, University of Bologna, 2003.

Padulosi, S., K. Hammer, and J. Hammer, eds. *Hulled Wheat.* Rome: IPGRI, 1996.

Paleologo Imbesi, B. *Cucina tradizionale di Calabria.* Roma: Gangemi, 1999.

Papa, S. *La cucina dei Monasteri.* Milano: Mondadori, 1981.

Patriarchi, G. *Vocabolario veneziano e padovano co' termini e modi corrispondenti toscani.* Padova, 1821.

Perez, G. *Vocabolario siciliano-italiano.* Palermo, 1870.

Perna Bozzi, O. *La Lombardia in cucina. Storia e ricette di piatti tradizionali lombardi.* Firenze: Giunti Martello, 1982.

Perusini Antonini, G. *Mangiare e ber friulano.* Milano: Franco Angeli, 1984.

Pitré, G. *Usi, costumi, credenze e pregiudizi del popolo siciliano.* Palermo: Pedone-Lauriel, 1889.

Placanica, A. *Storia della Calabria.* Catanzaro: Meridiana libri, 1993.

Platina, B. *De honesta voluptate et valetudine, manoscritto, Library of Congress, Washington.* Edited by E. Faccioli. Torino: Einaudi, 1985.

Politi, A. *Dittionario toscano.* Firenze, 1691.

Porcella, M. *Maggiolungo: storie dell'Appennino ligure-emiliano.* Genova: Sagep, 1996.

Prato, C. *Manuale di cucina.* Verona and Padova: Fratelli Drucker, 1906.

Prezzolini, G. *Maccheroni & C.* Milano: Rusconi, 1998.

Pulci, L. *Il Morgante.* Edited by G. Fatini. Torino: UTET, 1948.

Ratto, G. B., and G. Ratto. *La cuciniera genovese ossia la vera maniera di cucinare alla genovese.* Genova: Fratelli Pagano, 1893.

Redon, O., F. Sabban, and S. Serventi. *La gastronomie au Moyen Age.* Paris: Stock/Moyen Age, 1993.

Regesti di bandi, editti, notificazioni e provvedimenti diversi relativi alla città di Roma ed allo Stato pontificio. Vols. 1–7. Roma, 1920.

Rennis, G. B. *La tradizione bizantina della comunità italo-albanese.* Cosenza: Progetto, 2000, 1993.

Renzi, R., and D. Zanasi. *Bocca cosa vuoi? 20 maestri della cucina emiliano-romagnola.* Bologna: Cappelli, 1965.

Restivo, M. *La cucina della memoria. Cibi e tradizioni alimentari dell'antica Lucania.* Potenza: Ermes, n.d.

Righi Parenti, G. *La cucina toscana. I piatti tipici e le ricette tradizionali provenienti da tutte le province toscane.* Roma: Newton Compton, 1995.

Rohlfs, G., ed. *Vocabolario dei dialetti salentini (Terra d'Otranto).* München: Bayerische Akademie der Wissenschaften, 1959.

Romoli, D. *Lo scalco. Della qualità dei cibi e reggimento della Sanità.* Venezia: Tramezzino, 1560.

Ronzoni, G. *Le origini del tortellino e la tradizione modenese.* Modena: Aedes muratoriana, 1992.

———. *Un libro di cucina modenese dell'Ottocento.* Modena, 2001.

Rosenberger, B. "Les pâtes dans le monde musulman." In *Médiévales.* Vols. 16–17. Saint-Denis: Presses universitaires de Vincennes, 1989.

Rossetti, G. B. *Dello scalco.* Ferrara, 1584.

Rovetta, R. *Industria del pastificio o dei maccheroni.* Milano: Hoepli, 1951.

Sada, L. *Dolci bocconi di Puglia, storia folclore nomenclatura dialettale delle paste dolci.* Bari: Edizioni del Centro Librario, 1981.

———. *La cucina della terra di Bari.* Padova: Muzzio, 1991.

———. *Profumo del focolare gioia della mensa.* Bari: Edizioni del Centro Librario, 1980.

Salimbene de Adam. *Cronica.* Bari: Laterza, 1965.

Salomone Marino, S. *Costumi e usanze dei contadini di Sicilia.* Palermo: Sandron, 1897.

Savonarola, M. *Libreto de tutte le cosse che se manzano.* Venezia: Bernardino Benalio Bergomêse, 1515.

Scappi, B. *Opera di M. Bartolomeo Scappi, cuoco secreto di papa Pio V.* Venezia: Tramezzino, 1570. Reprint Sala Bolognese: Forni, 1981.

Scully, T. "Du fait de cuisine par Maistre Quiquart, 1420." *Vallesia, Bulletin annuel de la Bibliothèque et des Archives cantonales du Valais, des Musées de Valère et de la Majorie,* 1985.

Senzanonna, G., and O. Zanini De Vita. *Tradizioni vive. Il folclore e la tavola nella provincia di Roma.* Roma: Cucina & Vini, 2003.

Sereni, E. "I napoletani da mangiafoglia a mangiamaccheroni." In *Terra nuova e buoi rossi.* Torino: Einaudi, 1981.

Serventi, S., and F. Sabban. *La pasta, storia e cultura di un cibo universale.* Bari: Laterza, 2000.

Sottana, O. *Usi e costumi di vita andata nel mondo rurale trevigiano.* Crocetta del Montello, 1979.

Stancati, F. *Il mio paese: tradizioni popolari nella famiglia nella vita nell'arte.* Nicastro: Arti Grafiche Nicotera, 1949.

Starec, R. *Mondo popolare in Istria, cultura materiale e vita quotidiana dal '500 al '900*. Venezia: Regione del Veneto, 1996.

Statistica del Regno di Napoli. 1811.

Stefani, B. *L'arte di ben cucinare et istruire i men periti in questa lodeuole professione*. Mantova, 1662. Reprint Sala Bolognese: Forni, 1983.

Steiner, C. *Il ghiottone lombardo. Costumanze, tradizioni e ricette della buona tavola lombarda*. Milano: Bramante, 1964.

Tabanelli, M. *Noi contadini di Romagna. Usi, costumi, tradizioni*. Faenza: Lega, 1973.

Tanara, V. *L'economia del cittadino in villa del signor Vincenzo Tanara, divisa in sette libri, coll'aggiunta delle qualità del Cacciatore del medesimo Autore*. Bologna: Eredi del Dozza, 1658.

Tassoni, A. *La secchia rapita*. Bologna: Fratelli Masi, 1821.

Teti, V., ed. *Mangiare meridiano. Le culture alimentari di Calabria e Basilicata*. Cosenza, 1996.

Touring Club Italiano. *Guida gastronomica d'Italia*. Milano, 1931.

Truini Palomba, G. *La cucina sabina*. Padova: Muzzio, 1991.

Vialardi, G. *Cucina borghese semplice ed economica*. Torino: Roux e Viarengo, 1901.

———. *Trattato di Cucina Pasticceria Moderna Credenza e relativa confettureria*. Torino: Roux e Frassati, 1854.

Vinydes i Vidal, T. M. *La vida quotidiana a Barcelona vers 1400*. Barcelona, 1985.

Vocabolario degli Accademici della Crusca, con tre indici delle voci, locuzioni e prouerbi latini e greci, posti entro l'opera. Venezia, 1612.

Westbury, Lord. *Handlist of Italian Cookery Books*. Florence: Olschki, 1963.

Zanini De Vita, O. *Il cibo e il suo mondo nella campagna romana*. Roma: Provincia di Roma Editore, 2001.

———. *The Food of Rome and Lazio: History, Folklore, and Recipes*. Translated by M. B. Fant. Rome: Alphabyte, 1994.

Zanotti, M. *A tavola con Maria Luigia. Il servizio di bocca della Duchessa di Parma, dal 1815 al 1847*. Parma: Arte Grafica Silva, 1991.

INDEX OF PASTA NAMES

The following list includes all pasta names mentioned in the book: entry titles, names listed under "Also known as," and other pastas mentioned incidentally under "Remarks." Numbers in bold refer to the book's main pasta entries. Sauces, ingredients, and preparations in general are listed in the General Index, not here, except when they are also part of the specific pasta name.

Italian pronunciation is quite regular and follows a few simple rules. But even Italians have trouble knowing, or guessing, which syllable to stress. The rule is to stress the penult (next-to-last syllable) unless a different accent is written or unless the word is an exception, and there are many exceptions. Accordingly, where the stress falls on a syllable other than the penult, or where a non-Italian might not understand which syllable is the penult, we have underscored the vowel or vowels of the stressed syllable. Where a vowel cluster is underscored, it should be considered as near a diphthong as makes no difference, though bear in mind that the underscoring is present to help English speakers and may not reflect the correct Italian syllabification. A common mistake among English speakers is to mistake the *i* that softens a *c* or *g* for a separate syllable. Thus the name Giovanni should be pronounced Jo-van-ni, not Gee-o-van-i (the double consonant is pronounced too, but that is another problem entirely); the pasta *calcioni* has three syllables (cal-cho-ni), not four (cal-chee-o-ni). The pasta *brofandei,* and others ending in two vowels, follows the rule because the two vowels are separate syllables: bro-fan-DE-i.

GENERAL INDEX

The following index contains names of ingredients, utensils and pasta-making equipment, pre-pared sauces and pasta dishes, place names, festivals, historical personages other than authors cited in the notes or bibliography, and a small miscellany of other items. For names of pastas, as opposed to pasta dishes, please see the Index of Pasta Names. Most place names (provinces, towns, and physical features) are listed under the region in which they are found. Where a toponym cannot be easily assigned to a single region, it is listed independently. For the convenience of the reader, the two-letter abbreviation of each provincial capital is given in parentheses after the name, which is in bold.

California Studies in Food and Culture

Darra Goldstein, Editor

Designer: Lia Tjandra

Text and display: Dante MT

Compositor: Westchester Book Services

Indexer: Maureen B. Fant

Illustrator: Luciana Marini

Printer and binder: Maple-Vail Book Manufacturing Group